SEXUAL ABUSE OF CHILDREN

SEXUAL ABUSE
OF CHILDREN
A Human Rights Perspective

Roger J. R. Levesque

Indiana University Press

Bloomington and Indianapolis

This book is a publication of

Indiana University Press
601 North Morton Street
Bloomington, Indiana 47404-3797 USA

www.indiana.edu/~iupress

Telephone orders   800-842-6796
Fax orders   812-855-7931
Orders by e-mail   iuporder@indiana.edu

The paper used in this publication meets the minimum
requirements of American National Standard for Information
Sciences—Permanence of Paper for Printed Library Materials,
ANSI Z39.48-1984.

Manufactured in the United States of America

Library of Congress Cataloging-in-Publication Data

Levesque, Roger J. R.
    Sexual abuse of children : a human rights perspective /
Roger J. R. Levesque.
        p.   cm.
    Includes index.
    ISBN 0-253-33471-3 (cloth : alk. paper)
    1. Child sexual abuse.   2. Children's rights.   I. Title.
HV6570.L4   1999
0364.15'36—dc21   98-48401

1 2 3 4 5   04 03 02 01 00 99

Contents

Acknowledgments

So MANY HAVE contributed to my understanding of law and multi-disciplinary understandings of life that it is impossible to acknowledge my gratitude to all of them. I am particularly grateful, however, to Lowell Eayrs Daigle, who first taught me about the need to adopt critical and cultural approaches to pressing social issues. My life would be far less eventful and less fulfilling if it were not for her. She continues to encourage me, even though she has passed away.

I also appreciate the gentle mentoring of several other professors, particularly the late T. Franklin Grady, Jr., who, along with Lowell, prepared me for an academic life far from my little home town in rural Maine and its small but enormously "rich" satellite campus of the University of Maine. I have been particularly fortunate to have had other caring mentors. Daniel G. Freedman and Gilbert H. Herdt guided me through the University of Chicago's unique doctoral program, which understands the significance of cultural life; and Bert Cohler challenged me to think of "different life worlds." I also am grateful to numerous professors from Columbia University School of Law, especially Martha Fineman, Phil Genty, and Louis Henkin, who made me struggle with difficult human rights issues and learn to love the law. Professors at the University of Nebraska's Law & Psychology Program, particularly Gary B. Melton and Alan J. Tomkins, deserve credit not just for their continued personal support but also for solidifying my interest in children and family issues. Likewise, I tremendously appreciate a brief comment made by Vicky Weisz, a former colleague at the University of Nebraska, that led me to think of the need to adopt a more sophisticated cultural perspective if we are ever to understand child sexual maltreatment. Marc Fondacaro, while at the University of Nebraska, challenged me to make a real contribution; his friendly prodding continues to push me toward even more demanding projects. I am grateful to him and to several others who may not fully realize how their voices and passions fuel others.

I am most thankful to Professor Hal Pepinsky, and for the good fortune that I have him a few doors past my office in Indiana University's

Department of Criminal Justice. A brief presentation in his class on Children's Rights and Safety led to an e-mail to Bob Sloan of Indiana University Press, which quickly led to a book proposal. Hal's contribution, however, is much deeper. He continues to remind me of the real significance of working *with* victims and of taking children's experiences seriously, no matter where victims' voices land us and no matter how outrageous conclusions may be to those who take different perspectives.

As I work on other projects, I continue to be impressed by the excellent editorial support I received from IU Press. Bob Sloan, who inspired me to write this book, provided encouragement and guidance throughout the process. Michael Nelson contributed his editorial skills, which caught so many small errors that I wondered how I had managed to write so many articles before writing this book. Two anonymous reviewers also deserve considerable credit. Both reviewers provided nurturing feedback that made writing the sort of intellectual process it is supposed to be.

Although this book required that I spend numerous hours running around the libraries at IU and even more hours sitting alone with my computer and piles of books, I was never really alone. My wife, Helen, challenged my thinking and ensured that I did not forget the need to balance life and remain faithful to other demands. I thank God every day for her love. Marc, my son who was born at the same time I started this book, made me realize the urgent need for a world that takes children's issues more seriously. As I end this book, the sense of urgency and panic about what the future holds for our children again rises as we all await the birth of Marc's first sibling. The urgency, however, is somewhat quelled when I sit back and think of my own childhood and realize that loving parents and siblings can make such a difference in a life that others would perceive as extremely difficult and without much hope. For that peaceful feeling, my deepest and warmest thanks go to "Mom & Dad" and to Yves, Gilles and Linda.

Bloomington, Indiana
September 1998

SEXUAL ABUSE OF CHILDREN

1 | Invisible Acts
Child Sexual Maltreatment across World Cultures

The world community recently has recognized every child's fundamental human right to protection from sexual maltreatment. This chapter introduces practices that may fall under that protection and delineates issues that arise from the recognition that children deserve such protection. The chapter also highlights how sexual maltreatment largely involves "invisible acts"—how most of us are unaware of maltreating situations, how lack of awareness contributes to maltreatment, and how we remain unaware that various forms of maltreatment involve violations of international human rights law.

THE WORLD IS quickly coming to grips with the severity and breadth of the problems besetting today's children. Children are dying from random violence, poor nutrition, lack of appropriate medical care, and the sequelae of persistent and pervasive poverty.[1] When children are not dying, lack of education, and environmental challenges to physical and mental health hamper their opportunities for a fulfilling life.[2] In addition to being subjected to victimization from what appropriately has been called "socially toxic environments,"[3] children are individually targeted and intentionally maltreated. Although maltreatment takes different forms and derives from several sources, the destructiveness and pervasiveness of sexual maltreatment highlights well the exceptionally difficult circumstances some children must endure.

Child sexual exploitation illustrates particularly well how children's difficulties may be widespread and pose considerable challenges to policy-makers and child advocates. Reports estimate that up to three million children are prostituted in the Southeast Asian sex trade.[4] Although commentaries limit themselves to sex-tourism in the Third World, the practice is found in industrialized countries. In the United States, for example, government figures estimate that approximately 600,000 girls and 300,000 boys regularly engage in prostitution.[5] Admittedly, these estimates are hotly contested. Some contend that current estimates are gross underestimates. Other sources report that the statistics are somewhat exaggerated—for example, the United Nations reports that approximately 10 million Third World children are involved in prostitution.[6] Regardless of the controversy, commentators tend to agree that the global diffusion of this form of child sexual exploitation continues, that it constitutes a multi-billion dollar a year industry,[7] and that it spawns other forms of exploitation, such as child pornography.[8] Even though various forms of sexual exploitation are pervasively condemned, financial considerations lead runaways or throwaways to sell themselves to survive, parents to sell their children, abductors to get involved in the sex trade, pimps to indenture children, and poor children to "consent" to sexual activities to support their families.[9] The diversity of circumstances and forces that contribute to child sexual exploitation highlights well the need for a complex and careful societal response.

Children who are not bought or exchanged for sex are sexually used in other ways. A cursory examination of cross-cultural manifestations of child sexuality and sexual development reveals yet another group of practices subject to condemnation. In some societies, children have their sexual organs permanently disfigured and dismembered—a practice affecting up to 18 million girls and, although the mutilation is usually less severe, millions more boys.[10] In other societies, children's sexual partners are predetermined: child brides are betrothed at birth, or soon thereafter, and engage in prepubertal sexual relations with their husbands.[11] In other cultures, such as Sri Lanka and Turkey, girls routinely submit to virginity exams, a practice enforced by parents, future spouses, school officials, and a variety of state actors.[12] In still other societies, all boys must engage in oral or anal sexual activities with adults.[13] Although certainly a challenge to the comprehension of cultural "outsiders" (as well as some inside), these practices are not necessarily seen as sexual in nature, let alone as inappropriate. Indeed, cultures deem the practices necessary. All cultures impose their own meanings on apparently sexual behavior and can make sexual acts sexless: even the masturbation of children may *not* be sexual—several studies have reported that masturbation is used to help children sleep in Indian, Chinese, Japanese, Middle Eastern, Latin American, as well as native American societies.[14] Yet, in other societies, such practices are perceived as problematic and linked to disruptive outcomes.[15]

The cross-cultural record of how children sexually develop and are socialized into adult roles leads to heated debates that again do not evoke easy resolutions and responses. Unlike practices that clearly have been deemed exploitative—such as child pornography and prostitution—the cultural practices described above are pervasively condoned, encouraged, and viewed as necessary for a fulfilling life and successful community membership. Despite the broad cultural acceptability of these behaviors, several commentators view them as abusive.[16] Indeed, several external and some internal forces aim to prohibit and eradicate such practices. Taken out of their cultural contexts, they tend to be viewed as repressive and inappropriately torturous, degrading, and inhumane acts. Choosing the proper way to deal with these indigenous, culturally meaningful conventions becomes increasingly contentious with the apparent globalization of cultures.[17]

In other cultures, practices are condemned pervasively and forcefully, both inside and outside the societies in which they occur. Yet, the condemnation arguably does not make responding to children's situations any easier. In a recent survey of over twenty societies, up to one-quarter of adults reported that they had been sexually maltreated as children.[18] The instances of maltreatment are relatively clear, and although there may be disputes as to whether specific individual events occurred, the practices are roundly condemned. Prominent commentators note that, despite high numbers and near universal condemnation, it actually may be impossible to protect children from these abuses; or at least that the current approaches are severely misinformed and misdirected.[19] These are not popular sentiments. The continued abuse of children and the controversial reactions it elicits reflect the difficulty of properly framing and executing societal responses. They also reflect the challenge of enacting policies beneficial to children, especially when such efforts are enacted in their name.

Although some societies may seem very much aware of sexual maltreatment and may condemn the practice, they too are not immune from condoning some forms of interactions that may be deemed maltreating. In the West, for example, several forms of sexual maltreatment essentially go unrecognized and are even arguably encouraged. Researchers propose that girls' early sexual experiences are marked more by trauma than by enjoyment. They argue that legal sexual relations between youth may be far from consensual and actually result from peer pressure, fear, and force.[20] Indeed, surveys reveal that over half of girls report consenting to unwanted sex and, surprisingly, over one-third of boys do so as well.[21] Coercive relationships do not necessarily appear in dating contexts: a U.S. national sample of sexually abusive youth revealed that the most frequently reported age of adolescent sex offenders' victims is 6.[22] It is no longer difficult to imagine the possibility of coercive sexual behavior even among preadolescents. Recent research indicates that girls and boys are sexually harassed in the full view of adults; yet, adults simply ignore or excuse the abusive behavior.[23] In yet other instances, youth are harassed because of their sexual orientation.[24] Remarkably, these behaviors tend to be condoned. Indeed, victims may not even realize they have been victimized until years later. These practices too do not evoke easy solutions. The extent to which such behaviors are to be proscribed, tolerated, or even recognized and encouraged, has yet to be debated seriously.

That sexual maltreatment takes different forms, some of which proceed unnoticed and unremarked, is exemplified by rapid changes in social mores. For example, in the United States, the past few years have witnessed dramatic changes in adolescents' attitudes toward nudity, privacy, and sexuality. Yet, the change has gone largely unnoticed. High school students in the 1980s regularly took group showers after physical education classes. The practice went unchallenged. Indeed, it was virtually inconceivable that youth would not shower after rigorous exercises; those who did not were viewed as troublemakers or simply maladjusted. More recently, this form of showering has dwindled rapidly, largely in response to increased erotization of bodies and concern for protecting youths' privacy.[25] Arguably, requiring children to shower together could be interpreted as maltreatment and violation of children's rights. In fact, although such a finding would undoubtedly be controversial, the practice has been challenged successfully when framed in that manner.[26] This development exemplifies not only changes in youths' perceptions of their bodies and societal attitudinal changes toward sexuality, but also the manner in which the legal system adapts, responds, and assists in those changes.

The number of ways children are maltreated, and the numerous responses these events evoke, raise several questions and concerns as the notion of children's rights and the manner in which children are treated are becoming key policy issues on a global stage. What is abnormal child sexual development? What are abnormal child sexual relations? What role do communities and families play in encouraging or discouraging certain sexual activities? Should countries influence the internal workings of another country to the extent that they determine their peoples' sexual behavior and views of human development? What role do children themselves play in determining their gendered development, their sexual activities, and their own sexual futures? What exactly is meant by sex, maltreatment, and childhood? Arguably, some of the practices described above are simply part of sexual development, some are tolerable, and some are abusive.

The proposal that some forms of maltreatment are tolerable certainly is controversial and should not go ignored. Determining degrees of toleration will be a major thrust of our investigation. For now, it is important to emphasize that the extent to which certain sexual or sex related behaviors will be viewed as tolerable indelibly hinges on one's particular psychological, social, and cultural perspective. Psycho-socio-cultural factors clearly contribute to the meanings placed on sex-related behaviors. Consider the now familiar example of teen dating violence. Partners involved in sexually violent relationships often view their abusive relationships as normal, and actually obtain support from their immediate and extended social groups that reinforce the maltreatment as proper. It is difficult and arguably impossible to disentangle each partner's own psychological reasons for involvement in such relations from the societal factors that contribute to the violence.[27] A similar example is the manner in which sexually harassed girls and boys tend to define their abuse as normal, a process that parallels the feelings of children seduced into sexual relations with adults.[28] Yet another example involves the extent to which parents and children actually are in genital contact: existing research from nonclinical samples in the United States indicates that more than fifty percent of eight- to ten-year-old daughters touched their mother's breasts and genitals, and more than thirty percent touched their father's genitals, while more than forty percent of eight- to ten-year-old sons touched their mother's genitals, and about twenty percent their father's genitals.[29] Regardless of the particular child's perspective and relationship with abusers, societal forces clearly aim to intervene when behaviors are viewed as too abusive, just as societal forces support relations society does not view as abusive.[30]

Globally, the number of sexually maltreated children, the diversity in the ways they are maltreated, and the apparently different meanings individuals and societies use to define maltreatment complicate efforts to devise universal principles, enact standards, and implement policies that may be used to protect all children from all forms of child sexual maltreatment. Yet, the global community has given itself the mandate to do so.

The world community recently has recognized every child's fundamental human right to protection from sexual maltreatment.[31] This right has been expressed in recent declarations, conventions, and programs of action. Indeed, the right to protection from sexual maltreatment is now entrenched so strongly in international human rights law that no country can relinquish its obligation. The protection has become part of customary international law.[32] As such, the rights have become *erga omnes*: all states, all world citizens, have an interest in their recognition and enforcement.[33] Arguably, these acts are now considered in the same category as war crimes, such as willful killing, torture, genocide, and enslavement. Most recently, draft protocols have taken the seriousness of the acts further. Since the offense is considered to be contrary to the interests of the international community, it would be treated as a delict *jure gentium* whereby all Nation States would be entitled to apprehend and punish offenders in their own courts. The result would be a universal jurisdiction that would ensure that no cases go unpunished.[34] The extent to which diverse forms of child sexual maltreatment practices are understood and recognized as violations of customary law is important: the major advantage of customary international law over other laws is that it binds all states, including those that do not recognize it.[35] Yet, when we hear of a child sexually abused, exploited, tortured, or maimed by peers, family members, or strangers, most of us are unaware that these situations may involve violations of international human rights law.[36]

This development in human rights law is momentous, yet ominous. Undoubtedly, halting the sexual maltreatment of a child is a praiseworthy endeavor. Yet, the dangers of intervention are now well known. Intervention in allegedly abusive families remains controversial, as reflected in the backlash against the child protection movement[37] and the various "moral panics" failed societal interventions have produced in several countries in the forefront of massive intervention efforts, most notably the U.S., Britain, and Australia.[38] Outsider attempts to intervene in other societies remain equally factious. Well-intentioned intervention quickly can be framed in terms of cultural imperialism and thinly disguised expressions of racial and cultural superiority. Likewise, attempts to save children in the name of international human rights arguably can be viewed as new excuses for old strategies of cultural destruction.[39] Yet, it is becoming increasingly difficult to protect children and counter human rights abuses without challenging established notions of state sovereignty[40] and its equally privileged counterpart, family sovereignty.[41]

Just as efforts to penetrate different forms of sovereignties in control of children's lives become awkwardly difficult, so do attempts to curb both children's and offenders' behaviors. Protecting youth from potentially harmful influences may conflict with the expression of youths' sexual behaviors, as revealed in current attempts to broaden youths' access to birth control services,[42] to explicit sexual information, including pornography,[43] and, even more radically, to sexual relations with adults.[44] Likewise, intervention in the lives of offenders remains problematic. The protection of children does not vitiate, for example, other people's right to privacy and their right to certain materials. Although it would be difficult to argue that some individuals have the right to maltreat others,[45] individuals who maltreat others have rights which do make the uncovering and halting of abuse difficult.[46] To complicate matters even further, although youth may not have a right to services related to sexual behavior, to sexual information, and to sexual relations with adults, it is undeniable that they often do have access to these relations, services, and commodities. Even more problematic are the nebulous forces that contribute to maltreatment and the recognized right of societies to raise their children according to their own cultural ideals. Yet, each child clearly possesses the individual right to protection, and the global community continues to commit itself to protect its children from sexual maltreatment.

Legally, the formal progress toward recognizing the need to protect children from sexual maltreatment is nothing short of phenomenal. Yet, much more change is needed in the manner in which legal systems treat children. Legal recognition of social issues coupled with extensive law reform does not necessarily advance children's causes. In fact, despite developments and apparent global commitment, it remains uncertain how the new domestic and international efforts marshaled to protect children ultimately will foster action most beneficial to them. Furthermore, once agreement has been reached regarding theory and even policy, implementation problems inevitably follow. Indeed, well-intentioned, extensive formal legal reforms may sometimes be counterproductive and leave certain children at greater risk.

There are clear examples of potential negative repercussions emanating from benevolent mandates, at both domestic and international levels. Internationally, strict law enforcement that protects children in some Western countries seems to increase exploitation in other countries, as revealed by increased efforts to obtain child pornography and hire child prostitutes in Third World countries.[47] Legal reforms also have iatrogenic effects that lead to the maltreatment of children within countries, although the harms tend to be more subtle, or at least more ignored. For example, the rise in statutory rape legislation arguably leaves entire groups of girls essentially unprotected from unwanted sexual relations.[48] Likewise, attempts to curb access to sexual materials arguably has lead uncounted numbers of adolescents to early deaths: youth unaware of how to deal with sexual feelings have the highest suicide rates,[49] and youth who do not have proper access to educational and medical services are placed at higher risk to contract deadly diseases.[50]

Moving from theory to practice undoubtedly remains difficult. The right to protection from sexual maltreatment certainly serves as a prime example of the need to proceed carefully and cautiously. Several countries have enacted extensive laws that forcefully prohibit sexual interactions with children. Indeed, the right to protection from certain forms of sexual maltreatment was one of the earliest recognized international children's rights that existed even before the founding of the United Nations.[51] Yet, inappropriate sexual interactions continue. Given existing laws and information about the plight of sexually maltreated children, the most pressing issue undoubtedly becomes how we are to deal properly with existing information and enact more effective laws and policies.

This book looks to human rights law to help detail what could and should be done to protect children from sexual maltreatment. This ambitious goal will be met by exploring diverse forms of sexual maltreatment, comparing societal responses to existing research and policies, uncovering basic themes, and framing directions for future endeavors. This is not an attempt to survey the exact incidence and existence of child sexual maltreatment around the world; such an investigation is impossible and would not necessarily be useful. Rather, this effort examines the ways sexually maltreating activities in different countries and societies are linked with one another and the ways diverse societal views of children place them at risk for maltreatment. Throughout this endeavor, an effort is made to bring together several intersecting debates that concern different areas of social science and the law. As a consequence, the different chapters concentrate on different aspects of maltreatment, childhood, and the law. Each chapter seeks to be sufficiently independent to enable readers to focus on the topics which touch their interests, but the more general arguments run throughout the book as a whole, with the individual chapters building onto one another. Each chapter pragmatically considers human rights law as a tool enlisted to combat child sexual maltreatment.

Chapter 2 places children's right to protection from sexual maltreatment within a broader human rights perspective. It examines critical developments in an increasingly comprehensive international human rights legal framework. The chapter highlights what the current international children's human rights movement asks of us: the enactment of child protection *and* liberation policies that take the child's perspective seriously and actually approach child policy-making from the child's point of view. The chapter also evaluates critiques of rights and addresses concerns regarding cultural relativism and emerging criticisms of the utility of framing social claims, interests, and responsibilities in terms of "rights." It is proposed that, in its effort to energize children's rights, innovative human rights law actively confronts and assimilates these critiques as it aims to create a global yet diverse culture that takes children's interests seriously. Lastly, the chapter focuses on drawing the legal consequences of the globalization of modern society[52] in the form of globalized social problems like sexual maltreatment that require different approaches than national problems and challenge existing notions of personhood, citizenship, nation, sovereignty, and state.

Chapter 3 sets the stage for our analysis of the right to protection from sexual maltreatment. The chapter addresses the reasons for the very existence of childhood and explores how childhood is not a "natural" fact—how there are indeed varieties of childhood determined by ecological forces. The reasons for childhood and its social construction help highlight why sexual maltreatment comes in diverse yet systematically related forms; they also help us appreciate that neither childhood nor sexual maltreatment can be examined or addressed in isolation from its systemic, ecological context. The chapter also delineates three broad forms of sexual maltreatment: sexual use, abuse, and exploitation. The categories of maltreatment are used for heuristic purposes and to highlight critical points and themes that span all forms of maltreatment and suggestions for proper societal responses. The chapter proposes that the suggestions are reflected in the policy framework that international law encourages us to take. It argues that the framework, rather than essentialist views of "rights," makes the current international statement of children's rights particularly useful and momentous.

Chapter 4 examines the sexual exploitation of children. Although this form of maltreatment arguably includes more traditional notions of abuse, the notion of bartering or economic gain is used to emphasize the approach. The chapter examines the domestic and international dimensions of several interrelated forms of exploitation, particularly sex-tourism, pornography, prostitution, international abduction, and sexual slavery. Although sexual exploitation remains the form that has received the most formal international attention and the form of maltreatment most directly amenable to international reaction, it continues to pose some of the most intractable problems. The chapter concludes with an examination of obstacles and opportunities for reforming the commercialized maltreatment of children.

Chapter 5 examines practices most foreign to Western audiences: the "sexual" use of children. These practices include bodily mutilation, sexual relations during rites of passage, religious practices that leave children at risk for sexual maltreatment, child marriages, and other practices that dictate the sexual relations of children and adolescents. After the practices are placed in their cultural contexts, which often do not denote sexual behavior as conceived in the West, they are reexamined through the lens of international human rights law. The chapter aims to pinpoint contradictions and difficulties, and to consider emerging strategies for dealing with polarized debates. It will be proposed that human rights law urges us to approach cultural issues in a manner similar to other forms of maltreatment, that international law asks us to focus on the "cultural child."

Chapter 6 explores the category of sexual maltreatment most familiar to Western audiences: sexual abuse. The analysis reviews the current understanding of child sexual abuse and analyzes different sociolegal responses to this form of maltreatment. The examination then places sexual abuse in the context of human rights violations and policy-making. The chapter elaborates upon the potential benefits and pitfalls of the formal international approach to protecting children from sexual abuse. The discussion highlights how the children's rights movement seeks to re-image the role of states and their regulation of private behavior, and how the movement calls for a societal transformation in perceptions of children. Importantly, the demands for transformation in the West are as great as those made on other cultures that engage in "traditional" practices deemed as maltreating by Western standards and observers.

Chapter 7 focuses on Western forms of abuse that remain largely ignored: victimization by peers. Although considerable research reveals the ubiquitousness of children's sex play,[53] only recently has there been more sustained interest in examining the abusive peer incidents the chapter examines.[54] The chapter focuses mainly on child sexual harassment, acquaintance rape, relationship violence, and juvenile sex offending against younger children. Although legal systems, particularly international law, ignore the deleterious effects and pervasiveness of these maltreatments, the chapter proposes that domestic legal systems, buttressed by insights from international law, can be marshaled to assist victims and address offending behavior. Again, the analysis points to the need for greater social transformation in perceptions of childhood, sexuality, and maltreatment.

Chapter 8 reiterates themes and highlights lessons learned. The chapter details recent transformations in the regulation of childhood and culture, and shows how these transformations appropriately address major reasons for the traditional failure to protect children from sexual maltreatment. The chapter then pinpoints counterproductive consequences of prevailing ideologies of childhood, sexuality, maltreatment, and the law, and suggests directions for reforms that develop a more child-centered vision of human rights. The discussion remains intentionally provisional, as it aims to suggest ways of making connections and asking better questions rather than to provide complete answers to pressing issues. In brief, the chapter develops a stance that allows us to take children's rights seriously, rethink victimology, and reinforce the need for culturally sensitive approaches to child protection and liberation.

The investigation necessarily delves into diverse social science and legal approaches to childhood, an attempt at comprehensiveness that undoubtedly constitutes an enormous undertaking. The risk of overgeneralization certainly abounds. Yet, because both children and sexuality have not been dealt with comprehensively but rather as disaggregated in anthropological, psychological, sexological, criminological, and human rights research, the current state of the law, policy, and social sciences warrants a study of the interlocking forces and approaches. The disaggregation will become apparent as we proceed, particularly when areas of study or legal responses comprehensively cover certain issues while ignoring others. To reduce the risk of improperly portraying sexually maltreated children and emerging responses to assist their plight, it is necessary to risk some overgeneralization in the process of piecing together the forces that shape variable forms of sexual maltreatment. Likewise, it is necessary to take a risk to break the cultural silence that keeps many of the hardships children suffer under the cover of custom and tradition, as well as the most "liberal" forms of socialization and even the more "enlightened" reactions to maltreatment.

"Invisible Acts" indicates more than acts that comprise the silent ecology of sexual maltreatment, such as the seduction of children into sexual activity, the coercion of others so they "do not tell," and the enormous difficulties encountered by attempts to uncover maltreatment. Invisible acts are part of the culture of silence that fails to distinguish among childhood experiences, varieties of sexual maltreatment, and the interrelationships of diverse forces that constitute the social reality of childhood and child sexual maltreatment. This book asks us to enact rather radical policies that must truly challenge and counter every society's unsuspecting belief that adults *and* children would not maltreat children and to uncover conditions that allow maltreatment to flourish without much resistance. It asks us to make more visible what the global community has recognized: children's human right to protection from sexual maltreatment.

2 | Transforming Legal Conceptions of Childhood

The Global Human Rights Revolution

International human rights law now protects children against sexual maltreatment. Yet, the nature and power of that protection remains invisible to general public consciousness. This chapter details sociopolitical developments that have laid the foundation for the current children's rights movement, the nature and content of children's human rights, and the numerous methods of enforcement that recognize the role played by states and the international community in fostering community, family, and individual protection. The discussion highlights how developments recognize the inseparability of civil, political, and cultural rights, the need for local application, and the demand that societies affirm children's inherent sense of human dignity and bestow upon children their own rights.

Introduction

Children are part of an unparalleled effort to establish and maintain a global community based upon universal but evolving standards of human decency, morality, and dignity. The principle of how children should be treated, and of how they treat themselves, reflects the revolution in the manner the world views children, family, and community life. Although this development in human rights undoubtedly constitutes one of the greatest social transformations ever imagined, it certainly does not fit the popular image of individual human rights. We reserve our mental image of international human rights for the international community's effort to pressure oppressive regimes to stop violations that involve prisoners of conscience, political torture, and disappearances. International law still clearly centers on individuals, on their own human dignity and equality to others, and on the power of countries and the international community to press for reform. Now, however, the international human rights movement also focuses on the need to recognize and respect the centrality of every individual in every family and every society. The movement further aims to re-image the important role played Ŀ, munity and family life in fostering individual protection and fulfillment.

The new image and new role of human rights law in the form of importance placed on every individual and on every individual as a family and community member is not just recognized and accepted by a small number of nations. A record number of countries officially have accepted this conviction as they have ratified and signaled their acceptance of international human rights standards. In addition, these countries obligate themselves to monitoring human rights and to encouraging their implementation.

Formal agreements, impressive developments, and the increasing power of international human rights have not been immune from criticisms. Human rights face attacks and challenges from all sides. Some challenge the universality of human rights, others accept universality but decry the divergence between espoused norms and actual standards, others reject the notion of rights altogether, while others simply debate the involvement of the United Nations.[1] These debates rage over the role that law can play in responding to complex social relations; all sides of rights discourses continue to be met with considerable resistance.

Controversies are even more pronounced when children's rights are involved. The extent to which children should determine their own lives and the point at which they no longer are children remains exceedingly controversial. Equally contentious is the determination of exactly who or what will protect children while also ensuring their eventual liberation: conflicts exist among the power and role of the state, parents, and children themselves. As expected, some view the framing of children's issues in terms of rights as counterproductive and as an obstacle to nuanced, sensitive, and desirable outcomes.[2] With respect to the development of a system of universal human rights and child policy, these issues become exceedingly problematic. The persistence of controversies and concerns makes the framing of children's rights complex and hampers effective implementation of child policies.

Despite their theoretical and practical difficulties, both criticisms and accolades must be taken seriously. Instead of playing down these continuing controversial issues, the current international children's rights movement directly confronts and assimilates them. The question has become less one of which "sides" of the debates are right, and more one of applying the insights of the debates to particular strategies and campaigns for children. Regrettably, that forthright approach has fueled yet another round of criticisms. Critics complain that the inclusion of different approaches, the balancing of interests, and respect for diversity essentially dilute children's fundamental human rights.[3] Yet, children's issues inevitably must involve more than children's concerns. Children's special status arguably calls for a different formulation of rights currently bestowed upon autonomous adults, especially as we begin to recognize that adults, too, are far from being autonomous.

This chapter investigates developments in children's rights and explores how the modern children's rights movement addresses the above difficulties. To accomplish this task, the analysis situates children's rights within the greater human rights agenda; for evolving conceptions of children's human rights simply cannot be understood apart from their broader theoretical and sociopolitical foundation. The evaluation focuses on whether the current move makes practical sense, particularly with respect to the way it frames children's issues in terms of rights, the necessary difficulties encountered when applied to diverse cultural conceptions of humanity, and its nonconfrontational and seemingly weak enforcement mechanisms. The discussion serves as a background for determining whether emerging legal ideologies of childhood offer hope for sexually maltreated children.

Modern Conceptions of Human Rights: The Sociopolitical Context of Rapid Developments

The eventual success of efforts to transform approaches to legal conceptions of childhood rests on the international community's ability to define and accept rudimentary universal standards and principles that regulate how humans treat one another. Although it is a daunting task, the foundation has been emerging for the past five decades as the international community continues to define and fine-tune basic notions of human rights. Efforts already have resulted in the construction of a substantial edifice of human rights law. In fact, such a wide range of human rights concepts have been invoked that no particular culture or political group can claim that its understanding and interpretation of those guarantees is exclusively fundamental.[4] A discussion of current conceptions of children's human rights, then, appropriately begins with these important developments in conceptions of human rights law and policy.

Although barely over fifty years old, the human rights movement already includes thousands of human rights conventions, declarations, and policy statements.[5] Despite the phenomenal number of human rights instruments and their impressive history, all modern human rights instruments derive from and complement a handful of important human rights documents. The Universal Declaration of Human Rights[6] originally set the basic standards and principles. The Universal Declaration, however, was supplemented by two highly influential international covenants: the Covenant on Civil and Political Rights[7] and the Covenant on Economic, Social and Cultural Rights.[8] Taken together, these three documents constitute the International Bill of Rights.[9] Although the International Bill is exceedingly comprehensive, other important extensions have been made to strengthen and actually expand international law's reach. The most notable addition has been the almost universally ratified United Nations Convention on the Rights of the Child.[10]

The substance of the rights protected in the International Bill and the Children's Convention reflects the entire gamut of imaginable rights. These rights have evolved at such a rapid rate that there are now said to be four generations of rights. The nature of these four generations has been influenced by changing concerns about global issues relating to the power of nations and their roles in recognizing and ensuring basic human rights. Each generation represents a novel phase in the history of human rights. Although each generation reflects the concerns of its time, taken together, their goals and reach encapsulate a comprehensive and coherent vision of human rights.

The foundation for what would become known as first generation rights emerged in the wake of World War II.[11] The end of the war meant that Western nations and Western political concepts would dominate the policy-making agenda and ensuing documents. The war also would galvanize concern for preventing similar atrocities, particularly the violations of basic standards of humanity by Nazi Germany. In the wake of the Nazi Holocaust's totalitarian abuses, a global audience was ready to support the nascent human rights agenda. Thus, the same concern for world peace and the need for international promotion and protection of human rights that actually led to the foundation of the United Nations also contributed to the landmark drafting of the Universal Declaration of Human Rights and the International Covenants.

Not surprisingly, the atrocities of war and concerns for peace fueled the development of human rights standards that would focus on the protection of the person's basic security against intrusion from state power. These protections are commonly known as first generation rights that center on the development of civil and political protections, and help shield individuals from abusive and arbitrary state interference and encroachment. These rights have a defensive character and are well known as "freedom from" rather than positive "rights to." The Universal Declaration and the Covenant on Civil and Political Rights exemplify these first generation human rights. For example, the documents emphasize notions of due process and the well-known freedoms of religion, expression, and association. Again, concern centers on preventing the atrocities of state power and protecting people from the state.

As the negative rights were being formulated, a set of positive "rights to" also were incorporated into human rights policy-making. These second generation rights were championed primarily by socialist and welfare states and are best known as social and economic rights. Historically, these rights were designed to help overcome the increasing impoverishment and proletarianization of the masses. As reflected in the Covenant on Social, Economic and Cultural Rights, these rights are considerably expansive. The rights include the right to employment and fair working conditions, to a standard of living that ensures health and well-being, and to social security, education, and the right to participation in the cultural life of the community. Unlike first generation rights that assume all individuals will be protected equally, second generation rights include special rights for vulnerable groups, including the unemployed, the disabled, the sick, the widowed, the elderly, and children.

The contrast between the two approaches to human rights has been the subject of a formidable and extended controversy as nations seek to devise and adopt universal human rights standards. The extent to which the rights diverge is highlighted by the inability to mesh the approaches into one enforceable document.[12] This is important. Each International Covenant actually delineates substantive rights and establishes monitoring and enforcement mechanisms. Each attempts to move beyond the Universal Declaration's simple "declaration" that the rights exist and begin the process of enforcement and implementation. The conflicts of values that emerged among participating nations had been subdued when nations were persuaded that the Universal Declaration's rights could not be legally binding;[13] but such would not be the case for the Covenants that followed.

Given the focus on actually ensuring that rights are respected, the disagreements became particularly intense. Yet, disagreements are unsurprising: they revolve around the fundamentally different values and visions of state involvement in everyday life. The negative rights-bearer is imagined as self-determining, unencumbered and unconnected to others by choice—thus suggesting a state which would aim to respect "the right to be let alone."[14] On the other hand, the positive rights-bearer is imagined as a person situated within and essentially constituted by relationships with others. In the positive vision, the rights are programmatic:

States take on the obligation to actively facilitate individual fulfillment and affirmatively promote social welfare.

Although the focus on individuals in their social contexts may be appealing, discussions of how to envision these international human rights became bogged down in a highly controversial debate fueled by political and ideological tensions of the Cold War. These tensions helped tailor debates about human rights ideologies in terms of issues that highlighted the East-West conflict. Not surprisingly, the dialogue consisted of disputes over which rights should be accorded priority, the civil and political rights or the economic, social, and cultural rights. Notions of what governments were to do, or not do, for their constituents were contentious matters.

By the time the two major covenants were adopted, the nature of the United Nations had changed. Many new countries from the Third World,[15] particularly those from Africa and Asia, had joined the United Nations. Although these new member nations' resources and general outlook on international problems and human rights considerably differed from those of the West or East, Cold War tensions still dominated the human rights agenda. The new members acted cautiously and aligned themselves with East-West factions. The alignment muffled the governments most likely to propose the expansion and alternative visions of human rights.

With the growing demise of the Cold War, Third World countries sought to champion their own causes. Several proposed that the very notion of human rights, or at least certain specific rights, was Eurocentric, and that current conceptions of rights inappropriately addressed their own needs. The Third World countries posed an important challenge. These efforts were instrumental in championing what would encompass the third generation rights, what now have become known as the right to "solidarity" or "development." These rights reflect a commitment to an equitable socioeconomic order and to a sustainable environment. Since this conception of individual rights cannot be separated from the collective context of the rights,[16] it clashes with the more narrow conceptions of negative rights.

Most recent, and still in the process of being formulated, are the fourth generation rights of indigenous peoples. These rights aim to "socialize" individualistic conceptions of rights through adapting current conceptions of rights to suit indigenous peoples' own needs. They embrace the focus on protection from state powers, but do so through a collective context. Thus, this conception of rights aims to protect *peoples'* rights to political self-determination and to grant *peoples* control over their socioeconomic development.[17] Propagation of fourth generation rights is fueled by indigenous peoples' claims that their rights are threatened within existing traditional state frameworks.[18] Likewise, even minority groups throughout the West are seeking greater recognition and accommodation for their cultural differences.[19] Considerable evidence supports their claims; the result has been a series of important declarations and international meetings that champion indigenous peoples' rights.[20]

It should be no surprise that the end of the Cold War witnessed a rise in attention to social development, concern for indigenous peoples' rights, and a new intensity in debates about the cultural relativity of human rights. The notion of human rights has now entered into the cultural schemes of meaning of peoples everywhere. Clearly, the four generations reflect the revolutionary move toward greater global respect for human rights, although heated disagreements continue over what the term entails.

Given the impassioned debates and the growing list of human rights, it is becoming clear that all generations of human rights necessarily must be included in any legitimate interpretation of current "human rights." The generations certainly are indispensable to an analysis of the human rights document that concerns us most, that which champions all generations of human rights and relates explicitly to children, families, and community life: the Children's Convention.

The international children's rights movement and its crown jewel—the Children's Convention—also owe a large part of their success to the Cold War. The end of the Cold War did more than give a new lease on life to notions of human rights and directly contribute to the development of so many generations of human rights. The Cold War actually instrumentally fostered a fortuitous combination of circumstances that would lay the groundwork for the drafting and eventual unprecedented endorsement of international children's rights. The ultimate result would be the immensely successful adoption of the Children's Convention.

The evolution of the Children's Convention, in terms of both its drafting and its adoption, reveals well how Cold War politics actually hastened the development of children's rights. The first draft of the Convention was in the form of a proposal made by Poland in 1978. Poland limited its effort to an attempt to adapt the provisions of the formally nonbinding 1959 Declaration of the Rights of the Child into a more suitable and binding treaty. History reveals that the attempt to make the Declaration binding was introduced partly in an effort to seize some of

Jimmy Carter's booming human rights initiative. Poland orchestrated the effort to elevate the economic and social rights to which, as we have seen, Communist countries wanted to accord priority. The rights of the child seemed an ideal topic for the purpose.[21] Poland's move was forceful enough to cause the U.S. to marshal its resources and seek to stall and stifle the Convention's early drafting process.

The U.S. ignored or obfuscated the drafting process until the mid-1980s. At that point, it became apparent that the notion of children's rights was garnering enough support to ensure the eventual adoption of an international treaty. Given the increase in world interest, the United States quickly adjusted its stance. The U.S. moved to include civil and political rights that it accused Communist countries of downgrading. Arguably, the United States' motivation was more than an effort to offer the world's children important first generation rights. These rights, such as the freedoms of speech, religion, and association, are not even fully bestowed upon children in the United States.[22] An arguably more critical part of the United States' attempt to influence the drafting of the Children's Convention was to make Poland's undertaking less appealing to its original sponsors and their allies.[23]

As the Cold War reached its end, nongovernmental organizations played an increasingly active role in preparing the Convention.[24] International organizations, UNICEF in particular, generated more active participation of developing countries in the drafting process. The result was the enhancement of the acceptability of the draft to those countries. Given that more nations had been included in the drafting process, the Convention gained even greater support.

Once the draft Convention was in place, world conditions were again propitious. By the end of the 1980s, formerly communist countries were eager to demonstrate their concern for human rights. No other document would better suit their desire to show their newfound attachment to a comprehensive package of international human rights norms. Likewise, a sense of hope grew as countries quickly leaped toward democracy. Rapid changes bolstered the optimistic sentiment that a significant change in the treatment of children was within the world community's grasp. The new era could mean the diversion of massive resources from military expansion toward the amelioration of children's survival prospects in many countries and of deteriorating conditions of children's environments worldwide. Equally propitious was the timely switch in U.S. presidential administrations, from Ronald Reagan to George Bush. This development removed the likelihood that the U.S. would prevent the final push to adopt the Convention. Indeed, the United States had changed its opposition to such an extent that it hosted the 1990 World Summit for Children in New York.[25]

The World Summit was convened to ensure that the Children's Convention generated more than a statement of lofty principles and hollow promises. In several regards, the Summit was a remarkable success. No other event has ever been attended by such a large number of heads of state—virtually all nations had a representative. The participants did more than simply meet. Participants adopted an ambitious Declaration and Plan of Action for Children in the 1990s.[26] In effect, an unprecedented number of countries committed themselves to preparing national programs of action to achieve the goals agreed upon in the Summit Declaration.

The World Summit and its Declaration highlighted how the plight of the world's children was deteriorating rapidly. Children in especially difficult circumstances included those "trapped in the bondage of prostitution, sexual abuse and other forms of exploitation."[27] The world community was at a turning point. Although the plight of children was alarming, there was significant room for hope. The world's societies seemed ready and willing to reassess the traditional relationships between childhood, family, and the state in matters relating to children's well-being. In the end, the global community committed itself to implementing the Children's Convention. Properly framed, the Children's Convention certainly fits the task—it provides a creative, timely, and effective response to the challenges facing today's children, youth, and families.

Convention on the Rights of the Child: A Comprehensive and Radical Vision for Children's Rights

The Children's Convention will likely dominate discussions of the nature of international children's rights. No other treaty has drawn such global interest and support. The unprecedented rapidity with which Nation States have ratified or acceded to it and the sheer number of States Parties it has attracted underscores the Convention's importance.[28] The only major country remaining outside the treaty regime is the United States, which has taken the first important step toward full recognition: in 1995, the U.S. signed the Convention and noted its intention to proceed with ratification.[29]

In addition to having been exceptionally well-received, the Children's Convention makes the international interest particularly momentous. The Convention contains all four generations of rights. In fact, the Convention is the most detailed and comprehensive human rights treaty in force: it enumerates the entire range of civil, political, economic, psychological, social, and cultural rights.[30] The world community has granted the role of standard bearer of children's rights to the Children's Convention.

The Convention raises vitally important challenges, and its complexities and proposals have yet to be understood entirely. Although the Convention bestows upon children all generations of human rights and seeks to balance those rights with other important interests, it continues to be presented as a unidimensional document. Not surprisingly, these analyses have fostered exceedingly polarized debates. Regrettably, these debates impede compromise, mutual understanding, and the discovery of common ground that must be reached before the Convention can have its intended impact.

Both opponents and supporters tend to propose that the Convention contains a single, unified philosophy of children's rights and that the Convention consists of recipes that resolve inevitable conflicts and tensions that arise among the different recognized rights.[31] Likewise, both camps characterize the role of individuals involved in children's lives as clearly defined and delineated. The result is that some view the Convention as Eurocentric, antifamily, repressive, and opposed to parental rights. These commentators view the Convention as misguided, improperly concerned with "abandoning children to their autonomy."[32] Others hail the Convention as a new Magna Carta that will protect children in the New World Order.[33] Given the intense level of debates, the problems are far from being resolved. The polarized debates, for example, largely account for the United State's failure to ratify the Children's Convention.[34] Supporters of ratification propose that the Convention, with a few minor exceptions, would not have an impact on U.S. law. At the other extreme, critics maintain that ratification would open the United States to unprecedented foreign influence and radically transform the United States' approach to children and family issues by bestowing numerous positive rights and children's freedoms, particularly regarding abortion, education, and discipline. Currently, opponents clearly have the upper hand. Although the process of securing United States ratification of human rights treaties is a well-established part of American history,[35] no other treaty has attracted such a strong and well-organized opposition that imperils the treaty's eventual ratification.[36]

Several reasons help explain the expected longevity of debates. A major reason for continuing controversies is the general tendency of countries that do ratify the Convention to do so simply to demonstrate their ostensible commitment to children; countries ratify yet attempt to avoid taking their treaty obligations seriously.[37] Politicking and divisive debates also contribute to the expectation that the Convention will not impact children's lives as quickly as expected. These debates inevitably postpone the need to deal with pressing yet politically sensitive issues. Lastly, the most important reason is most likely that the Convention actually does not solve major dilemmas. With a few exceptions, the Convention simply does not mandate a particular solution or outcome to controversial issues. The roles, obligations, and privileges bestowed upon children, families, local communities, states, and international communities have been delineated and defined in a much more complicated manner. Simply put, framing the Convention in simple terms injuriously promotes unrealistic expectations and ignores the reality of children's lives. The history of children's rights is replete with examples of campaigns for law reform that, rather than leading to the elimination of violent and discriminatory practices, often reinforce and rigidify positions of those who defend the practices.[38] Just as importantly, the Convention ignores how laws function: law seldom is a simple instrument of social engineering, nor of liberation or oppression, but rather is a complex and contradictory force. Feminist writers have shown well how law not only reinforces current power structures, but also provides important sources of resistance and change.[39] The Convention is no exception.

Several examples illustrate how the Convention is far more complex and multidimensional than prevailing characterizations would imply. Most fundamentally, recognition of and respect for all generations of human rights reflect the complex and often contradictory nature of the Convention. Although commendable for their inclusiveness and extensiveness, the generations of rights remain somewhat problematic. The problem with the comprehensive approach is that rights cannot simply be a wish list of different protections and approaches. The use of cumulative listing and the process of addition fail to mediate and reconcile the inevitable differences between opposing views and sometimes conflicting values. Simply stated, the simplicity of wish-listing is deceptive. Critics rightly have suggested that the approach leaves unaddressed too many issues pertaining to the nature of rights and the extent to which some rights are "trumps" that override other concerns.[40] Yet, it would be unwise to formulate rights in a stark, unqualified fashion—such conceptions improperly foster the illusion that the rights in question are more secure than they actually are.

Although the Convention is the subject of immense criticism and is admittedly quite complicated, it would be premature to propose that it cannot fulfill its aspirations. The Convention does not provide easy answers to pressing children's issues, but it does provide a framework for addressing children's concerns and a range of important issues affecting children. The enumerated rights simply cannot be interpreted independently of others. Indeed, to be at all useful, children's rights must be interpreted from the standpoint of the entire Convention as well as other documents and developments in international human rights.[41] As several human rights commissions, international organizations, and world conferences have lamented, there is a pressing need for comprehensive interpretations of children's rights from an international perspective.[42] Such examinations are necessary if we are ever to develop a better appreciation of the nature and complexity of children's rights at the global as well as the national, local, familial, and individual levels.

An interpretive reading of human rights documents reveals that the Convention is more than a document with some rules for how nations are to behave. The Convention puts forth an important *vision*. Although it is important to reiterate that the Convention rarely dictates clear-cut answers to pressing children's issues, the treaty does express basic values about the treatment of children, their protection, and their participation in society. The vision is reflected in its agreed-upon guidelines, major principles, and reverberating themes. These developments are truly visionary. The rights enumerated in the Convention and the principles used to guide their interpretations urge us to rethink fundamentally ingrained ideologies of childhood, families, rights, communities, and international law. It is important to understand the way the Convention urges us to rethink these ideologies; they guide the current children's rights movement and have important consequences for efforts to combat child sexual maltreatment.

A fundamental vision found in the Convention and every international human rights document is respect for human dignity and equality.[43] The Convention, like all core international documents, recognizes "the inherent dignity and equality of *all members of the human family* as the foundation of freedom, justice and peace in the world."[44] Through the Convention, the international community reaffirms its belief that the fundamental essence of human rights is that they are the entitlement of every human being. All civil and political rights as well as economic, social, and cultural rights recognized by these and all other international documents derive, as necessary implications or practical manifestations, from the inherent dignity and integrity of every person.

Respecting Children's Personhood:
Recognizing Children's Interests and Liberation
under Human Rights Law

It is often difficult to appreciate the Convention's proclamation that children are to be regarded as people with equal worth and dignity. Although this may sound like a truism, it is, as we will see, a radical idea. As human beings, children have the same inherent value as adults. Yet, the inherent value does not mean that they have rights equal to those possessed by parents or others acting *parens patriae*. Instead, children's dignity is to be protected and their equality ensured through consideration of their own interests and recognition of their voice in matters affecting them. These two considerations provide the necessary ingredients both to promote special protections against children's vulnerabilities and to foster their liberation.

The familiar principle of "best interests" represents well how the Convention aims to recognize the centrality of children's concerns.[45] In terms of international law, the best interests standard serves as an umbrella provision that plays several critical roles exemplified by the Children's Convention. The first role is simply interpretive. The best interests of the child is simply an element to be considered when implementing other children's rights: the standard supports, justifies, and clarifies other articles. The second role is that of mediator. In that regard, the standard assists in the mediation of conflicts that arise in the interpretation of rights; arguably the child's best interests would be a major factor weighed in considerations of children's issues. The third role is the important, yet often ignored, role of evaluator. The Convention's best interests standard serves as an important benchmark upon which to compare and evaluate the laws and practices of all societies. In this regard, the best interests standard is a primary principle not only in the Convention itself, or in notions of children's rights, but also in the overall human rights context. Other treaties, declarations, and policy statements must take children's best interests into account.

Taken from any of these perspectives, the Convention's basic principle that children's best interests be a primary consideration is rather far-reaching. The Convention essentially obligates all nations to follow children's best interests in the design and implementation of policies affecting children and families. Through the Convention, all societies have agreed to the primacy of the best interests of children in "all actions concerning children."[46]

However, the Convention does much more than obligate nations. Its language is expansive; it seeks to apply to more than just official actions of governmental bodies. The best interests standard applies to *all* actions involving children. As it stands, the Convention leaves no doubt that it would apply the best interests provisions to actions of parents and guardians. For example, some articles have a strong version of the principle. The article regulating parental rights and responsibilities enjoins parents and legal guardians in exercising their primary responsibility for the upbringing and development of the child to have "the best interests of the child [as] their basic concern."[47] Likewise, other international documents support the interpretation and arguably offer even stronger protection: the Convention on the Elimination of All Forms of Discrimination Against Women mandates that, in the context of parental rights and responsibilities, "the interests of the children shall be *paramount*" (emphasis added).[48]

The Convention has not only breathed new life into the best interests standard which most societies already have "on the books."[49] Arguably even more revolutionary is the manner in which the Convention adopts a new principle to ensure children's rights, the new principle of dynamic self-determination. This central principle in the way children's rights are now framed bestows upon children increasing rights as they develop. In theory, the principle is quite simple: *all* children must participate in decisions that affect them.[50] In reality, the task of including children in decision-making is much more difficult than it may appear: the right arguably applies in several different contexts.[51]

The Convention clearly bestows upon children a voice in legal and extralegal proceedings. The potential ramifications of this approach are momentous. The principle could, for example, influence the prosecution of sex crimes against children by giving victims the right not to participate in proceedings, giving them the prosecutorial veto often given adults.[52] Although already partly implemented in some jurisdictions, that proposal could be extremely contentious. That contentiousness could certainly pale in comparison to other possibilities. As with the best interests standard, the Convention grants children a voice in more than legal proceedings. For example, the principle could influence children's right to consent to sexual relations and all that consent would entail.[53] At the very least, for example, it would make it more difficult to impose paternalistic protections upon children. Given that parents, like society, have an interest in their children's sexual relations, it remains unclear how the right to self-determination ultimately will be fostered in family settings.[54] Yet, the Convention offers protections in all fora that affect children's lives.

The focus on all actions affecting children is not just a significant development in the best interests standard and recognition that children could benefit from increasing self-determination as they develop. The developments are revolutionary for international law. The Convention consciously breaks new ground, as it creates an important addition to human rights jurisprudence—the notion of autonomy-based individual personality rights for children.[55] Giving children a voice in decisions that affect them and considering their best interests necessarily means that their voices would be heard in settings heretofore beyond the reach of international law. For example, to ensure children's right to self-determination, international human rights law has created a new focus for intervention: in the name of human rights, the international community may "intervene" in families and ensure that caretakers recognize and respect children's rights.

The significance of this development toward new forms of intervention simply cannot be overstated. For example, the focus on dynamic self-determination, buttressed by other principles, essentially challenges the private, patriarchal nature of families. International law aims to open families to public scrutiny and ensure each individual family member's greater equality within families.[56] This new principle provides a legal mechanism for opening up the private household, parental behavior in particular, to new forms of surveillance. The approach makes the family more visible to social regulation, not just from formal state structures, but also from neighbors, relatives, communities, and even the international community. Although it would be erroneous to argue that the international community aims to control and pry open individuals' families, the development clearly indicates that countries are obligated to enact policies that would allow local communities to do so. The openness is not just limited to families. The practices of welfare professionals also are arguably made more visible and subject to new forms of monitoring and accountability. This effort is a critical example of how the Convention encourages attempts to rethink family and welfare paternalism.

Like the best interests standard, the emerging focus on children's individual self-determination essentially seeks to re-image children's personhood. Children are not necessarily passive, defenseless, and in need of protection by state agents who know what is in children's interests. Likewise, children do not just "belong" to their parents; children belong to themselves. The practices of states and families are no longer assumed to be inherently benevolent. Approaches to family life are now to focus on individual family members, how their interests might diverge, and how those interests must be disaggregated to ensure that children and young family members may make distinctive rights claims. In this regard, the Convention is the first serious international attempt to redress potential imbalances in family life.[57] It is also the first time children's rights have been taken seriously enough and not simply identified with a unified notion of family welfare, including, as we will see, Nation State welfare.

What emerges from the new re-imaging is a reconstitution of children as persons in their own right. The international movement aims to recognize children's own legal personhood. Children are no longer possessions over which power is exercised. What is significant, and to a large extent historically radical, about this move is that rights are bestowed upon children,[58] as opposed to being conferred upon parents or the state. Indeed, what the Children's Convention does confer upon parents, the state, and every individual is the duty to ensure that children's rights are respected.[59] Simply stated, children are no longer mere *objects* of rights; they are the *subjects* of rights.

As new subjects of rights, children essentially have been granted different rights than familiar phrases suggest. Conceptions of children's best interests are strongly rooted in the self-images of families and cultures.[60] The focus on self-determination, though, contributes something important. The notion of best interests no longer is equivalent to collective, familial, or cultural self-determination. It appeals directly to each individual child within each family and culture; it demands that such a child, as it develops, be allowed space within the culture to find its own mode of *individual* fulfillment. Arguably, for example, a society that would take this obligation seriously would protect youth who adopt different lifestyles from ridicule and violent harassment; such societies would not necessarily encourage, but would at least allow, exploration without discrimination.

This momentous development cannot be underestimated. Because much violence against children—including, for example, virginity exams, circumcision, prepubertal marriages, and prostitution—is committed or condoned by purely private actors, most notably family members, states often have maintained that such acts of violence are outside the scope of state responsibility, and hence beyond the reach of international law.[61] The children's rights movement has moved forward one of the central challenges to the human rights movement: it has expanded the traditional human rights framework and now holds states accountable for violations carried out in the private realm.

It is critical to emphasize that the dynamic self-determination principle does not aim to support a global view of socialization; it allows for cross- and intra-cultural differences and challenges essentialist, or singular, representations of children's experiences.[62] Taking self-determination seriously translates into the need to develop a skeptical attitude toward decisions that will affect children and the necessity to be more tentative and open-ended in the actual process of decision-making. The presumption is that the best response to whatever issue has arisen may lie *within* the child. This approach aims to help direct children as they accommodate to their social world. Rather than manipulating the social world in hopes that the child will respond appropriately, the approach aims to include children even though they may need direction to an accommodation with the social world that surrounds them.[63]

Self-determination is a mode of optimally positioning children to develop their own perceptions of their well-being as they enter adulthood, rather than a foreclosure on the potential for such development. This is what is fundamentally meant by children as rights-holders: the focus is on furthering children's own interests. The result is that socialization forces beyond the family are emphasized, as reflected in a strong emphasis placed on education, the sharing of ideas, and increasing access to information.[64] This undoubtedly constitutes a radical move, but it is, as we will see, a move which makes considerable sense for developing programs of action aimed at child protection and liberation.

Children's right to self-determination in their own interests gives most people cause for concern. The argument for denying participation rights to children has two interrelated themes. Critics argue either that children are not rational or capable of making reasoned and informed decisions or that children simply lack the wisdom born of experience. Consequently children are viewed as error-prone, a perception that legitimizes the rejection of their right to participate and make decisions for themselves. From those perspectives, the law benevolently acts as it protects children from their own incompetence.[65] Indeed, because children do not even necessarily have legal rights, families are assumed to protect children's interests.[66]

Arguments used to deny children's rights claims have been met in two ways. The first approach proposes that children do possess the qualities that critics allege they lack. The second approach concedes that if children do lack the skills and qualities necessary for participating in decision-making, they lack them to no greater degree than adults who are not disqualified from participation.[67] An overwhelming amount of recent social science research supports *both* approaches.[68] Even infants engage in self-determined behavior, a finding that has revolutionized psychological approaches to child development.[69] Yet, adults' behaviors are not necessarily self-determining; adults are far from being the mature individuals they hold themselves up to be.

The rebuttal, however, does not necessarily advance discussions.[70] Critics' concerns have considerable practical merit. Simply bestowing upon children the right to self-determination would be problematic. Familiar difficulties would arise. For example, children could be vulnerable to adults, as is well revealed by the persistent efforts of NAMBLA's (the North American Man-Boy Love Association) to liberate children from what they perceive as repressive sexual laws that prohibit adult-child sexual interactions.[71] In addition, children could risk being burdened with the guilt of adverse outcomes, such as those that arise in custodial battles, particularly when a parent allegedly abuses family members. There is also the formidable practical problem of accurately understanding the child's decisions. Assuming that the child is capable of deciding at all, other concerns arise. It remains difficult to convey to children the nature of available alternatives. The quality of the information they are provided and their providers' subjective biases indelibly affect decision-makers. Children's articulation of the decision will be influenced by how they think the decision will be accepted, the promises about what they should or should not say, and support from friends or siblings. In contexts of more formal decision-making—e.g., those conducted by or for state officials—the decisions would be influenced by where the interview occurs and the manner in which it is conducted, a finding that has led to tremendous controversy and legal reforms.[72] Practical obstacles to self-determination are simply enormous.

Although numerous, the difficulties can be misleading. The familiar obstacles often form the basis for denying children a voice in important matters affecting their lives. Certainly, the dynamic self-determination principle does not stipulate that decisions be simply foisted upon children. Including children in decisions that affect them is far from a recommendation that decision-making concerning children should simply be delegated to children themselves. Just as importantly, children already make difficult decisions, even without the benefit of adult guidance. As with other children's issues, the children's competency debate has been narrowly constrained to "liberation" concerns, such as those that involve access to reproductive materials and services.[73]

Even in the context that has dominated the self-determination debate—reproductive decision-making—issues are far from clear. Several have challenged the legitimacy of requiring judicial regulation of teenagers' reproductive decision-making.[74] More importantly, despite being denied access to reproductive services, children and youth continue to make complex decisions regarding sexual activity. When it comes to sexual maltreatment, for example, children do act competently, possess rational thought, and make informed choices. Before disclosing maltreatment, children who have been sexually abused make complex assessments of the consequences for their families. In these circumstances, children display remarkably sophisticated decision-making skills in the systematic evaluation of outcomes, as revealed in the number of years they often need to take before revealing the abuse.[75] Children also develop strategies to deal with harassers at school and to avoid other forms of violence outside the home.[76]

The existence of children's coping strategies should not be news. But, the strategies have been recognized only recently, a recognition influenced by taking children's perspectives and concerns seriously. Without adopting this stance, we still would not fully recognize the alarming extent to which children are victimized in schools and in close, romantic relationships.[77] Just as importantly, the developmental roots of aggressive and maltreating behavior still would elude us.[78] The Children's Convention simply reflects the move toward taking children's voices and interests seriously. That is, given that children's interests are at stake, the Convention attempts what should be intuitively obvious: it refocuses concern on children. By doing so, it attempts to construct a new consensus related to the respective role and responsibilities of the state, families, and communities (all broadly defined) in the upbringing of children.

The refocus on children rather than those holding "parental status" (e.g., parents, guardians, and state officials) is quite revolutionary and momentous. For example, children now have a right to remain in their families and to maintain ties with their parents. This focus on relationships is likely to revolutionize international family jurisprudence in that it could lead to the recognition of children's rights "in" and "to" relationships.[79] This approach allows for envisioning policies that aim to keep children in their homes and with their families. A possible result could be, for example, giving children a right not to be sent to brothels, since that would violate their right to be with their families. As we will see, this right could be ensured in several ways. A most obvious approach could be the creation of societal support services. A more radical approach would be to argue that families actually are entitled to resources. Society (even the global community) arguably has an obligation to assist parents and families to ensure children's rights (e.g., the responsibility to support families that would otherwise sell their children).[80] Although these general rights and obligations could be interpreted narrowly, parents and communities clearly have become responsible for ensuring children's rights.

The scope of human rights now includes not just what nations do to one another or what nations do to their citizens, but what citizens do to one another. Although several children's rights violations do fit easily into formal international human rights analyses, much maltreatment is part of a larger cultural framework that renders children systematically vulnerable to private power. The Children's Convention has roots in the insight that states create and sustain the conditions under which children are victimized and therefore should be accountable for the level of violence, as much as in the challenge to the public/private dichotomy that emphasizes the importance of state intervention to regulate violence in the private sphere of the family.[81] Thus, the Convention properly recognizes that states are far from being the greatest direct threat to the life and liberty of citizens, and that states reinforce the power that threatens children's interests.

These are powerful developments. The standards clearly seek to revision how societies are to approach children's issues. As such, the standards require us to rethink how different cultures view children and the place children actually have in families, different societies, and the international community. The revisioning even requires the reallocation of resources and responsibilities, not just in societies but in families as well as interpersonal relations. That is quite an innovative move for international law. Although the full import of this move has yet to be imagined, the attempt to revision *all* societies already faces numerous obstacles, simply because it aims to do just that: transform all cultures. Although the manner in which international law aims to transform cultures will be addressed in chapters to come (most explicitly in Chapter 4), it is important to introduce the reasons why concern for protecting cultural rights may be losing its saliency while there remain important reasons cultural forces need to be taken seriously.

Children's Rights:
What's Culture Got to Do with Them?

Numerous commentaries debate the cross-cultural applicability of international human rights norms.[82] Although contentious,[83] the debate is critical if the notion of human rights is ever to be taken seriously.

Respect for international human rights standards is likely to become effective only if the standards relate directly to, and where possible are promoted through, local cultural, religious, and other traditional communities. Indeed, failure to consider deeply held beliefs and customs largely accounts for the inability of previous efforts to eradicate even heinous practices.

Regrettably, the need for local acceptance and implementation of human rights also intensifies debates. Critics view international human rights as arbitrary, intrusive, and elitist. They propose that international norms should not be the basis of value judgments in other cultural contexts. Their belief that human rights norms do not transcend cultural location and cannot be readily translated across cultures reflects the skepticism about the availability of universal norms. Most commonly, critics contend that international instruments are based on the Western conception of the autonomous individual, which, they further argue, is foreign to other societies' conceptions of humanity.[84] These critiques have enjoyed renewed popularity as they provide pointed criticisms of Western colonialism and challenge the justification of "civilized" nations to conquer and control "savage" nations for the good of the latter: the white man's burden is to mind his own business. At the extreme, these commentators seek to deprive human rights advocates of the very foundation of human rights: the category "human" does not enable cross-cultural assessment of human practices or state actions.[85]

While these commentators rebuke conceptions of international human rights on the grounds that the dominant Western discourse of rights is antithetical to the norms in non-Western societies,[86] others argue that conceptions of human rights similar to those in international documents can indeed be found in all societies.[87] Commentators challenge the purity of the "collectivism" said to be found in traditional cultures. For example, Africanists propose that placing a high value on "individual effort, integrity, wealth, and achievement is as indigenous to Africa as it is to the West."[88] Others who report African law and society emphasize, for example, that it may be true that Africans have a greater group identity than some other peoples, but the "group identity never means individual submergence, much less individual nonexistence."[89] Likewise, some note that despite questioning the reliance on social groups to protect individual rights,[90] even the indigene in traditional Africa relied on intimate groups—extended families or clans—to manipulate the political and social forces to secure *individual* rights.[91] These arguments are important. They help legitimate the use of international human rights norms since, it is argued, even Western notions of rights can be found in indigenous concepts of justice.

Both sides of the debate have considerable merit. Yet, it would be a mistake to espouse extreme views. While human rights language may derive from Western sources, its present currency is no longer unproblematically and solely Western. As we have seen, there are now several generations of human rights. Likewise, modern conceptions of human rights seek to include more holistic approaches to human rights, an approach exemplified by the Children's Convention. The Convention seeks to balance the priority given to the individual over society or community. Yet, it still aims to privilege the community. Although there are attempts to balance individual with broader community interests, a balance that is particularly meaningful for children's rights, both established and emerging principles still assume that the rights are universal for all human beings.[92] Viewed from this perspective, heated discussions and attacks on mainstream human rights discourse are somewhat overdrawn. Yet, although obvious from a historical perspective, it has proven politically difficult to recognize diversity and even more politically difficult to accept that universality is not a static concept but one that evolves and responds to changing configurations of interests and needs.[93]

It is not self-evident why, in addition to being overdrawn, the debate takes place on the more general level of the status of rights and their universal application. Presumably, and perhaps more fruitfully, the debate could just as well take place on a level of substance and interpretation of the rights themselves, such as a child's right to protection from sexual maltreatment. Yet, differences frequently are translated into the rhetoric of universality versus cultural relativism, imperialism versus cultural self-determination. The practical appeal to broader principles persists and permeates human rights discourse.

Despite controversies, the debate's concerns are increasingly becoming moot. A single inward glance at Western conceptions of rights reveals the imprudence of holding to extremes. Commentaries frequently ignore the fact that Western norms of individuality and morality are as diverse as norms found in non-Western cultures. Characterizations of the West as the bastion of unbridled individualism are somewhat misleading. For example, although the prevailing social ethic in the United States has been aptly identified as individualism, individualism actually takes various forms. Just as it would be inappropriate to conclude that there is no concern for communal aspects of life in the West,[94] it would be improper to view Western rights discourse as individualized. Even the

United States has extensive "programmatic rights" that were established after the World Wars and expanded dramatically during the "Great Society" years. The Social Security Act is a powerful case in point; it was an extensive statutory entitlement which court decisions have essentially promoted to constitutional status.[95] In addition, it is important to recognize that many in the West are critical of liberal individualism. Feminist writers have emphasized the prevalence and importance of communalism, both in interpersonal relations and in larger society.[96] Their efforts have gained considerable support from research indicating that community life and a sense of obligation to others are strong aspects of modern life, even in North America.[97] These social relationships clearly influence rights discourse. In fact, multiplicity of beliefs often thrives within a single community or family group—conflicts over the legitimacy of abortion or the role of children and women in family life illustrate the complexity of translating imperfectly shared assumptions into broader normative standards.

In addition to the diverse (yet sometimes conflicting) discourses found in individual societies, communities, and families, it is also important to recognize that societies are no longer insular entities. It would be naive to ignore the wide variety of external forces that influence countries and societies.[98] Although historical patterns of difference and distinctions between East and West have been arguably overdrawn, the extreme differences that may have once existed are likely to be erased in the evolving convergence of global culture.

As political boundaries lose much of their former significance in the current international economic order, there are numerous indications that a new transnational legal culture is developing. In this process, economic and cultural forces arguably develop a universal body of legal norms and processes, and even a "common world-wide legal consciousness."[99] This globalization of law converges several legal systems to create a modern legal culture that stresses fundamental human rights.[100] Others view the changes as going even further, and focus on "governance without governments."[101] These are phenomenal changes. The changes reflect a move toward "positive peace"—in the sense of a mutual approximation to an agreement of basic values, as opposed to "negative peace" in which a particular culture's ideals are taken as mandatory achievements of universal human rights and which creates, at best, a truce between cultures and countries to prevent war. Economic and political developments forcibly move international law toward positive peace.[102] Clearly, the admittedly Western bias continues to dissipate as the South gains international representation. These forces inevitably impact interpersonal relations. As they do, they contribute just as much to the transformation of children's rights as do the recognition and legitimization of claims of cultural imperialism and the benefits of other approaches to human development.

Given these rapid changes, it is important not to presume that all members of society will benefit equally from social change. Social change often means that children are confronted by adult risks and opportunities. For example, the media exposes both adults and children to similar images and addresses both as independent actors; yet, children's legal status does not match how they are, in some respects, less socially differentiated from adults.[103] Just as it is important to recognize risks inherent in social change, it is important not to be blind to subtle or blatant oppression in societies that oppose change. For example, it is important to question the power to constitute dominant cultural norms and explore the gendered nature of society.[104] Indeed, as we will see, only through confrontation of gender issues on local and global levels can the plight of oppressed children be addressed satisfactorily.

Yet, there are aspects of cultural relativism in human rights that are important to incorporate into any serious analyses. Simply dismissing cultural relativism and refusing to engage with other critiques of international human rights discourse can lead to a strategy relevant only to a minority of privileged people around the world. Just as fundamental conflicts buried beneath presumptively universal norms must be addressed, so must cultural biases. If culturally based arguments about human rights norms are not embraced, important concerns may be silenced and important aspects of human rights struggles in non-Western and Western contexts may be overlooked. It is important not to suppress and devalue cultural diversity. Cultural relativism in human rights scholarship and practice poses important challenges which can produce constructive insights for the project of using international human rights protections for children.

The diversity of world legal systems provides cause for both hope and fear in national and international human rights communities. Culture, inevitably linked to customs, customary law, and traditions, provides a political base for child protection. For example, in some cultures, traditional extended family systems provide essential social safety nets that operate far more effectively than government programs.[105] Indeed, innovative child protection efforts aim to rebuild communities and foster social networks instead of formal governmental systems.[106] Yet, culture also has been used to defend forced marriages of young girls, genital circumcision, and other arguably cruel and dangerous practices.

Societal transformations make the protection of human rights even more pressing. For example, as traditional African economies develop, capitalism expands.[107] These transformations demand much more than concomitant changes in relations between individuals and the state; they transform interpersonal relations. Indeed, it is becoming increasingly clear that, with global societal transformations, there is a growing need for a concept of individual human rights, as defined in the international legal sphere. Social change in the modern world involves a more complex division of labor, industrialization, and the emancipation of many individuals from prior social roles that both restricted and protected them. Thus, human rights protections that take an "individualistic" approach become increasingly important as traditional rights and attendant responsibilities are loosened by the breakdown of geographical and cultural ties that traditionally bound and protected individuals. To be sure, modernization has not inevitably led less developed societies to assimilate readily individual rights and accordingly change behavior; Japan, Singapore, Taiwan, and South Korea continue to grapple with notions of individualism, individual freedom, and equality.[108] Yet as the role of modern Nation States continues to decline, there is a concomitant increase in the role for a new mix of actors, including international financial and development institutions, the private sector, regional and local governments, and individuals. The increasing difficulty of identifying the main actor responsible for policies and programs makes more urgent the need to shift focus toward individual rights and not leave people's fundamental needs at the mercy of changing programs, policies, and politically unaccountable actors.

Considerable evidence supports the claim that the need for rights protection within and among states increases dramatically once the individual moves outside the traditional sources of security, such as kin, village, and ethnic associations. This is especially the case with sexually maltreated children who are trafficked across Nation States or who adapt to foreign invasions in the form, for example, of businessmen seeking prepubescent sexual partners or children to engage in pornographic and other sexual performances.[109] Indeed, these children's need for international human rights protections is especially strong precisely because they have already been denied protections in both customary and national law.[110] Of course, implications of the converse situation make many uncomfortable: prestate societies that use children in sexual ways may buffer children from other forms of maltreatment, but the protections may not vitiate the need to consider intervention.

Cultural values, across countries with widely diverse legal systems as well as with legal systems with diverse customs, are an important factor not only in the interpretation but also in the eventual application of human rights norms. In this regard, it is important to understand the ambiguities and ambivalences of international human rights law and the flexibility that will be required for its effective implementation. That is, now that we know what human rights law asks of us, it is important to understand how it can ensure that the global community takes human rights seriously.

The Energizing Power of International Human Rights Law

International human rights law operates in a paradoxical manner. Its norms must be sufficiently clear, comprehensive, and inflexible to provide the international community with some basis upon which to constrain states and other actors that undermine or circumvent minimal standards of decent behavior. Yet, human rights promulgations must remain flexible and adaptive if they are ever to address an exceedingly wide variety of issues that involve the relationship between the state, the family, and individuals, including children.

Contrary to several analyses and critiques of human rights law, indeterminacy and flexibility do not inevitably result in paralysis. These qualities simply underscore the importance of institutions as a means through which to pursue the interpretation and implementation of human rights and the need to develop a better understanding of the different cultural dimensions of relevant norms. This attempt to situate individual rights in social contexts reveals how international law entitles each human being to individual respect; it also properly views individuals as necessarily *social individuals*. The resulting image of rights—what they are and how they are to be ensured—necessarily focuses on social institutions besides the state. At a minimum, the effort forces policy-makers to look at the effects of laws and policies on the individual's social environment. For example, as several human rights policies emphasize, the family is treated as a "fundamental unit of society"[111] to be enlisted in protecting human rights. Strictly individualistic approaches to rights would enlist state powers at the exclusion of familial interests.

Although there is a need for flexibility to reach and ensure individual rights, this does not necessarily mean that the new international human rights, as enumerated in agreed-upon treaties, are toothless tigers. For example, under Article Four of the Children's Convention, states that ratify the treaty undertake the following forceful obligation: "States Parties shall undertake all appropriate legislative, administrative, and other measures, for the implementation of the rights recognized in this Convention." Undoubtedly, global support for the Convention is likely to remain meaningless without adequate compliance and careful monitoring to ensure that obligations are taken seriously. The significance of monitoring did not escape the Convention's drafters. Ratification of the Convention necessarily opens societies to domestic and international scrutiny based on agreed-upon international norms. Although ratifying countries may carefully circumscribe their duties to enforce the Convention's basic standards,[112] they cannot avoid the obligation to publicize, report on, and monitor the enforcement, and failures of enforcement, of all rights found in the Convention.[113] This reliance on international monitoring is one of the most remarkable aspects of the Convention.

The Convention explicitly enumerates its monitoring mechanisms. The Convention follows the standard international law practice that requires parties to submit periodic reports outlining the progress that the nation has made toward the Convention's implementation.[114] Unlike previous international treaties, the Convention offers the monitoring committee extra tools to pursue its mandate. Pursuant to Article 45, specialized agencies are entitled to be represented; likewise, the committee may request technical advice or assistance from those agencies, may request that the Secretary-General undertake studies on specific children's issues, and may make suggestions and general recommendations directly to States Parties. In addition to these differences, the Convention is less accusatory; it aims to be supportive, as reflected in the focus on educational efforts and information exchanges rather than on the provision of complaint procedures for noncompliance.[115]

Commentators often play down the significance of the cooperative and educational approach to enforcing international law. Although this reliance may seem to be a rather weak method of enforcement, it is a major weapon in the struggle to ensure human rights.[116] Human rights treaties seemingly function best indirectly—they offer norms that are comprehensive and flexible yet rigid enough to provide the international community some basis on which to constrain governments that circumvent internationally recognized standards. If nations fail to respect standards, the international community typically encourages, pushes, prods, and ultimately embarrasses states into taking steps to guarantee the proper implementation of rights.[117] In addition to foreign parties themselves, it is important to note the growing effectiveness of nongovernmental organizations (NGOs), which have appropriately been characterized as "tugboats" in international channels.[118] The dynamic and innovative involvement by NGOs in international systems is not the only force.[119] It remains difficult to underestimate the growing power of citizens to form local social movements that ultimately have global repercussions and even more difficult to ignore how charismatic individuals can play important roles at international policy-making levels.[120]

When examining how the global community can ultimately attempt to influence other countries' domestic policies, it is important to recall the impact of international treaties on obligations to foreign parties. The attachment of reservations confines a treaty's domestic effect to the existing requirements of the ratifying Nation State's own domestic laws; they do not affect the treaty in terms of obligations to foreign parties. For example, although Nation States may circumscribe their obligation to implement certain of the Children's Convention's articles in their own states, the provisions do not negate their international obligations. In this regard a basic requirement in the law of treaties—"good faith" in efforts to implement its core values and standards—becomes crucial.[121] That is, other Nation States may use the Convention as a lever to influence *any* other country's approach to children. To be sure, the black letter obligations set forth in the Convention may not impose direct obligations on the States Parties or subject them to foreign jurisdictions,[122] but the rights enumerated in the Convention are, nonetheless, rights. And, as human rights that have been negotiated among Nation States, they are *erga omnes*: all states, all world citizens, have an interest in their recognition and enforcement.[123]

The extent to which the Convention's standards could influence States Parties' laws and policies depends upon the extent to which governmental and nongovernmental organizations most susceptible to societal influences can be encouraged to support the Convention's principles. Many disparage the Convention for failure to provide for judicial enforceability and formal complaint mechanisms. Such criticisms, however, adopt an unnecessarily narrow conception of rights. The Convention's judicial unenforceability should not discourage efforts. Even unenforceable policy statements have enormous potential.[124] For instance, in the United States, the most significant legislation that provides for social service delivery to children and families, the Adoption Assistance and Child Welfare Act of 1980,[125] essentially offers no method of enforcement, since the Act has been interpreted as failing to give individuals the "private right of action" necessary to judicially challenge the implementation of the statute.[126] Despite failing to create rights that were judicially enforceable, the Act revolutionized the manner in which federal, state, and local governments respond to families and children in crisis.[127]

Clearly, then, domesticating international rights through the executive and legislative branches—federal, state, and local—offers fertile ground for implementation. In this regard, it is important to recall that statutes and regulations, especially those dealing with child welfare issues, necessarily leave considerable discretion to those entrusted with their implementation.[128] Thus, thousands of national and local decision-makers who have discretion to enforce, interpret, and implement laws could be encouraged to administer laws in the more progressive manner consistent with the Convention.

In addition to administrators and other actors (e.g., social workers, psychologists, and teachers) who help implement legal standards, private actors cannot be ignored. For example, professional societies often place burdens on their members to act in certain ways; ethical codes are a prime example. Equally important, and perhaps more critical to children, are the actors with whom they are in daily contact—family, peers, and community members. All have an obligation to "take appropriate steps" to ensure that private actors will respect children's basic rights.[129]

The developments are revolutionary; their impact, including whether they can and will be taken seriously, remains to be seen. Yet, it is clear that modern international law, much like other children's policy-making, takes into account domestic avoidance devices that states may devise to ignore their obligations, and finds several methods of breathing legal life back into international human rights law. These methods of energizing international law are quite significant—they allow for progressive interpretations and implementation of the Convention. Thus, in addition to encouraging direct policy-making, the approach to enforcement has the effect of legitimizing a broader human rights debate and raising the prospect that children will become legitimate foci of concern. Essentially, the movement asks for a social revolution that must begin with a reconstruction of childhood.

Efforts that will transform legal and social approaches to childhood undoubtedly rest on the international community's ability to define and accept rudimentary universal standards and principles which will then be domesticated by the world's cultures. As Nation States move toward legitimizing basic standards of how children should be treated and how they should take part in society, several basic norms have emerged. The most persistent and arguably universal norm is the prohibition against child maltreatment. Concern over child protection has become a flash point for national and international debates over the nature of international human rights and the extent to which they can be taken seriously.

The "Simple" Commitment to End Child Sexual Maltreatment

Attempts to combat, prevent, and react to sexual maltreatment have a long history. Few rights have received such attention. In addition to receiving attention through several of the Convention's articles, the right to protection from sexual maltreatment has been championed by children's advocacy groups and other nongovernmental organizations (NGOs),[130] has elicited policy commitments from international agencies and organizations with an international reach,[131] and has prompted numerous world conferences dedicated to its implementation.[132]

The Convention forcefully states that ratifying States Parties are to take appropriate "national, bilateral and multilateral measures" to prevent the sexual exploitation and sexual abuse of children.[133] These are strong words, the impact of which has yet to be fully envisioned. However, there are indications that the effort will be taken seriously. The urgent need to combat the sexual maltreatment of children already has led to palpable results. The Commission on Human Rights recently charged a Special Rapporteur to report on the sale and prostitution of children, including child pornography.[134] The urgency also elicited new international instruments.[135] In 1993, the United Nations World Conference on Human Rights reiterated the urgency; in its Vienna Declaration and Program of Action, the United Nations urged all States to cooperate to address the acute problem of children enduring especially difficult circumstances. The U. N. found that

> [e]xploitation and abuse of children should be actively combated, including by addressing their root causes. Effective measures are required against . . . harmful child labor, sale of children . . . child prostitution, child pornography, as well as other forms of sexual abuse.[136]

The efforts have been fruitful. In 1996, the First World Congress on the Exploitation of Children was held to call even more attention to the sexual maltreatment of children.[137]

Clearly, few international child and family policy issues have been met with the same desire and eagerness to protect children and youth as the current attempts to prevent and abolish child sexual maltreatment. Recognition of the issue, however, does not dictate solutions. The nature of sexual maltreatment remains exceedingly controversial. Indeed, exactly what is meant by "child" or "sex" is even more controversial! We turn to these issues in the next chapter.

Conclusion:
A New Legal Image of the Child Person

The investigation thus far reveals the emergence of an image of the child that human rights discourses address at several levels. The basic premise is that notions of human rights must begin with the basic value of independence and individuality of *every* human being. At the same time, however, a full-fledged understanding of the rights of the child must take into account the sociability of human beings. The necessary flux between the two legitimizes the need to accommodate competing individual and public interests. Relatedly, the image of the child in social interaction with its environment supports the basic insight that rights absolutism cannot be justified and that a balance between rights and responsibilities must be reached. The new image of the child person addresses the entire range of established human rights and takes note of the tension among private interests, between private and public interests, and among competing groups and cultures. Importantly, no one element of the legal image of the child person can dominate to the exclusion of any other; if this were to happen, the result would be an ideological appropriation of children's human rights, an imperialism that would inevitably undermine the universal validity of human rights. The extent to which the legal image is practicable, useful, and realistic remains to be investigated.

3 | Deconstructing Childhood and Sexual Maltreatment

This chapter explores the importance and central determinants of socially constructed images of childhood. The investigation notes that essentialized images of childhood persist despite strong evidence that conceptions and realities of childhood vary according to economic, demographic, political, and religious concerns. These societal forces pose the greatest challenge to the international movement that aims to make all children visible and all their problems worthy of consideration. The chapter highlights the tendency to narrow images of childhood, the nature of dominant images, and how they help render certain children and forms of maltreatment invisible. The chapter ends with a delineation of the basic forms of sexual maltreatment that will undergird the following chapters' analyses of how children are sexually treated across societies and the responses that have been and may be made available. Throughout the analysis, the chapter emphasizes the need to consider the multiple ecologies of childhood and their contributions to maltreatment.

Introduction

A discussion of child sexual maltreatment in the world's cultures first necessitates some clarification of key terms and development of working definitions. The world's cultural diversity means that different criteria define child development and the period of childhood. The different criteria make investigations conceptually messy and require that we examine definitions along with an effort to "deconstruct" children's issues and the notion of childhood itself. The themes, now commonly described as "discourses," that emerge are important to consider for they show how terms come from socially organized frameworks of meanings that define and essentially dictate what is said and done, along with what can be said and done.

Given the need to socially situate definitions, the following discussion clarifies the reasons for the very existence of childhood, explores how childhood is far from a "natural" fact, examines how sexual maltreatment comes in diverse yet systematically related forms, and proposes that neither childhood nor sexual maltreatment can be examined or addressed in isolation from systemic, ecological contexts. The argument is simple. Children, childhood, and the maltreatment of children are constructed through contexts that are intrapersonal, interpersonal, cultural, historical, and political. These areas and modes of construction must be considered not just in examinations of phenomena, but also in proposals for reforms and in their actual implementation.[1]

The Most Basic Challenge to Children's Rights: The Simple Reason for Childhood

Every society necessarily sets rules and standards that proscribe or encourage certain behaviors, even thoughts and emotions. The international children's rights movement seeks to influence the nature of those standards and universalize determinations of exactly what are children's rights and wrongs. The internationalization process continues even though we have yet to determine such sociocultural fundamentals as self, person, identity, society, and culture.[2] Indeed, the movement proceeds despite facing the most basic obstacle and challenge to children's rights: the social regulation of the value and number of children.

One does not need to believe wholeheartedly in evolutionary theory to recognize that every sexually reproducing species must find ways to create copies of its adult individuals. Somehow, adults must be able to nurture those copies at least long enough that they, in turn, are able to produce viable offspring. Given the importance of the effort, it is no surprise that efforts to meddle with the process are extremely contentious. Yet, all societies seek this end result, although all social groups use somewhat dissimilar means.

To ensure that they indeed do reproduce, any sexually reproductive species may adopt essentially two main strategies. The first generates as many offspring as possible, with the expectation that at least a few will survive to adulthood. Through this strategy, parents need not invest much effort in protecting and raising their offspring. The alternative approach generates a small number of offspring. In that scenario, parents necessarily devote considerable energy to ensuring that their offspring will successfully reach full adulthood.[3]

Humans are characterized by the second strategy, although there is considerable range within human populations and among individuals.[4] The extent of the range depends on a host of factors, such as infant mortality rates, the symbolic value of having children, the particular economy, sociopolitical structures, and other cultural value systems. Although often ignored, the principle is straightforward. The carrying capacity of the ecosystem determines whether individuals will have offspring and how well the offspring will be treated. Social changes influence neonatal and post-neonatal survivorship.[5] Likewise, children's conditions intricately relate to similar factors that make up the social ecology and its ability to support child development.[6]

Intact communities responsible for their own self-preservation spontaneously manage the process of social regulation. For example, when ecological conditions are harsh, the result is also harsh for some children. Anthropologists have documented well how societies under ecological stress may not even welcome children into their social communities until the child's chances for survival are established more firmly, as symbolically reflected in the failure to name children until they survive infancy.[7] In other societies, some children will be specifically targeted. Categories of childhood are systematically more vulnerable to maltreatment: illegitimate children, adopted children, deformed children, and female children tend to be more vulnerable to cultural stress. The most typical responses to "unwanted" children continue to be abortion, infanticide, and abandonment.[8] Clearly, not all children are equally esteemed by adults, and their elimination serves important social functions rather than fulfillment of individual members' maliciousness.

The manner in which children are "disposed of" tends to be subtle. Where some forms of dealing with unwanted children are prohibited, others emerge, such as the "deferred infanticide" of girls whose parents are pressured to keep some children alive while stinting them of food, clothing, and other necessary material resources.[9] Indeed, males almost universally benefit from more parental attention and receive a greater share of scarce societal resources such as food, education, and medicine.[10] In several Asian communities, the female child is disadvantaged, for example, by the priority accorded to boys in relation to access to schooling, which decreases girls' choices and increases their risk of involvement in prostitution.[11] In other communities, children are warehoused in orphanages, a practice that overtly leads to death of girls "by default."[12] Two-thirds of the children in the South who do not attend primary school are girls.[13] Such discrimination between boys and girls appears to be attributed to factors such as family size, birth order, and ratio of sons to daughters, all of which determine children's differential current and future economic value to parents.[14] Forces that similarly lead to the denial of girls' opportunities also are at work in the North:

important studies document the extent to which girls suffer for lack of certain educational opportunities.[15]

Although ecological conditions lead to harsh consequences for vulnerable members of social groups, few societies could survive the difficulties that result from indiscriminate care for all children, and for that matter, all adults. Yet, it is difficult to imagine how any society could have survived without making sure that children were raised by parents or community groups that took responsibility for them. Likewise, it is difficult to imagine how those targeted for parenting could have survived without strong community and cultural bonds.

The children's rights movement essentially attempts to counter the potentially harsh consequences of social reproduction, and increase investment and concern for *all* children. From this perspective, the movement clearly faces impressive obstacles. Attempts to reconcile protections of the weakest and most vulnerable face severe challenges when balanced against the need to develop and sustain social programs for children. The entrenched human rights belief now is that the global society, not only parents and their immediate communities, has an obligation to provide for *all* children. In addition to championing the belief that children must be provided with supportive environments, the global community supposes that supportive environments will produce happy and productive adults.[16]

Arguably, the idealized vision of what children's lot should be, which only recently became standard in the industrialized nations, is a historical aberration.[17] This construction of an idealized childhood in which all children are to be highly valued is in practice bound both historically and culturally to the social and economic conditions that prevailed in Europe and North America in the advanced industrial period. Although idealized images may seem much more humane, it is important to realize that the notion of childhood is much more complex and that idealized images can be counterproductive. The most problematic aspect of idealized ideologies of childhood is that children who do not fit into preconceived notions are often symbolically or literally defined as outside of childhood. These cloaked layers of preconceptions and idealizations of who are valued children must be penetrated if we are to investigate the nature of childhood and help sustain proper reforms.

The Children of Childhood

Western society embraces the romantic vision that children merely should be "children." In this view, children simply are to play, spend time in school, or otherwise be unproductive; children are to be economically and sexually inactive and are not allowed to decide how to spend their time. A child's only obligation is to be happy.[18] This romantic vision portrays children as innocent, frail, and necessarily dependent on the protective care of parents, school officials, and other caretakers.

The romanticized concept of childhood creates much confusion and angst. Adults spend considerable energy separating children from the "adult worlds" of politics, work, sexuality, and independence.[19] Children who move prematurely into adult worlds are perceived as having "lost" their childhoods, or as having had them "stolen" or "destroyed."[20] For example, children beyond childhood often include those who are beyond the direct constraint and surveillance of adults, families, schools, and other authorities. These children portray a disturbing image of youth. These are the street children who band together in urban streets, independent of adults and sufficient in each other's company. Although this popular image of street children is largely inaccurate,[21] these children have entered the forbidden adult areas of sex, work, and crime. They have lost their childhood innocence; they are outside of childhood.

The focus on childhood as innocence and as a period marked by fun and leisure also leaves several other children essentially outside of childhood. Children who are poor, sick, or harmed pose problems for the romantic imagery. Ironically, even though their weakness and dependency status actually provide exemplars of childhood, their experiences mean that they cannot be the bearers of joy and guileless innocence, and that they do not have the abilities to develop to their fullest potential: They are not truly "children"; they too are outside of childhood.[22]

Children outside romantic images of childhood make the mythology of childhood difficult to sustain. Yet, there is no need to resort to examining only the extremes. Western societies seemingly exclude a growing number of children from the idealized social category of childhood. For example, schools now exclude their pupils; children work; latchkey children fend for themselves; children are abused and maltreated.[23] Likewise, several have shown the particularly racialized nature of the landscapes in which children grow.[24] The disjuncture between romantic ideals and the everyday lived reality is immense. Given the enormous number of actual exceptions to mythologized images of childhood, those searching for prototypical children would be hard pressed to find them. Yet, the cultural image of childhood as a state of weakness, dependency, and incompetence persists. Indeed, children's powerlessness is even exacerbated by their limited access to economic resources and their exclusion from political participation and other decisions affecting their quotidian situations.

The experiences of children in developing countries further subvert the modern, mythologized understandings of childhood. In several countries, the most commonly portrayed group of children outside of childhood are street children and child laborers, two groups prone to sexual maltreatment. Commentators who study the lives of street children demonstrate how Western conceptions of childhood that stress domesticity and dependency necessarily place street children outside of childhood. For example, commentators appropriately document how Western concepts of childhood idealize the notion that childhood occurs "inside"; e.g., inside conventional society, inside a family, inside a private dwelling.[25] The result is that concepts of childhood exclude children who are not in families and in private dwellings—these children become defined as outside of society. Ironically, the Western focus on children's domesticity and private upbringing also leads to the exclusion of other children from protection; for example, domestic child labor, especially girls' labor, tends to be undervalued and ignored.[26] It is assumed that children inside families do not work, that they are protected from exploitation. That is, children inside families are assumed to be prototypical, happy, and economically idle children.

Paradoxically, the images of dependency, vulnerability, and suffering figure prominently in appeals for assistance and societal mobilization, and even in foreign aid campaigns, not only for children but also for their adults and societies. The media's quintessential child is the vulnerable child (particularly the girl child) in need of assistance. The image of a child sexually held hostage or sexually abused is that of a female child.[27] The idiom has become psychologically effective in enlisting the assistance of local and international organizations. In Belgium, for example, where four girls had been held hostage and the judicial system seemed to have difficulty prosecuting offenders, several thousand ordinary citizens took to the streets in protest. The incident even led the United Nations to consider making such crimes international crimes with international jurisdictions: perpetrators could be sought and brought to justice in essentially any country.[28] Similar efforts have been reported in individual countries: in the U.S., it took the abduction and rape of an eleven-year-old girl to enlist aggressive law enforcement campaigns that have led to the development of a national register for known sex offenders.[29]

Given the emotionally charged nature of child sexual abuse, it is difficult to consider, let alone appreciate, how such reactions could be counterproductive. Think instead of how the idiom of the female child is used in other ways, as highlighted well by scholars who make use of critical theory. These commentators describe how the idiom of the starving Southern child has been used to obtain financial and development assistance from the North. The idiom's ability to mobilize resources has been particularly effective. Yet, critical theorists emphasize how the images are problematic for those receiving and bestowing assistance. The representation of lone children in aid appeals works to pathologize their families and cultures, positioning these as failing to fulfill their duties.[30] In order to qualify for "help," the parents and cultures are either invisible or infantilized as incapable.[31] The pictured children elicit sympathy for passive suffering rather than active struggle. The imagery reinforces the North as competent donors who have the power to help the helpless unfortunates from the South.[32]

The images of childhood used in aid appeals parallel the images of sexually abused children. Child victims are represented as alone. Blame is not placed on the community for ineffective child protection. The way communities contribute to the maltreatment, even unwittingly, remains ignored. The images foster disappointment and outrage with justice and child protection systems. At the international level, Western assumptions of abuse and perceptions of how to react to abuse through justice systems are readied for export. There is a general failure to see how Western systems fail in their own recognition and responses to maltreatment, how Western cultures render some forms of maltreatment invisible.

Analyses of images of childhood, particularly of children who fall outside of childhood, highlight how childhood is not solely an individualistic, private experience; nor is childhood solely a period of interaction with parents and private family life. Children have a cultural life; children play a large part in the economic, social, and political life of communities. Private and public worlds of childhood remain linked, despite attempts to maintain distinctions and dichotomize influences.[33] Economic developments, public policies, and ways of imagining the world clearly interact with ways of thinking about childhood and the actual experience of being a child. Children unmistakably participate constructively in, and are under the undeniable influence of, overarching sociocultural processes.

Defining Childhood:
Finding a Suitable Marker

If anything can be learned from conceptions of childhood, it is the need to see children for what they are and not adopt culturally free child development models. Given this need, recent comparisons of childhood, both within and outside of cultures, have tended to focus on chronological age as a marker. For example, the Children's Convention defines a child as "every human being to the age of 18 years."[34] As expected, the Convention allows for some flexibility: where appropriate, "custom or local law" may lower the age of childhood below eighteen.[35] Despite flexibility, the use of age as a marker for childhood raises considerable difficulties, both within and across cultures. These difficulties are important to consider, especially since age is the marker we will adopt.

Reasons for caution in marking childhood

A fundamental danger faced by the broad inclusion of all persons under any designated age in the concept of childhood is that it obscures the inherent diversity of children. Clearly, children are not a homogenous group with uniform needs; as we have seen, the very young, poor, and disabled have different needs. In addition, the broad age boundary embraces the most rapid and extensive period of an individual's physical, emotional, and intellectual growth. In that period, children develop a wide range of skills and competencies, and express a divergent range of needs which fit difficultly into broad age ranges.

In addition to difficulties arising from the heterogeneity of childhood, difficulties arise with respect to differences within the homogeneous groupings. For example, the age boundary between childhood and adulthood is established at different ages in different spheres of activity. Thus, children may reach the age of criminal responsibility by the age of ten yet still not be adults politically until eighteen. Differences may also occur within spheres of activity. Thus, children may be able to engage in sexual activity with people their own age, but not with those who are a few years older or younger.[36] Broad chronological definitions do not necessarily take into account individual children's needs or activities; nor do they take into account how children's relationships with adults change dramatically as children progress through childhood.

Even more difficulties arise when one examines the notion of age across cultures. Simply put, no obvious age or status category can be used to study childhood across cultures, or even classes within the same society.[37] The state of physical and mental immaturity or incompleteness changes, in duration and in character, to fit societal demands and expectations.[38] Just like those in developed societies, the great majority of children in developing countries assume a wide range of adult responsibilities before the age of legal majority. Unlike industrialized countries, however, traditional cultures use various means to determine the state of childhood.

Anthropologists point to the many-sided aspects of life course development classification. Cross-culturally, categorizations differ tremendously. Only industrial societies have introduced ideals of childhood that accord a tremendous importance to chronological age. In other societies, "age" derives from social and cultural meanings in addition to biological markers. Chronological age is less relevant than, for example, the attainment of states of biological maturity.[39] Indeed, biological markers are often a better indicator of an individual's early life milestones. In addition to biological markers, some societies use birth order. For example, it is often of greater importance to be the eldest son, the youngest child, or the first daughter to attain puberty in a domestic group than to have attained a certain chronological age.[40]

Cross-culturally, another factor complicates the use of chronological age as a marker for childhood. Although age hierarchies may be important, they tend to be valid for specific gender roles. For example, it may not be necessary for a girl to attain a particular age or even a certain physical maturity before she is encouraged to be self-sufficient in her daily routine or to take on domestic responsibilities. In terms of her development, her training and inculcation into feminine roles may occur even before she reaches the threshold of puberty.[41] Indeed, even for the social ritual that so often marks full adulthood—marriage—sexual maturity may be irrelevant. In contrast, a boy's adulthood may be postponed for many years after puberty and sexual maturity.[42] Yet, the postponement of adulthood does not imply that a boy has less power and influence than a girl of the same "age." As we will see, the implications of the differential duration of childhood for boys and girls are far-reaching and carry considerable significance to cultures.

In addition to differentials between sexes, variations clearly exist within sexes, their societies, and their institutions. For example, although recent studies of "girlhood" assume that girls' social and sexual development is doubly marginalized by their status as children and as future women, the main socialization forces—family, school, peers—differ tremendously.[43] Not only do the socializing agencies differ among one another, they differ considerably among girls of different social milieux, particularly based on whether the girls are from advantaged or disadvantaged backgrounds.[44]

Clearly, the temporal point at which childhood ends and adulthood begins varies among cultures and national legal systems. Importantly, though, no international standard has made operative provisions to define "child" or to prescribe the age of consent even in the limited context of sexual maltreatment.[45] Uniformity of definitions remains elusive.[46] The heterogeneity of children makes attempts to address and establish a uniformity of needs and rights difficult.

Age as a reasonable investigatory marker

Regardless of the difficulties and the need for caution, an emphasis on children's chronological age does highlight important features of childhood and child welfare. Although there undoubtedly is diversity within childhood, an examination that includes *all* children below a certain age category ensures the inclusion of all children. Including diverse conceptions of childhood and not ignoring entire groups of children allows for not only a more informed investigation, but also more workable policy-making.

Just as the use of age as a marker functions to include broader notions of childhood, age as a boundary emphasizes important distinctions between children and adults. Children are necessarily dependent upon adults. Socially, and especially legally, children's status means that all their needs and rights are subject to actions of adults, and the remedies for their suffering tend to lie in adults' actions. For example, differences in age highlight well how children lack power: children are denied access to decision-making processes and are thus less able to change conditions that may lead, for example, to their abuse. In that sense, then, children are weaker and more vulnerable than adults. Although children now have acquired rights that bring them closer to adults, it is important to recognize that they also are pervasively victims of adults, and that adults must assume important roles in alleviating children's suffering, even when children's peers cause the suffering.

Using age as an upper marker for investigation does not necessitate accepting that those below a certain age are all "children." Clearly, as we have seen, child development varies considerably. Children's rights are not based solely on age, but on a correlation between age and some relevant index of certain needs. Our use of age simply allows us to examine the indices and not limit the notions of rights.[47]

As we have seen, then, the "age" of majority is a social, religious, cultural, or legal device by which societies acknowledge the transition to adulthood. Definitions of children, as well as the varied childhoods which children experience, are social constructs formed by a range of social, historical, and cultural factors. Being a child is not a universal experience of any fixed duration, but is differently constructed as it expresses the divergent gender, class, ethnic, or historical locations of particular individuals. Childhood is not constituted similarly across and within cultures. Since distinctive cultures and segments of those cultures construct different worlds of childhood, childhood cannot be studied apart from society as a whole. Equally important, legal responses to children's issues must not focus on a singular category of childhood but must capture how children may occupy simultaneous membership within broad social groups—gender, race, religion, physical ability, and/or sexual identity—and that membership in given categories serves to advantage or disadvantage children within particular communities.[48]

Child Sexual Maltreatment

Given that ideologies of childhood are embedded in wider sociocultural contexts, it should not be surprising to find that conceptions of maltreatment and sexuality are equally culturally constituted. Yet, the present knowledge of child maltreatment, including sexual maltreatment, is based almost exclusively on research and clinical experience conducted in Western nations. The international organization that studies child abuse and negect, for example, makes use of Western definitions and concepts.[49]

Despite rising interest in other cultures, in protecting indigenous societies, and in preserving cultural traditions, few have examined what would constitute maltreatment across cultures. Cross-cultural comparisons of maltreatment have tended to focus on the incidence rates, intervention strategies, and service delivery systems of Western nations.[50] It would be imprudent to assume that such comparisons are appropriate and that notions of what constitutes maltreatment do not differ among societies. Clearly, certain practices deemed acceptable by one culture may be abhorrent to another. For example, a father's cultural peers would deem him abusive if he would "protect" a child from painful but culturally mandated initiation rituals. Failure to allow a child to proceed through initiations essentially denies the child a place as an adult in that culture and compromises the child's development. Despite a certain degree of relativity, though, it is important to emphasize that each culture sets its limits. While each culture necessarily varies in its definition of child maltreatment, each society nevertheless has criteria available to identify behaviors that are outside the realm of acceptability. For example, in cultures where sexual relations between adults and initiates are part of rites of passage, relationships that would continue after rites would be "abnormal."[51]

Given the paucity of cross-cultural examinations, and despite unprecedented international interest in protecting children from maltreatment, there are not yet agreed-upon definitions of maltreatment.[52] Nor are there even universal standards for optimal child rearing, even for sexual development. The world community operates on the conventional wisdom that cultural boundaries have no impact on notions of child maltreatment, that maltreatment is easily recognizable and ascertainable. The received wisdom is quite problematic.

The lack of agreed-upon conceptions of maltreatment and child development presents a familiar dilemma faced by those who conduct culturally informed investigations. Failure to include a cultural perspective increases the danger of considering our own set of cultural values and practices preferable to others. At the same time, a stance of extreme cultural relativism that suspends judgments of humane treatment of children would be counterproductive to promoting the well-being of the world's children. As with notions of rights, cultural sensitivity is a necessary component of a proper examination of maltreatment; cultural sensitivity helps broaden the range of social and ecological conditions that Western notions would afford.

Given the need to consider different cultural conceptions of maltreatment and the obvious salience of culture to different peoples, it is important to come to terms with notions of what exactly constitutes maltreatment. Regrettably, the task of defining sexual maltreatment has been obstructed by the numerous imprecise derivatives that commentators use to describe children's conditions. Terms range from sexual assault, sexual abuse, sexual exploitation, sexual violence, prostitution, rape, incest, and sexual harassment to, most recently, teasing. To exacerbate matters, the terms often can relate to similar experiences. The differences in terminologies make an examination of the cross-cultural and international dimensions of sexual maltreatment exceedingly difficult.

Although differences in terms and emphases complicate comparisons, they are nonetheless instructive. The differences in terminology and approaches to sexual maltreatment continue largely because of the different perspectives and approaches that commentators wish to emphasize. For example, some early commentators preferred "sexual victimization" to the terms "sexual assault" and "sexual abuse".[53] Their focus on victimization emphasized that the child was a victim because of its age, naivete, and relationship with perpetrators rather than a victim of only physical violence. While these researchers wanted to de-emphasize physical violence and essentially broaden the recognition of sexual maltreatment, other researchers preferred to use the terms "assault"[54] and "child rape"[55] to underscore the inherent violence caused by sexual maltreatment. More recently, some commentators have chosen the term "sexual misuse" to emphasize the need to adopt a mental health perspective and to rehabilitate victims and families; these researchers view sexual maltreatment as arising from normal relationships gone wrong and emphasize the need to correct relationships.[56] Other experts focus on the need to alleviate the stigma suffered by children involved in criminal activities and thus opt for phrases that place the blame on adults; some focus on the "prostituted child" rather than on child prostitutes,[57] while others play down the sexual nature of prostitution and focus on the "working girl."[58] Others prefer to distinguish between extra-familial and intra-familial sexual abuse, in hopes of emphasizing the need to take different approaches to dealing with the effects and prevention of arguably different forms of maltreatment.[59]

Different approaches to delineating sexual maltreatment and their different emphases highlight not only the complex nature of sexual maltreatment but also the importance of adopting different approaches to deal with different manifestations and concerns about maltreatment. To explore the international dimensions of sexual maltreatment, the following chapters adopt a similar stance.

Readers familiar with international children's rights may recall that the prevailing approach simply protects children from sexual exploitation or sexual abuse.[60] No definitions are ever offered. For our purposes, we will first distinguish sexual exploitation, which primarily involves the commercialization of child sexuality. Then, we will examine sexual use, a term that helps distinguish sexual maltreatment deriving from "traditional" cultural practices and helps emphasize different issues that inherently cultural practices raise for children's rights. Lastly, we will distinguish sexual abuse, which involves practices directed at individual children and which communities generally agree are maltreating even though they may be ignored. Clearly, the three forms of maltreatment are interrelated; the tripartite division simply offers an analytical strategy rather than absolute categorization. Although not distinct in significant ways, the divisions help emphasize important points and surmount hurdles in the way of achieving a balanced sense of proportion in perceptions of sexually maltreated children.

The different categories are important to the extent to which international and domestic laws offer mechanisms for dealing with these manifestations. To be sure, international law remains better-suited to dealing with inter-state behavior than intra-state action. Yet, there is a growing focus on using international law to influence domestic behavior. The extent to which either area of policy-making—international and domestic—can be used to protect children from maltreatment varies considerably, depending on the form of maltreatment, the actors involved, and the social conditions that contribute to maltreatment. Yet, both are clearly related: A great deal must be done both within countries and internationally to combat, for example, feudalistic notions and practices that place children at risk.

Differentiating distinct categories also helps highlight the potential conflicts that may exist between children's right to protection from sexual maltreatment and other rights. For example, although no one has the right to sexually maltreat children, there are other rights or interests that hamper the discovery of maltreatment or obfuscate children's right to obtain assistance and recovery. These rights include, for example, the right to family privacy, the right to practice one's traditions, the right to engage in consensual sexual relations, and the right to obtain medical services.[61]

Distinguishing between forms of maltreatment also helps identify the communities' willingness to recognize certain behaviors as maltreatment. No social policy can be considered in isolation from attitudes and values; customary practices and traditional values will crucially affect both the priorities and the nature of programs. The socialization and care of children is of massive significance in every culture. Many circumstances and beliefs of specific communities and societies give rise to some of the most serious child welfare problems. Although female circumcision provides a very clear example, there are many other widespread practices whose eradication would equally challenge ingrained societal beliefs. In the industrialized world, for example, child harassment and dating violence continue at very high rates; yet as we will see in Chapter 7, cultural forces that contribute to these forms of maltreatment are ignored and make impossible the fruition of attempts to appropriately address adult forms of harassment and domestic violence.

Differentiating the forms of maltreatment also highlights the extent to which communities actually are willing to commit resources to intervene and combat these forms of maltreatment. For example, although many factors affect the welfare of children, poverty repeatedly emerges as a condition that adversely affects children. Indeed, it is poverty in the widest sense, and the social implications of that poverty, that provides the prime context in which child welfare must be considered. Poverty of material resources is often exacerbated by poverty of services and opportunities. Although variations exist in the extent to which countries exhibit internal inequality, disparities challenge all societies. Inequality exhibits its devastating consequences not only in terms of access to the economic rewards of development but also in the implementation of social policies and social welfare measures. For example, sexually exploited children are not simply victims of men preying on children; they are also ancillary victims of global and local patterns of development, underdevelopment, and social change.[62] Despite the impressive impact of poverty, the tendency to attribute all exploitation and other social ills to poverty is manifestly misleading. Many destitute girls do not become prostitutes, and many poor families do not abuse their children. How alternatives that lead to victimization are taken is understandable; but we know little about why some people choose not to take them. The extraordinary resilience is just that: extraordinary.

Conceptually separating the different forms of maltreatment also reveals their differential amenability to intervention. The actual ability to combat maltreatment once it has been recognized differs among the forms of abuse. This aspect deals more with the details of social service administration. Precisely how child welfare services are to be administered remains a complex issue. For example, failures continue for lack of will to confront controversial issues. A most obvious example is the failure to take education regarding sexual issues as forthrightly as is needed to help children face the pressures of harmful sexual activity.[63]

Lastly, the different forms of maltreatment help emphasize the extent to which deep societal reform will be needed, since maltreatment symbolizes deeper problems. For example, pornography has been allowed to flourish without much resistance partly because of society's unsuspecting belief that an adult would not attempt to sexually exploit children for commercial profit. Violence operates at all societal levels. Violence can be deeply embedded in social and material structures that are often taken for granted as normal, natural, just, humane, reasonable, and even enlightened.[64]

Although distinguishing among the forms of maltreatment is important, it is just as important to consider converging themes. Responses to maltreatment highlight well the need not to ignore commonalities. As we will see, the themes that will emerge are reflected in the policy framework that international law encourages us to take. Briefly stated, the themes include the need to rethink youth's participation in sexual activities, to increase support for families and other caretaking units, to focus on the reintegration of victims, to offer flexible approaches to dealing with maltreating behaviors, to incorporate children in efforts to assist them, and to encourage societal change and redevelopment through increasing every individual's participation in cultural life. Regardless of the particular society, each of these factors plays a critical role in determining the nature of maltreatment and the proper response to it.

Conclusion:
Recognizing the Multiple Ecologies
of Childhood and Maltreatment

Different ideologies and images of childhood make it necessary to think more carefully about the ecology of human development. It is not enough to study a developing child alone. Likewise, it is not enough to study a child within the setting of a family, for children and families are crucially affected by conditions in a host of interconnected environments.[65] Just as an individual identity and well-being is influenced by conditions within families, families themselves are sensitive to conditions within their own surrounding networks: neighborhoods, workplaces, churches, schools, and other associations. Importantly, just as local environments influence individuals and families, so do international political economies and global conditions impact local environments and their children.

The pressing need to reflect the broad ecology of child development in deliberations about children's issues is especially important in discussions of child maltreatment. Emerging themes and reasons for differentiating among forms of sexual maltreatment essentially amount to the need to consider the significance of the ecology of sexual maltreatment. Global, local, and individual ecologies undoubtedly must be considered in attempts to understand and react to maltreatment. For example, families and communities do not necessarily secure child welfare. Children can be abused and neglected in their families. Beyond the undoubted problem of individual failure to care for children within particular families, there are more generalized issues. Children are as often victims not of parents or other adults around them, but of patterns of development, underdevelopment, and social change. Examining factors in different cultural contexts that increase or decrease the propensity for sexually maltreating behavior expands and enhances the understanding of sexual maltreatment.

An approach to childhood and child maltreatment from multi-ecological perspectives undoubtedly opens itself to considerable obstacles. The hurdles are much more than theoretical. Several practical challenges arise, for the approach raises uncomfortable issues about adult power and responsibility, the structure of the Western nuclear family, motherhood, fatherhood, male sexuality, cultural imperialism, and the actual participation of children in cultural life. These challenges form the basis of the exploration that follows. To a large extent, then, the following chapters explore issues and behaviors involved in child sexual maltreatment from perspectives not considered in the current child development or sexual maltreatment literature. The cross-cultural record and international approach to children's rights which urges us to approach child maltreatment from the child's perspective allow us to consider childhood and sexual maltreatment from a broader range of social and environmental conditions than that afforded by a consideration of Western nations alone.

4 | The Sexual Exploitation of Children

The international community reserves its most ardent condemnation of child sexual maltreatment for actions that are most clearly exploitative, particularly child prostitution, sex-trafficking, and child pornography. These forms of maltreatment are recognized as universal wrongs and increasingly subjected to strict prohibitions and comprehensive regulations that have a global reach. Yet, the exploitation continues and even thrives as it adjusts to new mandates. This chapter critically examines the nature of exploitation, trends in existing legal mandates, and the need for reforms that allow exploitation to be even more visible and worthy of concern. The exploration reveals several emerging themes: the disruptive forces of modernization, the difficulties of policing despite pervasive agreement about practices, the need to recognize global and local structural forces that contribute to maltreatment, and the children's rights movement's potential.

Introduction

Previous chapters identified the beginning of the most radical shift ever imagined in conceptions of childhood. Instead of viewing children as property owned by adults and the state, the modern children's rights movement aims to view and treat children as persons in their own right. These developments provide the foundation to begin the exploration of child sexual maltreatment. The new ideology helps focus attention on children who are, yet should not be, exploited as exchangeable commodities through child pornography, child prostitution, and child sex-trafficking.

Although other forms of maltreatment discussed in the following chapters include dimensions similar to those found in exploitation, commodification serves as the central factor in sexual exploitation and distinguishes it from other forms. The focus on commondification is important, for it provides the basis upon which to acknowledge that the

60

practices are maltreating and may be the subject of local and international control. The impressive laws aimed to regulate and combat this form of child sexual maltreatment reflect well how these practices are clearly condemned. Yet, exploitation continues despite widespread condemnation, extensive laws, and an emerging ideology that aims to respect the inherent personhood of all children. Difficulties in combatting sexual exploitation persist although this form of maltreatment consists of dimensions directly amenable to domestic and international prohibition and control.

The enigmatic nature of sexual exploitation—the pervasive extent to which societies view it as wrong, have extensive laws that respond to the problem, and yet still allow the practice to continue—presents a major theme in responses to child sexual maltreatment. To move beyond simply highlighting enigmas, this analysis evaluates reform efforts in light of current ideologies of childhood and emerging notions of children's rights. The analysis suggests that, although current efforts provide important steps to stem the tide of exploitation, more radical changes in the ways children are perceived and greater infusions of economic and social development resources will be needed to reverse the trend toward increasing levels of child sexual exploitation. Although the eventual implementation of these changes undoubtedly would face formidable challenges, there exists considerable room for hope. Available evidence suggests that properly crafted policies consistent with the international shift in images of childhood can be used more effectively to combat sexual exploitation.

Pornographic Maltreatment

Numerous commentators analyze the place of pornography in modern society.[1] Although these analyses detail important debates, the most contentious and central controversies involve the nature of, and possible responses to, pornography's link to harms—such as coercion and abuse in the creation of pornographic materials, the use of pornography as a blueprint for sexual violence and degradation, and pornography's effect on attitudes toward sexual violence and sexual subordination.[2] Several challenge the claims of harms arising from a free market in pornography and emphasize the unproven or lack of readily identifiable harms.[3] Beyond challenging proof, some opponents of regulation stress pornography's educative and liberative functions, while others emphasize the dangers regulation creates as it uses civil and criminal law to encroach on private moral choices,[4] even in cultures characterized as repressive societies.[5] These debates tend to exclude child pornography, simply because most societies condemn the use of children in pornography and accept the proposal that child pornography exploits children because children are unable to consent to, and suffer harms in, pornography's production.[6] Thus, although issues remain contentious for adult pornography, evidence more conclusively reveals that child pornography harms children, and societies tend to concur.

Despite widespread condemnation and the belief that the involvement of children in pornography violates children's human rights, the place of children in pornography and censorship debates still is important to consider. First, close links exist between child and adult pornography. For example, some question whether child pornography can be eliminated without also regulating adult pornography. Support for this claim derives from the finding that adult pornography can be used to initiate children into taking part in the production of pornographic materials; likewise, pornographic materials actually often play a part in adolescents' initiation into sexual maturity for both boys and girls.[7] Second, regulation of children's participation in child pornography involves adults' rights—most notably their right to privacy and freedom of expression, as well as adults' rights to receive pornographic materials when attempts aim to limit access to those materials in order to protect children from viewing them. Third, conceptualizations of child sexual maltreatment tend not to include child pornography, just as they ignore the potentially instrumental role played by pornography in other forms of sexual maltreatment.[8] Lastly, and increasingly more importantly, the very reason that children are excluded from the pornography debate—children's apparent inability to consent—may run counter to the general movement in children's rights that aims to include children in the realm of rational moral agents, not entirely lacking the capacity to make their own choices and decisions.

The nature of pornographic exploitation

Child pornography is best understood as the visual depiction of children involved in sexually explicit activities.[9] Although this would seem to end the discussion—since sexual activities with children tend to be illegal—the matter does not stop there. It is important to better understand why this form of exploitation is so problematic in order to respond more properly to existing problems and to those that will arise. To do so, several concerns are important to investigate, especially children's ability to participate in pornography, the children who are the objects of pornography, as well as child pornography's uses and production. In examining these concerns, it is important to emphasize that current research examining child pornography remains limited and based on a range of sources that must be culled for information; the most obvious sources include clinical work with offenders, research relating to prostitution, and child pornography itself. Although limited, existing research does seem conclusive in several respects.

CHILDREN'S ABILITY TO PARTICIPATE IN CHILD PORNOGRAPHY

The general ability to consent to participate in pornographic activities clearly places children at a disadvantage and indicates the abusiveness of child pornography. If individuals could be involved legitimately in these activities, at least two forms of consent would be necessary: consent to being the subject of pornography, and consent to the sexual acts and relationships. Arguably, adults are currently in a better position than children to consent and enter into binding, legal contracts with their photographers or to engage in sexual activity. Indeed, contracts with children are still generally void *ab initio*.[10] Likewise, it is difficult to argue that children can meaningfully consent to engage in pornographic activities. This is especially true given that children essentially have little legal status and arguably less knowledge or experience to determine the nature and consequences of sexual actions. Although these two factors should not be used to oppress children and dominate their lives, the factors are quite important to consider in this context, for they exacerbate the already vulnerable status of children who are lured into pornographic work.

In addition to consent issues, another way to approach concerns about children's abilities to participate in child pornography considers the activities children perform. For example, the acts performed by children set them apart from those in adult erotica. The contents of pictures and films range from posed photographs of naked and semi-naked children to more explicit shots of their genitalia being massaged, and to explicit sexual activities with adults, children, and animals. Catalogues describe pictures that involve children of all ages, including infants being ejaculated upon.[11] These depictions support the claim that, if ever there have been explicit examples of pornography as a means to objectify sexuality and treat people as objects, this undoubtedly would be a prime candidate.

THE USES OF CHILD PORNOGRAPHY

The uses of child pornography also highlight its exploitative nature. Child pornography seems inextricably connected to child sexual abuse.

The sexual abuse of children during pornographic production is only part of the exploitation. Much of child pornography's utility derives from its use to lower children's inhibitions and encourage children to engage in activities similar to those depicted in pictures and magazines. Pornography helps groom children and persuade them that they would enjoy certain sexual acts. It provides children with instructions about how they are to behave, including how to pose or enact scenes. Likewise, child pornography also helps excite children and arouse their sexual curiosity. Children reluctant to engage in sexual activity with adults or hesitant to pose for sexually explicit photos can sometimes be convinced by viewing other children apparently having fun participating in the activity.[12] Just as importantly, pornography provides a powerful tool to help convince children that what they are being asked to do is "all right." Pictures legitimize abusers' requests and help normalize the abuse. All of the uses help pornographers trap children in abusive situations. Once children are trapped, threats of blackmail and threats to send pictures to authorities and parents reinforce the pornographer's hold. Clearly, the threat that materials may be distributed can be damaging. The awareness that such a record could be circulating or may continue circulating can cause irreparable emotional and psychological harm.

Pedophiles use child pornography to endanger children in still other ways. Child pornography helps pedophiles expand their sexual activities. Although pedophiles can preserve a child's youth through pornographic pictures, they also may look for new children by advertising in magazines and on computer bulletin boards. Child pornography helps pedophiles form underground networks that allow them to locate new children and exchange child pornography. After contacts are made through this network, pedophiles trade pictures of exploited children, obtain new pictures for their collections, and increase opportunities to meet new children.

An equally destructive and often ignored aspect of child pornography is the manner in which pedophiles use pornographic materials to legitimize abusive behaviors to themselves. Evidence reveals that child pornography induces viewers to commit sex crimes on children.[13] Its intended and most direct effect is to produce sexual arousal. Pornography enables pedophiles to construct a different version of reality, one in which they continually reinterpret victims' actions and responses. Just as it allows children to normalize abuse, pornography helps abusers normalize their behaviors by suggesting that children are seductive, that they receive pleasure through sexual interactions, and that they desire sexual relationships.[14] Likewise, child pornography helps abusers increase their own sexual arousal before abusing children and helps them reinterpret their victim's behavior to support their abuse. In some studies, over a third report being incited by pornography to commit an offense, and over half of those who committed child sexual abuse indicated that pornography was deliberately used in preparation for the offense.[15] These results find corroboration in studies of juvenile victimization; as one important study reveals, even when researchers do not ask victims of sexual abuse about pornography, approximately one-quarter of respondents incidentally volunteer its use by the adult offender before the sexual acts.[16] These findings help counter the popular misconception that child pornography acts in some way as a "safety valve," a theory inappropriately based on a Danish study that found a link between the availability of hard-core adult pornography and an apparent decrease in child molestation of preschool girls.[17] The new studies certainly help refute the theory that pedophiles can use child pornography safely to indulge fetishes without abusing children.[18]

THE PRODUCTION OF PORNOGRAPHY

An analysis of child pornography's production also helps to distinguish it from other forms of pornography. Commentators rightly indicate that child pornography cannot be produced without the sexual abuse of a child. These observations gain support from more recent modes of production. In the 1970s and early 1980s, child pornography generally was a commercial enterprise; oftentimes it involved adults posing as children.[19] Partly because of the criminalization of child pornography, individual pedophiles who recorded their abuse of children replaced commercial distribution.[20] The pedophiles sell, barter, or exchange materials with other abusers. A study by Chicago police supports the view that those who use child pornography are pedophiles who engage in sexual activities with children.[21] In almost 100 percent of their child pornography arrests during a recent year, detectives found photographs, films, and videos of child pornography customers engaged in sexual activities with children. The pictures had been taken by the men themselves and were used to document their pedophiliac careers.[22]

Although the bulk of child pornography is produced through a "cottage industry" run by self-producing pedophiles,[23] it would be a mistake to view commercialized child pornography as a problem of minor proportions. Although arguably now only a relatively small part of child pornography, commercialized dealing still remains a multi-billion-dollar industry. The American government identifies child pornography as one of the world's largest cottage industries. The Department of Justice estimates the market to range between $2 billion and $3 billion a year.

In addition to generating significant sums of money, commercialized child pornography exploits large numbers of children. The Department of Justice estimates that pornographers have recorded the abuse of more than 1 million children in the United States alone.[24] Statistics from other countries also reveal that child pornography involves more than self-producing pedophiles; e.g., Germany's annual sales reach beyond $250 million, with up to 40,000 consumers.[25] Other countries, however, serve mainly as points of trade and clearinghouses for pornography en route to the United States. The single largest geographical source of commercial child pornography has been Scandinavia, particularly Denmark. Since these countries have severe penalties for producing child pornography, most dealers buy films in Asian countries and other developing countries where operations can be easily run and there is an abundance of potential victims.[26] Recent commentaries emphasize how the actual production of international, commercialized pornography increasingly exploits children from poor and often black countries.[27]

Arguably, personal computers have replaced magazines and videotapes as the primary means of distributing child pornography. Pedophiles using computers may obtain images through international organizations and sophisticated networking. The result is that several countries, especially the United States, have become major markets for computer-linked pornography from networks originating in Denmark, Norway, Sweden, Switzerland, and the Netherlands.[28] These international organizations do not necessarily transfer only images. Computers allow for the maintenance of secrecy and the creation of covert underground networks that assist in child exploitation. For example, the international "Orchid Club" involved "virtual molestation," in which members molested actual children while requesting pointers from others in the chat room.[29] Again, the production of child pornography links to the abuse of children.

THE OBJECTS OF PORNOGRAPHY

Consideration of who is abused also helps us discern the abusiveness of pornography. In this regard, three significant points emerge. First, children abused through pornography tend to also suffer abuses in other ways, most notably through prostitution. An early study of child prostitution discovered that every one of the young people interviewed had been solicited to pose for porn photos or appear in films.[30] Other researchers do not produce such stunning findings; but they do indicate that a high number of those who eventually do become prostitutes experienced childhood pornography for commercial purposes and/or the gratification of the photographer.[31]

Second, child pornography clearly has a global reach. Children from around the globe are trapped and "abused" in other parts of the world. The exploitation of black children from Third World nations raises several important questions. Several commentators highlight that, when dealing with international issues, racism and Western economic and cultural imperialism undoubtedly play important roles. For example, some have argued that it is "easier" to abuse children from other countries, because they are not seen as "our" children.[32] White consumers are more readily able to see these children as "non-persons." Likewise, as other commentators have suggested, the thriving exploitation contributes to perceptions that black children are erotically exotic.[33] These commentaries highlight important points. Child sexual exploitation derives not only from children's powerlessness in relation to adults but also from the conjunction of sexism, racism, and imperialism. In this regard, it is important to view the objects of child pornography as more than children who engage in pornography to counter the attention and affection absent in their families; it also is more than simple alienation of children from traditional values.[34] Yet, parallels and connections exist between children exploited in the Third World and those in rich Western countries. A most basic similarity is that the vast majority of the children are simply trying to find ways to ensure their own physical survival. Child pornography involves cultural, political, and economic international relations.

A last point to emphasize about the objects of child pornography is that considerations of who or what the objects actually are become considerably complicated with computer-created pornographic images. The computer-generated "child" does not actually exist. Computer artists may create images of what appear to be children engaging in sexual activities.[35] These computerized sexual depictions are likely to become increasingly problematic.[36] Tactile feedback devices needed for "virtual sex" already exist: researchers have devised body suits in prototype forms that are embedded with fiber-optic sensors meant to be useful for erotica and sexual therapy.[37] Although they may seem like all-too-surreal fantasies, these developments are within the range of possibility. Virtual reality allows one to sensually interact with one's computer and simulate acts that would be crimes if actually carried out, but that in actuality take place only inside the computer and the imagination of the user. Although the images and the virtual sex of the future may not exploit actual children, computerized child pornography still remains problematic. Given what we know about the use of pornography, it is difficult to argue that "virtual pornography" would not have an impact on child sexual maltreatment and constitute sexual exploitation.[38] The devastating effects of child pornography do not begin and end with photographed and "virtual" victims. Pedophiles use child pornography to aid in the sexual abuse of other children.

Protecting children from pornographic exploitation

NATIONAL AND COMPARATIVE TRENDS

A primary issue in the regulation of child pornography begins with acceptance that pornography involving children is distinguishable from that involving adults. Courts and legislatures typically agree with the findings presented above and recognize the need to differentiate between the two forms of pornography. For example, in the groundbreaking 1982 case of *New York v. Ferber*,[39] the Supreme Court held that states may prohibit the depiction of minors engaged in sexual conduct. The purpose of the challenged New York statute at issue was "[t]o prevent the abuse of children who are made to engage in sexual conduct for commercial purposes. . . . "[40] Importantly, the case dealt with a film that did not involve illegal acts. The film simply showed two boys masturbating, a legal act that was apparently noncoercive. The Court found the following dispositive: the film could encourage abuse if it was used to initiate children into sexual activity; the prohibition properly dealt with the financial gain involved in selling and advertising child pornography as the production of materials through activities that are prohibited throughout the U.S.; and adults' right to privacy and freedom of expression is overweighed by the potential harm to children's physical and psychological well-being. The case continues to be of considerable significance. *Ferber* distinguishes child pornography from adult pornography, which is subject to greater protection from regulation.[41] The case recognizes the aggravated harm of repeated showings of films, and does so without evidence of coercion. More important, the case reflects an important move to allow intrusion into any individual's private life in order to restrict immoral behavior.[42]

The move to restrict one's behavior in one's private affairs is significant and considerably broadened by a critical and controversial point of intervention: the actual possession of child pornography.[43] The 1990 United States Supreme Court case of *Osborne v. Ohio*[44] reflects well why statutory efforts may be allowed to actually reach into the privacy of one's life and criminalize the possession of child pornography. The state's overriding need to protect children from exploitation and harms involved in the production of pornographic materials provides the basis for intervention. In that case, the Court accepted Ohio's three arguments for upholding the ban on the possession of child pornography in order to protect children from sexual exploitation: (1) child pornography production had been driven underground, and criminalization would decrease demand and supply; (2) criminalization would lead to the destruction of existing child pornography in response to the destructive effects of pornography as a permanent record of abuse that would haunt children for years to come; and (3) criminalization would prevent pedophiles from using child pornography to seduce other children into sexual activity. These developments are particularly significant, especially in terms of the law's receptivity to social science evidence regarding the potential harm of child pornography and the willingness to intervene more meaningfully in potential perpetrators' lives in order to protect children.

The Court's support for regulating child pornography has led several states to pass legislation dealing with child pornography.[45] Less than five years after the Ohio decision, for example, nearly half the states had passed laws to prohibit the possession of child pornography.[46] In addition, federal legislation dealing with child pornography increasingly became available to combat all aspects of child pornography. For example, federal laws now make it an offense to possess more than three copies of any materials that may be construed as child pornography.[47]

The focus on possession is an important tool to use in efforts to protect children from child pornography. However, the United States' approach remains an anomaly. Most countries that do regulate child pornography focus on its distribution or production.[48] For example, the U. K. Protection of Children Act of 1978 made it an offense for a person to take, or permit to be taken, any indecent photograph of a child, or to distribute or show such photographs, or to possess such photographs with a view to their being distributed or shown to others.[49] Even the most recent amendments do not move away from focusing on distribution efforts.[50] Importantly, even the laws in the U.S. still focus on distribution, as revealed by new laws that necessitate possession of at least three copies of child pornography to make possession a crime[51] and other more traditional provisions addressing child pornography.[52] Although these approaches may be limited, they represent important developments. These countries legally recognize the harms of child pornography.

In addition to these efforts, there have been international cooperative efforts aimed at combatting child pornography, particularly its international distribution.[53] For example, in November 1984, the United States Senate conducted its first hearing on the importation of child pornography from foreign countries. The customs service maintained that the Netherlands, Denmark, and Sweden were the source of about 85 percent of all pornography imported into the United States. After the hearing, the United States Interagency Group to Combat Child Pornography visited the three countries. The result was an intensified focus on prosecuting distributors.[54] Although fraught with difficulties, efforts have been fruitful. For example, efforts eventually resulted in a series of successful crackdowns on child pornography. In Operation Long Arm, Danish officials identified potential pedophiles and reported the names to the Customs Service, which then launched successful raids on those suspected of obtaining prohibited materials.[55] In *U.S. v. Kimbrough*,[56] following Operation Long Arm, the defendant was sentenced to a term of imprisonment of seventy-two months on charges involving receipt and possession of child pornography.[57] In Britain, Operation Starburst involved an international investigation of a pedophile ring thought to be using the Internet to distribute graphic pictures of child pornography. Nine British men were arrested as a result, not including other arrests in Europe, South Africa, the Far East, and America.[58]

Although there are several examples of successes, efforts still face several challenges. Tougher legislation is not necessarily enough to deal with the exploitation. A study conducted after apparently tougher legislation was enacted revealed that at least 264 different magazines depicting sexual acts involving children were produced and distributed in the U.S. every month.[59] Although the study's findings may be high, and subject to scrutiny for the way they were interpreted, the study does reflect the high number of circulated materials that largely go unnoticed; for the study did not include clandestine operations in which pornographers simply exchange materials or in which pornography is produced and exchanged by computer. As we have seen, technology increases the availability of materials that exploit children, such as computer-generated fantasized images of children.[60] Importantly, these modern technological advances in pornographic work provide the most challenges and exacerbate difficulties faced in efforts to criminalize traditional forms of child pornography.[61]

The regulation of computers—the most recent area of legal activity—illustrates the new challenges child protective efforts face. Efforts to curb computerized access to pornographic materials have proven considerably difficult for at least three reasons. First, the legislation must be responsive not only to the government's compelling interest in the protection of children but also to the legitimate interests of both computer users and computer communication businesses. For example, in December 1995, Compuserve suspended access to more than 200 sex related newsgroups. The action was taken in response to a direct mandate from

German prosecutors. German authorities aimed to investigate news-groups and other Internet content providers in an attempt to locate child pornography and other pornographic materials illegal for minors.[62] The ban was heavily criticized, especially by on-line users. Compuserve quickly restored access. The event highlighted the extent to which the emergence of virtual communities in cyberspace poses complicated challenges in the most basic determination of jurisdiction.[63]

Second, efforts generally aim to protect minors from computerized access to sexual images, rather than protecting them from becoming the sexual images.[64] And efforts aimed at limiting children's access to computer materials suitable for adults—i.e., those perhaps indecent but not obscene—have proven unsuccessful. For example, concern for protecting children formed the major impetus for the enactment of the Telecommunications Act of 1996.[65] The clear purpose of the act was to restrict access by minors to offensive depictions of sexual or excretory activities that might be available over interactive computer services, including materials on the Internet.[66] Although the Act contained exceedingly broad language, public and scholarly commentaries narrowed to protecting children from access.[67] In fact, the Act was so broad that the statute never went into effect; less than a year after its enactment, the Supreme Court struck down the attempt to have Internet users limit their transactions for fear that exposure to minors would bring criminal sanctions.[68] Although the Act failed in the U.S., it reflects and exemplifies well other countries' efforts; England, Australia, and New Zealand are considering similar proposals.[69] Given the nature of the Internet, prior attempts to regulate, and legal precedents established in the U.S., it seems likely that future efforts to regulate minors' access will place primary responsibility for children's on-line activities solely in the hands of adults who watch over them.[70] This characterized both Internet service providers' response before the court ruling[71] and the approach adopted by the Supreme Court;[72] it also reflects the difficulties service providers face.[73]

Third, materials made to look like child pornography but not created with the use of minors generally do not qualify as child pornography. Early problems with this approach to regulation involved adults posing as children. Such materials were not deemed illegal; for example, in the U.S., most child pornography statutes still require that the subject be below a specific age—only one state, Arizona, statutorily prohibits the visual depiction of adults engaging in sexual conduct who "masquerade" as minors.[74] Even pseudophotographs are not directly prohibited in the United States;[75] the only exception would be materials deemed obscene, in which case they could be addressed by laws regulating obscenity, but not child pornography.[76] Thus, computer-generated images *may* not, in some circumstances, be impermissible. In other countries, "constructed" child pornography is explicitly not criminalized, for their laws protect children only from sexual crimes committed during the production of the pornographic materials.[77] The United Kingdom provides an important exception; British statutes were amended in 1994 to include pseudo-photographs of children, a development that addresses computer-generated pornography.[78] Rather than simply being concerned with the actual abuse that may occur during production, the new developments concern themselves with the way photographs may be used as tools for further molestation of children. Countries that have not yet responded to the new forms of pornography may also regulate new images through obscenity statutes.[79] In sum, despite impressive laws and societal concerns, certain forms of child pornography may still not be considered "child pornography."

DEVELOPMENTS IN INTERNATIONAL LAW

Given the often global dimensions of sexual exploitation, international law could become an important tool to fight this form of sexual maltreatment. Until very recently, no international document directly addressed the need to protect children from child pornography. The 1923 International Convention on the Suppression of the Circulation and the Traffic in Obscene Material, as amended in 1947, required only that States Parties "take all measures to discover, prosecute and punish" those who produce, distribute, and exhibit obscene material.[80] The International Convention did not specifically address child pornography. Since then, however, there have been decisive steps taken to protect children from pornographic exploitation.

The most notable developments are in the Children's Convention. The Convention addresses long-standing gaps in protecting children from child pornography. Unlike previous documents, several of its articles explicitly address child pornography. These provisions clearly require that States Parties take all national, bilateral, and multilateral measures to combat sexual exploitation. For example, Article 34 explicitly urges Nation States to prevent "the exploitative use of children for pornographic performances and materials." In addition, Article 36 offers protection against "forms of exploitation prejudicial to any aspects of the child's welfare." Likewise, Article 32 "recognizes the right of the child to be protected from economic exploitation" and Article 39 forcefully finds that "States Parties shall take all appropriate measures to promote physical and psychological recovery and social reintegration of a child victim of: any form of neglect, exploitation, or abuse." Given the number of provisions that aim to combat child exploitation, the Convention clearly aims to prohibit the exploitative use of children in pornographic performances and materials.

Developments in children's human rights law are significant for several reasons. The developments reflect the extent to which human rights organizations and Nation States recognize the importance of protecting children from this form of exploitation. As we have seen, countries already have responded to the need to develop international cooperation to deal with the increasingly sophisticated methods of distributing child pornography.[81] As part of the cooperative efforts, several countries now have legislation to combat child pornography, and those without anti-child-pornography legislation have, in theory, ways to deal with the problem under existing obscenity statutes.[82] The Convention provides extra impetus to further cooperation. The international condemnation of child pornography facilitates support for furthering international developments to protect children from sexual exploitation. For example, concern for preserving national autonomy is less a problem when the form of maltreatment is offensive in a multinational ambiance.[83] Likewise, international attempts to control child pornography emphasize that some aspects of child sexuality are not culturally relative. These considerations are significant, and are best reflected in difficulties encountered in policing efforts. For example, the geographical and cultural area with the closest ties, the European community, finds policing matters controversial.[84] The Maastricht treaty has furthered the general idea of supranational competence (jurisdiction) for criminal law and policy by defining areas of common concern in the general field of criminal policy.[85] Although current focus remains primarily on money laundering initiatives involving illegal substances and insider trading, commentators expect to find child pornography added in due course.[86] The efforts help focus the attention of States Parties on sexual exploitation through pornography.

The developments are also significant in that they require that Nation States themselves enact domestic laws to do more than criminalize child pornography. Given existing difficulties faced by the criminalization of child pornography, especially its possession, its distribution, and the emergence of technological developments, it is important not to ignore the need for other efforts. The new mandates reveal how international law can help prevent the creation of child pornography by addressing its roots causes. Although these dimensions of modern human rights law will be detailed in later chapters, it is important to note here that international law can indirectly combat child pornography through antipoverty programs that alleviate the need for some children to be involved in exploitative activities.[87] Likewise, international law can be enlisted to address the social structures that reinforce exploitative dispositions, such gender discrimination and other cultural beliefs that ignore exploitations that inappropriately sexualize children,[88] sexualize materials that are directed to children,[89] or do not even recognize pornography.[90]

The developments in international law are perhaps even more significant in how they reveal a new concern for protecting children's sexualities. The Convention reveals this controversial development through several curious facets in its protections. For example, the Convention prohibits only "exploitative" or "unlawful" use of children in pornographic performances and materials.[91] These contentious provisions suggest that prostitution can be other than exploitative and that, for example, children sufficiently mature but still under the age of official majority could be free to engage in pornographic performances. Although striking when brought to attention, the significance of the "limitations" reaches beyond the important attempts to protect children. The limitations reflect the unprecedented effort to remain consistent with provisions that respect the child's right to self-determination, a theme that will recur throughout the analyses that follow.

The import of the attempt to protect children's right to sexual self-determination can not be overestimated. The development reveals an effort to recognize children as able to participate in their own development into social beings. The concern also reflects the reality that the major task of childhood is to deal with sexual issues, and that protecting children from all sexual activities will not necessarily be productive if they warp child sexuality. The recognition is reflected in emerging commentaries that point to the possibility that attempts to curb access to pornography actually may increase harm to vulnerable children.[92] Lastly, the development serves to highlight an equally important point about pornography—pornography is not monolithic. We are dealing with different types of pornographic materials, some of which may be necessary to engage children in efforts to protect themselves from exploitation and to address their natural curiosities. Overregulating children's access to sexual information raises important issues which must be considered in attempts to combat the pornographic exploitation of children.

Prostituted Children

The prostitution of children involves situations in which children engage in systematic sexual activity for material benefits for themselves or others. As with child pornography, it is commodification of child sexuality that distinguishes it from other forms of sexual maltreatment. Again, although there is a focus on commodification, child prostitution involves several dimensions. A surprisingly complicated set of factors actually contributes to children's selling their bodies—multiple forces sustain the lives of young prostitutes. To a large extent, as most evident in examinations of the diverse forms and international dimensions of child prostitution, child prostitutes are part of institutionalized arrangements—sustained, patterned social structures that foster the sexual exploitation of children for profit.

This section first examines the international forces that foster child prostitution and recently emerged policies that combat this form of exploitation. The analysis highlights several themes—most notably the difficulty of implementing reform efforts and the increasing institutionalization of practices. The difficulties identified at the international level are then examined at the domestic level. The analysis of intra-country prostitution focuses on the United States' efforts to combat this form of maltreatment; for the U.S. has a substantial number of laws and policies aimed at alleviating the prostitution of children. The section ends with highlights of how domestic and international law may assist in developing policies to help alleviate the problem of domestic child prostitution.

International sex tourism

THE EXTENT OF SEX TOURISM

International attention to the prostitution of children comes mainly in the form of sex tourism: men traveling to foreign countries to engage in sexual activities with children. Although it remains impossible to assess the magnitude of sex tourism with any precision, even the United Nations estimates that a high number of children are involved: over 800,000 children in Thailand, 400,000 in India, and 250,000 in Brazil.[93] A conservative estimate by UNICEF reports about 20,000 child prostitutes in the Philippines, two-thirds of whom are street children and runaways exploited by pedophiles.[94] The global result is that over 1 million children a year are forced into what is becoming known as the global child sex market, a $10-billion-a-year industry.[95] Figures alone do not tell the social crisis represented by this development in the way children are exploited. The International Campaign to End Child Prostitution in Asian Tourism (ECPAT) reports that entire villages and rural regions of the world are empty of children.[96] Other organizations report that AIDS contracted from adults increasingly threatens to destroy an entire generation of youth.[97] Still others report individual horror stories of children killed, maimed, and tortured to fulfill tourists' passions.[98] These anecdotes are buttressed by reports from other human rights groups that emphasize the systematic nature of child prostitution. For example, in Sri Lanka, where ethnic violence has frightened most tourists away from lavish hotels, beach resorts frequented by pedophiles still report full occupancies. Roughly 10,000 "beach boys" between the ages of eight and sixteen are controlled by syndicates; the boys regularly move from resort to resort and are exploited sexually and financially.[99] In other well-known destinations, such as Pagsanjan in the Philippines, sex tourists have established permanent relationships not just with local boys, but also with their families: wealthy pederasts buy expensive items, such as cars, homes, and even businesses, for the boys' parents.[100]

Evidence also reveals the need to consider the extent of international abductions and trafficking. Although these practices have a long history,[101] the United Nations reports that the practices continue. For example, girls procured in one state are auctioned and sold at transit centers and then sent to markets in other states, and from there to red-light areas. The Working Group on Contemporary Forms of Slavery reports that thousands of minor girls from Bangladesh and Nepal are exported to Indian brothels.[102] At any given time, it is estimated that 20,000 girls are being transported from one end of India to another for prostitution.[103] Human rights organizations also report the smuggling of girls between Thailand and neighboring countries, particularly Burma,[104] and that about 1 million Asian children are involved in the sex trade.[105] Despite international focus on Asian countries and those in Latin America, the International Labor Organization emphasizes that five major international networks traffic children to destinations including northern Europe, former Russian countries, Australia, New Zealand, and China.[106]

THE DYNAMICS OF SEX TOURISM

As expected, poorer countries receive most of the tourists that seek child prostitutes. Customers are relatively rich, whether they come from rich or poor countries. Because their activities, if exposed, could ruin their lives at home, many pedophiles rely on what the United Nations Children's Fund describes as "the economic power and effective information systems"[107] of clandestine pedophile networks to find the safest destinations and to learn to avoid detection. Through extensive networking, pedophiles can obtain lists of locations where they can engage in pedophilia without fear of repercussions, and lists of legal limits in each receiving country.[108] Human rights groups reveal how industrialized countries continue to allow the advertisement of exclusive sex tours, despite repeatedly noting their dissatisfaction with countries that continue to receive tourists who sexually exploit children.[109] Importantly, the information is readily available, as reflected in efforts by the Coalition Against Prostitution and Child Abuse in Thailand (CAPCAT) to force a U.S.-based company to remove advertisements offering teenage commercial sex from its Web site.[110]

Given the obviously important role played by tourists, commentaries that have examined potential ways to deal with sex tourism tend to focus on the tourist and tourism industry.[111] The tourism industry certainly remains a major contributor to the expansion of sex tourism. Human rights advocates highlight well how multinational conglomerates operating tours and publishing guides, as well as airlines and hotels, benefit from the significant income generated by child prostitution, much like the benefits received by those engaged in the underground economy run by pimps, procurers, and organized crime.

The result of the focus on tourist industries has been an increasingly successful effort to lobby for criminalizing the participation of sex tourists. Although measures have been successfully lobbied and legislated, their implementation remains more problematic. Narrowly directed attempts to deal with this form of exploitation seem futile. The exploitation continues, as revealed by the United Nations' recent optional protocols to the Children's Convention that finds "the sexual exploitation of children through prostitution, pornography and trafficking has assumed new and alarming dimensions at both national and international levels."[112]

The major reason the exploitation still assumes "alarming" proportions is that, despite increased criminalization, prostituted childhoods are multi-determined. In addition to the contribution of the tourism industry, exploitation also must be attributed to the global economy that exploits the inequality inherent among nations, sexism, mythologies of childhood and sexuality, and even unintended results of apparently beneficent attempts to help countries deal with internal strife and economic development. These dimensions are worthy of emphasis, for they are central to efforts to combat child prostitution.

Mythologies of childhood play important contributory roles in the prostitution of children. Although this form of sexual maltreatment is the one most generally viewed as wrong, some cultural beliefs fail to support the condemnations and tend to portray sexual interactions with children as beneficial. In parts of India, for example, sex with a virgin or a child is commonly believed to cure venereal disease.[113] Perhaps more prevalent is the belief that young sex partners are less likely to have or to spread deadly diseases, such as AIDS.[114] Although mistaken—children actually do have higher rates of HIV infection than other prostitutes, and even HIV-drug users, because sexual intercourse is more likely to cause lesions and injuries in children[115]—these beliefs still drive the expansion in child prostitution in the form of sex tourism. The mistaken belief, coupled by the formal prohibition of sexual interactions with children, fuels efforts by men to travel to foreign countries to engage in clandestine sexual practices with children.[116]

In other societies, customs have been perverted to supply children. For example, Indian children command a price three times that of older women. To supply the sex market, girls as young as twelve are recruited and become *devadasis*, "slaves of god." The seventh-century religious practice in which girls were dedicated to temples for lives of dance and prayer has been distorted so that tens of thousands of girls, with the full knowledge of their parents, now pledge fealty to the goddess Renuka at puberty and then are shunted off to brothels.[117] Although the practice has been outlawed, in parts of India it continues unchecked.[118] During the festival of Marg Purnima in 1989, over 3,000 minor girls were induced into the Devadasi system near Belgaum, Karnataka. Far from stopping the prohibited ceremony, the police directed traffic and managed festive crowds. The practice's cultural roots make the system difficult to prohibit and control. In Karnataka and parts of Maharastra, the Devadasi system requires families to dedicate their daughters to Goddess Yellamma; they are exhorted by tradition and scriptural injunction to produce sons.[119] Religion requires that the girls are barred from marriage and discarded by their community. The girls eventually fall prey to pimps and procurers. Clearly, several cultural forces continue to play a major role in this form of exploitation.

Sex tourism has had reverberating effects other than the perversion of local customs; it exacerbates sexism. Several examples are illustrative. First, in some countries sex tourism has interacted with the open acceptance of polygamy and reservations regarding prostitution. Sex tourism has helped vitiate traditional reservations about prostitution; that is, many now feel that what is good for tourist entertainment is also good for themselves.[120] Second, as traditional sources of adult females in the sex trade have shifted to cater to foreign tourists, a supply shortage has been created for local consumption. Additionally, prostitutes become less affordable to locals. Children are recruited to fill the gap, because in some areas they are cheaper and more plentiful. Social forces beyond children's control determine not only whether they will be subjected to prostitution, but also what they are worth.

The forces that distort local customs and gender relations are powerful; they even wrench benevolent efforts to offer assistance. For example, some attempts to offer humanitarian and military assistance to countries have inadvertently led to an increase in child prostitution. Several have analyzed the contribution of the U.S. military forces to prostitution in general, and child prostitution in particular.[121] The most commonly cited example occurred during the Indochina War. In that war, the U.S. signed a Rest and Recreation treaty with Thailand; the goal of this effort was to provide respite for U.S. military troops who were fighting in the Vietnam War. These events led to the transformation of prostitution into a lucrative industry.[122] Even the United Nations' unprecedented peacekeeping efforts have had similar impacts. Commentators report that the Cambodian experience is illustrative. With a budget of $2.8 billion, 15,900 peacekeeping troops, and 600 administrators, peacekeeping efforts in Cambodia have been the largest field operation in the history of the United Nations. They have also led to the most flourishing environment for child prostitution. Child prostitution became an important part of the trade, with children kidnapped, raped, bought, and sold.[123] The Special Rapporteur on the Sale of Children, Child Prostitution and Child Pornography noted how there were recurrent complaints against peacekeepers for exploiting local girls.[124] Similar patterns around U.S. military bases where American servicemen call into port for "rest and recreation" are found in other areas, such as the Philippines.[125] Importantly, commentators also note that domestic militaries create similar demands: since the civil war in El Salvador, the number of prostitutes in its capital, San Salvador, has doubled to 19,000 under the demand of a large military.[126]

The corruption of efforts to offer assistance also are reported in attempts to assist children caught in war zones and suffering as a result of warfare. For example, inter-country adoption was initiated as a humanitarian gesture to foster war orphans.[127] Regrettably, the efforts have been thwarted by some as the practice commercialized. Sometimes children who are supposedly being adopted are in fact used for sexual purposes. Popular press reports recently revealed the ease with which children can be adopted abroad and then brought to the United States to be sexually abused.[128] Although precise numbers for the sale and trafficking of children are not available,[129] the demand in the developed world compounds problems; adoptive parents bypass officially recognized authorities and act through their own means, unwittingly helping to create and support clandestine and illegal channels.[130] The practice is markedly similar to the fake marriages used to lure young women into prostitution[131] or to practices in which young children are indentured to wealthier families only to be diverted to brothels in distant cities; others lose their positions and resort to prostitution as a means of survival.[132] The practice of adoption for sexual purposes has become significant enough that it now falls within the mandate of the Special Rapporteur on the Sale of Children, Child Prostitution and Child Pornography,[133] and contributed to the development of the 1993 Hague Convention on Protection of Children and Cooperation in Respect to Intercountry Adoption.[134] These practices have been characterized as particularly problematic, given that recent changes in the nature of military conflicts have brought women and children to the forefront of most contemporary wars. The conflicts not only threaten and cause harm to women and children, but they also remove resources on which they depend for survival, and make them particularly vulnerable to abduction, sexual violence, as well as prostitution and marriage enforced by a military.[135]

Economic aid also has been known to bolster child prostitution. In Thailand, the World Bank and the International Monetary Fund encouraged the government to supplement its exports with tourism; the goal was to stimulate the economy by attracting wealthy visitors.[136] Although the economic incentives appear innocuous, they apparently contribute to the prostitution of children. Several have persuasively shown how the tourism policy advocated by the World Bank and Thai government indirectly subsidized the sex industry and promoted "tourism with a sex package"[137] in which child prostitution was viewed as a "service attraction" sanctioned by government agencies.[138] Again, the pattern finds parallels elsewhere.[139]

Economic inequality between nations reveals the overwhelming circumstances faced by children involved in sexually exploitative activities. In developing countries, they are adversely affected by urban migration, an overspending military, a lack of natural resources, unequal economic development, and industrial changes in the form of a compulsive drive for rapid modernization. Under pressure from all sides, governments cannot afford to ignore the money generated by tourism: they have to pay foreign debts, and acquire expensive technology, commodity goods, and weapons that finance rapid industrialization.[140] As several commentators have suggested, these factors inevitably lead to the nuclearization and fragmentation of families and to rampant poverty. The poverty that results has long been identified as one of the fundamental reasons children prostitute themselves to foreign tourists. Indeed, economic hardships within the household often prompt family members to approve of, if not take an active role in, the induction of their children into prostitution.[141] Many children voluntarily enter the sex trade to support their families out of a long-standing cultural perception of familial obligation; they attempt to strengthen family ties.[142]

Although economic inequality and the resulting poverty encourage segments of societies to allow their children to engage in child prostitution, it is difficult to argue that the choices of families and their children are voluntary. Financial pressures result in much more than the breakdown of the family unit. Poverty results in illiteracy, undereducation, a lack of marketable skills and employment opportunities, and ultimately a lack of real and effective choices. Poor families become particularly vulnerable to pimps and other procurement agents. Agents on commission from bar and brothel owners coerce or entice parents from slums and poor villages to surrender their children on the promise that they will be given legitimate positions in restaurants or hotels. Instead, the reality is that the children are sold into prostitution. Although recruiters typically descend on villages and persuade unsuspecting poor farmers to allow their children to "work" in cities, at times it is the migrants who return to their home villages and entice their neighbors to let their children leave. Once these children are brought to cities, they too are quickly introduced to the sex trade.[143] In other instances, girls are committed by their parents to procurement agents who lend money in exchange for the girls' work in brothels until the loan and interest is paid. Children face usurious interest rates, charges for room and board, and various other fraudulent expenses, making the prospect of ever actually working off loans appear quite illusory.[144] The United Nations' Working Group reports that, given the highly lucrative nature of child prostitution, crime syndicates from the United States, Germany, Australia, and Japan have been intensely involved in Southeast Asian organized prostitution. As the Working Group noted, the child prostitution industry is being maintained and promoted by a marketing system usually controlled by those who already control a great deal of wealth and power.[145]

Although poverty may help explain why some children are involved in prostitution, many families and children show extraordinary resilience in their ability to resist child prostitution in the face of hardship and desperate social and economic conditions.[146] Remarkably, only one empirical study has examined resistance to prostitution. A longitudinal study in Hawaii traced the lives of several young people living in poverty. The common denominators in the lives of children who resisted prostitution, drugs, or delinquency had simply been unconditional acceptance by an adult. Regrettably, this does not make the situation any easier. Providing job placement, training, and even money may be easier than unconditional acceptance of a child by street educators and social workers. It means not only changing the children, but changing the views of workers and child activists.[147] These findings reveal how economic intervention programs may not be successful, and arguably should not even have the highest priority, since it is difficult to imagine events that would lead to the actual restoration of a more justly managed world economy. Inner resources within children, families, and communities are just as important as broad social development programs in designing appropriate prevention and rehabilitation strategies.

Protecting children from prostituted exploitation

Given the often global dimensions of sexual exploitation—especially the tourist and trafficking dimensions—international law could become an important tool for fighting this form of sexual maltreatment. International cooperation among national and international law enforcement and service agencies on a multilateral, regional, and bilateral basis constitutes one of the more important strategies to counter the transnational aspects of child prostitution. Five articles in the Children's Convention explicitly address child sexual exploitation. These articles clearly require that States Parties take all national, bilateral, and multilateral measures to combat sexual exploitation. Article 34 explicitly urges Nation States to prevent the inducement or coercion of children into unlawful sexual activity, including the exploitative use of children in prostitution. In addition, Articles 35 and 36 respectively offer protection against the "abduction, the sale of or traffic in children for any purpose or in any forms" and against "other forms of exploitation to any aspects of the child's welfare." Lastly, Article 32 "recognizes the right of the child to be protected from economic exploitation," and Article 39 forcefully requires Nation States to take all appropriate measures to promote physical and psychological recovery, and social reintegration of child exploitation victims.

In addition to eliciting this straightforwardly strong language, child prostitution breaches several other rights recognized by international human rights law. The more notable violations include the infringement of the child's right to life and liberty of the person; freedom from torture and cruel, inhuman, or degrading treatment or punishment; prohibition on arbitrary or unlawful interference with the child's privacy or family; the enjoyment of the highest attainable standard of physical and mental health; education; and protection from economic exploitation.[148] Clearly, the affronts to moral, spiritual, and physical dignity and integrity entail significant breaches of children's human rights. The world community seemingly agrees.[149]

An amalgam of laws address issues directly related to child prostitution. Since the early part of this century, the international community has adopted a number of antitrafficking and antislavery conventions designed to suppress the traffic in persons and the exploitation of the prostitution of others, and to prohibit slavery.[150] These international instruments seek to assure children equality of opportunity, self-sufficiency, and citizenship. For example, there are several international legal instruments dealing with slavery and the slave trade,[151] most notably the Convention for the Suppression of the Traffic in Persons and of the Exploitation of the Prostitution of Others,[152] which aims to suppress prostitution and the accompanying trafficking of women and children and which dictates that states prohibit child prostitution even with the consent of the child. The Convention requires contracting parties to punish "[a]ny person who, to gratify the passions of others, has hired, abducted or enticed, even with her consent, a woman or a girl who is a minor, for immoral purposes . . . "[153] Likewise, the Convention on the Elimination of All Forms of Discrimination Against Women[154] seeks to end the suppression and exploitation of women by eliminating discrimination against women in marriage, family, employment, health, and education in order to eliminate gender stereotypes and gender inequality. In addition, several international organizations have confronted these issues. The International Labor Organization adopted conventions concerning forced labor and the minimum age for admission to employment that its Committee of Experts on the application of the conventions has used to report how the use of children for prostitution is "one of the worst forms of forced labor."[155] Lastly, the prohibition gains support from the International Covenant on Civil and Political Rights, through its prohibitions against slavery.[156]

The comprehensive international legislative framework that seeks to abolish the impugned practices and to punish perpetrators already exists. It is the Convention, however, that provides a new catalyst for developing international laws to protect children from sexual exploitation. The effectiveness of previous mandates was undermined by the antiquated nature of some of the instruments, the modest number of ratifications and accessions by countries, and the lack of effective implementation by States Parties to the international treaties. Just as important, previous instruments largely failed to adopt preventative approaches to tackle the root causes and offer incentives to help change local practices. In this regard, the Convention and the renewed interest in children's rights have energized important developments.

A most promising development of the new international standards and attention to child prostitution has been the focus on the travelers themselves. The new standards encourage countries to prohibit their own citizens from traveling to engage in sex tourism. Several countries recently have criminalized foreign travel with the intent to engage in sexual activity with children: the United States, Australia, Sweden, France, Germany and England now have enacted legislation.[157] Admittedly, these laws are exceedingly difficult to enforce and implement. Although several would be quick to enact more aggressive law enforcement measures,[158] extraterritorial jurisdictions, evidentiary standards, and the accumulation of physical and testimonial evidence complicate prosecutorial efforts.[159] Political and economic forces and cultural ideologies that permit and even condone the exploitation of child sexuality further exacerbate matters.[160] Yet, despite these overwhelming obstacles, the efforts are far from futile and not merely symbolic. Several countries already have prosecuted men who have violated the new codes.[161]

The most impressive legislative initiatives have emerged from the Philippines. While formerly the age of consent was only twelve and all forms of prostitution were criminalized, children below the age of eighteen who engage in prostitution are now exempt from criminal liability. The child is now considered an exploited party who may seek protection. Other changes have been more dramatic. New statutes create a number of criminal offenses targeting clients, such as a new rebuttable assumption whereby an adult found in a hotel room with an unrelated child is deemed to be engaged in sexual exploitation.[162] In addition, convicted foreigners must serve any custodial sentence imposed by the court before deportation.[163]

Difficulties faced by criminal justice approaches are rampant in countries that prohibit child prostitution. For example, Thailand boasts extensive laws that impose penal and monetary damages for prostitution and several related acts, including those aimed at trafficking and those targeting places where prostitution occurs, as well as laws dealing with statutory rape.[164] Yet, the country continues to be cited repeatedly for its most egregious exploitation of children. Likewise, in Sri Lanka, where child prostitutes cater to tourists despite drops in other forms of tourism due to internal war,[165] there are a number of laws that can be used to punish those engaged in child prostitution. In addition to important legislation regulating child labor, the Vagrancy Act of 1841 prohibits the "picking up" of young children, and the Ceylon Legislative Enactments of 1889 prohibit the managing and keeping of a brothel. Yet, the exploitation continues. Laws suffer from weak and inconsistent enforcement.[166] The reasons for the underenforcement of the laws are manifold. The United Nations reports that, in the context of rapid economic modernization drives, the lure of tourist dollars induces governments and law enforcement officials to look the other way. Low-paid law enforcement officers are prime targets for bribery by affluent foreign tourists and the well-organized sex trade industry. For example, Asia Watch recently condemned police and government officials for profiting from the forcible recruitment of thousands of Burmese women and girls into Thai prostitution.[167] Another concern for enforcement is that when traffickers and those who engage in sexual activity with children are convicted, sanctions tend to be minor. For example, tourists usually are simply deported.[168] Legal loopholes and lacunas also contribute to enforcement ineffectiveness, such as the absence of laws regulating the roles of parents in prostitution. As with other sex crimes against children, convictions are hampered by the unwillingness of prostituted children to cooperate in police investigations—fears of persecution and possible retaliation are well-grounded and exacerbate the trauma of being sexually exploited. The United Nations Children's Fund and the Working Group on Contemporary Forms of Slavery have reported well the permanent psychological trauma, physical harm, illness, and stress sustained by children who render sexual services.[169]

Perhaps even more problematic in dealing with victims of prostitution and involving the criminal justice system is victims' tendencies to normalize the sexual assaults they endure. For example, in a recent study conducted by Thai police, an incredibly low number of prostitutes, 2.1 percent, indicated that they had been "forced."[170] These prostitutes treat their sexual interactions as providing a service for entertainment. Again, difficulties in determining consent and lack of force hamper efforts not only at intervention, but also at recognition among those ostensibly exploited.[171]

Although the traditional problems encountered by the criminal justice system pose significant challenges, the most important challenge deals with the victims themselves, not the offenders. Efforts that do not prevent exploitation must deal with the reintegration of identified victims. Reintegration of victims, as mandated by the Children's Convention's Article 39, remains exceedingly difficult to imagine. One influential commentator put the child prostitute's situation and chances for recovery as follows:

A young girl not yet in her teens forced to receive thirty to fifty customers a night will be so severely traumatized after a single week that
the possibility of rehabilitation is almost non-existent. Those who
have worked to try and give child prostitutes a new start in life despair
at finding any real solution for a life which is virtually over before it
has begun.[172]

The negative effects and dire conditions reverberate and exacerbate children's earlier living conditions. The child's early social environment has
produced a host of life-threatening and health-damaging experiences,
not the least of which are physically and emotionally damaging infancy
and childhood experiences, persistent poverty and degrading life experiences, powerlessness, victimization, loss of self-esteem, loneliness, social
isolation, and social marginality. These factors suggest not only that traditional law enforcement may have a difficult time dealing with child prostitution, but also that other efforts are likely to be equally problematic.

In addition to the severity of victimization, there is the counterintuitive finding that prostituted children do not even reach out to organizations that offer assistance. Organizations which try to render relief
through rehabilitation or prevention are actually little patronized. For
example, even if boys attend vocational classes it is difficult for them to
focus on learning skills; they apply themselves in a desultory and listless
fashion, and have difficulty understanding lessons.[173] Moreover, they lav-
ishly spent the money they had previously earned, and programs that
provide only teaching without the accompanying ability to earn money
while learning hold little appeal for such boys.[174] Likewise, there is no
question that researchers, as well as those who seek to rehabilitate children, are exposed to grave dangers from corrupt and powerful bodies.[175]
Several incidents have been reported in which organized crime syndicates
have harassed and beaten children's rights workers.[176]

To complicate matters even more, measures that seem effective do
not necessarily translate well to children's difficult circumstances. For
example, AIDS is now a major threat to the health and survival of prostituted children, and its impact is expected to grow. The World Health
Organization (WHO) consultation on AIDS and prostitution acknowledged that successful interventions to prevent HIV infection have been
directed at prostitutes and clients, but that these have been most effective
where prostitutes are empowered to determine their working conditions.
For children and adolescents, this is not the case. Children do not determine their working conditions. The gap in knowledge continues; even
the WHO points to the need for further research and for new forms

of information and education for adolescents and children in prostitution.[177]

The difficulties encountered by attempts to deal with the recovery of victims help highlight the significance of another critical area of progress in international law, most notably the Children's Convention right to development, which finds support from numerous other documents that recognize the world's obligation to developing countries[178] and to children inside developed countries that have not developed equitable national programs.[179] The right is located in Article 2(3) of the Declaration of the Right to Development: "States have the duty to formulate appropriate national development policies that aim at the constant improvement of the well-being of the entire population and of all individuals, on the basis of their . . . meaningful participation . . . in the fair distribution of the benefits resulting therefrom."[180] The Declaration further defines the right to development as "an inalienable human right by virtue of which every human person and all peoples are entitled to participate in, contribute to, and enjoy economic, social, cultural and political development in which all human rights and fundamental freedoms can be fully realized."[181] The right finds further support in the International Covenant on Economic, Social, and Cultural Rights that requires allocation of resources without discrimination toward "progressive" implementation of positive rights that include housing, food, shelter,[182] and protection of children from economic and social exploitation and harmful employment.[183] These mandates encourage the development of programs to help alleviate the need for some children to be involved in exploitative, money-making enterprises.

The antipoverty and social service development programs are significant in light of the fact that countries most affected by child prostitution through sex tourism lack social subsidies to support families. Addressing basic material needs of children, parents, and the local community, in conjunction with educational measures, remains necessary to empower families and children so they may make informed choices and protect themselves from the cycle of poverty and exploitation. To be sure, other important forces beyond poverty place children at risk for involvement in sexually exploitative situations: excitement and curiosity are often ignored,[184] while there is a focus on problems within family networks, such as sexual abuse, family disintegration, and desires to escape the danger and disparagement at home.[185] For example, the "beach boys" of Sri Lanka who cater to tourists are drawn not only from the marginalized and poverty-stricken or from the ranks of neglected, abandoned, and destitute children. They also come from middle- and upper-class homes where the lure of money, drugs, and favors attract adolescents.[186] Yet, despite these possible exceptions, it seems clear that comprehensive programs still would go a long way toward alleviating this form of maltreatment.[187]

The developments reflect a new role for the international community. The new standards, as they encourage states to control their own citizens during foreign travel and to reassess social development programs within and among countries, aim to influence intra-country behavior. International treaties provide an objective standard for the regulation of citizens' behaviors, and by doing so also provide a standard against which the actions of nations can be judged. By applying the objective standards, international and national organizations may attract the attention of both the international community and the offending nation in order to further reform efforts.

Child prostitutes exploited by domestic men

The currently popular focus on inter-country sex tourism and the extensive pornography networks is an important step toward ensuring that children are protected from sexual exploitation. These developments, though, should not blind us to other forms of sexual exploitation. Although it would be unwise to play down the need to focus on inter-country behaviors, it does tend to draw attention away from intra-country exploitation to the extent that existing discussions of how international law and policy may be used to combat child prostitution focus exclusively on its inter-country dimensions at the expense of prostitution occurring solely within countries.[188] Despite that focus, as we will see shortly, international mechanisms can be used to combat even localized prostitution.

The point that intra-country prostitution should not be ignored is of significance. Available statistics reveal that children from both wealthy and poor countries are exploited by "native" men. In countries renowned for their sex tourism industry, native men also are involved in sexual exploitation. For example, in Thailand, where estimates of children involved in child prostitution go beyond 800,000, the majority of those purchasing services are native men who travel to cities to take part in the sex market.[189] Researchers report that high numbers of children also are exploited in even the wealthiest societies. For example, in Paris, it is estimated that about 5,000 boys and 3,000 girls below the age of eighteen are involved in prostitution.[190] In large countries, such as the U.S., up to 300,000 boys and 600,000 girls are involved in sexually exploitative activities.[191] Of those figures, the United Nations reports that at least 100,000 are involved in underground, commercialized child prostitution.[192] Research further shows that "stables" of boy prostitutes between the ages of twelve and fourteen have been found in every U.S. major city.[193]

Again, however, research providing estimates is rare, and existing figures are subject to several challenges. For example, estimates of children involved in prostitution often derive from the number of youth who are runaways. Those estimates remain highly controversial. In the U.S., for example, the most recent figures from the National Incidence Study of Missing, Abducted, Runaway, and Thrownway Children reveals that the number of children who are "policy focal" (children without familiar and secure places to stay), including runaways and thrownaway children, reaches only slightly above 200,000.[194] Although that study was the most careful and comprehensive to date, it has been challenged as underestimating the number of children at risk for exploitation.[195] Likewise, it remains unknown how many children at risk actually engage in prostitution and how many not at risk do.[196]

Just as there have been few reliable estimates of the number of children involved in prostitution, few have actually investigated the nature of child prostitution.[197] The major concern of existing research tends to be the determination of whether conditions leading to runaway and prostituting behavior relate to individual differences and inadequacies or to inadequate, abusive families. One position maintains that child prostitutes are incapable adolescents who drop out of their families and communities because of individual inadequacies. Another position holds that prostituted children are simply victims of their families' failure to integrate their children into the family system due to family conflict, violence, and neglect. A more recent line of research points to youth maltreatment carried out not simply by parents or caretakers, but also by peers who reject youth.[198]

Existing research supports the three major explanations as factors that lead to runaway behavior and child prostitution. For example, a high number of child prostitutes have escaped from abuse at home. Although little is known about the abusive experiences of runaway youths either at home or on the street,[199] existing research points toward some expectable patterns. An important study of 200 street prostitutes found that over 60 percent were under the age of sixteen. Of these children, over half reported that they had run away from home because of sexual abuse.[200] Female runaways are more likely to be running away from sexual abuse than males: 73 percent to 38 percent.[201] Other researchers report that the majority of young prostitutes were sexually abused or psychologically maltreated while they were growing up,[202] and that run-away episodes involved maltreatment.[203] Though evidence consistently points to high levels of rape, incest, and other kinds of sexual trauma in the backgrounds of young prostitutes, recent reviews of early research and current theoretical thinking suggest that the purported link between sexual trauma and prostitution arises from failures of intergenerational attachments and/or inappropriate parenting behavior.[204]

Although it would be inappropriate to emphasize one causative fac-tor, the most consistent research finding points to the important role of parental maltreatment as a foundational element in running away.[205] Three recent studies revealed that over 80 percent of runaways experi-ence severe forms of abuse by parents and other adult caretakers.[206] Im-portantly, only 50 percent report running away *because* of abuse. Youth cite difficulty in getting along with caretakers and feeling unloved as equally important reasons for leaving. Researchers interpret these findings as consistent with the suggestion that the psychological aspects of living in a dysfunctional family have more negative consequences than actual physical abuse.[207] The important role played by families is reflected in other research that indicates that families of runaway and homeless youth demonstrate patterns of poor conflict resolution, inadequate com-munication, and ineffective parental supervision.[208]

Existing research, then, contributes an important and undoubtedly obvious point: relationships to parents and caretakers matter. Research convincingly indicates that entrance into child prostitution is a problem manifesting deviance that is caused by a number of possible variables, such as sexual abuse, dysfunctional families, low self-esteem, and drug/alcohol abuse.[209] Yet, the research remains limited. Although the factors may explain why youth get to the street, they do not necessarily dictate that youth will engage in prostitution.

Engagement in prostitution depends on the length of time on the streets, the intensity of survival needs, previous encounters with sexual maltreatment, and the influence of friends and street peers.[210] In terms of actual entrance into prostitution, other prostitutes play the more signifi-cant role. However, even that varies—entry into prostitution exhibits a clear sex difference. Boys are more likely to learn and be influenced by peers engaged in prostitution. Adolescent girls are more likely to be ap-proached by pimps, a party which is rarely mentioned in studies of child prostitution. Yet, victimization prior to leaving home also still plays an important role. The consequences of running away, such as involvement in crime or repeated victimization, appear to be most severe for those youth who have already experienced victimization at home prior to running away.[211] Likewise, sexually abused female runaways are more apt to engage in delinquent activities than nonsexually abused female runaways.[212] Sexual assault at home prior to running away increases the probability that both boys and girls will be sexually assaulted while on the streets.[213] Importantly, familial economic status does not necessarily factor directly into child prostitution, in contrast to what has been found to operate most prominently in sex tourism. Contrary to popular belief, child prostitutes are not primarily children from lower socioeconomic circumstances. An important National Institute of Mental Health study reported that 70 percent were from families of average or higher incomes.[214] Another study focused on juvenile prostitutes reported that nearly one in four has parents with college educations.[215] Yet another study reported a "phenomenal" increase in the number of "affluent and overindulged" child prostitutes.[216] Although they may be from more advantaged backgrounds, children finding themselves outside of families, without resources, become at risk for exploitation.

Although research reveals important sex differences in the way children actually move from runaway to prostitute and highlights how youth come from different social environments, the research still remains significantly limited. The variables provide little insight into the more fundamental processes that contribute to children's continued involvement in prostitution and the factors that present barriers to exiting street life and prostitution. For example, little research examines child prostitutes' involvement with social service delivery systems, simply because until recently, rehabilitation programs were virtually nonexistent. Indeed, recent research reveals that no more than one in three of these youths ever receives shelter once on the street, and no more than one in twelve is ever actually identified or cared for in any way.[217] Unfortunately, homeless and runaway youth live in fear that use of even the available resources will result in automatic, involuntary returns to their families.[218] A study of 195 runaway youths that examined the severity as well as the incidence of violence revealed that, for most types of violence, the street is a haven of relative safety when compared to the abuse suffered at home by the runaways. Not only are homes more abusive, but the abuse is more severe.[219] This is an important finding that, at the very least, highlights well how the disruptiveness of home lives pushes youth to the streets. Yet, it would be important to not minimize the disruptiveness of their street lives, which places them at high risk for infectious diseases, drug use, and violence.[220]

Barriers to exiting street life illustrate well the problems youth face, for barriers reveal a host of other variables which have remained ignored.

Several factors that are not easily indexed have been identified: the disenfranchisement of youth, the mixed messages about sexuality that target youth, the inability of social services to provide assistance to street youth, the disintegration of communities and of the families within them, and the climate of futility in which many young people grow up. For example, running away disrupts education and prematurely thrusts youth into the role of sole provider—a role that youth are ill-prepared to undertake. In sum, these forces constitute two critical factors identified by researchers: shelter and unemployment.[221]

As we have seen, then, juvenile prostitution is a complex social problem. Its complexity is due, in part, to its interrelationship with such other social problems as physical abuse, sexual abuse, family disruption, and running away. It is a lifestyle that attracts both males and females, although differences exist between male and female juvenile prostitutes. These factors make juvenile prostitution a difficult problem for policy makers to address.

Protecting child prostitutes from domestic exploitation

THE ROLE OF DOMESTIC LAWS

The United States exemplifies progress in the countries that have unusually strong legal arsenals to combat child prostitution. Attempts to offer assistance to child prostitutes tend to take a two-pronged approach. The first approach makes use of criminal statutes to penalize adult participants who engage in or encourage prostitution with juveniles. That approach is complemented by the second, which makes use of civil statutes that aim to identify juvenile prostitutes more promptly to offer them necessary services. The two-pronged approach is important to consider, for it is part of what the Children's Convention encourages State Parties to adopt: measures that offer children's services while still targeting offenders. As such, it helps us understand how the approach may help alleviate sex tourism by focusing on the child prostitute. As currently implemented, however, the approaches have severe limitations.

The criminalization approach has several problems. Numerous commentators have shown how it may be simplistic to believe that punishment of customers will eliminate the problem, since such an approach has failed with adult prostitution.[222] A major reason is that few resources of local authorities are ever directed toward the customer.[223] Juvenile prostitution exacerbates the potential for continued failure. Many statutes allow for the mistake-of-age defense, which results in lighter sentences if customers can prove that they were reasonably mistaken as to the age of the juvenile.[224] In addition, the application of the law to status offenders (minors who break laws by actions that would not be criminal if committed by adults) remains far from gender-neutral. When law officials apprehend runaways and juvenile prostitutes, attention must be directed to both male and female juveniles. Intervention must help runaway boys as well as girls; runaway boys are more likely to be ignored by police.[225] When they are not ignored, as research suggests, boys are at greater risk of verbal and physical abuse from the police.[226] Relatedly, when there is intervention and child prostitution is targeted, researchers note that the policing may lead to a loss of "safe" clients, informal support, and warning networks, and thus actually increase the risks faced by youth.[227]

Likewise, attempts to combat child prostitution through crackdowns on pimps leave entire groups of children without protection: boys tend to operate with peers, not pimps. Thus, apparently sound legislation, such as the Mann Act in the United States, which is best designed to address the inter-state aspects of prostitution, essentially limits itself to girl victims who are transported across state lines.[228] A focus on patrons is the only criminalization approach that addresses the reality of juvenile male prostitution.

Other assumptions hamper the law's response to juvenile prostitution. The use of social services provides another case in point. Recent legislation aims to attack acts of child prostitution by making it a reportable offense. Thus, the Child Abuse Prevention and Treatment and Adoption Reform Act includes juvenile prostitution as a form of child abuse which must be reported to appropriate agencies when the acts involve parents or caretakers. The shortcomings are obvious: the Act limits itself to acts perpetrated by parents and caretakers. Only sexual exploitation perpetrated by parents, caretakers, or persons "responsible for the child's welfare" is a reportable condition. Acts of prostitution prompted by any other family member, or by extra-familial third parties such as pimps, are outside the ambit of the reporting legislation. In contrast to sex tourism, parental involvement in juvenile prostitution is not a frequent occurrence: the timing of youths' entrance into prostitution suggests little significant correlation with direct parental involvement. Juveniles begin prostitution after they have left home, when they need money to survive, and when they are induced by peers or others to engage in prostitution. Again, however, the factors do not necessarily translate across societies. For example, Turkey—a country with a population of about 51 million—over the period of five years, charged over 3,000 people with prostituting children, and another 2,000 with the more serious offense of prostituting children for whom they were responsible.[229]

To be sure, it would be misleading to suggest that legislation that aims to prevent child abuse is ineffective in combatting child prostitution. The original objective of the legislation—to encourage reporting of abuse—is essential in the prevention of juvenile prostitution, since abuse is one of the primary factors contributing to juvenile prostitution.

The federal focus on preventing child prostitution essentially focuses on runaway youth. For example, the special national clearinghouse established by the Missing Children Act to facilitate identification of missing and runaway children seeks to locate runaways soon after they have left home. This is a sound effort; the more prompt the identification, the less likely it is that the child will turn to prostitution.[230] In addition, the Federal Runaway and Homeless Youth Act[231] funds a national network of short-term shelters for adolescents, and provides hot lines. Some states make specific statutory provision for runaway and homeless youth services.[232] Yet, problems still run rampant. The Missing Children Act relies on family reports of missing children; and, as we know, families with abused children, or families that have disintegrated may not report. In addition, throwaways are not likely to be reached. To exacerbate matters, family reunification may not always be an appropriate solution. Current programs for assisting youth on the streets do not statutorily provide for transitional living services, intensive mental health and substance abuse services, and other services youth may require—and few shelters actually do provide them.[233] Despite federal calls for shelters, less than ten states statutorily provide for young runaways and homeless youth.[234]

Commentators report that the main failure of statutory provisions aimed to help homeless youth is the focus on reuniting families. Although it would seem to make sense to encourage children to return home, the focus is problematic for two major reasons. First, the approach assumes that juveniles will cooperate and want to return. The result, according to the most recent study of services for youth, is that youth may actually stay away from shelters: the survey funded by the National Institute on Drug Abuse and the National Institute of Mental Health revealed, for example, that on any given night, only 55 percent of available beds in youth shelters are occupied.[235] Thus, children are not only evicted by their families, but are also rejected or ejected by the public social welfare system which may not deal with youth. Or the shelters simply may be overwhelmed: the federal study revealed that the shelters investigated in the study have unwritten polices not to accept youth over the age of twelve.[236] Social service systems have failed to adapt to the problems faced by youth on the streets, and are unable to take a client-driven approach that often runs contrary to the interests or expectations of funding agencies and society at large.[237]

The second major flaw in approaches aimed at family reunification is that they run the danger of discouraging the provision of informal family and community shelter services to children in need. For example, research reveals that the largest resource of thrownaway and runaway children is nearby friends and relatives.[238] Yet, the federal law and most state laws actively discourage this kind of assistance. For example, some states still make it a crime or tort to knowingly or intentionally provide housing to a runaway child; most states prohibit children who do not live with their parents or guardians from attending public schools; nor can children obtain work if their parents or guardians do not give their permission.[239] These are important concerns. The balance toward broadening social supports to relieve stress within the family unit and improve the quality of its caregiving will be returned to in later chapters, for it is a major part of national and international approaches to preventing child maltreatment in homes.

THE ROLE OF HUMAN RIGHTS LAW

The legislative experience to date with juvenile prostitution has provided lessons that might improve future reform efforts, including the role that could be played by international human rights law. To a large extent, the issue of children's right to protection from exploitation fundamentally remains an issue about resources and their distribution. Whether they are poor children who sell themselves or children from wealthier families, children engage in prostitution largely to survive. Securing rights for children will require governments to reallocate resources in their favor. Likewise, prevention requires an infusion of resources in the form of, for example, the family support and youth services alluded to above. The right to protection from child prostitution continues to be undermined and eventually denied by poverty.

Although it does not receive as much attention as expected in the fight against juvenile prostitution, it is important to revisit the international positive right to social services, particularly to protections against homelessness. The Universal Declaration finds that

> Everyone has the right to a standard of living adequate for health and well-being of himself, including food, clothing, housing and medical

care and necessary social services, and the right to security in the event of unemployment, sickness, disability.[240]

The Declaration affords each child the rights that should safeguard her from homelessness and place correlative obligations on governments and states.

The Children's Convention likewise confers upon every child the right to social security and an adequate standard of living, including adequate housing.[241] Regrettably, the Convention calls upon states to assist parents in the realization of this right and emphasizes that parents or others responsible for the child have primary responsibility to do so, "within their abilities and financial capacities." The failure to bestow the right more completely on the child has important repercussions. Commentators appropriately have called runaway and homeless youths "illegal aliens in their own land" who are denied access to schools, medical care, and other rights children have if they remain with their parents.[242] Runaway and homeless children simply do not have anyone "responsible" for them.

Under the International Covenant on Economic, Social and Cultural Rights, the call for shelter for all people is actually even stronger: States Parties "recognize the right of everyone to an adequate standard of living for himself and his family, including adequate food, clothing and housing."[243] Likewise, the "States Parties will take appropriate steps to ensure the realization of this right, recognizing to this effect the essential importance of international cooperation based on free consent."[244] From this perspective, the child has a rather expansive right to basic services, including the right to housing for himself as well as his family.

The Special Rapporteur on the Right to Adequate Housing has enumerated well the nature of the obligations.[245] States must first recognize and respect the right to housing as a human right, which at least requires that governments abstain from taking measures that may diminish the legal status of the right, and that states must undertake steps to ensure universal enjoyment of this right. In addition to eliminating legislation or policies that may compromise the right, states must protect the right from violations by third parties who harass, discriminate, and threaten those in need of housing. In addition, states must promote the right by formulating state laws and policies that will ensure the realization of the right and take affirmative action on behalf of disadvantaged groups.

Being homeless and a runaway means not only lacking adequate housing, but often living in life-threatening and degrading conditions. Thus, other rights come into play, for the condition also jeopardizes effective enjoyment of the most basic rights, such as the right to life and personal security, the right to freedom of movement, the right to privacy and, where applicable, the right to family life.[246] The nature of these human rights and the critical role they could play in protecting children are examined in the chapters that follow.

Conclusions

Child sexual exploitation is remarkable in being internationally condemned. Even countries that host the most egregious exploitation recognize the need to combat this form of maltreatment. Yet, the recognition, coupled with the perceived need to react appropriately, has yet to diminish the incidence and destructive effects of the practice. Indeed, indications are that the practices are increasing and becoming even more complex, particularly with the impact of advanced technology in both developing and technologically advanced societies.

A first conclusion and recurring theme underscores the proposal that more aggressive and harsh law enforcement has its place in child protection; yet, criminal law can not address all the needs of child victims of sexual exploitation. Simple criminalization leaves children unprotected, and their reintegration becomes highly improbable. The examination makes it difficult not to become critical of criminal justice systems. Stricter penalties for adult participants, though an apparently needed response to pressing problems, arguably do not have the broad intended impact. For example, to deal with international sex tourism, increased criminalization may work only when coupled with massive antipoverty programs to support families and communities.

A second theme involves the increasing recognition that an emphasis on prevention and treatment is a necessary component of attempts to assist victimized youth as well as those at risk. As we have seen, few services currently exist that target children themselves. Evidence supports the need to rethink services and to consider children's perspectives. Services should reach children not only while they are on the street, but also while they are still in their families, schools, and communities.

A third important point is the need to reconsider the prevailing image of childhood. Ideologies of childhood have an overwhelming tendency to regard children who prostitute themselves as individual failures. This tendency shifts attention to them and improperly draws attention away from the social institutions which they flee, such as families, foster homes, and schools; these institutions may play important roles in the encouragement of exploitation.[247] To a large extent, children involved in pornography, prostitution, and trafficking challenge the dominant allegiance to family values, schools, communities, and work. Like other "exiles" from dominant social institutions, exploited youth would benefit from law reform that enables them to obtain assistance from a variety of sources and that moves away from the ideology that families are the best source of care and support for victimized youth. Sexually exploited children offer critical perspectives and views that are frequently disparaged as deviant and that are conspicuously silenced.

Lastly, to combat child sexual exploitation, a rethinking of what constitutes sex is necessary. Combatting child pornography requires more vigilance in recognizing the manner in which children are sexualized, especially the way deviant adults perceive as sexual depictions of children that nondeviant adults perceive as nonsexual. Combatting child prostitution warrants concern for the manner in which children are sexually treated at home, in the community, and on the streets. Addressing exploitation also requires making links between how children are sexually treated and conditions that foster maltreatment—such as gender discrimination and poverty—and the way these factors contribute to sexual development, expectations, and eventual exploitation. Importantly, although maltreating conditions seem to call into question any notions of consensuality,[248] the most important development involves balancing children's developing right to sexual self-determination. The need for balance comes to light when dealing with regulating youth's access to sexual information that may be prohibited by efforts to protect children from indecent materials. The right becomes more obvious in the following chapter, which examines cultural practices that are locally condoned yet internationally condemned.

5 | The Sexual Use of Children

This chapter discusses the international community's ability, willingness, and rationale regarding the extent to which it will intervene in the following practices that are pervasively condoned in certain cultures: the altering of children's sexual organs, the active "sexual" use of children in initiation rites, the premature selection of children's sexual partners, and intrusive sexual purity exams. An emerging trend reveals that the balance between cultural rights and internationally conceived notions of children's individual rights to protection from these practices increasingly moves toward the latter. Developments in international children's rights seek to transform locally condoned practices, particularly those that are publicly violent, have violent outcomes, and exacerbate gendered violence. Discussion of the manner in which the international human rights movement seeks to catalyze the transformation—through recognizing children's right to self-determination and greater participation in determining cultural life—serves as a springboard for the analysis of the practices.

Introduction

Investigations increasingly document how cultures exhibit tremendous variety in how they treat children and how those treatments relate to child sexuality and adult development.[1] This investigation places importance not so much on actual types or kinds of behavior found in different cultures as on understanding incidents of maltreating behavior in terms of their inconsistency with the reality defined by the relevant cultural theory of sexuality. From a cultural perspective, then, victims of sexual maltreatment can be individuals subjected to "sexual" experiences beyond social expectations. Or victims can be individuals whose socialization has been so different that their personal social realities diverge from those of other societal members who constitute the norm.[2] From an indigenous cultural point of view, practices that form the focus of this chapter are *not* necessarily sexually maltreating. Indeed, some of the practices are not even perceived as "sexual" in nature.[3] The practices are embedded in and condoned by indigenous cultures, or large segments of those cultures,[4] that interpret these practices as requisite to children's normal development. The customs from which the practices derive and which foster belief that the way the children are treated is normal distinguish the practices from sexual exploitation and abuse. In the next chapters, practices that do deviate from internal cultural norms are examined as sexual abuse. This chapter focuses mainly on exogenous norms—the perspective of an emerging culture of international law—that view the culturally salient practices as maltreating.

Developments in international law actually challenge numerous practices that sexually involve children or that affect children's sexual development in ways inconsistent with emerging international norms yet fully consistent with the indigenes' theories of sexuality and cultural life. Most of the interest and concern centers on practices that exist across groups of cultures, that seem highly resistant to cultural change, or that represent particularly pernicious violations of children's human rights. Such practices include the altering of children's sexual organs so that children may assume their proper cultural roles, the premature selection of children's sexual partners, the encouragement of child prostitution by leaving selected children without social supports and resources, the use of virginity exams to determine and control girls' sexual purity, and, although less examined, the active use of children in initiation rites that include sexual activity. Commentators, including several who report under the auspices of human rights groups and the United Nations, argue that these pervasive, culturally condoned practices diverge from several international developments in children's rights. The customs variously have been construed as violating children's rights to health, to freedom from torture, to bodily integrity, to sexual autonomy, and, more recently, to protection from child sexual maltreatment. Given overall developments in human rights, it would seem that the practices at least conflict with the major thrust in human rights thinking that there now exists a universal standard by which to judge all cultures and to encourage reform more consistent with international conceptions of children's rights.

Despite apparent disparities between international norms and more localized cultural conventions, attempts to rethink observed practices from the perspective of human rights law have been highly contentious and continue to engender exceedingly polarized debates. At one extreme, some propose that respect for these practices fundamentally jeopardizes the concept of human rights.[5] Indeed, even though the practices remain culturally meaningful and human rights activists continue to champion cultural sensitivity, discussions among human rights advocates and officials tend to term the practices torturous, barbaric, uncivilized, and inhuman.[6] Abolitionists urge respect for internationally negotiated conceptions of human rights and increasingly frame arguments against intervention as inappropriately making entire areas of private rights irrelevant, an approach similar to accusations that rhetoric of nonintervention in private family matters results in the denial of women's rights.[7] These challenges reflect an important point: notions of human rights cannot simply be based on limited ideologies of particular societal values and mores. Extreme cultural relativism seemingly places children in jeopardy and, as several increasingly argue, leads to culturally condoned child sexual maltreatment.

In contrast to the need to move toward universally based notions of child treatment, the other extreme champions the need to respect and ensure culturally meaningful practices. Cultural sensitivities and concerns about the cultural mooring of universal rights actually have significant roots in the development of modern notions of human rights. The American Anthropological Association's early plea to the Drafters of the Universal Declaration of Human Rights illustrates well the need to consider cultural forces in attempts to ensure human rights. The Association properly argued that individuals realize their personalities through their cultures, that respect for individual differences necessarily entails a respect for cultural differences, and that the step of defining the rights and duties of human beings and groups toward one another can only be taken once individuals possess the right to live in terms of their own traditions.[8] The challenge has resurfaced more forcefully as Third World countries have joined the United Nations and vigorously championed their own causes, in the form of minority, cultural, and indigenous rights.[9] These rights make for important and distinct theoretical moves that rein in the unprecedented progress toward universal conceptions of rights as envisioned by more dominant cultures. The move highlights the potentially broad impact of abolishing traditional customs. Ending practices may mean ending the practicing group's existing culture, since cultures construct the questioned practices as central to cultural conceptions of child development, cultural participation, and cultural life.

These divergences lead to debates beyond notions of child sexual maltreatment. The emerging issues fundamentally challenge conceptions of the nature of cultural diversity; of respect for minority cultures' customs; and of the status of children's citizenship, rights, duties, and equality before international and domestic human rights law. In fact, the rise in efforts to protect and respect "cultural rights" runs parallel to a renewed focus and interest that aims to abolish condoned cultural practices. Given broad issues and concerns, then, a prelude to analyses of cultural practices that commentators view as children's international human rights violations must detail the precise way modern international law may approach the developing notion of cultural rights, respond to charges of imperialism, and allow for and actually depend on cultural applications of children's rights. The previous discussion of the development of human rights law, found in Chapter 2, noted how debates rage over the cross-cultural applicability of human rights norms, and highlighted how international law offers an energizing power that aims to transform people's perceptions of children. This chapter elaborates upon that discussion to highlight international law's actual approach to the notion of culture and the actual way international law provides for resolution of controversial matters. After they are located in recent international developments, the culturally condoned practices are examined in light of existing arguments regarding the need for change. The exploration aims to expose the cultural roots of maltreating practices, to help identify practices that could be construed as maltreating yet are currently condoned, to emphasize the need to consider the important cultural rules that must be confronted in order to combat practices deemed maltreating, and to elucidate some of the factors contributing to maltreatment in the observing culture by moving beyond considering the observed societies' social constructions of sexual practices.

The Cultures of Cultural Rights

Few reified social science terms have spread into public, political, and legal discourse like the anthropological notion of culture. Anthropologists have contested and debated exactly what "culture" may signify for over a century. Anthropologically, the notion of culture conceptualizes the manner in which people engage in the continual process of accounting for what they do, say, and think. From this perspective, cultures are essentially a person's second nature; cultures liberate human beings from strict biological determination. Cultural concepts provide a new source of determinacy that helps determine courses of action and related notions of the meaning of these actions in a given context. As such, then, cultures simply provide general guidelines for behavioral dispositions. Since anthropologists generally concern themselves with exploring the nature of these guidelines, notions of culture simply serve as useful analytical abstractions.[10] And as abstractions, cultures are not necessarily authentic, consisting of individual, autonomous, and internally coherent universes. Anthropologists' deliberate abstractions are not meant to be essentialist. Cultures are not merely attributes of totalities, but attributes that express contradiction as much as cohesion.[11]

Outside of anthropology, culture has gained a more concrete meaning. The term has been transformed to identify fundamentally different, essentialized, and homogenous social groups, a use that fixes the boundaries between groups in an absolute and artificial manner.[12] Instead of being a perpetually changing process of meaning-making, culture has become a reified entity that has definite substantive content and assumes the status of a quality certain people possess or thing to which people belong. The reification makes practical and legal sense: it helps determine who belongs to a certain group and helps effect mobilization, as reflected in the anti-universal-rights and pro-culture alliances in international law.[13]

Although the mobilization and legal developments are found at international levels, international law actually possesses various views of culture. Two conceptions are particularly significant and prominent in the Children's Convention and children's rights movement.[14] The first conceives of culture as an accumulation of a particular group's material heritage. These materials include monuments, artifacts, and various forms of information. In this form, the right to culture would ensure access to this accumulated cultural capital. For example, the Children's Convention recognizes the child's right to information and cultural activities: governments should "encourage the provision of appropriate and equal opportunities for cultural, artistic, recreational and leisure activity."[15] Interestingly, the right even includes access not just to children's own cultural materials but also to those of others, as seen in the focus on obtaining access to global information, most prominently encouraged in international cooperation in educational matters.[16]

International law's second, broader approach to culture derives more directly from anthropology. This perspective interprets culture as the sum total of the material and spiritual activities and products of a given social group which distinguishes it from other similar groups. In this manner, culture consists of the system of values and symbols reproduced by a specific cultural group, a system that provides individuals with the required signposts and meanings for behavior and social relationships in everyday life. In this sense, culture simply is the weave of meanings associated with each belief and practice that necessarily resonate together. These practices carry meaning in terms of the culture itself, as distinct from an external perspective. For example, the Convention recognizes a child's right, "in community with other members of his or her group, to enjoy his or her own culture."[17]

Both approaches to culture cause concern for those seeking a neat, universal, and readily applicable definition and approach to combatting sexual maltreatment. For example, what constitutes maltreatment becomes problematic if we consider the modern commentaries' approach to notions of culture. The notion that cultures are constantly constructed, reconstructed, invented, and reinvented by ever-changing subjects makes the term's use particularly problematic.[18] This approach places emphasis on the manner in which people perceive their culture, on the discourse about culture, rather than on the culture itself, which, by this approach, has no objective existence outside of the individual's subjectivity.[19] These apparently flexible approaches pose considerable obstacles, for they fail to advance the legal debate. Either sexual interactions can be challenged, since cultures can change and practices often lose their meanings, or, given that cultures are subjective and personally meaningful, practices should be preserved.

In addition to existing concerns about conceptions of the nature of culture, and although the international community now recognizes the need to respect cultures, international law has yet to reach a consensus about criteria for a definition of cultural membership, specifically in terms of who belongs to a certain cultural group and who is excluded from it.[20] For example, a primary impediment is the notion of "cultural identity"[21] that gives rise to every cultural group's right to maintain and develop its own specific culture. The focus on "group" rights is particularly problematic for traditional international law. At issue is whether this concept of cultural rights can be adequately encompassed by a notion of individual rights, or whether it must be complemented by a different approach. As recognized in the International Bill of Rights, the rights clearly relate to the rights of individuals.[22] To complicate matters, the International Bill also establishes the right of peoples to self-determination.[23] These rights relate more to political self-determination, as the right of peoples to achieve statehood and independence or the rights of peoples against their own government.[24] Yet, as we will see, the collective rights clearly would affect individual rights. It remains particularly difficult to separate the two.[25]

Although the balance between individual and group, or cultural, rights remains contentious, recent trends indicate that the balance seems increasingly settled. The manner in which the Children's Convention attempts to counter some problems relating to cultural rights and practices illustrates the most recent approach: international law focuses on individual rights. Recall that the Convention recognizes the more group-oriented rights of peoples, particularly indigenous peoples, and every culture's right to protection.[26] Despite concern for the group, the current move conceives rights as fundamentally concerned with *individual* children situated in their own cultures. The focus on every child's individual rights, as seen in Chapter 2, reflects the children's rights movement's aim to have policies and decisions affecting children's lives become more consistent with children's best interests and their right to self-determination. The Convention also protects the right of *individual* children who belong to a minority group or to one of the indigenous peoples,[27] and broadly bestows upon children their *individual* right to enjoy their own culture.[28] Most fundamentally, then, the current move urges societies to rethink the way children are to be perceived and included in their cultures. The rethinking is important, for it reveals the manner in which human rights operate and aim to reach all cultures. Given that the aim is particularly ambitious and still contentious in practice, it makes sense to first situate analyses of customs that may be conceived as sexually maltreating in the more general way international law, particularly children's rights law, seems to respond to charges of cultural imperialism.

Rethinking Cultural Imperialism

Recognition of certain children's international human rights protections conflicts with prevailing cultural conceptions of childhood. The clash becomes most apparent when efforts aim to apply international human rights standards to foreign practices, particularly those found in the South, that are locally condoned yet anathema to cultural outsiders and the broader international human rights community. In such instances, human rights are resisted and calls are made to respect cultural autonomy and to embrace more relativistic approaches to children's rights. The resistance often involves charges of cultural imperialism, a move that provides a powerful defense against the imposition of external values and outsider conceptions of human rights.

Attempts to conceive and enforce universal children's rights need not inevitably be plagued by relativist resistance. Evolving conceptions of children's human rights, as well as modern approaches to international human rights law, move toward resolution of potential cultural clashes and help resolve contentious issues that arise when efforts are made to implement children's rights. The ways international children's rights attempt to deal with culturally enmeshed disputes are important to understand, for the ways are pervasive in the context of children's human right to protection from child sexual maltreatment.

An important starting point is to emphasize that children's human rights challenge all cultures. Although several focus on Western efforts to impose Western values on the South, it is important to note that several also notice the failure of Western countries to take children's rights more seriously. Two points regarding the universal challenge are worthy of emphasis. First, several of the problematic practices found in the South find counterparts in the North. For example, practices often are brought by refugees and migrants to countries that otherwise would not encounter such customs. Likewise, and particularly significant to our later analyses, similar practices and their correlates actually already exist in the North, yet go undetected and unremarked as potential violations of human rights. Second, countries from the North resist rights that infringe on their own cultural values. For example, the United States, arguably the most "Western" and imperialistic country, remains formally and essentially hostile to the children's human rights movement as articulated by recent international developments.[29] The resistance, although couched in terms of state and national sovereignty, still deals with the domestic application of foreign principles and visions of humanity. Children's rights, then, are intentionally imperialistic and, as we have seen, their ideals fundamentally challenge the internal workings of all cultures and demand a radical reformulation of how all cultures view and treat children.

Just as it would be erroneous to argue that international conceptions of children's human rights are not imperialistic, it is equally incorrect to propose that international law aims to inappropriately and decisively usurp cultural values. That is, although there may be domestic or cultural differences in the way children could be treated if international children's human rights were considered, it is important to recognize the diverse levels on which human rights operate. These levels have significant implications for the nature of respect accorded to cultural life; the levels reveal how human rights must be interpreted and eventually applied and enforced locally.

Interpreting and applying human rights

A most obvious level on which law operates to interpret and apply human rights comports with popular notions of how legal systems function. This level concerns itself with the manner in which courts, lawyers, and other legal actors—such as police or social welfare administrators—resolve disputes. At this level, law and its interpretations simply provide arguments for legal actors to use in justifying their actions, as well as versions of truth in legal propositions.[30] At this level, laws operate to articulate rules that describe enforceable claims of individuals or groups against the state, regardless of whether the state must affirmatively protect rights or refrain from interfering in the way people and institutions treat one another. Although this level deals with universal laws, what may seem universal still is applied situationally—normative interpretation of any rule must be situational.[31] For example, practitioners necessarily balance formal legal rules with situations through their own acts of interpretation, as revealed by an abundance of scholarly literature in the field of statutory interpretation concerned with methods of finding various meanings in law.[32] Differences in interpretations reveal how practitioners work in realms where all situational influences interweave; personal, legal, political, and other cultural domains are at work. It is within these networks of factors and forces that norms come into existence. In this regard, it is important to emphasize that states and local jurisdictions actually make international law, not just individual actors.[33]

The common conception of how law functions provides only a partial view of human rights law, and only a restricted view of how international norms are interpreted and applied locally. Human rights law operates at other critical, yet related levels that are necessary to help resolve deeply rooted cultural disputes. Clearly, rights need not be judicially or administratively enforceable; several commentators document well how rights violations may not be realistically redressable by judges and other state officials.[34] In terms of international law, for example, the Children's Convention does not provide petitioning mechanisms. As we have seen in Chapter 2, the Convention relies on reports, record-keeping, and more cooperative approaches to ensuring that states follow the international community's mandates. This mode of operation, one arguably more critical to human rights law, involves using laws and images of rights to provide sources for consciousness-raising. This function allows individuals and groups to imagine and act in light of rights that have not been formally recognized or enforced. This level of rights-formulation, the more transformative role of human rights law, plays a central role in the resolution of cultural disputes.

Human rights allow for and even catalyze dispute resolutions through the provision of a common vocabulary that community members use to interpret and reinterpret their relationships with one another. Conceptions of human rights that transform relationships begin with simple consciousness-raising.[35] The consciousness-raising vocabulary provides the base that helps mobilize cultural change, the already occurring processes that anthropological investigations so aptly have revealed in their conceptions of culture. Human rights law, then, can best be conceived and understood as a process, as part of the process through which cultures change. Like the cultures they imbue, the resolutions that law institutes and reflects are never fixed, but always precarious. Law necessarily results from, and is on the edge of, a grinding process of accommodation and competition among diverse interests, diverse groups, and diverse social needs and forces.

From both perspectives of the manner in which human rights law works, law is progressive and offers the possibility of its own radical renewal and the possibility of reforming the cultural structures in which it operates. That is what is meant, for example, when we speak of constitutions as living documents and when the Children's Convention is viewed as a constitutional document.[36] Human rights law may be viewed as an autopoietic system that dynamically and imperceptibly spreads over interstices located between emerging social values and well-established legal rules.[37]

The emergence of human rights law that affects local social values and already established legal rules does not mean that modern human rights law does not contain universals.[38] As currently conceived, for example, human rights focus on deliberation and the protection of deliberation.[39] This is a necessary foundation of human rights law: given widespread social disagreements over what justice and rights require, human rights law allows considerable scope for experimentation and debate. The main concern is to secure basic commitments to impartial deliberative principles that ensure the preconditions that allow for a process-perfecting, deliberative society.[40] By embracing these commitments, societies are able to keep political participation and processes open—free of the process of prejudice—and assure equal concern and respect for everyone alike. The law and its processes allow for deliberation about the justice of basic institutions and social policies, and about how to live lives. Most fundamentally, although the process historically concerned itself with political self-government,[41] it rests on personal self-government (self-determination). The emergence of the perception that human rights are all-inclusive, covering all members of the human family, clearly parallels the ascent of a world community composed of all nations and based on the principle of equal rights and self-determination of peoples. The emergence also means that individuals, as the Children's Convention proclaims, will be "fully prepared to live an *individual* life in society, and brought up in the spirit of the ideals proclaimed in the Charter of the United Nations."[42] In sum, human rights law champions deliberative processes involving individuals with each other, and involving groups with the international community.

The transformative power of local interpretation

The conception of human rights highlighted above—whether or not interpretations and applications involve or go beyond traditional legal actors—views human rights as the by-products of cultural struggles over shared cultural experiences to articulate norms about how individuals treat one another. Social meanings and interpretations contained in social ambiguities and contradictions in the way people treat one another fuel law's fundamentally interpretive process as they provide the arenas for struggles and interpretations.[43] Law thus reflects a social reality that derives from constant reformulation and analysis of inherited meanings that are applied within local contexts.[44]

The process of developing human rights necessarily deals with interpretive communities and places considerable faith in the power of discourse. Although international actors may bluntly demand rapid changes, such approaches contradict the principles that offer international law its legitimacy: respect for state, cultural, and personal sovereignty.[45] That is the reason legitimate human rights law cannot operate counter to deeply held cultural values.[46] Rather than directly supplanting cultural forces, international law simply provides guiding principles in the rethinking of cultural values. Concern for ensuring the consideration of children's interests provides a good example of how such law aims to operate. The belief is that, as children's interests are considered and reconsidered, cultures will change. In the transformation, the interpretations of law, the meaning that it develops, will occur inside and outside formal legal institutions. Everyone will engage in legal activity, not simply lawyers, judges, and those formally trained in law: normative meanings will be nurtured inside and outside official legal culture.[47] Through law and discourse about rights, people will engage in meaning-making through communal narratives, summon a sense of potential community, and transform personal relationships.[48] That is the goal and operation of human rights law. Formal and informal human rights law flows into and filters the process of communication and meaning-making. Through this process of meaning-making, new rights emerge and gain legitimate authority. The law thus helps to create communities; to establish shared discourse; and to provide contexts for linking the past with the future, and for bridging creativity and change with tradition.[49]

Human rights law and the power of rights in regard to children's rights, then, derive from the manner in which they provide methods of public resolution of real and imagined (not yet publicly or privately accepted) injustices. Human rights simply give power to those who previously were ignored. Human rights aim to make interests visible, to integrate those who make claims into their communities, and to involve people's interests in communal debates; human rights assert and acknowledge membership. Rights structure attention and compel an equality of attention as they take aspirational language of society seriously and begin processes that promote and sustain change. These claims assert a right and thereby secure the attention of the community through transforming existing conflict. Since legal developments are processes by which meanings change, the critical role of participation again emerges as fundamental.[50] Through participation, social actors may draw on law, an ensemble of symbolic resources, to claim self-determination and to articulate new identities and knowledges. This is, as we have discussed previously, the most radical concept of international law ever imagined in terms of children's rights: the participation of children in determining their own lives.

In terms of violence and maltreatment involving children (as we will also see in the next two chapters), human rights law demands public debate about existing patterns of private power, aims to provide children public voice, and seeks to renegotiate relationships. As human rights aim to increase attention, they provide a common language. The most obvious example involves calling children "innocent," which, by definition, presupposes that they should not be punished or harmed.[51] Other important legal articulations involve calling rituals torturous, which presupposes that the customs are wrong; or calling practices unhealthy, which presupposes that change is needed to ensure health. The labeling leads to different reconceptions and actions—it generates new moral certainties. Although considerable effort has been made to identify universal moral certainties in the search for core human rights and in the identification of universal human rights,[52] the examination that follows rests on the more fundamental notion that the thrust of human rights simply aims to make things visible. By providing mechanisms that ensure visibility (e.g., by labeling practices unhealthy or torturous), human rights lead to transformation and appropriate protection of human rights.

This resolution of the traditional dilemma facing universal laws and domestic application that relies on ensuring visibility through participation opens itself to several challenges. The approach may be equally disturbing to those who champion cultural diversity and cultural rights as well as to those who embrace universal conceptions of children's rights.

The former who resist change may find little solace in the proposition that all cultures are asked to adjust and accommodate, and horror in the thought that ingrained social practices are doomed to disappear. The latter may reject the sluggish approach and argue for more immediate implementation. But, international law necessarily mediates between the two extremes; that is how international law must work—deliberately, legitimately, and effectively.

Although the resolution offered by international law will be developed further with examples of culturally condoned practices, several factors that support this interpretation can highlight how the focus on participation and cooperative transformation has become central to international law. First, international law clearly focuses on cooperation, rather than, for example, individual petition.[53] This often is viewed as a limitation; however, many of the contributing causes of the violations of children's rights are structural, and international law has not developed procedures akin to what would be called class actions in national jurisdictions. Importantly, as we also have learned, such actions do not necessarily advance children's rights in societies that are unwilling to commit to the movement.[54] Second, communities do not accept standards unless they have gained local legitimacy. Human rights gain their legitimacy from being rooted in the people, in humanity. The increasing prohibition of female genital mutilation, and the extent to which the mandates actually are followed, serves as a powerful example of the need to gain local legitimacy in order to ensure children's rights.[55] Third, it is important to keep in mind changes in the constitution of communities. No culture remains isolated; cultures are dynamic forces. Progress in recognizing and ensuring human rights over the past half century provides clear examples of the fundamental force of human rights—examples include the rapid move into the private sphere;[56] the new wave of national constitutions that incorporate international law into domestic law and judicial practice;[57] and the new conceptions of international relations that focus on individuals, groups, institutions, and transnational actors that exert different pressures on local, national, and international governments.[58] Fourth, the faith in discourse actually reflects what both historical and modern developments in international law are all about. The basic faith in human interactions characterized by visions of a humanity that champions equality, inclusion, and respect for human dignity forms the very foundation of human rights law. The democratic principles apply not only to what governments should strive for, but also to individuals in their everyday interactions.[59] Lastly, the system of state sovereignty that guides international law is based on a system of legitimacy, and legitimacy is measured in conformity to international standards. That is, Nation States demonstrate their sovereign right to their citizens, not only by serving their citizens' interests, but also by observing exogenous universal principles heralded by the international community.[60] The following discussion reveals the significance of the way these developments in human rights law operate.

Altering Children's Sexual Organs

The practice of altering children's sexual organs

Physical manipulation of children's bodies is part of a series of life cycle events that some societies celebrate as essential to the cultural processes through which individuals achieve full personhood. The rites are central to the particular society's concern with the body and its physiological functions and to the society's concerns of morality, politics, cosmology, and societal regeneration. For example, the Tahitians' rite of passage that involves superincision—a longitudinal dorsal cutting of the penis foreskin—condenses several meanings, functions, and symbolic events.[61] Likewise, the circumcision and subincision of Pintupi youth— practices that essentially split a child's penis as the incision lays open the urethra from the tip of the glans to the base of the scrotum—also involve life course events marked by the transmission of myth and ceremony.[62] Anthropologists document well how these multivalent transfers of tradition actually incorporate the concept of a cultural memory into the very structure of the initiates' social identity and humanity. These deeply meaningful practices have not been the concern of human rights groups.

The form of bodily manipulation that has attracted attention has been female genital circumcision or, as it is more controversially known, genital mutilation.[63] The prevalence and broad geographical reach of this practice certainly justify attention. World Health Organization (WHO) estimates reveal that over 130 million women in the world have been subjected to some form of circumcision, and that 2 million girls are subject to the practice each year, a rate of 6,000 per day.[64] Forty countries around the world, including more than twenty-six countries in Africa alone, are home to most genital circumcisions.[65] Although small segments of Western societies do perform female circumcisions,[66] the practice continues mostly in societies in Africa, the Middle East, and to a lesser extent Asia, Australia, and Central and South America.[67] Importantly, where such bodily manipulations are practiced, the procedures are far from universal. Research from selected geographical areas reveals that the practice may be dominant but not universal. For example, esti-

mates in Egypt range from one-third to one-half of the female population.[68] Clitoridectomy is performed on 80 percent of the female population in Senegal and Mali, and on 60 percent of women in the Ivory
Coast.[69] Yet, in the Sudan, early research revealed female circumcision to
be nearly universal, although various forms were practiced.[70]

Although contentious and widespread, genital circumcision involving girls actually is simple to describe: the procedure requires the partial
removal of sexual organs. The practice, however, varies considerably,
which makes use of the term somewhat misleading, in that it may imply a
unitary practice. The term "female circumcision" euphemistically stands
for a variety of operations conducted on girls as young as two or three
months old or on girls who have reached puberty or young womanhood.
The practices may be categorized into four main types.[71] *Circumcision*
is the circumferential cutting away of the clitoral prepuce, although in
some cultures it also means cutting away parts of the labia minora. This
is the least mutilating of the three procedures and corresponds most
closely to male circumcision. The second form, *excision* or *clitoridectomy*, involves the removal of the clitoris, and may also include removal
of part of the labia minora. *Infibulation*, also known as *Pharonic circumcision*, is the most radical of operations, and involves cutting out the vul-
val tissue and partially closing the vaginal orifice. The two sides of the
wound are stitched together, leaving a small pinhole opening for the passage of urine and menstrual blood. Lastly, *introcism* involves cutting into
the vagina or splitting the perineum.

Just as the practices are varied, so are the justifications given by societies that perform these operations. Many cultures perform the procedures for a variety of reasons. Despite the differences in practices and
in the percentage of girls who participate, all forms of genital circumcision are justified on traditional grounds. Among the most often cited and
culturally persuasive reasons is the need to ensure girls' virginity before
marriage and their chastity afterwards, as well as the need to undergo
a rite of passage necessary for marriage.[72] These practices are deeply embedded in cultural thinking, particularly the customary jurisprudence
that still rules and clashes with the law of the modern state.[73]

The importance that customary African jurisprudence places on virginity and fertility reveals the centrality of customary law to the practices. Although customary law has evolved in different ways in different parts of Africa,[74] contracts of marriage and family patterns in many
African societies are structured on these two concepts.[75] For example,
in traditional societies, a good marriage is one contracted with a virgin bride. The virginal state of the bride is based on her genitalia and

symbolizes both purity and economic value. Virginity status is the standard upon which the marriage is contracted and determines the value of the bridegroom's dowry.

Commentators have shown how concerns for virginity and fertility result in a preoccupation with the appearance of the female genitalia. The genitalia have to be re-created to indicate and ensure purity. For example, excisions remove areas of the female genitalia considered inimical to purity. Infibulation most prominently indicates the high value placed on the reason for purity: virginity, assured by the stitching of the vagina. When the woman is married, a midwife or her mother usually defibulates her in order to facilitate intercourse.[76] Ideally, though, it is the husband who deflowers his wife, often with the aid of a knife. Repeated sexual intercourse is then necessary to ensure the reopening of the vulva to allow functional sexual intercourse and consequent childbirth.[77] Reinfibulation is usually performed after childbirth, divorce, and widowhood.[78] Concerns about appearance, purity, virginity, and economic life closely relate to one another.

In addition to what may be viewed as jurisprudential and purity arguments, related arguments propose that the practices are necessary to maintain gender roles foundational to concerns about appearance, virginity, and economic values. These arguments suggest that not having undergone the operation leaves girls "masculine," in that they still have vestiges of male sex organs. One common theory traces the origin of both female excision and male circumcision to an ancient belief in the bisexuality of gods and humans. The "female part" of a man's soul resided in the male foreskin, which needed to be removed at circumcision. In the same way, the "male part" of a woman's soul was located in the labia or clitoris. Excision was practiced, therefore, not to detract from a woman's identity, but to make her fully female; it was a step toward full gender identity.[79] It is even thought in some cases that girls who are not circumcised will be unable to undergo pregnancy and childbirth. Other beliefs maintain that the clitoris is not only a "masculine" feature which requires excision to create true femaleness and to ensure fertility, but also actually poses a danger to the health of a fetus.[80] Simply stated, the practices are important parts of the process of socialization and initiation into womanhood and of the process of gender differentiation.

Other, more controversial justifications include the need to continue these practices for religious purposes.[81] Indeed, research indicates that those who undergo the operation insist that it was required by the dictates of their religion, Islam.[82] Although the rituals clearly have deep religious roots,[83] the association with religion continues to be challenged.

The religious grounds have been interpreted as manipulations of knowledgeable, male religious elites who continue to perpetuate the delusion that female circumcision is a formal religious requirement.[84]

These criticisms, however, have been challenged by non-Western feminists who protest the charge that women lack civil rights "under Islam" and who contest the tendency to see them as inescapably oppressed by a sexist religion and culture.[85] These critics maintain that religion is improperly portrayed as a complete picture of the social system as opposed to simply a component of a Muslim culture. Likewise, several have shown how Islam, as a religion, may actually hold promise for women's rights, and has gradually ameliorated the status of women.[86] These critics further propose that Western feminists must dispense with stereotypical images and paradigms of Third World women and must be willing to think differently about the variety of modes of being female, including their own.

Regardless of the justifications, the arguments for continuing the practices reveal that groups that condone female circumcision view these practices as necessary prerequisites to healthy development and full societal participation. Simply put, without the procedure, children become outcasts. Indeed, the major justification for the practice is tradition and heritage, rather than religious demand, health and cleanliness, and the demands of marriage: virginity, virility, and sexual pleasure.[87]

The extent to which the practices are culturally meaningful certainly is highlighted by the difficulty of eradicating these traditional practices. In societies where marriage for a woman is her only means of survival, and where circumcision is a prerequisite to marriage, convincing women to relinquish the practice for themselves or for their children is an exceedingly difficult task.[88] The overriding fear among mothers is that their daughters will be unable to find husbands or to have children and consequently will become social outcasts. Marriage provides the exclusive opportunity for women to attain any degree of social acceptance and economic security. In addition, girls undergo the surgery to preserve their virginity in order to maintain the honor of their families.[89] Their fears are well-placed. In some societies, women who have not had any children are not given final funeral rites.[90] Such interpretations help reinforce arguments that the custom is the ultimate form of female oppression.[91]

Despite growing opposition,[92] the willingness to preserve this practice continues. Women remain the practice's most vocal proponents. Many women perceive it as part of the creation of a special and exclusive "women's space."[93] The extent to which it is culturally emphasized by women is evidenced by Western-educated women who oppose the

practice and yet succumb to social pressures to have the surgery performed.[94] Demands from men to ease the practice are often resisted as
inappropriate intrusions into women's affairs. Although women's concerns for continuing the practice are often framed in terms of "false consciousness," women are the ones who perpetuate the oral tradition that
contains the justifications for the practice, who demand it for their
daughters, who perform the practice, who criticize or ostracize those
who resist the procedure, and who ask that it be performed on themselves after giving birth.[95]

Protecting children from genital operations

The strength of the arguments to continue the practice is reflected in
the explicit failure to label genital operations human rights violations.
Despite its long history, its enduring prevalence, and the capacity of such
practices to arouse emotional responses, for example, the literature on
practices that alter children's sexual organs was surprisingly scant until
approximately two decades ago. The issue had been so controversial that
several organizations, including the World Health Organization and the
Children's Defense Fund, ostensibly refused to examine or take an official stance on the issue until the 1980s.[96] In response to widespread
publicity and efforts from nongovernmental organizations, U.N. bodies
and official conferences have adopted resolutions and declarations that
explicitly condemn female genital circumcision; yet, the documents do
not flatly state that the practice amounts to a human rights violation.
Even the Working Group in Traditional Practices Affecting the Health
of Women and Children, which was established to study the practice,
evaded the issue and simply noted that cultures involved in the process
were "at variance with new standards defined by various international
instruments relating to human rights" and were in the process of changing and undermining the significance of the practice.[97] It was only in
1988 that the Sub-commission on Prevention of Discrimination and Protection of Minorities determined that the practices violated "the rights
of women and children."[98] Yet, the official position is far from straightforward. The Children's Convention and other regional children's rights
documents still do not explicitly prohibit the practice, an omission which
reflects the fact that significant segments of societies still favor it.[99] Likewise, the Declaration on the Elimination of Violence Against Women,
adopted by the General Assembly in 1993, recognizes female genital circumcision as a form of violence against women, and therefore as a *bar-
rier* to the full enjoyment of women's human rights and fundamental

freedoms.[100] Current enforceable law, then, does not *directly* find genital operations as violative of children's rights.

Despite evasive efforts, several international legal norms could support a human rights case against female circumcision. The protections which circumcision typically might transgress are the right to health, the right to protection from torture, and the right to corporal and sexual integrity. These arguments, however, are not without their own limitations.

A most frequently cited approach condemns female circumcision as unhealthy.[101] The argument against female circumcision on right-to-health grounds clearly rests on the list of health complications that result from the surgeries performed even under the best conditions. Several negative health effects have been documented. Disease, infection, bleeding, and reproductive dysfunction challenge propositions that circumcision promotes health.[102] The ritual often results in severe pain, shock, infection, and malformation. In the long term, the practice may result in physical and psychological trauma accompanying sexual intercourse, increased vulnerability to the AIDS virus, difficulty in childbirth, and increased risk of sterility and infant mortality, including the risk of death to the female from the direct effects of the operation.[103] Given the obvious connections, the health argument recently has been championed by several organizations, including the World Health Organization, which has condemned the practice as a serious health risk.[104]

Descriptions used to show the extent to which practices may be unhealthy certainly seem to encapsulate what the Children's Convention seeks to eradicate: "traditional practice prejudicial to the health of children."[105] There is considerable support for this approach; indeed, the Convention's Travaux Preparatoires reveals that this may have been the intent of the article.[106] This argument finds support from the person who chaired the Working Group during the entire period the Convention was drafted and who bluntly states that the Convention explicitly prohibits the practice through this provision.[107] From this perspective, the protection has considerable legal weight: the right to health has been universally recognized, even in the Universal Declaration of Human Rights[108] and subsequent international documents.[109]

In addition to finding support from numerous human rights instruments, the health argument, as a strategic move, has several advantages. First, a focus on observable health hazards provides a compelling reason for intervention—practices that do not seem dangerous are more readily tolerable. Second, campaigns for health are less likely to raise fears of Western cultural imperialism than are notions of children's or women's rights. Third, the approach provides a cross-cultural language that is neither inflammatory nor accusatory. It is no surprise that commentators who advocate adopting a cautious and culturally sensitive approach accept the health argument, and herald the low-key approach aimed at gradual change as an important example of how human rights bodies may appropriately address cultural practices.[110]

Although apparently robust, the health perspective remains limited. A critical limitation of the approach is that current experiences with the operation in wealthier, urban areas show that new medical technologies can prevent some of the severe health dangers associated with female circumcision. The attendant complications that exist in current circumcision practices do not seem peculiar to female circumcision, but rather seem typical of all operations where crude tools are used in unhygienic settings. Thus, Western medical techniques could essentially eradicate unhealthy consequences,[111] with the important exception of health complications that materialize later, such as vaginal infections, infertility, painful intercourse, and infant mortality.[112] The argument is equally limited in light of the nature of the right to health. If it could be argued that circumcision falls under the right to health, Nation States are only under a duty to implement the right progressively.[113] Preventative health care measures, aside from all cultural obstacles, are also often costly. Money remains a scarce resource in many of the countries that still perform the surgeries.

Some have argued, though, that the right to health argument is buttressed by claims that the operation is "completely unnecessary from a medical viewpoint."[114] This proposal, of course, vitiates the need to provide costly resources: the obligation simply would be to do nothing. This argument, however, still remains problematic. Proposals that circumcision is medically unnecessary could be countered by claims that circumcision is simply a form of cosmetic surgery that enhances a woman's sexuality.[115] Others have argued that circumcision has an aesthetic effect that excision of the clitoris gives the vulva.[116] As for several of the other arguments, commentators also have challenged the genuousness of cosmetic arguments. Such counterarguments propose that cosmetic arguments simply view women as conforming to what men find attractive and fail to acknowledge that female circumcision actually denies women sexual pleasure and satisfaction.[117] Abolitionists have argued that circumcision denies women any sexual pleasure, since the main erogenous zone is removed. Others have rebutted that this argument takes a narrow view of sexuality by focusing on sexual pleasure instead of, as in the African context, on fertility. In the African context, it is women's fecundity that gives them sexuality. The female sexual organ is not perceived as a site for sexual pleasure, but as a site for conception; reproduction is the primary purpose for sexual intercourse.[118]

The core of the response to the cosmetic and pleasure argument, then, challenges outside observers' notions of sexuality, and proposes that arguments improperly concentrate on the need to derive pleasure from sexual intercourse and inappropriately view reproduction as women's oppression. One anthropologist insightfully listed the procedures to which Western women submit themselves to produce "perfect" bodies and concluded that "a central question epitomized so horribly by the practice of female 'circumcision' is why female bodies in virtually every society should be subject to laceration, maiming, mutilation, and control."[119] Likewise, anorexia and bulimia have been identified largely as part of the current cultural struggle over female identity, in terms of perceptions of beauty and of women's control over their lives. Although some theorists do grapple with answers and explanations for the continued physical alteration of bodies, few conclusions are satisfactory.[120] Even fewer account for male genital modification, such as modern surgical procedures performed by North American plastic surgeons to elongate penile shafts and augment girth, or the traditional practices, found in Southeast Asian cultures, of sewing objects into penises, including bells, rings, rowels, pins, and rods,[121] and the spread of some of these practices to contemporary America.[122] Those who have examined these practices note how body modifications tend to be viewed as a means of empowerment, initiation into groups, and beautification. These evaluations reveal how body modifications may be a means of bodily self-determination, an approach which parallels justifications for female genital circumcision.[123]

The challenges to the health argument that views the practices as simply unnecessary from a medical standpoint are limited in other significant ways. First, health is actually a luxury that few already enjoy, and the medical fact that surgery may not be necessary is not dispositive. Second, the arguments do not confront what lies behind the moral condemnation from a human rights perspective. The failure to properly condemn means that the practices continue. For example, the Egyptian and Sudanese governments already recognize female genital operations as a health concern and even ban all but the mildest forms.[124] Third, the approach does not attempt to understand why the practices continue and why women defend them. Ritual activity and mythic beliefs do not necessarily correspond to objective facts or empirical reality; they do not respond to attempts to falsify them simply because they serve multiple purposes—

such as the creation of a sense of community and of solidarity among women, and the inculcation of cultural values and personal identity. In sum, the focus on health issues and calls for abolition based simply on the allegation that the practices are not medically necessary ignore and avoid the more difficult problems of changing cultural norms.[125]

Other probable arguments against genital operations are considerably more difficult to make than the health arguments. For example, some have proposed that circumcision is simply a form of torture and constitutes degrading treatment.[126] Clearly, the operation may be torturous. Regrettably, it does not satisfy the requirements of international definitions of torture as currently conceived. The authoritative definition of torture, found in the UN Declaration on the Protection of All Persons from Being Subjected to Torture or Other Cruel, Inhuman or Degrading Treatment or Punishment,[127] places emphasis on punishment and political torture. A major limitation of the torture argument is that the forms of torture that are prohibited are those involving state action, not individual actions like those performed in circumcision rituals.[128] Admittedly, changes in conceptions of children's rights seem to be moving toward holding private parties accountable as they expand the notion of state action.[129] Such expansion would certainly help provide a stronger basis for approaching genital circumcision with a view to ban at least the most extreme forms. Yet, practical limitations still remain. Approaches that characterize circumcision as torturous, degrading, and mutilating undoubtedly offend many who practice their cultural traditions since circumcision is such an integral aspect of African cultural identity.[130] These approaches are particularly problematic in that they inevitably would control those who are targeted to be liberated. Women perform the practice; they would be the ones simultaneously harmed and assisted.[131]

The stronger argument could be that the practice is degrading rather than torturous. The operations are seemingly done coercively, particularly because of the use of actual force and because of the prospects of suffering degrading treatment and economic sanctions for not being marriageable without the operation. That is, when the "choice" for a girl is between having the operation and being treated degradingly, it cannot be said that the practice respects and promotes her fundamental dignity and freedom. Again, though, the argument does have considerable limitations. From an insider's point of view, the practice may not be degrading. Female circumcision is a deeply rooted cultural practice that confers upon women a high social status. Social privileges and benefits derived from circumcision are the reasons put forth by women who subject themselves and their daughters to the range of practices, including the main cultural value of women's fertility, which deemphasizes female sexuality and protects women from male violence.[132] Likewise, social privileges protect girls from the most dramatic operations. In the Sudan, for example, the most drastic operations, the Pharaonic, took place in illiterate families, while educated parents opted for milder forms.[133]

The most difficult argument, and yet the most critical in terms of eliminating the practices as well as the beliefs that support them, simply proposes that female circumcision may thwart a girl's bodily and sexual autonomy. Although there is no explicit right to that form of autonomy, the argument gains merit when viewed as a link between nonconsenting female circumcision and the actual philosophical core of all international human rights law: the universal protection of individual autonomy. The principle regarding the right to protection of individual autonomy essentially finds that bodies cannot be interfered with without the consent of the persons concerned, as best reflected in prohibitions against slavery, torture, and arbitrary punishment and arrest. Thus, female circumcision violates human rights in that it fails to respect the right to corporal noninterference.[134]

It actually remains difficult to make the argument that a female child should not be subjected to the practice because she has a right to control her own body and to develop and pursue her own sexual life. Several possible challenges readily emerge. First, the proposal rests on Western views of women's rights to equality. Second, the argument assumes a right to acceptance and toleration of a diversity of sexual preferences and practices. Third, the approach plays down the important role that social forces inevitably play in the construction of sexual choices: it posits autonomous beings, which children rarely are. The last point—the cultural embeddedness of rituals—remains critically problematic. The operations tend to be performed before the girl's first menstruation, between the ages of three and eight.[135] Girls justify the surgeries on the grounds of preserving their family honor, which reveals a great concern for the group, even at one's own expense.[136] Girls recall their circumcision "as if it was something sweet"; it proves that they are members of their communities.[137] From an outsider's perspective, it seems difficult to argue that these young girls possess the intellectual and psychological maturity to be informed and freely decide whether to undertake the operation.[138] It remains to be determined how their consent to the operation can be well-informed, independent, mature, free, and real.

Although seemingly grounded in numerous problems, the argument based on bodily and sexual self-determination remains important to consider. From this perspective, consenting female circumcision is *not* a human rights violation. The importance attached to this approach is that it recognizes the significance of protecting the right to self-determination. From this perspective, international law would bar any use of coercion to prevent a person from freely choosing to follow one's culture. The proposal is congruent with recent arguments that propose that eradicating the practice may conflict with children's newly recognized right to participate in their own cultures, a right that arguably includes the right to traditional practices.[139] Likewise, the approach would be congruent with arguments that abolishing culturally embedded practices may conflict with a growing international focus on preserving and protecting cultures, and on recognizing "group rights" and cultural self-determination.[140]

Given developments in international law, it is clear that laws enacted to control female circumcision must, on the one hand, prevent infringement of the rights of individuals to cultural determination and protect those who choose to exercise their right to be circumcised. On the other hand, laws must protect children against abuse, protect their freedom to elect not to be circumcised, guarantee their right to proper information concerning circumcision, and ensure informed and expressed consent. Most fundamentally, the approach clearly reflects the emerging need to involve the child in decision-making regarding the practice, rather than simply viewing the child as a passive recipient of the practice. It is not clear whether the practices will continue when children are involved. Parts of Ethiopia provide one of the few instances of an actual, clear-cut rejection of the practice. In that case, girls had joined the Eritrea People's Liberation Front, which opposed clitoridectomy and which had removed the girls from their villages. Upon the girls' return, they all refused to be circumcised. The practice was eradicated within five years. The dramatic changes are a testament to the cultural changes that can occur when girls' self-conceptions of abilities and roles change.[141]

The changes that occurred in Ethiopia reflect a clear global trend away from practices that involve routine modifications of girls' sexual organs.[142] The process of change, however, tends to be slower and less spectacular. Two factors reflect the need to proceed deliberately and focus on the need to change behavior in a long-term fashion. First, both governments and women's organizations place emphasis on information and education, a long-term process.[143] Second, laws that have emerged to combat the practice, even though they may criminalize certain forms of genital modifications, as in parts of postcolonial Africa,[144] have not been the subject of rigorous enforcement; there have not been any trials.[145] The long-term approach differs considerably from encounters with the practice in developed countries, where the practices are less culturally salient and have been the site of important trials involving migrant families that continue the practice.

Genital operations in the West

It remains impossible to ascertain accurately the incidence of genital operations in developed countries. Given the silence and secrecy that shroud the issue, the paucity of concrete evidence is hardly surprising. Evidence does indicate that the practice is occurring; given the experience of several of the countries with migration patterns, it is difficult to assume that Western countries are immune from the practice. For example, genital operations have a long history in the U.S.[146] Contemporary evidence indicates that physicians and families still practice female circumcision in secrecy within several immigrant communities, particularly in Detroit, Atlanta, New York, and Los Angeles.[147] Although immigrants have left their native cultural groups, the cultural pressures to continue the practice remain strong. Many families continue to hold on to the idea that they will return to their "home country," hold on to idealized images of their countries, and understandably want to continue practices that are part of their cultural life.

Efforts to deal with the practices have been less contentious than might have been anticipated. In general, three legal strategies address the practice.[148] All strategies criminalize the practices and include efforts to protect women and children from the operations and social repercussion of refusing to undergo the surgeries. The approaches and the arguments involved in the three legal strategies are important to consider, for they highlight several of the issues involved in efforts to control the practices in countries where they are more pervasive.

The first general approach aims to prosecute offenders under existing child abuse and neglect laws. Experiences in France are illustrative of the approach. France successfully convicted several women involved in female circumcision by using laws prohibiting violence against minors.[149] The trials highlight the nature of Western debates for and against the practice.[150]

Those who defended the women typically relied on cultural relativist theories and respect for cultural diversity. For example, they focused on the danger of incautiously imposing Western ways of thinking and of living on foreigners who do not necessarily share them. Just as importantly, defenders emphasized the danger of penetrating the intimacy of family life, framed circumcision as a private matter, and labeled the prosecution an attack on family intimacy. Lastly, they highlighted attempts to eradicate the procedure as the continuing abuse by hegemonic Western power of peoples it had once colonized; such efforts destroyed the right to practice the customs of one's own culture without interference from the "outside."[151] Legally, these arguments make considerable sense. Respect for customs of cultural minorities and customary practices constitutes the prime reference for the establishment of legal doctrine and jurisprudence in the absence of a specific legal text. Customary practices are legally tolerable. To sharpen the argument, the focus on family and on protecting families adds considerable moral and legal weight. The argument thus becomes one in which "mutilation" is a relative notion, determined by Western cultural conditioning, inappropriately applied to a practice legitimately based in cultural and familial practices that confer upon it redemptive value.

Arguments by those who challenged the practice and encouraged the use of criminal trials are also illustrative. Antirelativists proposed that those who wanted the practice to continue simply wanted to maintain segregation and encourage ghettoization.[152] They proposed that universal human rights are ostensibly the same for all, and that female genital circumcision fundamentally conflicts with human rights law. The approaches use different methods to reach similar ends. One group focuses on criminalization and argues that bringing legal pressure remains the most effective way to end excision; another group opposes criminalization in favor of working with the families concerned, providing information and support rather than taking legal action against women in the name of women's rights. Both approaches, however, reject defenses of the practices based on the grounds of race, culture, or tradition.[153]

The second general approach to dealing with female circumcision involves distinct criminalization of the practices rather than reliance on existing legal mandates. Several countries recently have adopted this approach and enacted significant legislation: Great Britain, Australia, Sweden, and the United States.[154] The United States' effort, which actually builds on the approaches of other countries,[155] illustrates well the approach. Although several states had banned the practice[156] and it could have been punishable under existing state child abuse laws,[157] a series of efforts to federally criminalize the practice recently passed, criminalizing the practice in the entire United States.[158] The U.S. law bans any genital cutting on girls under the age of eighteen, and provides a prison sentence of up to five years for parents who arrange for the procedure, as well as for the people who actually perform the cutting.[159] Importantly, arguments against the ban, based on freedom of religion and the venerable family right to privacy, were superseded.[160] This is an important development. The statute reflects how the state's interest in child welfare trumps concerns of parental rights, religious liberty, and multiculturalism.[161]

Although criminalization through national legislation provides an important development, the extent to which it is useful in dealing with the practice has been the subject of considerable debate, much of which criticizes the approach. The first criticism points to the use of the statute. Prosecutions are infrequent, as suggested by the failure to prosecute individuals under the oldest national statute, Britain's 1985 Prohibition of Female Circumcision Act.[162] The lack of prosecutions is attributable to several cultural factors, including the difficulty of obtaining evidence against parents in cultures that exhibit and highly value family honor, unity, and loyalty.[163] The second major criticism pertains to the fear that punitive legislation might drive the practices underground and dissuade practioners from seeking medical assistance when necessary.[164] The third argument pertains to the possibilities of raising issues of political power through the criminal justice system. For example, the role of law in judging individual and not collective behavior is exceedingly suspect from a feminist point of view; individual behavior is in any case judged not from a neutral point of view but within a culturally and politically loaded context, according to collective criteria. Individual behavior is never the only element brought into play; collective assumptions and political power relationships are always relevant and will have direct bearing on any verdict. The fourth and most problematic point is that trials mean addressing issues of women's rights by putting women on trial: the law tries individual acts, not collective practices. Since women are the ones who are tried, the result is that women not only are the vehicles of their own oppression, but also end up paying for it through the process of "liberation." Operations are conducted by women, behind closed doors with only women taking part; indeed, it is men who primarily support and express preferences for less dramatic forms of circumcision.[165]

Given the difficulties and criticisms associated with the approach that nationally criminalizes the practice, it would seem difficult to find utility in the statutes. The limitations suggest that the greatest contribution of national approaches that criminalize the practice is simply the heightening of social awareness concerning the practice.[166] Importantly, all new statutes recognize that without concurrent educational outreach efforts to change immigrant's beliefs, legal penalties will accomplish little. In the United States, for example, recent legislation would require the Secretary of Health and Human Services first to compile data on the number of female victims of female genital circumcision residing in the United States, including the number of minors, in order to identify practicing communities. The next step would be to carry out outreach and educational programs regarding the health effects of female circumcision, and to make recommendations for the medical profession.[167] Another proposed law would require that the Immigration and Naturalization Service make available to all aliens who are issued visas from countries where female genital circumcision is commonly practiced information on harms caused by the practices and on potential legal consequences.[168] This approach, then, despite efforts that seem to use criminal law to abruptly stop practices, actually recognizes how laws must gain local legitimacy. Although the current legislative efforts do not remain immune from criticisms,[169] the approach reflects actions taken by international human rights law and by countries that more frequently practice female circumcision.

The last effort to deal with female genital circumcision involves asylum law and the grant of refugee status to protect women and children from operations.[170] Protections from practices have not neatly fitted into immigration law. The traditional definition of refugee adopted by the United Nations Convention Relating to the Status of Refugees[171] did not include women as a protected class. The Convention described qualifying refugees as "any person who, by reason of a well-founded fear of persecution for reasons of race, religion, nationality, membership in a particular social group or political opinion."[172] Under this approach, claimants must satisfy two criteria. First, claimants must have a well-founded fear of persecution. Second, the fear must be based on membership in a particular group. Although developments since that initial definition have aimed to include protections from genital operations, the developments remain limited and protections are difficult to obtain.

Rigid and strict interpretations of the Refugee Act continue to hinder the granting of refugee status to women who have suffered female circumcision, despite commentaries that accept gender-based persecution as complying with international refugee law.[173] In cases of genital circumcision, a finding of refugee status would depend on the characterization/recognition of the circumcision as a form of gender-based persecution, which the United Nations recently recognized. The recognition has come in two parts that address the two components of the traditional definition of refugee. Claims of gender-based plight gained legitimacy in 1985 when the High Commission for Refugees commented that "women who face harsh or inhuman treatment due to their having transgressed the social mores of the society in which they live may be considered as a 'particular social group'" within the meaning of the Convention.[174] Recognition that genital operations could lead to persecution of the "particular social group" came in 1993, when the High Commission for Refugees recognized sexual violence, including "female genital mutilation," as persecution.[175] Although the recent developments remain recommendations by the High Commission, the development reflects a slow change in immigration regulation that permits some women to gain asylum to protect themselves or their children from persecution that would ensue from practices involving female circumcision.

The eventual impact of the recommendations remains to be determined. Few asylum cases actually have been granted on the grounds of genital circumcision.[176] None have been granted in France, which was the first country to establish that the threat of genital mutilation was sufficient grounds to grant women refugee status; Canada, which pioneered guidelines expanding the basis of refugee claims to include gender-based persecution, granted one case; and the United States, which only recently reformed its laws, granted two cases.[177] Two reasons explain the difficulties encountered by those seeking asylum. One difficulty involves the production of evidence to prove persecution or fears of persecution. Claimants may not want to discuss the topic in public forums; physical evidence may not be obtained if the claimant has not undergone the procedure; and evidence of similarly situated and persecuted women from the country of origin, required to comply with the "particular social group" requirement, may be difficult to obtain.[178] The second difficulty, which has diminished somewhat with recent developments, involves the inability of claimants to avail themselves of protections in their own countries. This difficulty arises from the need to show a state connection and to demonstrate that authorities tolerate, refuse, or prove unable to offer effective protection.[179] The two limitations reflect well how laws aimed to condemn cultural practices remain difficult to implement.

The three approaches to dealing with female genital circumcision and the resulting trials and legislative actions represent significant steps toward rethinking the practice. If anything, the developments garner considerable publicity and lead to discussion of women and children's positions in society as well as to a recognition that the operations are questionable. The efforts provide ways to think of children's issues and to offer assistance when practices have become questionable.

Both the extent to which public awareness continues to increase and also the way human rights have a tendency to expand are reflected in recent efforts to ban male circumcision. Although the immense cross-cultural variation in male circumcision remains ignored, efforts have been made to platform the rights of young boys. First, commentators actually have noted that the recent national bans on genital operations pervasively exclude boys, even though worldwide, five out of six children who are circumcised are male.[180] Recent research reveals that the average removal of foreskin actually involves half of the skin of the penis,[181] although several rightly have argued that some forms of female genital circumcision are considerably more intrusive than the male practice.[182] The significant extent of the intrusion on male anatomy is exemplified by the recent recognition by pediatric associations, most notably Canadian and Australian, that involuntary circumcision should not be routinely performed and may contravene human rights.[183] The significance of recognizing boys' rights is reflected in the general finding that no cases of female circumcision exist without the concomitant practice of male circumcision,[184] and a number of children's rights advocates continue to associate infant male circumcision with the practice of female genital circumcision.[185] It is important to remember that all genital circumcision practices remain integral parts of female and male existence and, as such, cannot be treated in isolation as single issues destined for elimination. As we have seen, circumcision is implicated in the eventual validation of full adult standing and community membership, as it prepares children for marriage and completes social personhood.[186] The practices clearly relate to the roles social systems have defined and circumscribed. It would seem that neither practice will be alleviated without rethinking male development. In this regard, the Children's Convention's focus on nondiscrimination offers important points for consideration. The Convention clearly finds that children are not to be discriminated against based on their sex,[187] a statement that reaches back to the Universal Declaration of Human Rights's proclamation that "[A]ll are equal before the law and are entitled without any discrimination to equal protection of the law."[188] Therefore, a human rights violation occurs if boys continue to be discriminated against while girls have greater protection. In addition to explicit prohibitions, there is a developing trend toward using international law to influence gender roles; the argument proposes that the only way to achieve equality is to include the way boys are treated since that largely dictates how practices will affect girls. For example, from the human rights agenda, the Women's Convention provides an important opportunity to alter social environments that disadvantage women. Most particularly, the Women's Convention, Children's Convention, and other international instruments aim to remedy private discrimination, through, for example, equalizing parental roles in families; this undoubtedly will influence children's own gender roles.[189] These are significant points that derive support from the claim that the most effective way to achieve equality is to consider practices that impact both men and women, and that the particular nature of discrimination against girls and women warrants a legal response.

Determining Sexual Partners: Child Marriages

Just as the phrase "genital circumcision" covers considerably different practices, so does the general rubric of child marriage refer to diverse traditions. Such marriages may be physically forced, arranged with consent, or arranged without consent. Likewise, the ages of the partners vary considerably, from age-mates to those who are considerably older. In addition, the age at which the child is exchanged in marriage also varies, ranging from prebirth, infancy, and childhood to adulthood. Since several of the practices involve the marriage of infant or unborn children, not all marriages involve sexual relations between partners. All of the marriages, however, do determine children's eventual sexual partners, and essentially their sexual relations.[190] The image that emerges from the study of child marriages is one in which marriage is by nature a process that evolves over many months or even years through a sequence of events, ranging from installments on bridewealth to the birth of a child.[191] Importantly, justifications for the different practices are equally numerous and ambiguous, ranging from religious mandates, criminal law sanctions, to considerations about welfare expenditures. Despite variations in the practices and their justifications, international law aims to prohibit these practices. Developments in international law indicate that all forms of child marriage may involve significant violations of children's right to protection from maltreatment.

The nature of child marriages

Taking the full heterogeneity of child marriages into consideration leads to the conclusion that the practice is surprisingly widespread. The best-known cultures that practice these marriages belong to some Aborigine groups of Australia, several African societies, and Indian societies.[192] Industrial countries such as the United States also allow for versions of child marriages.

Although different permutations exist, the most well-documented practice involves gerontocratic marriage: the marriage of prepubescent girls to men who are considerably older. Jane Goodale provides the best ethnographic description and analysis of how child marriages are central to traditional cultural life.[193] Her important account explores practices of the Tiwi who live on Melville Island, North Australia. In Tiwi society, betrothals of most females for first marriages are made even before they are conceived; contracts are made when the as-yet-to-be-conceived girl's mother commences menstruation. Once the marriage contract is made, the husband-to-be becomes a member of the family. He joins the family camp and works for them with the expectation that when a daughter is born, he will receive her as a wife. There is no fixed chronological age at which the young girls actually are given to their designated husbands, but it occurs after they are able to undertake household and other economic responsibilities, but well before their first menstruation. The father decides when she is mature enough to be taken to her husband and instructed to sleep with him.

Tiwi husbands begin sexual relations with their prepubertal wives early. The Tiwi consider sexual intercourse to be necessary for breast formation, growth of pubic hair, menarche, and subsequent menstrual periods. When the girl experiences her first menstrual period, the physiological event is ritually noted, and her future daughter is promised in marriage to a specific male adult. The event confers considerable status upon girls. The young wife is simultaneously recognized as both a potential mother and mother-in-law with a dutiful son-in-law to serve her and her husband. These practices, and versions of the marriages, were found among many Australian Aborigine groups.[194]

The practices found in parts of Africa and India have received more attention from human rights commentators, although less-detailed cultural analysis. Cultural analyses that do exist tend to focus on the practices' centrality to religious life and religious law.

Practices in Northern Nigerian towns have received the most scrutiny. In these societies, it is not uncommon for women to be married at age ten to men three or four times older than themselves. According to one study, one-quarter of all women in Nigeria are married by the age of fourteen, one-half by the age of sixteen.[195] Not all are married voluntarily. For example, Hausa parents frequently give away their prepubescent and adolescent girls in arranged marriages, even though girls attempt to run away, or express objections.

Under Muslim family law, fathers are assumed to be "fond of their offspring," without "sinister motives in arranging their [children's] marriages."[196] Thus, girls' wishes fall to the side as fathers orchestrate their daughters' unions with prospective husbands and their families. Fathers have the right to give their daughters in (first) marriage regardless of their daughters' age or consent.[197] After the first marriage, however, daughters are given the power to consent; and divorces are not infrequent.[198] Although divorce may be permissible and ostensibly provides child brides with some protections, it does not necessarily protect the daughter's best interests. The nature of the protections divorce offers is understandable from the impact of early marriages on girls' eventual health and the consequences of ill health for women.

Commentators who report the negative consequences of child marriages that involve prepubescent girls and older men highlight how most child brides engage in sexual relations with their husbands immediately after marriage, and how many give birth before they are physically mature. Pregnancies and births may have potentially devastating consequences for mothers who haven't reached appropriate maturity, including illness and death from childbirth.[199] For example, in Nigeria, women younger than fifteen years of age are four times more likely to die during pregnancy and childbirth than women aged fifteen to nineteen.[200] Those who do survive are sometimes abandoned by their husbands when medical complications arise. Recent estimates reveal that over 20,000 women who had been married and pregnant at an early age in predominantly Moslem Northern Nigeria suffer from vesicovaginal fistula, a disability resulting from a ruptured uterus and accompanied by tearing of the intestine or bladder; the condition is caused by obstructed labor.[201] Long-term health, social, and economic consequences often result.[202] Young brides are then not only abandoned by their husbands but also ostracized by their natal families. The social and economic consequences are undoubtedly devastating.

The articulated rationale for gerontocratic marriages like those found in Nigeria has been that it ensures that girls are married before they reach puberty in order to avoid the risk of out-of-wedlock pregnancy.[203] The social stigma attached to premarital sex is reflected in the contemporary attitude of many Hausas, who believe it shameful to have a daughter at home who has started menstruating. The danger is that she may embarrass her family by becoming pregnant out of wedlock while still residing in her father's home.[204] Again, there is an important parallel to practices aimed to control girls' sexuality. Child betrothal also aims to ensure purity of the bride, much like female circumcision does in other cultures.[205] Where cultures practice neither child betrothal nor circumcision, the concern for purity and protection from pregnancy is reflected in other attempts that rely on prohibiting premarital relations.[206]

The Nigerian example is again illustrative of how religious beliefs may provide rationales for practices that are actually deeply embedded in cultural life. Gender role expectations clearly drive the institution of child marriage. In addition to concern with children's virginity, the practice reflects images of what girl children are to be. For example, children are expected to adopt the traditional domestic roles of childbearer and family caretaker. The result is that formal education for the girl child is generally considered unimportant. Child brides are frequently withdrawn from schools, while their brothers continue with their education, in order for them to assume the status of the head of their households.[207] Thus, although laws may prescribe a minimum age of marriage for either males or females, young boys are rarely married off, with or without their consent.

These cultural traditions are further exacerbated by economic pressures. According to nongovernmental organizations and social service groups, Nigeria's worsening economy under military rule has contributed to earlier and earlier girl child marriages. Families simply want fewer children to feed. Even in cases where the immediate impetus is economic necessity, however, underlying gender stereotypes create an environment where early marriages of daughters is considered an acceptable economic survival strategy.[208]

It is important to note that studies from other regions of the world also reveal how the social structure—in the form of economic, political, religious, and familial forces—takes a toll among young girls who become child brides. In India, for example, the higher death rate for females in their late teens and early twenties is partly attributable to early childbearing and to adjustment difficulties. For example, a government report for the state of Gujarat found that over half of the women who committed suicide were below age fifteen. The police reports used in the government study indicate that in many cases of alleged suicide, the victim had actually been poisoned, beaten, drowned, burned, or hanged. Those who did commit suicide did so to escape their husbands or mothers-in-law, whose harsh treatment deliberately aimed to do away with them.[209]

Although the above forms of child marriage practices receive increasing interest, other forms receive even more condemnation from the international community, particularly the United Nations. For example, international law has become increasingly concerned with religious practices that have a tendency to result in the prostitution of children. The United Nation's Special Rapporteur on the Sale of Children recently highlighted Nepalese customs and criticized practices in which girls are offered to temples to become goddesses, or to be "married to God."[210] He concluded that these children inevitably fall prey to coercive sexual practices and ultimately prostitution, and further noted that some communities have taken such traditional practices and "distorted [them] conveniently to legitimize prostitution as a cultural practice."[211] The potentially problematic effects of these forms of child marriages are well-known and even condoned despite local laws that prohibit the practices. The "Devadasi" system provides a powerful case in point.[212] Although several commentaries actually ignore how the tradition leads children to prostitution,[213] these child bride customs reveal well how traditional practices may provide a cover for legitimizing prostitution. Researchers indicate that the Devadasi account for an average of 15 percent of the prostitution in India, and up to 80 percent of those living in the southern regions of the country.[214] Those who examine the roots of child prostitution report that what leaves young children vulnerable to prostitution actually is not difficult to understand. After the child is devoted to her god, she lives with her parents. However, she does not have means to support herself after she leaves the family environment. In addition, anyone marrying her is considered a social outcast since she is perceived as the property of the god. Since the girl is never offered any job, she is forced to work as a temple prostitute and to become part of commercialized prostitution. Although these traditional practices are banned by the government, they continue.

Other cultures practice similar customs that involve religious beliefs. In parts of Africa where women are viewed as mediums of exchange and their reproductive labor is viewed as belonging to the family, young female virgins are given away as "gifts" to oracles and shrines to pacify gods for offenses allegedly committed by other members of their families. For example, in Ghana, girls as young as ten years old are left with the shrine's chief priest. In these instances, girls are forced into marriage to the priest and forced to serve their husbands sexually. Even running away is not an option; the children know that no member of their families would take them back. They are, in essence, trapped and unable to leave their priest/husbands. Child brides fear not only repercussions from their spouses and families; they fear the wrath of gods.[215]

The problems associated with child marriages and young girls' sexual relations recently have become contentious in industrialized countries. For example, attempts to deal with teen sexuality by encouraging early marriages have become controversial ways of coping with the behavior of "problem girls." Efforts in the U.S. are illustrative, for they reflect divergent attempts to deal with girls' sexuality. One approach attempts to recognize the sexual relations between early teenagers and their adult sexual partners as child abuse and rape, with the result of prosecuting offenders.[216] The effort was prompted by recent research indicating that at least half of babies born to school-age mothers are fathered by adult men who are, on average, more than four years older than their adolescent partners.[217] The other approach aims to recognize the relations as legitimate and encourages marriage: even thirteen-year-old girls have been encouraged to marry much older adults.[218] The encouragement comes not necessarily from parents, who have the ability to consent to such marriages, but from states attempting to save welfare expenditures and to deal with the apparently deleterious effects of teen pregnancy.[219] It is likely that neither approach is effective, as highlighted by reproductive health care providers who find good reasons not to pursue either strategy: it may discourage pregnant, sexually active, and/or abused adolescents from seeking medical care.[220] The new focus on teenage pregnancy and parenthood has resulted in shifts in policy priorities and ideological rhetoric.[221]

Protecting children from child marriages

It would seem that traditions that involve the marriage of young children result in the infraction of several human rights norms. Yet, one is hard pressed to find explicit language that finds child marriage a human rights violation. For example, the Children's Convention fails to address the issue of child marriage. Likewise, the 1994 International Conference on Population Development and its Program of Action, the most recent statement in the progress to secure international attention to women's rights to make reproductive and sexual decisions, stresses that child marriage is an undesirable practice that governments should seek to eradicate, but does not denounce it per se as a human rights violation.[222] However, the United Nations has made a nonbinding recommendation, in the Draft Recommendation on Consent to Marriage, Minimum Age of Marriage and Registration of Marriages.[223] The thirty-year-old draft asks that member states "take legislative action to specify a minimum age for marriage, which in any case shall not be less than fifteen years of age. . . . "[224] The non-binding recommendation's impact is revealed by how it has been essentially ignored by recent documents dealing with children's violence and children's rights.

Despite the difficulty of locating explicit, usable language that relates directly to child marriages, other important documents do relate to marriage. The Women's Convention recognizes women's "right freely to choose a spouse and to enter into marriage only with their free and full consent. . . . "[225] Likewise, the Women's Convention calls upon States Parties to set an "appropriate" minimum marriageable age.[226] In addition, the International Covenant on Civil and Political Rights requires parties to "undertake to respect and ensure"[227] that "[n]o marriage shall be entered into without the free and full consent of the intending spouses."[228]

These provisions appear rather strong. For example, when actual or threatened force is used to coerce girls to marry, current international documents obligate governments to protect the victims regardless of their age. The government could be improperly complicitous in a child's forced marriage if, for example, a child bride sought police or court assistance and subsequently was turned away. Regrettably, girls tend not to turn to government officials. Most of the cases of child marriage documented by Human Rights Watch involve girls who did not seek outside assistance. Few girls can even conceive of raising objections since child marriage is a socially accepted institution. Most young girls either "agree" to marry for economic reasons or "consent" to the marriage in order not to bring shame and dishonor to their families.[229] The pressure of cultural norms and expectations replaces the physical force and violence that might be expected to "coerce" young girls to marry. Given these considerations, the international instruments' focus on force and consent are not as helpful as they may appear. Thus, in the majority of cases where there is no physical force, it is difficult to determine exactly when and how state governments must intervene in child marriages. This is made even more difficult to determine since international law has studiously avoided specifying minimum age for marriage, even as it calls upon governments to do so in the Convention on the Consent to Marriage, Minimum Age for Marriage and Registration of Marriage.[230]

To complicate matters, other difficulties abound in efforts that already offer state protection from marriage at an inappropriate age. India's attempt to prohibit child marriages provides a striking illustration. India's Child Marriage Restraint Act of 1929 reveals why such statutes are so difficult to enforce. The Act specifies that prosecutions could only be initiated by complaints from private citizens. First, as we have seen, it is difficult to obtain complaints from private parties: wives, their parents, or their friends remain reluctant to register complaints due to the social boycott that might follow. Second, there remains the difficulty of ascertaining the age of the girls: imperfect or nonexistent birth registrations complicate matters. Third, the practice continues simply because poverty plays an equal role in encouraging early marriages and prostitution. Commentators conclude that attempts to reform the institution of child marriage actually have had few concrete consequences, except to reinforce class and gender distinctions.[231]

Another possible approach to dealing with child marriage condemns the practice on the grounds that it places girls at risk of forced sex or rape in marriage. In addition, it is arguable that this risk has serious outcomes, most notably bodily injury associated with early childbirth. As with child marriage, however, there are no clear-cut violations of sexual relations with young children, particularly in the case of young child brides married without overt use of threat of force or violence. Child brides "consent" to have sex with their husbands whether out of a deeply ingrained sense of social obligation, or for lack of any alternative. Under international human rights law, there is no treaty provision or other authoritative guidance that sets forth a minimum age below which sex with minors constitutes statutory rape.[232] Without this standard, it is difficult to hold governments accountable for failing to prevent and punish marital sex involving young girls. In the United States, for example, a look at the age of consent to sexual relations and the age of consent to marriage statutes reveals that some states will allow a minor to marry with parental permission at an age when the minor cannot engage in sexual activity, while others allow minors to engage in sexual activity when they are unable to marry without parental approval.[233] Taking action is especially difficult given that governments have a competing obligation to uphold the right to privacy and to protect family life.[234]

Another approach proposes that the practices violate the right to life itself, particularly since child marriage often ends in avoidable maternal death. Although numerous human rights documents affirm that "every human being has the inherent right to life,"[235] the actual reach of the right remains to be determined, and attempts to expand it remain limited by the usual reticence to develop positive rights. The accepted approach restricts the ambit of the right and frames it in essentially negative terms—for example, the right not to be deprived of life by the state without due process of law—rather than asserting a right to absolute preservation of life itself. Yet, even this approach may offer assistance. By providing that "[n]o one shall be *arbitrarily* deprived of his life,"[236] international provisions suggest that programs should not be abolished, withheld, or terminated capriciously. From this line of reasoning, protection could impose, for example, a requirement that existing programs, such as family planning, not be depleted of resources without a conscientious procedure. A more expansive approach would suggest that international practice supports the proposition that the right to life encompasses positive features. The most obvious example would include the right to health, which, as we have seen, has independent content in international law. The Covenant on Economic and Sociocultural Rights finds "the right of everyone to the enjoyment of the highest attainable standard of physical and mental health."[237] This approach seems more consonant with the Children's Convention, which not only recognizes that "every child has the *inherent* right to life" but also that States Parties "shall ensure to the *maximum* extent possible the survival and development of the child."[238] By focusing on the inherency of the right (and on the only right that is expressed in terms of inherency) and the maximum efforts, the Convention comports with proposals that the right applies to children not by operation of law, but by the very fact of the child's human existence.[239] However, as revealed previously, these positive rights have not been the subject of much enforcement.

Relatedly the right to found a family figures prominently. Several Conventions recognize the "right of men and women of marriageable age to marry and to found a family."[240] The Women's Convention further amplifies the content of this right and obligates States Parties to ensure men and women the "[s]ame right to decide freely and responsibly on the number and spacing of their children and to have access to the information, education, and means to enable them to exercise these rights."[241] The right is rather expansive, as it embraces not simply the right to conceive, bear, and rear children; the provision also bestows the right to space and maximize the number of children, and even arguably includes the right to sex education. The result is that it may provide legal grounds to postpone childbirth and sexual activity until the child is more physically ready.[242]

The last alternative is to hold child marriages as violations of children's rights to physical security and inherent dignity. Clearly, children's right to control their bodies is fundamental to their dignity. Physical security and inherent dignity are protected in a host of international documents, most notably the Universal Declaration, International Covenant on Civil and Political Rights, and the Children's Convention.[243] The right to privacy, for example, arguably includes a sphere of personal autonomy, whereby the right to privacy could include the right to make the most intimate decisions regarding marriage and sexuality free from state interference.[244] As currently conceived, the ban on state intrusion into individual privacy does not prohibit parents from regulating the conduct of minors. The Convention, however, in a move that is somewhat radical, also would require parents to respect the *child's* privacy. Although there have yet to be arguments proposing that children would possess the right in these situations, the effort to bestow rights upon children indicates that this is a possible direction consistent with broader conceptions of children's rights.

The potential power of urging a greater respect for children's privacy and self-determination are illustrated well by the recent "moral panic" over teenage childbearing in the West. One emerging outcome has been efforts to marry girls to provide relief for welfare rolls. Although unmarried teenage mothers are not necessarily separated from their children's fathers, existing research questions whether the state's effort to force marital relations addresses the issue. Commentators demonstrate that teenage parenthood is not associated with the availability of welfare benefits. Instead, it is most likely to be associated with poverty, unemployment, low self-esteem, lack of hope for the future, and victimization at home.[245] Clearly, then, policies that focus on the provision of information about contraceptive services and that provide access to services are most likely to be helpful. Thus, the policies most likely to reduce levels of teenage pregnancy, the need for parenthood, and the need for early marriage are likely to be those that aim to increase educational and employment opportunities for young people, not those that seek to restrict access to services.[246] For example, reviews of literature that investigate effects of reproductive health and sex education programs on young people's sexual behavior indicate a delay in the start of sexual activity and a more effective use of contraception; this research includes programs in developing countries.[247] The respect for privacy and self-determination seems to have an impact.

Although some Western societies seem to be able to deal with early pregnancy in ways that do not involve circumcision or early marriage, the ability to do so does not necessarily dictate the need to begin an export of Western practices. Clearly, though, addressing the practice of child marriage inevitably will result in changes in gender status and must address notions of equality. For girls' reproductive decisions to be in any real sense "free," rather than compelled by circumstances or desperation, requires the presence of certain enabling conditions. They include material and infrastructural factors, such as child care, economic supports, and comprehensive health services that are accessible, humane, and properly staffed. These conditions constitute the foundation of sexual rights. The conditions also reflect the extent to which respect for children's rights actually may require a radical reformulation of societal structures, and the extent to which societies respect children's right to self-determination. Without concomitant societal reforms, as several have noted, imposed measures may prove counterproductive and give rise to new social problems in addition to those addressed.[248] It is not surprising to find that, as societies change in terms of urbanization, economics, religion, and education, they also change in terms of marital patterns; as social conditions ameliorate, age at first marriage, in law and practice, increases.[249]

Virginity Exams

The nature of the issue

Human rights activists recently identified practices in which girls must undergo intrusive exams to determine whether they are virgins. Practices in Turkey provide the best-documented example. Parents require girls to submit to virginity exams for a variety of reasons. Parents often choose to have the exam performed if they fear an accident unrelated to sex may have robbed their daughter of her virginity, and thus wish to obtain proof that the physical damage to the hymen was not attributable to sexual intercourse.[250] Parents may also do so to bring criminal charges against a girl's sexual partner and to force the girl to marry, since Turkish law provides for the removal of criminal liability for certain sex crimes if the man charged marries the victim of his crime.[251]

Parents usually do not act alone. Parents often conduct the exams in conjunction with school authorities.[252] In some instances, schoolgirls who live in state dormitories are required to undergo virginity exams after significant lengths of time spent outside their dormitory.[253] The practices also are conducted by police and other state actors, such as prison officials.

By Western criteria these practices may be seen as abusive and coercive. Yet, ethnographic accounts of their institutional and ideological contexts help understand how they conform to local ideals, and how parents believe they are acting in the best interests of their children. To judge such customs without considering their indigenous meanings and the parental attitudes that accompany their enactment places international law on precarious grounds; such considerations must play in attempts to intervene.

Parents and state authorities view such exams as necessary to maintain girls' reputations.[254] Culturally, fear of the consequences of damaged honor is well-placed. Consequences include not being able to marry or being rejected or mistreated by family members.[255] These potential repercussions motivate girls to act in accordance with family and community expectations of proper behavior. Thus, invasion of psychological and corporal privacy is tolerated to ensure female purity and virginity as well as to uphold differentiated gender roles.

Although the practice arguably may be extreme, the practice and its rationales are not much different from the pressures faced by girls in other societies deemed less oppressive. The United States and several other Western countries provide noteworthy examples. In those societies there remains a focus on chastity in the form of the "double standard" and on efforts to prevent teenage pregnancy. Although it is important not to trivialize the experiences of women who undergo forced virginity exams, similar mechanisms are at work in other societies. Virginity and its preservation are central to ideas of premarital sexual morality. For example, girls are thought of as in danger, as in need of keeping their sexual drives under control, as pursuing men and provoking them into sexual activity. Those that are so perceived often suffer consequences. To foreshadow a later discussion, these perceptions allow girls and boys to be victimized through date rape and sexual harassment, and allow sociolegal structures to fail to offer protection, let alone harness prevention efforts.[256]

Protecting children from virginity tests and double standards

Because international law does not expressly guarantee a right to sexual autonomy,[257] the denunciation of forced virginity exams as a human rights violation rests on an argument that such practices violate other internationally recognized human rights. One approach focuses on the states' roles in carrying out and condoning the practice of forced virginity exams. The other focuses on family members' duties to respect the privacy and individual bodily integrity of its members.

The argument based on the state's role rests on the prohibition against cruel, inhuman, and degrading treatment. The Torture Convention and the Children's Convention are directly on point. To reach the level of inhuman or degrading treatment as defined by international law, a practice must satisfy various elements. First, there must be a clear connection to the state. For example, public officials or other persons acting in an official capacity must consent, acquiesce, instigate, or actually commit the act. Second, the practice must be unjustifiable. Third, the practice must cause mental or physical suffering, including that brought on through humiliation.[258] Simply put, then, virginity exams that are carried out by state agents have no legitimate justification; they seriously harm or humiliate victims, and may constitute degrading and inhuman treatment prohibited by international law.

Turkish girls' description of the physical and mental suffering they experience when forcibly examined demonstrates that their experiences may be protected under international law. School and hospital authorities employed by states are often the ones who perform the examination, even when initiated by private individuals. Likewise, it is difficult to argue that the exams meet the legitimate justification standard required by international law. In addition, it is difficult not to view the practices as humiliating and their effects degrading: several reports of suicide have been made in connection with the exams.[259]

Again, international mechanisms are limited. Where women "consent" to virginity exams under pressure from their families, or where parents decide that virginity exams are in the "best interests" of their minor daughters, international human rights law does not provide concrete and direct grounds for condemning the practice. The question of how extensively families may regulate their daughters' behaviors remains open. This is particularly the case with minor girls, whose parents are entrusted to make decisions in their interest. These limitations reveal the importance of designing laws to better reach parental and family practices, for they play a central role in concern for virginity.[260]

Lastly, the human rights framework does not directly address the ultimate source of the problem. That is, it does not address the emphasis on women's chastity that leads families and communities to regulate girls' lives and control their private decision-making. It is difficult to protect from state, family, and community interference. Although no explicit protections exist, the practices serve to highlight the importance of privacy and the actual philosophical core of all international human rights law: the universal protection of individual autonomy. The principle regarding the right to protection of individual autonomy essentially finds that children's bodies cannot be interfered with without their consent. Thus, intrusive exams that control girls' sexuality violate human rights in that they fail to respect the right to psychological and corporal noninterference.[261]

What has emerged from our discussion is every child's *individual* right to protection. The right seemingly outweighs other forms of rights—family, group, cultural, and socio-economic rights—against which it is usually pitted.[262] Importantly, the failure to protect young girls from intrusive exams reflects well the limitation of the traditional focus on state responsibility. To protect girls from the consequences of double standards, communities and families cannot avoid responsibility. Yet, again, it remains difficult to divorce the individual child from her family and culture. Recent developments and our previous discussion of genital physical manipulation and child marriages, however, suggest that greater involvement by those who are subjected to the practice in determining the manner in which and the extent to which the exams are conducted would be an important step toward protecting these children's rights. Again, although the practice could not be directly banned, increasing participation would begin the process of cultural transformation that would lead to greater child protection. The next section examines practices that make it quite difficult to distinguish between cultural groups and their children, particularly in terms of their rights, since the practices are even more clearly central to cultural experiences and existence. Yet, despite the cultural embeddness of the practices, it is important not to underestimate the role played by attempts to increase children's self-determination in transformations of cultural life.

Ritualized Sexual Interactions

Readers not accustomed to anthropological investigations may find it difficult to dislodge the notion that adults' sexual relations with prepubescent children are other than abusive. Yet, the cross-cultural record indicates that societies do not necessarily attach deviancy labels to such behaviors. Importantly, although interactions may be condoned and allowed, they nevertheless operate under strict proscriptions that, from a cultural insider's view, protect children from maltreatment. For example, in a Southwest Pacific society, East Bay,[263] some older men often took, with the father's consent, nonrelated boys as relatively permanent passive sexual partners for anal intercourse. From the perspective of members of the East Bay society, the boys who become partners to older men are understood to be substitutes for females, not homosexual partners. The passive role accepted by the boy is not considered deviant or harmful to psychosexual development. Indeed, the close relations are meant to have positive effects on a boy's development. If the man did not fulfil his expectations, he would be accused of mistreatment and the boy would be taken away. Similarly, restrictions also applied to the homosexual relations reported from ancient civilizations. Several commentators report widespread adult sexual activity with young boys in eighteenth-century China, Arabia, Turkey and India.[264] An oft-cited practice found in ancient Greece was conducted in a very prescribed manner. In that society, pubescent boys were solicited, seduced, and sodomized by warriors who were viewed with contempt if they adopted passive roles.[265] Indeed, historical proscriptions against sexual activity with children related mainly to young males: sexual activity with young girls seems to have been widely accepted and has only recently emerged as deviant.[266]

Given the current movement in children's universal legal rights, it would be difficult not to argue that the acts would not violate children's right to protection from maltreatment if they were practiced elsewhere. Doubtless, there exist many other relationships that international law would regard as violative of children's rights. In place of an inventory of relationship abuses, which is not yet feasible, an obvious, widespread, and relevant example will serve to highlight significant points: initiation ceremonies. The discussion will be further limited: it necessarily focuses mainly on male initiation since female initiations outside of practices that involve circumcisions remain largely ignored.[267]

The nature of ritualized sexual interactions

Adult sexual behavior with children has received some attention from anthropologists who study Melanesian ritualized or obligatory homosexual activities with male children. The leading expert, Gilbert H. Herdt,[268] estimates that 10 to 20 percent of Melanesian societies practice ritualized homosexuality or have practiced it in the recent past.[269] Varieties of these practices are characteristic of Papuan-speaking societies of the southwestern New Guinea coastal fringe and certain islands to the east of New Guinea. Despite some variations in forms of sexual activities, all practices are condoned or prescribed by broader social rules with powerful symbolic connotations, and are structured by age and kinship rules and taboos.

The most thoroughly researched and publicized society is the Sambia of the fringe highlands of eastern New Guinea, who practice obligatory homosexual fellatio in secret societies. These activities and relationships are meant to make men out of boys by separating them from all women, especially their mothers. The rationale for separation emerges from the Sambian belief that girls mature and become women "naturally" (that is, with limited cultural assistance), whereas boys do not, in part because they were raised by women. Men instill their values in a manner constructed largely in opposition to women's interests, most notably by giving boys oral inseminations as well as magical ritual treatments.

Sambia boys' initiations consist of six initiation stages. It is during the first and second stages of initiation that boys fellate older bachelors (third-stage and older initiates) in order to obtain the semen they will need for maturing into manhood. Herdt writes that the boys engage in these practices on a daily basis, first as fellator, and then as fellated, for a period of ten to fifteen years.

The motivation to fellate stems manifestly from the teaching that bachelors have what the boys need: biological masculinity in the form of semen. Sambian beliefs view semen as the source of all fertility. Sambia cultural meaning systems largely reflect an elaborate value structure concerned with the value of semen. Semen is a scarce resource that is necessary for a boy's growth and for his own later use in fathering children; relations with women are seen as particularly semen-depleting. The growth-inducing properties of semen are reflected in Sambian symbolic worlds: their myths equate the penis with secret flutes and with women's breasts.[270]

Although the belief is culturally embedded, most boys interviewed recounted experiencing both revulsion and significant fear when first told that, in order to become men, they needed to fellate older boys.[271] The relationships are embedded in violence. The extent to which violence and fear operate at the experiential level of boys' initiations in societies with boy-man sexual practices is striking:

> The bachelors get soundly thrashed and nose-bled, and they otherwise suffer much. This is how it should be, the elders assert, for the youths must become "strong" and "angry" because of what has been done to them. But they can "pay back" that anger by doing to younger initiates what was done to them: beating and otherwise traumatizing them. In addition, they can do something equally laden with power: they are urged to channel that anger and relax their tight penises, by serving as dominant fellateds.[272]

Other anthropologists have reported similar accounts of violence. Some cultures force initiates to imitate nosebleeding by using sharp objects and to emulate older men who push U-shaped, lengthy pieces of cane down their throats and into their stomachs, sawing them back and forth before withdrawing to induce vomiting.[273]

In addition to the violence, it is important to consider that the practices are strictly prescribed. There is a clear focus on the creation of age inequalities and hierarchies. These homosexual behaviors are promiscuous only within certain limits; the practices are strictly age-graded, with boys starting at age seven, or somewhat older, by performing fellatio on older men. Homosexual contacts are not permitted among age-mates, fellow clansmen, matrilateral kin, or ritual sponsors. In the context of boys' initiations, a hierarchic ideology models and undergirds the relationship between boys and bachelors. Initiates are forced to accept the elder's conceptions of manhood; they must be passive to initiates who have gone before them. It is noteworthy that homosexual taboos are closely related to heterosexual (incest) taboos, as ritual sponsors are viewed as "parents." In addition, the taboo on age-mates reflects the asymmetry of heterosexual relations between the strong male and weaker female. As a boy becomes older and further initiated, he switches from fellating to being fellated. This activity continues until he fathers children. Similarly, marital relations are begun with fellatio, which continues until the woman is "strong enough" for vaginal intercourse and the bearing of children.

Perhaps a most outstanding feature of these societies that practice institutionalized homosexual eroticisms between men and boys is the degree of gender polarity and antagonism. What is being effected through boys' initiation is growth—both in the sense of physical growth and in the sense of teaching boys how to become culturally masculine. Thus, beliefs about the polluting effects of women's bodies are common, as are negative images of women in myth and idiom. Women are socially constituted as dangerously polluting. Women are viewed as contaminated and men must practice sexual purification procedures. Succumbing to a woman's charms could be fatal; all heterosexual contact is deemed harmful without purification. For example, men are taught to ingest special leaves, to place leaves in their noses to prevent inhalation of women's fluids, and not to swallow their partner's saliva.[274] Importantly, the ideologies that are transmitted through male initiation practices focus on the proper distance and relations between men and women, and on the supremacy of men over women. There is a strict separation of labor along gender lines, and residential separation as well. Women do not participate much in public affairs, often have no choice in the selection of marriage partners, and have little control over their economic products. These factors, coupled by patterned responses to warfare and men's aggressive training, relate to the high incidence of wife-beating and marital arguments, which themselves proximally contribute to a suicide rate for females three times higher than the male rate.[275]

Other societies that practice ritualized homosexuality exhibit different features within a similar cultural framework. Among the Big Nambas of North Vanuat, an island near New Guinea, ritualized homosexuality also occurs in a context of extreme male ideology.[276] In that situation, though, the leading man of each village has an almost complete monopoly on the labor and sexual services of the women and the teenaged boys of the village.

The Kimam Papuans of southern New Guinea also exhibit ritualized homosexuality; but in this instance it involves anal intercourse with young boys.[277] The younger brother of each boy's mother is the preferred mentor who performs this task. They also preferentially select young girls, as young as eight years of age, for sexual activities designed to produce semen to be used as medicine. Girls of marriageable age are tested sexually by many men in succession to ensure their fitness for marriage.[278] Among the Marind-Anim of southern New Guinea, boys are taken to live in the men's houses when just past infancy.[279] As the boy's puberty approaches, he is introduced to anal intercourse by his mother's brother, who "feeds him" for three to four years. The Marind-Anim also have fertility rites in which girls copulate with large numbers of men in succession at marriage and at the first menstruation following pregnancy. The mixture of semen and vaginal fluids also is collected and thought to have potent medicinal qualities.

Several other societies in this area practice ritualized homosexuality or employ homosexuality as a mythic theme. In general, all of these societies perceive sperm as creating growth and strength in prepubertal boys. Although variation and diversity prevail, the method of "sperm-feeding" varies over these societies. Societies that practice some form of ritualized "homosexuality"[280] tend to vary in the manner in which sex is allowed; some employ anal intercourse, some fellatio, and some masturbation and the smearing of sperm on the boy's skin. These practices are condoned and encouraged and have become ingrained in their societies' cultural fabric. Yet, strict rules dictate the nature of relationships between partners as well as the times when certain forms of sexual activities are permitted to begin and when they properly cease. Different societies do not always approve of their neighbor's methods.[281] Thus, all societies still recognize the concept of sexual offending and deviancy.[282]

International protections

Initiation rituals highlight well the challenges faced by efforts to address culturally embedded practices that are purposefully violent and shocking to children, involve nonconsensual relations, and intentionally invade children's physical integrity. Convincing reasons may provide international law the authority to intervene; the rituals seemingly violate a number of children's rights. Most notably, protections from torture and from cruel and inhumane treatment seemingly would apply.

Although the practices may seem to violate an extended list of rights, the total cultural embeddedness of the practices provides causes for rethinking whether the actions do violate children's rights. In addition, the consequences for abolishing the practices are quite dramatic: the elimination of the culture. Clearly, these considerations give cause for rethinking intervention. Yet, the practices already reach extinction. The Sambia, for example, have been the recent subject of rapid Westernization through education. The Sambia no longer practice extreme forms of initiations.

The importance of considering the ritualized initiations rests not so much in how international law can intervene, as in how the practices highlight the importance of cultural life in determining the experience of maltreatment. For example, the rituals serve as clear examples of the cultural embeddedness of maltreating behavior, of how practices that are most violent may be defined as normal. The rituals also highlight well the socially determined nature of children's psychological and corporal integrity. Equally important, the practices reinforce the human rights contention that some basic level of child protection does seem universal: all societies place boundaries on what people do with children. Likewise, the nature of and concern for physical and sexual boundaries emphasizes well the importance of considering gender roles and the social construction of child development in efforts to understand child sexual maltreatment. Lastly, the move toward the extinction of the practices reveals well how changes in conceptions of childhood and the place of individuals in cultural life must play the critical part in ending cultural practices that relate so deeply to cultural existence.

Conclusions

Evolving conceptions of children's international human rights and variances in the ways different cultures deal with child sexuality make cultural explorations to uncover ideologies that contribute to child maltreatment especially informative. In terms of child sexuality, the investigation reveals the critical point that one society's sexually deviant and prohibited practice may be another's socially condoned practice. Cultures determine the amount and nature of acceptable coercion or force in the initiation and continuation of sexually related activities.[283] Cultures have the power to define violent practices as normal. Even the public nature of violence and its gendered embeddedness essentially may remain invisible to cultural insiders. The investigation reinforces how practices involving children and their sexuality remain important parts of the process of socialization and initiation into adulthood and of the process of gender differentiation. In terms of international law, the current approach aims to broaden the basis and role of international law in influencing cultural practices. Thus, although some practices may be condoned locally, international law increasingly construes these culturally condoned practices as violative of children's rights. Outsiders view the behavior as maltreating, damaging to mental health, or most likely as shocking to the conscience, and as barbaric and uncivilized.[284]

Although international law may construe these practices as important human rights violations, the recognition does not dictate quick results. Those who champion traditional international law that focuses on formal state action should not be surprised when it fails to protect children. Families, communities, and private actors must be enlisted to help protect children's rights from private wrongs as well as from state inflicted harms. Since the goal remains to transform private relationships, international law must reach and focus on private behavior. Yet, there still remains the need to focus on broader structural changes, such as levels that would impact gender, economic, and political relations. Inevitably, the international movement must be able to reorient the thinking of adults and children and the ways in which they perceive their own societal roles. To dislodge problematic practices, international law must aim to reach different arenas that may promote change.

Human rights workers and the international community should not be surprised when demands to abandon cultural traditions in order to comply with external norms elicit indignation, resistance, and even reinforcement of traditional practices. However, contrary to popular perceptions, intervention does not necessarily aim, or need, to eliminate or criminalize practices. Modern international law recognizes that new rights must be embraced and respected as part of the culture and traditions of the given society; cultures must be engaged in the process of change and transformation. Only through a cultural transformation, initiated and developed by people within those cultures where the practices are found, can the customs be transformed. The multifaceted approach makes sense when dealing with multifaceted systems that do change— even practices apparently fundamental to cultural life disappear. Documented changes reveal well how cultures clearly are recursive systems that react to a variety of influences, both internal and external, that reach the core of traditional cultural life. In the process of change, international legal action is imperative; legal developments provide an affirmative statement for those who attempt to transform their cultures and for those who attempt to resist. To that end, international law has moved to endow children with legal personhood. The effort properly reflects the need for a greater movement that seeks to erase the notion that a child is a piece of property, even cultural property, that can be passed from one adult to another.

The insight emerging from the way international law may approach cultural practices parallels lessons offered for the West. First, the analysis reveals the extent to which numerous practices are essentially ignored. Several anthropological investigations mention practices that Westerners most likely would see as improper or simply barbaric if they were practiced in the West. These practices may include, for example, customs in which boys sit with decapitated heads between their outspread legs to ensure proper sexual development and reproductive capabilities,[285] customs in which gender role socialization involves giving boys sticks to push up girls' vaginas,[286] or more commonly, practices aimed at sexual development that allow, tolerate, or encourage sex play[287] and early, prepubertal intercourse.[288] Although these practices involve the active sexual use of children in rituals or invasively control children's sexual lives, those interested in international law essentially ignore the customs that allow the practices to continue. More importantly, practices that relate to those that are the subject of investigation remain essentially ignored; e.g., addressing male circumcision seems essential to addressing properly the cultural forces that make female circumcision so difficult to combat. A second helpful contribution from cultural analyses involves recognizing that the forces contributing to what international law increasingly construes as maltreatment also may be found in the West. Despite variations in the type and amount of sexual activity with children that cultures permit, similar mechanisms work in all forms of traditional practices that control children's sexuality. For example, the important attempts to control girls' sexual activities we have examined thus far all image girls as at risk for pregnancy, as potential sources of shame or embarrassment, or as burdens to families and societies. These underlying concerns run through all examined practices, including genital circumcisions, early child betrothal, and concerns with teenage pregnancy in Western societies. A third important insight deals with the way countries that look to foreign practices and find them maltreating may approach their own conceptions of sexual maltreatment. Empiricists and several theoretical researchers who have started to examine cultural factors in relation to offenses against children tend to focus on those that allow the adult to minimize or cognitively distort the harm done to the child, and on those that serve to sexualize children.[289] Rather than focusing on individualized, pathological approaches to maltreatment, cultural investigations highlight important culturally embedded factors that include the cultural value of children, beliefs about specific categories of children, beliefs about age capabilities and developmental stages of children, and beliefs about sexual and gender development.[290] Although these factors may not assist in identifying specific practices as maltreating, they do help emphasize major themes at work in all societies that may lend themselves to maltreating behaviors. A prime example involves the process of male socialization and the manner men may learn to associate control with sexuality, and the attitudes and beliefs men may learn about children in general in a culture. These considerations are not divorced from the role of women, parental rights over children, and cultural attitudes towards violence. All cultural values inevitably influence the amount of intrusion in children's lives and the need to protect children from such practices. A last insight involves the extent to which the investigation reveals the significance of viewing practices from children's perspectives. In that effort, international human rights law provides important principles. International children's rights require a focus on self-determination, equality, and respect for difference, all of which allows for examination and reform of traditions by those who live them. At the very least, the human rights movement asks us to explore the difficulties of recognizing, promoting, and protecting children's sexual rights and consider the ways in which social and cultural attitudes toward child, female, and male sexuality create the context for maltreatment to occur.

6 | Abuse by Adult Offenders

A largely invisible development in international law addresses child sexual abuse suffered at the hands of adults, particularly family members and caretakers. Although neither fully recognized nor developed, the momentous progress provides an opportunity to rethink current domestic efforts to combat the sexual abuse of children as experienced and conceived in the West. This chapter first presents the current empirical understanding of the extent, nature, causes, prevention, and outcomes of sexual abuse. The discussion serves as a background for an analysis of the state of the art in the major sociolegal responses to this form of maltreatment. The responses are followed by advances and obstacles to formal international developments and a delineation of what the international movement seems to ask of the global community, States Parties, families, and individuals. The discussion highlights how the movement seeks to re-image the role of states, increasingly moves toward regulating private behavior, and demands cultural transformations in views of and supports for children.

Introduction

The form of sexual maltreatment most recognizable to Western audiences falls under the wide umbrella of sexual abuse. Indeed, the world community frames this form of maltreatment into an explicitly Western paradigm. The paradigm derives from C. Henry Kempe's now classic definition of child sexual abuse: "involvement of dependent, developmentally immature children and adolescents in sexual activities they do not fully comprehend, to which they are unable to give informed consent, or that violate the social taboos of family roles."[1] It is undeniable, however, that diverse definitions of child sexual abuse continue to be accepted. Although several now have expanded upon the definition,[2] definitions continue to encompass at least two factors: (1) sexual activities involving children and (2) an abusive condition, such as coercion or lack of consent.[3] Clearly, these two factors do not distinguish sexual abuse from the practices reviewed in the previous chapters. What does seem to set the current practices apart is the extent to which local communities actually condemn the acts, actively seek to prevent them, and actually have extensive laws designed to address the occurrences that do arise. Furthermore, the practices are distinguishable from those analyzed in previous chapters in that, until very recently, international law ignored these practices. Human rights law's move toward regulating intra-state and private behavior that could respond to sexual abuse in domestic arenas and in family life actually reflects one of the most cutting edge areas of international law and children's human rights. The extent to which international law currently recognizes and provides a framework to respond to sexual abuse remains highly controversial.

The chapter begins with an examination of the state of the art of our understanding of the extent and nature of child sexual abuse and then details its causes, consequences, and prevention. After delineating the most common sociolegal reactions to the research and rediscovery of sexual abuse, the chapter briefly details how the international movement aims to guide reforms, including a discussion of the advances and obstacles facing the international movement in its effort to construct and reconstruct child welfare systems. The chapter ends with a discussion of how the international movement can guide the rethinking of sociolegal responses to child sexual abuse. The analysis suggests that the international approach actually asks for radical societal changes, arguably equal in extent to demands that have been made on some countries to change their cultures and to stop traditional cultural practices that amount to child sexual maltreatment as conceived by the broader international community.

Understanding Child Sexual Abuse

The extent of abuse

Despite considerable interest in and widespread condemnation of acts considered sexually abusive, the extent to which children in different countries experience abuse remains essentially speculative. No epidemiological studies compare the cross-national prevalence of sexual abuse. Despite the lack of systematic comparisons, individual countries have examined the prevalence of sexual abuse, even through national probability surveys.[4] The empirical studies are actually quite impressive, particularly in terms of the solid empirical nature of the research, the actual findings, and the extent to which results reveal abuses official statistics fail to uncover.

Extant evidence from over twenty countries indicates that at least 7 and 3 percent of women and men respectively report sexually abusive histories.[5] Importantly, these estimates are minimal rates. Several countries report considerably higher estimates that reach as high as 36 percent for women and 29 percent for men.[6] It is significant to note that those estimates do not rely on official reports derived from criminal justice and social service intervention.[7] The studies that have been used to estimate comparative trends use samples from the general population or from specific groups (e.g., college students) which tend to result in rates that reach much higher levels than those currently reported through official reports.

Given often wide disparities between epidemiological data and official crime or child protection statistics, estimates remain controversial.[8] The continuing controversy reveals the extent to which sexual abuse remains naturally difficult to quantify. A result of these difficulties is that methodological and definitional differences make actual comparisons among countries essentially impossible.[9] Differences in samples studied, methodologies used, questions asked, and the extent of substantiation— let alone the actual definitions of abuse—can deflate or inflate results.[10] To all these problems, as in the estimation of any crime, must be added differences in societal perceptions and the central dilemma of victims' recognition and actual willingness to report. In addition, high rates may reflect societal recognition and societal attempts to combat abuse, just as low rates may reflect the simple failure to recognize; e.g., it is difficult to determine the implications of a recent report revealing over 80 percent child molestation prevalence rates in Berlin.[11] These ethical and practical issues inherent in multifactorial research designs are formidable, and as yet have not been solved.

Regardless of the interpretations and sources, existing research warrants at least one important conclusion. Sexual abuse is far from rare and may exist in locales where lack of official reports and limited professional interest seem to indicate otherwise.[12] In every country where researchers have asked about childhood exposure to sexually abusive behavior, important percentages of adult populations recognize abuse as part of their childhood experiences. Regardless of the amount of publicity devoted to child sexual abuse, all countries have adults willing to report childhood sexual victimization.

The nature of abuse

Difficulties faced by attempts to measure the extent of abuse resurface in research that aims to clarify the actual nature of sexual abuse. Despite difficulties and controversies, accumulating evidence paints a relatively complicated picture of the nature of sexual abuse. Investigations make the currently used umbrella term "child sexual abuse" problematic; for the term obscures several experiential differences. Despite differences, several trends and notable patterns emerge in experiences reported from numerous sources of data. Research reveals several important themes regarding the following aspects of sexual abuse: potential sex differences, victims' relationships with offenders, the methods used by offenders, and the actual types of acts involved.

In contrast to the perpetrators of other forms of sexual maltreatment, abusers are most likely acquaintances and family members, rather than strangers. Parental figures account for one-third to one-half of girls' abuse.[13] Acquaintances account for another 40 percent.[14] Likewise, children's own homes are the primary location of threats to their safety. Several reports reveal that up to half of the abuses children suffer actually occur in their own homes. The remaining places of abuse tend to be places children frequent, such as schools and day care centers.[15]

Research highlights the difficulty of uncovering abuse. Victims generally are reluctant to disclose; they rarely speak out quickly. Not only do victims hesitate reporting, very few actually do report. For example, an important retrospective study found that only 11 percent of male victims and 24 percent of female victims reported their assaults;[16] those who do report often deny or recant allegations.[17] The international data suggests that less than half of the victims disclose the experiences to anyone, let alone to authorities and those who can offer formal assistance.[18] It remains difficult to predict which children will disclose, as well as when, how, and to whom. The general trend that emerges from research suggests that disclosure tends to be less common with more severe levels of assault and when the assailant is related to the victim; disclosure is least common for the types of assault that produce the greatest psychological distress.[19] Even when the abusers are strangers, however, it is not clear that children will disclose, particularly if they are the ones most likely to be abused by strangers: boys.[20]

Another important finding highlights that boys also suffer from sexual abuse. It is true that boys are one-and-a-half to three times less likely to be abused than are girls.[21] Yet, when not comparing them to women and focusing solely on men's experiences, estimates often reveal very high percentages; up to 31 percent of males report sexual abuse.[22] Formally substantiated cases also reveal high rates of male victimization.[23] Despite these important rates, researchers and commentators overwhelmingly focus on girls. Several investigators now emphasize the negative consequences of the failure to consider male victimization: boys are assumed to be less vulnerable, their abuse is viewed as less damaging than that of girls, prevention programs fail to address boys' needs, and boy victims do not receive help for abuse-related issues when they reach adulthood.[24] Perhaps the most consistent finding is that offenders tend to be male. Male perpetration is undoubtedly high. Every international report shows offenders to be disproportionately male, from 90 to even 100 percent.[25] Yet, child sexual assault by female perpetrators does seem to exist. Few, however, have investigated the nature of abuse by females; and those that do report that female perpetration may offer important insights into the nature of sexual abuse.[26] This direction of research is of significance, given that prevailing theories place gender and male power at the center of child sexual abuse analyses,[27] that victimization tends to be an important contributor to males' future sexual offending,[28] and that abuse by female perpetrators is not less severe than abuse by males.[29]

Research also begins to better understand the nature of the sexual acts and the different types of force used by offenders. Reports indicate that the most common sexual act is exposure, followed by touching and then by attempted assault.[30] Only a very small percentage involves actual coitus: about 3 percent.[31] Findings also reveal an important inverse relation between the amount of force employed and the degree of the relationship between the offender and victim.[32] Given the higher incidence of related abusers, overt physical force is not likely to be as prevalent as commonly believed. Offenders "seduce" and psychologically trap their victims.[33] Although offenders do not necessarily use physically violent force, psychological coercion and other forms of "force" undoubtedly have profound effects on the child and contribute to the silencing of victims.

The way children get involved in sexually abusive situations, the place where the majority of them are abused, the relationships they have with abusers, and their hesitancy to reveal that they were abused, all make attempts to respond exceedingly difficult. Some commentators appropriately have viewed these characteristics as constituting the silent ecology of child sexual abuse.[34] Part of the silent ecology is that offenders are "normal" people who maintain everyday relationships with children. As we will see, the need to address the silent ecology of sexual abuse guides legal responses and the understanding of the causes, consequences, and prevention of sexual abuse.

Causes of abuse

Factors leading to the onset of sexual abuse have received considerable attention. Regrettably, growing evidence indicates that "we have no great insights"[35] into what might cause pedophiliac offending. For example, one influential researcher reviewed research on personality dynamics of child sexual abusers and attempted to identify factors that predicted who would become perpetrators. The review included factors such as physiological measures of deviant sexual arousal, biochemical measures of testosterone, personality measures, and other clinical measures such as history of sexual victimizations.[36] The effort resulted in little success, except that a history of sexual aggression was the most accurate predictor of future sexual aggression.[37] That finding tends to be consistent and is complemented by findings of a history of victimization: studies that compare different forms of pedophilia and sexual offenses to community control groups find child sexual and physical abuse common except for the control group.[38] Despite these two findings, researchers generally conclude that psychiatric, intellectual, and neurological problems characterize only a small minority of offenders,[39] that traditional categories of sex offenders essentially are meaningless,[40] and that even "sexual predators" are not readily distinguishable from other types of offenders.[41] Available research suggests greater similarity than difference between sexual offenders and nonoffenders.[42] If anything, then, existing research indicates how critical it is to take a more holistic approach; a focus on single factors and select groups of offenders does not further the appreciation of either the wide variety of ways adults offend against children or of the variety of reasons they do so.[43]

Given the limitations of the search to identify singular causative variables, research has expanded and models have been presented that incorporate a number of causal factors, each of which may contribute to the development of sexual offending against children. Although increasingly comprehensive, all models have been the subject of criticisms for failing to emphasize important factors, for attempting to categorize offenders, or for moving the focus away from perpetrators to their environment.[44] Despite these criticisms, models that focus on the processes that motivate and enable perpetrators to offend, or that inhibit offending, have been particularly influential and have helped guide research dealing with prevention and therapeutic efforts.[45] This area of research actually has been rather fruitful and has identified four important points.

The first critical point in the causation of sexual abuse deals with the abuser's *motivation* to relate sexually with children. Research reveals that people who engage in sexual activities with children have unusual needs for power and dominance, and that sexual relations with children satisfy those important emotional needs. Equally importantly, perpetrators must be sexually aroused by children and not have available alternative sources of gratification. For example, individuals who engage in sexual activities with children often have difficulties with adult sexual relationships and demonstrate unusual levels of sexual arousal to child stimuli such as children's clothing and pictures of children. Evidence suggests that perpetrators tend to exhibit distorted thinking, deny victims' feelings, and have irrational justifications for sex offending.[46] These distortions provide offenders with an interpretive framework that permits them to construe the behaviors and motives of their victims as sexual and to justify their behaviors to themselves. These findings are reinforced by recent research that links a focus on cognitive deficits and interpersonal skills to effective rehabilitative approaches.[47]

The second condition to consider in attempts to understand causes is the need to overcome *internal inhibitors*. These inhibitors provide mechanisms that lead to avoidance of sexual arousal to child stimuli. Numerous factors facilitate the overcoming of inhibitors. We already have seen how the sexualized portrayal of children in the media may have an impact. In addition, the use of alcohol, stressful life events (e.g., unemployment and divorce), emotional dysfunction, and lack of strong community sanctions all serve to reduce inhibitory factors. Relatedly, research reveals that abusers cognitively approach children differently: they perceive more benefits to the child and greater cooperation on the child's part.[48] This evidence helps clarify why perpetrators report how, during acts of victimization, they perceive their victims not as persons, but as objects.[49]

The third general factor that ordinarily allows abuse to occur is the lack of *external inhibitors*. The perpetrator must, for example, have access to the child. Research has documented well how maternal physical or psychological absence places children at increased risk.[50] Although the absence of other individuals is not dispositive, even early research revealed the importance of considering caretaker absences.[51] Importantly, this research remains controversial in that it may inappropriately blame mothers for the abuse, as reflected in a recent refocus on mother's roles as contributing to the child's vulnerability, rather than finding her responsible.[52] This developing line of research emphasizes, for example, that offenders must have an erotic interest in underage children which motivates incestuous acts, rather than a bonding failure with the mother or other adults.[53] This area of research also tends to focus on how families that lack cohesion, concern between members, and organization may fail to supervise children adequately and may expose them to more opportunities for sexual abuse.[54] The result is that abusive families are often reported as lacking clear grasps of normal family relationships and find behaviors acceptable on some level even though they may not like their occurrences.[55]

The last factor that helps us understand the process of victimization concerns the need to overcome the *child's resistance*. This research derives mainly from studies that have interviewed convicted child sexual abusers to determine how they engage children in sexual activities.[56] Results of these studies indicate that perpetrators tend to engage children who could be described as passive, troubled, or lonely and in need of attention and affection, or who are overly friendly.[57] Varieties of methods are used to ensure compliance. Perpetrators use games, provide toys, give special attention, and use other activities to gain children's trust. Importantly, they also use force and weapons, but more often simply use threats, including threats to divorce a parental figure, to hurt love objects, and to withdraw love. Victims' accounts of the manner in which perpetrators initiate sexual relations closely resemble those provided by perpetrators themselves: offenders shift from normal activities to more physical interactions and suggest that the behaviors are not sexual or simply are acceptable.[58]

The focus on the inhibitors and motivators helps explain the need to take a broad view of sexual abuse. The emerging research is part of a move toward understanding broader social forces, toward establishing an environmental psychology of sexual abuse.[59] The effort importantly places renewed interest in broader, sociocultural factors that foster distorted beliefs about children and support victimization,[60] a development that reflects the difficulty of dealing with child sexual abuse that is grounded in silence maintained by secrecy and that is hidden from public life.

Sexual abuse prevention

Responses to sexual aggression against children remain clearly weighted toward victim-centered prevention, a focus on victims that is unique when compared to prevention programs for other types of crimes and forms of violence against children, such as child physical abuse.[61] Given the considerable societal and empirical attention granted to the prevention of sexual abuse, programs have developed rapidly and have considerably expanded their reach.

Early prevention programs mainly centered on children as the source of prevention. Child-centered programs continue to be the primary source of prevention measures. The majority of these programs have been school-based and vary in their presentation of prevention information. Despite variability, there is an emerging consistency in program objectives: all attempt to explain the forms of inappropriate relationships, describe perpetrators, focus on empowering children through personal safety skills, and promote disclosure.[62] Research suggests that most preschool age children can benefit from participating in developmentally appropriate personal safety programs. Yet, reviews also warn that children should not shoulder the full responsibility for prevention, particularly since the most difficult skill for young children to acquire is telling adults about inappropriate touching situations.[63]

Given the limitations of relying solely on children, the prevention movement rapidly has expanded to include parents and other caretakers. Parent-focused efforts aim to inform parents about the problem of sexual abuse, offer ways for them to educate their children, have parents assist in identifying victims, and teach appropriate responses to disclosures of sexual abuse. Recent research indicates that it remains difficult to get parents involved in prevention efforts: one study reported that only one out of 250 families explicitly discussed with their children the nature and proper reaction to unwanted sexual attention.[64] Yet, researchers continue to argue that parents could be highly effective in preventing and responding to sexual abuse.[65] Likewise, attempts to include other caretakers, especially professionals, have expanded dramatically. Although the focus has been on reporting suspected cases, several programs now aim to include teachers, social workers, law enforcement, and medical professionals in prevention efforts. Although these experts continue to be underutilized in primary prevention efforts, researchers report considerable hope that they can assist.[66]

Despite progress, debates about prevention programs continue.[67] Some commentators propose that child-centered prevention programs are ineffective and essentially misguided,[68] while others argue that children do learn important concepts and that prevention efforts are on the right track.[69] For example, the focus on children has been criticized for omitting potentially embarrassing topics such as incest until children reach adolescence, a point far past the time when the programs could have been useful to most victims.[70] Although more timely programs could be developed, some continue to argue that it is unclear whether greater knowledge will help children prevent abuse, that it is unclear what kinds of skills are needed to prevent abuse, and that prevention programs may have negative effects on children.[71] Others importantly note that, although rightly child-centered rather than focused on the pathology of abusing adults, the effort inappropriately draws attention away from adult responsibility for care, watchfulness, and restraint.[72] Despite debates, however, the general finding tends to be that children can benefit from participating in developmentally appropriate personal safety programs and that efforts must be expanded so that children do not shoulder the full responsibility of prevention.[73]

In addition to debates concerning the potential efficacy of child-centered prevention models, societal reactions, especially legal interventions, have been the subject of considerable criticisms. For example, critics claim that society still tends to focus too heavily on "stranger-danger" and on investigating and uncovering abuse rather than engaging in more preventive measures and adopting policies that will assist victims.[74] In addition, the most common approach specifically aimed at preventing abuse, the incapacitation of offenders, also has come under fire by child advocates. Although incapacitation through long-term imprisonment has been a primary focus of the "punitive zeitgeist in child protection,"[75] research indicates that offenders are more amenable to therapeutic interventions than popular perceptions suggest. In a recent review of therapeutic approaches to the treatment of child sexual abusers, a leading expert concluded that "the emerging literature is encouraging in terms of desired change for those individuals who are identified."[76] Several comprehensive reviews reveal that appropriately tailored therapeutic approaches, particularly those with a cognitive-behavioral focus, report low recidivism rates for "child molesters."[77] Yet, there is a surging move toward eliminating offender treatment programs, despite knowing that offenders eventually will be released from incarceration.[78] Thus, it seems that the deployment of legal resources used to incapacitate offenders also lends itself to criticism.

Although emerging criticisms center on the improper focus of prevention efforts, it does seem that comprehensive efforts remain necessary. Focusing on punishing offenders, for example, addresses important societal concerns that offenders "pay" for their crimes, serves as a way to ensure that children can be protected from people known to be dangerous to them, and sharpens public consciousness about the problem. Likewise, it seems clear that children will benefit from learning skills that may not only protect them from abusers but also begin a socialization process that helps ensure that they do not become abusive themselves. Lastly, given what we have learned about motivators and inhibitors of abuse, it seems that a comprehensive approach is more than a politically sound move; it is a move necessary to combat different forces that factor into the largely silent ecology of sexual abuse.

Problems inherent in efforts that aim to break the silent ecology of abuse have led to interest in preventive efforts targeting potential perpetrators of sexual aggression, not the small minority of aggressors who have been adjudicated. We will see in the next chapter some of the promising interventions with adolescent sexual aggressors, the group of child sexual abusers who may not have ingrained patterns of sexually aggressive behavior and may be the most amenable to treatment.[79] Other efforts focus more on the potential perpetrators' environment, and advocate such interventions as preventing antisocial behavior via parent training[80] and molding peer environments in school settings.[81] Although increasing, perpetrator-oriented interventions have touched only the tip of the iceberg and have barely begun to move from focusing only on sexual aggressors who have been apprehended and convicted to boys and girls at all developmental levels. This important development recognizes and confronts the finding that sexual abuse is engaged in by many more than the abnormal individuals who are apprehended and convicted.

Outcomes of sexual abuse

Arguably the most important finding relating to outcomes of sexual abuse is evidence that points to a wide diversity of possible effects. Indeed, some (controversial) reports point to no effects: recent meta-analyses reveal that up to 30 percent of children show no more negative psychological symptoms than control groups who were not abused.[82] To a large extent, the estimates should not be alarming; actual trauma caused by abuse is multi-determined; harm depends on the child, perpetrator, supporting environment, and the nature of the event(s). Importantly, the actual sequelae of abuse remain difficult to understand precisely because of the multi-determined nature of outcomes.

Little is known about the mechanisms that facilitate individual adaptation and the factors that underlie successful adjustment in some individuals.[83] Yet, factors that significantly impact a child's response and adjustment to abuse have been the subject of considerable research. Indeed, attention to the study of sexual abuse during childhood primarily has focused on its emotional and social sequelae.[84] The list of negative outcomes is virtually interminable; the most noteworthy and frequent symptoms include depression, poor self-esteem, sexualized behaviors, post-traumatic stress disorders, and especially increased risk of revictimization in adolescence and adulthood.[85] Regrettably, the mechanisms that determine specific outcomes remain poorly understood.

Although several models recently have been developed to explain why certain effects occur or fail to occur, the models' broad conceptualizations of multiple dynamics have yet to account well for trauma. Influencing factors are so recursive and multi-determined that it is difficult to explain traumatogenic outcomes. Regardless of difficulties, researchers generally identify important groups of variables.

A first group of variables includes characteristics or descriptions of the abuse itself, such as type, severity, frequency/duration, as well as age of onset.[86] The results of this research have been both promising and disappointing. Among the most promising findings has been the conclusion that a significant number of sexually abused children (over 30 percent) quickly recover.[87] This encouraging finding, of course, is a double-edged sword. The failure of victims to present predictable symptoms makes abuse particularly difficult to uncover. Another important point about this research that is disappointing is that information on the ill effects of early child-adult sexual contact comes from children who are in therapy or involved in legal proceedings, or from adults who have entered therapy.[88] Such information probably represents the worst cases, particularly since there are twice as many studies of incest and since incest cases are probably the most detrimental forms of sexual abuse.[89] Yet, a recent review of both clinical and nonclinical research on psychological correlates of children's sexual experiences with adults found the presence of force or coercion as a major moderator to outcomes, and also reported a wide variety of reactions.[90]

A second group of variables identified as important to consider when examining the effects of child sexual abuse includes familial roles and general familial functioning. In this regard, research consistently points to the mother's support as the most powerful mediator of negative outcomes for abused children. Research contradicts the popular myth that familial sexual abuse is the feature of an excessively intact family: abuse is connected with family disruption, low levels of support, and separation from parents.[91] Poor outcomes consistently relate to more noxious family environments, particularly to family violence.[92] Research indicates a need for increases in familial support services.[93]

A third group of variables places concern beyond the family, in more general societal reactions. This research, for example, focuses on the process of shaming and stigmatization that occurs once sexual abuse has been discovered.[94] Some researchers point to a direct relationship between societal interaction and symptomatology: the more neighbors and family members become involved, the worse victims' symptoms become.[95] Clearly, however, the same process works before discovery and undoubtedly inhibits the disclosure of sexual abuse.[96] Another critically important but less frequently examined factor is the type of societal intervention. The majority of studies suggest that sexually abused children who testify are often harmed by their experiences in the legal system, particularly in the *criminal justice system*.[97] Several of the findings are counterintuitive and controversial.[98] Contrary to popular beliefs that defense counsel rarely intimidate or deliberately confuse child witnesses for fear of alienating juries, evidence suggests otherwise. One study reported that the stress of testimony produced not only tears but vomiting, asthma attacks, and epileptic seizures.[99] Despite increasing interest, it remains uncertain how dramatic these effects are for the vast number of victims, particularly given that only a very small number of children eventually do testify.[100] Yet, it is true that even the anticipation of testimony causes immeasurable stress: reports of suicide attempts and prolonged absences from school are not uncommon.[101]

A last group of variables focuses on victims' perceptions of abuse, rather than on external, objective perceptions of harms.[102] This research suggests that victims' subjective experiences and framing of events actually mediate the harms. For example, recent studies find that, compared to other variables, the manner in which victims perceive the severity of the abuse largely determines subsequent adjustment or maladjustment, not objective factors.[103] This finding has been recently corroborated by Dutch research that examined the extent to which children "consented" and perceived themselves as willing participants. That research revealed that nonconsensual adult-child sexual activity related to later mental health and interpersonal problems; consensual sex was associated with increased levels of sexual desire and fewer anxieties about sex.[104] Although the research remains highly controversial,[105] the findings underscore the need to proceed cautiously and not to assume that different sexually abusive events result in interchangeable and equally traumatic outcomes.

Taken together, existing research and current understanding of sexual abuse point to the importance of considering the ecology of varieties of maltreatment. Rather than viewing child victims as victims of sporadic abuse, current literature highlights the high frequency and variety of sexual abuses, the need to include a broad range of community members and to adopt more comprehensive approaches in preventative efforts, and the need to consider children's reactions to abuse and to offer victims assistance. Clearly, the extent to which societies offer assistance varies considerably. The responses, however, remain compelled by their legal systems, which themselves reflect the social perceptions and general views regarding the need to protect children.

The Legal World of Child Sexual Abuse: The State of the Art

Legal systems largely constrain societal responses to issue resolution. Although there are several types of legal systems, they tend to operate between two extremes.[106] One extreme emphasizes and privileges the protection of innocent defendants and their individual freedoms. This accusatorial model arrives at decision-making through the presentation of evidence by adversarial parties to a decision-maker who, largely constrained by the parties' presentations, eventually decides the dispute's outcome. The focus provides the accused protections as they proceed through the legal system.[107] Instead of privileging personal freedom, the other extreme emphasizes the common good and societal interests. This inquisitorial approach emphasizes the more active role of the decision-maker, the courts. These courts take considerable initiative: inquisitorial courts gather information, question all involved in the matter, and then determine who prevails.[108]

The different methods of deciding disputes necessarily determine their response to family life, the general treatment of children, and child sexual abuse. Although commentators champion various approaches and even variants of each, all approaches necessarily balance costs and benefits associated with sociolegal intervention. Rather than listing all variants, the following highlights how different systems impact societal attempts to address sexual abuse and how different countries exemplify certain emerging trends. Again, the focus necessarily concentrates on Western systems, for only they most recently have reacted to the recognition of sexual abuse.

Inquisitorial systems

These systems' central tendencies are to view abuse as a familial, not a societal or a legal, problem. The result is that the systems are characterized as family support systems in which policy and practice are driven by an emphasis on partnership, participation, prevention, and family support.[109] The approach also focuses on helping parents and children in the community in a supportive manner that minimizes policing, surveillance, and coercive intervention. Thus, rather than criminal justice agencies, mental health agencies deal most with child sexual abuse incidents. Rather than treating abuse as a criminal act, agencies adopt a therapeutic philosophy that focuses on a strong belief in families and their preservation. The focus on families is significant: it translates into a move that protects families more so than individual children within families.[110]

Child advocates champion the inquisitorial approach as more child-friendly.[111] By their very nature, inquisitorial systems seem less hostile to children.[112] For example, less focus on the prosecution of sex offenders undoubtedly reduces the number of children who may experience the possible trauma of providing live, in-court testimony. However, the focus away from punishment also remains fraught with problems. Given that these agencies are mostly family oriented, instances of extra-familial sexual abuse often are overlooked or seldom dealt with at all. The prosecution of sex crimes, whether intra-family or extra-family, is more infrequent.[113] It is the focus away from direct intervention, broader support of families, and their enactment of more child-friendly legal procedures that separates this approach to child welfare from the accusatorial.

The Netherlands' child welfare system provides a good example of how inquisitorial models focus on family support, rather than on individual child protection. Strong antagonistic feelings toward state interference in family matters characterizes the system. Child maltreatment, including sexual abuse, is viewed as a "family affair." The problems associated with this approach are now well-known. First, most suspicions of child sexual abuse, especially of young children, are not dealt with at all.[114] Second, when these abuses are investigated, they are investigated by social workers who usually do not interview the child about the alleged sexual abuse, for abuse is classified as a child-rearing problem, a family problem, or neglect. Third, even when mental health, medical, and criminal justice professionals may suspect sexual abuse, legal action is rarely taken. Last but not least, since there are no reporting laws, the extent of abuse remains essentially hidden. The failure to gather important data significantly reduces the chances of increasing societal will to intervene.[115]

Importantly, despite mandates that would suggest that sexual abuse remains outside of formal legal intervention, the Netherlands recently has undertaken a widespread, sustained revision of its morality laws. A most dramatic change deals with age-of-consent cases and their prosecution. The changes allow for the prosecution of nonviolent sexual contact. Importantly, the law provides that nonviolent sexual interactions with a child over twelve years of age and under sixteen will only be prosecuted upon complaint, unless the perpetrator has authority over the child.[116] Thus, the age of consent is sixteen, but the possibility of consent between twelve and sixteen emerges. The prosecutor is obliged to ask the minor's opinion of the desirability of a prosecution. In exceptional cases, the public prosecutor may override a child's wishes. A consenting child may refuse to complain, a child who wishes to complain may do so, and parents may complain on behalf of the child. To protect children from intra-family abuse, the Child Protection agency may complain on behalf of children in cases where children may have difficulty complaining against family members. These developments reflect well changes in the emerging societal recognition of the potentially negative consequences of sexual abuse. Despite the new laws, the inability of police to dismiss cases, and increased public awareness, recent research reveals that nearly half of sexual abuse cases proceed to prosecution and less than half of those cases lead to conviction.[117]

The Israeli system presents another important variant of the inquisitorial model. Unlike the Netherlands' approach, the Israeli system focuses less on family protection and preservation. Instead, the Israeli system responds to child sexual abuse in a manner that is shaped by the need to protect children from the perceived trauma of testifying in court.[118] The law presumes that testifying in court, particularly against family members, could be so traumatic as to cause "irreversible harm" to children, because the children might reexperience the traumatic events.[119] In order to prevent possible trauma, the system makes use of youth investigators.[120] Unlike mental health professionals, youth investigators hold extensive power to investigate child sex crimes and have a major role in their prosecution: they have the authority to determine whether the child can testify in court, can be asked to identify alleged perpetrators, and can be allowed to undergo medical examinations. Perhaps more importantly, when youth investigators conclude that it is not in the children's best interests to participate in court proceedings, the investigators evaluate the truthfulness of the children's allegations and so testify in their place.[121]

Although the Israeli system emphasizes the protection of children from the harms associated with formal legal processes, its laudable attempt is subject to challenges that highlight the difficulties encountered by efforts to help sexually abused children. A focus on protecting children from legal intervention results in a small number of prosecutions. In 1993, youth investigators found less than 7 percent of children qualified to testify.[122] Since children do not testify, prosecution rates are notoriously low. A primary reason for the paucity of prosecutions is that judges are unable to formulate informed impressions of alleged victims: there is no judicial check on youth investigators' decisions. To exacerbate matters, the legal system requires corroboration of alleged events. Given the private nature of sex crimes, the failure to obtain corroborating evidence abounds and allegations are dismissed frequently. In addition, youth investigators have been assigned to the unit of juvenile probation, the source of their primary training experience. Investigators are torn between conflicting roles and desires: as probation officers and youth investigators, they desire to provide therapy and also to conduct investigative interviews. Even though the investigators are given enormous powers, privileges and responsibilities, they remain overworked, under-trained and poorly compensated.[123]

The Israeli system's basic assumptions are important to emphasize. The effects of in-court testimony implicitly are considered more damaging than continued exposure to unpunished perpetrators, and more harmful than leaving perpetrators free to victimize other children. The high interest placed on not harming children is revealed further in the recent failure to consider innovative reforms. Although several reforms could alleviate concerns about the traumatogenic effects of court testimony,[124] proposals consistently have been rejected for fear that parliamentary debate of such controversial laws might lead to abandonment of all the special procedures designed to protect children.[125]

Norway presents another important example of the inquisitorial model and of the focus on shielding children from harm that may arise from legal intervention.[126] Statutory rules regarding the use of children witnesses in cases of sexual offenses were first enacted in Norway in 1926. Those rules, established due to concern for the adverse effects of in-court interrogation of the child, introduced the use of out-of-court judicial interviews of witnesses. Importantly, because the interview is not considered a court session, the parties have no right to be present. The examining magistrate reports the child's testimony, including his own personal impression of the child, particularly as it relates to the child's level of maturity and trustworthiness. The judicial report is read in lieu of the child's testimony. On some occasions, children are asked to appear in court to be examined by the presiding judge, not the parties. Remarkably, there have been only a few changes in the approach: children above fourteen are now viewed as sufficiently developed to be heard as witnesses in court, provided special protections are used; the magistrate will use trained experts to assist in the examination and the interview will be tape-recorded if possible. Importantly, the child-friendly and non-adversarial collection of testimony continues to result in the suspension of hearsay rules: nothing prevents the trial court from hearing testimony about the child's statement from parents, doctors, officers, and others. Clearly, the Norwegian approach conflicts with ordinary rules of Norwegian criminal procedure: trial courts neither see nor hear the witness, and the parties are deprived of their right to examination and cross-examination. The Norwegian experience highlights the extent to which even inquisitorial models go to protect children from abuse. Other countries that make use of the pretrial interview allow the parties to be present and observe the right to examine the child. Likewise, in those countries, defendants often have the right to be present, although their exclusion may be permissible.[127]

Germany also adopts the inquisitorial system.[128] Importantly, the German "principal of legality" requires police and prosecutors to investigate any criminal event they get notice of, and prosecutors' discretion in prosecuting are limited: they are required to accuse if there is a probability of conviction. Even if the prosecution is not in the child's interest, it is difficult to avoid prosecution in sexual offenses against children. This does not mean that there are no attempts to be child-friendly. There are no corroboration requirements and there are no formal age limits to being a witness. In cases of sexual offenses against children, experts or judges are used to interrogate the child witness. Cross-examination is an uncommon practice, although not prohibited by law. When children are under the age of sixteen, the judge will ask questions; others are only able to propose additional questions. The defendant can be excluded. Importantly, the child may opt out of prosecution altogether. The child may simply refuse to give evidence, particularly if the defendant is a relative. In addition, it remains impossible to coerce a child under the age of fourteen to provide evidence, because fourteen is the age of responsibility, and coercive measures, such as fines or arrest, are not imposed on those who cannot be held responsible. Just as importantly, the child must consent to be interviewed by experts.[129] Germany's approach to dealing with child victims demonstrates well the extent to which inquisitorial systems may go to protect children from the harms of intervention. It is important to emphasize that responses to the sexual abuse of children recently have begun to shift away from treatment-oriented intervention to more repressive approaches. Despite the move, there continues to be a reluctance to interfere with family life and only a small amount of sexual abuse by family members comes to the attention of the criminal justice system.[130] Perhaps more importantly, victims report that they would not contact private or public institutions for fear of negative consequences for themselves and their families.[131]

Inquisitorial systems, then, greatly emphasize the protection of families from criminal and other formal legal intervention. There is a desire to protect families from destruction and from public stigmatization when criminal laws are used.[132] Inquisitorial systems also focus on protecting children from judicial and criminal justice processes, even to the extent that children simply will be excluded or will be given the option to exclude themselves. As a whole, however, inquisitorial systems seem to bestow upon children little voice in actual legal proceedings. The goal is to avoid traumatizing a child witness at trial. Likewise, the approach does not necessarily give children a voice in their families. To a large extent, children's rights are coterminous with their familial rights. In inquisitorial systems, children's best interests relate firmly to family preservation, whether this is formally stated or simply the practical outcome of systems that do not criminally pursue the prosecution of sex crimes against children.

Accusatorial systems

Public concern about sexual abuse and the effects of legal intervention also galvanized support for reforms in systems that are characterized by adversarial approaches to dispute resolution. Countries adopting this approach tend to minimize the role of the state in private life, to restrain government spending, and to encourage individual and family responsibility and solutions. Although it may be an oversimplification to interpret trends in child protection along the lines of greater emphasis on the privacy of the family and on the diminution of the role of the state, the factors do help illustrate the predominant features of this model of child welfare, which focuses on individual responsibility and individual failure. These systems perceive abuse foremost as a problem that demands protection of children from harm; when systems function according to plan, allegations result in rapid "child saving" efforts and their removal from contact with abusers, including family members. In contrast to the inquisitorial model's focus on familial and community support, a focus on child protection clearly characterizes this approach.[133]

The accusatorial model's child protection efforts have been essentially two-pronged. First, it aims to uncover sexual abuse through the use of more aggressive mandatory reporting schemes that mainly encourage professionals to report suspicious signs of abuse. Second, it aims to determine whether abuse has occurred and to punish offenders. The model's twin aims reflect the attempt to criminalize sexual abuse and to treat such abuses differently from others whose impact could be equally devastating.[134] Both goals also aim to tackle the silent ecology of sexual abuse by sleuthing to uncover abuse and by providing clear statements regarding its prohibition. The focus on using the criminal justice system has had dramatic effects, particularly on perceptions of children as potentially credible witnesses. The shift has been particularly controversial, and often is viewed as conflicting with the venerable protections of individual freedoms, not the least of which is the protection from false accusations.[135] The emerging difficulties reflect the need to accommodate legal systems to children's special vulnerabilities and to maintain important adversarial systems' traditions, which, in contrast to practices in the inquisitorial models, have strong preferences for oral as against written evidence and have a natural distrust of expert evidence called by opposing parties.[136] Several countries have embraced these important trends: criminalization, reporting mandates, and differences in the introduction of children's testimonies.

Canada well reflects how societal recognition of the extent of sexual abuse directly impacts adversarial legal systems. For example, protection cases, criminal charges, and criminal trials involving sexual abuse were essentially invisible until the early 1980s.[137] Since then, statistics indicate that of every ten sexual assault victims known to police, four are teenagers and four are under age twelve.[138] Researchers attribute this impressive change to the discovery that child sexual abuse is much more prevalent than ever before imagined and to a concomitant removal of legal obstacles to uncovering abuse and to admitting children's testimony.

Although the clandestine nature of the acts remains, the legal rethinking about child victims successfully led to greater recognition and reaction. For example, previous statutes limited the offense of sexual abuse to sexual intercourse (1) with a female person between the age of fourteen and sixteen who was not the accused's wife and who was of previously chaste character, or (2) with a stepdaughter, foster daughter, or female ward. New statutes expanded the protection of children under fourteen years of age by voiding their consent to any kind of sexual activity with an adult. The result was especially significant for cases that involved extra-family relationships or other caretakers, particularly teachers and counselors. Another important change was the removal of the nonvirginity defense; the child's prior sexual behavior was no longer a defense. Equally important, statutes expanded the definition of abusive behavior to include sexual touching, initiation to sexual touching, and sexual exploitation. Like those of several other countries, the new statutes also aimed to reform child-witness laws. The statutes abrogated the need for corroboration, abolished the judge's duty to warn juries of the inherent unreliability of child witnesses, and expanded the use of videotaped testimony. Canada's efforts reflect well the vigorous move toward making child sexual abuse a crime more readily punishable.

Although clearly aimed to protect children from abuse and from the trauma of courts, Canada's reforms have not been free from controversy. One important challenge suggests that efforts to prosecute overshadow some of the protections child witnesses can have from the trauma of court testimony and investigative procedures. Several of the special protections that do exist actually have been shown to remain unused. For example, videotape testimonies are used infrequently simply because children must be present in court, accept the contents of the tape on the witness stand, and be subject to cross-examination. Another criticism emphasizes the failure to reform legal actors' attitudes. Research indicates that simply because the law sought to view children as more credible witnesses, it did not necessarily change the practice of attorneys and their need to convince juries and judges. The result is that children still experience considerable trauma about testifying. In fact, one study revealed that almost half of the children evidenced post-traumatic stress disorder.[139] Although there is hope that reforms will eventually counter some of these negative consequences of legal intervention, the challenges reflect the extent to which current accusatorial models remain concerned with protecting children from sexually abusive situations and the extent to which attempts will be made to accommodate their presence in the system rather than adopt a different approach to child protection.

Great Britain also enacted radical changes in its effort to take child sexual abuse more seriously. Recent years have seen important reforms in the law that governs the evidence of children in criminal proceedings. Recent statutes removed competency requirements altogether.[140] In addition, conviction on uncorroborated evidence is now permissible and there is no longer a duty to warn juries of the danger of accepting children's evidence. Likewise, reforms permit the use of child-friendly innovations; e.g., testimony behind screens, use of videotapes, and closed-circuit television have made testimony less stressful for some children. These recent innovations are part of the Criminal Justice Act implemented in 1992, a systematic attempt to expedite the prosecution of child abuse.[141]

Britain's legal reforms, however, also are subject to criticisms simply because formal legal changes do not ensure changes in practice in well-established legal models that reflect societal views of the way to deal with disputes. Several examples reveal well how legal rules meant to make children's accounts less suspect simply cannot reach their goal. Despite abolishing the corroboration rule, for example, judges still draw on it in a more discretionary sense as they tend to distrust children's evidence on its own.[142] Technological advances may not be that useful either.[143] Statistics regarding the extent to which children are involved in prosecutions, let alone how many prosecutions are failed or delayed and how children may be traumatized by them, simply are not available.[144] Ironically, recent research illustrates how efforts even may be counterproductive: Reforms seem to prolong rather than expedite cases[145] and attempts to curb rigorous cross-examinations have not abated their use.[146] Although it is difficult to determine the impact of these reforms, the

changes do indicate that the basic needs of the adversarial criminal justice system remain: e.g., despite efforts to make testifying more child-
friendly, the need to convince judicial decision-makers and to protect offender's rights continue to play key roles, and undercurrents of resistance
by all legal actors continue.[147] The currently failed introduction of technology reveals how legal system changes mask the need for basic attitudinal changes in the resolution of disputes.

Australia has also adopted an accusatorial approach.[148] Unlike other
abuses that are dealt with in children's or juvenile court, sexual abuse is
dealt with in criminal courts.[149] Three points are important to emphasize. First, like other countries, reform efforts have attempted to address
the difficulties children face in the criminal courts where the standard of
proof is high enough that children are *more* likely to need to testify.[150]
To counter limitations of criminal legal interventions, reforms have been
numerous and recent: actually allowing children to testify,[151] preparation
for court programs, and closed-circuit television are among the most
prominent innovations.[152] Second, and illustrative of accusatorial systems, Australia instituted mandatory reporting laws in most states.[153] Although reports skyrocketed, few were substantiated;[154] the result has
called into question the utility of these statutes and has led to charges
that important resources are likely to be funneled away from children
who truly need assistance.[155] Although the statutes remain controversial,
they indicate well the increased societal concern, awareness, and suspi-
ciousness about potentially abusive situations that have led to concerted
effort to protect all children from abuse. A last innovation involves
the flexible use of pretrial diversion from prosecution, in which offenders
who are the victim's parents, or spouses of the victim's parents, can enter two-year treatment programs. This alternative is adopted in instances
where the offender accepts responsibility, there was no violence, and
where it is in the best interests of the child. Arguably, it remains difficult
to understand how there would be no violence. Yet, the attempt to maintain flexibility and to ensure the best interests of the child certainly is
laudable and significantly reflects the extent to which even accusatorial
models do not necessarily omit innovations that opt out of predominant
legal models.

The United States' recent reform efforts also illustrate well the dynamics of accusatorial systems, particularly their potential aggressiveness. As in several other countries, legal responses to child sexual abuse
aim to punish perpetrators by uncovering instances of abuse and by involving children in the prosecution of crimes. The most recent child protection efforts, both at federal and state levels, reflect the prosecutorial

ethos that includes, for example, sex offender registration and castration legislation.[156] Society's compelling interest in the elimination of child sexual abuse through vigorous law enforcement has helped sway the balance away from defendants' rights.[157] Like several other countries that adopt an accusatorial model, the U.S. recognizes that children often suffer from court intervention[158] and has introduced legislation designed to protect children from the full rigors of the courtroom atmosphere.[159] These innovations include the provision of screens or closed-circuit television, and legal exceptions to permit the introduction of videotaped statements or other forms of hearsay.[160] Again, however, although these reforms may be available in theory, the practice of using innovative methods to protect children remains rare, particularly because defendants' rights still weigh heavily in decisions to protect children from in-court proceedings.[161] Given these limitations, perhaps more promising are the precourt preparation and empowerment programs offered to reduce the stresses on child witnesses.[162] Clearly, constitutional constraints place severe limitations on the use of innovative procedures. The predominant mode of resolving disputes limits innovations and the ability to use alternative approaches, even to the extent that, despite impressive reforms, commentators continue to view the legal system as hostile to child victims, and see existing structures of "proof" and evidence in law as inadequate to dealing with the crime and as actually leading to the denial of the existence of harm.[163]

The accusatorial systems present similar patterns in their attempt to deal with child sexual abuse and to make legal intervention more child-friendly. Reforms to accommodate child witnesses in court have occurred in three arenas: investigative interviewing, mandatory reporting, and preparation of children for court and courtroom accommodations. For example, these systems tend to implement innovative child witness techniques aimed to relax child competency laws and ease children's provision of testimony; they may, for example, use closed-circuit television or drop corroboration as a prerequisite for prosecution.[164] In addition, accusatorial systems are more likely to implement mandatory reporting laws to ensure societal intervention and are more likely to take punitive approaches. Regardless of the innovations, defendants' rights and family rights limit the use of innovations. Attempts to shield children from the rigors of the courtroom or to empower them to deal with courtroom demands remain attempts to ameliorate the decision to prosecute sex-offenders.[165] The systems are offender centered. Ironically, the success of innovative empowerment programs and child witness accommodations may encourage the view that criminal prosecution is the best or only way to respond to sexual abuse and thus may hamper the search for alternatives.[166]

Extralegal systems

Although it is difficult to imagine that some legal systems simply ignore or do not recognize sexual abuse, the majority of the world's children do not live in countries that could offer legal protection. For example, sexual abuse in developing countries remains relatively undocumented, uninvestigated, and essentially outside of legal arenas.[167] This does not mean, however, that the failure to recognize and formally react to child sexual abuse makes these countries nonillustrative. Although it would be unwise to reproduce western assumptions and ideas about sexual abuse as though they are universal and unquestionable, countries that are only beginning to recognize sexual abuse offer important insights.

The failed sociolegal recognition of child sexual abuse in India is illustrative. The extent to which child sexual abuse is a problem in India certainly remains unknown.[168] There are no accurate figures of the extent of child abuse simply "because incidents are neither reported nor punished."[169] Yet, one study of middle-class graduate students in Bombay reported that one of every three girls and one of every ten boys had been touched inappropriately or had had sexual intercourse with an adult relative or close family friend in childhood.[170] Again, where researchers inquire, there is an important percentage of individuals who recognize and willingly report abusive experiences.

Several beliefs play key roles in the failure to recognize and combat sexual abuse. Traditional themes of the sanctity of the family, prerogatives of parents, and children viewed as parental property have protected abusive families from societal inspection and intervention. To exacerbate matters, the failure to recognize the need for intervention makes the focus on intra-family child abuse even seem somewhat futile in the absence of intervention services, and given the failure to invest limited social service resources in preventive and parental education programs. To be sure, laws do protect children from neglect, exploitation, and cruelty. However, given the size of the child population in India (over 300 million below the age of sixteen),[171] the large majority of whom live in poverty, coupled with the country's limited financial resources, it is not realistic to meet the needs of children in especially difficult circumstances. Most resources simply aim to address the basic survival needs of children and families.

One recent observer reported that reforms are far from imminent.

Nothing in the literature or in discussions of directions for policy suggests use of the voice of children in the prosecution of perpetrators. There are no discussions of the need to accommodate child witnesses in the legal system; evidence "clearly suggests that child witnesses are not considered in the case of sexual abuse."[172] Sexually abused children remain largely invisible.

Preliminary conclusions regarding domestic legal interventions

Sociolegal responses to sexual abuse fall under two orientations that emerge from the way the problem is framed. Some systems perceive abuse as a problem of individual deviancy and responsibility while others tend to view abuses as dysfunctions that are responsive to services and public aid. The manner in which the problems are framed has considerable import. Intervention under the child protection model uses investigatory processes backed by legal powers of the state; in contrast, the therapeutic approach of the service-oriented systems uses members of the public authority as partners with families and children. Importantly, countries do not fit neatly into these two extremes, and countries often have various jurisdictions that adopt different approaches, which themselves are in a state of flux and constant development.[173] Existing differences reflect the social framing of abuses, and legal systems' attempts to accommodate.

Although remarkably different systems exist, it is important to note that they often produce similar results, both positive and negative. On a positive note, systems seem to provide similar protections. For example, the more legalistic, accusatorial systems tend to rely on mandatory reporting laws, while the family-focused systems do not. The absence of mandatory reporting systems does not mean that children are not protected: systems that reject reporting laws rely on well-developed and tightly knit social service networks in which children regularly come under professional surveillance of public service workers.[174] On a more negative note, one system formally protects children by excluding them from court appearances, while the other formally offers protective court systems yet excludes children by means of the very small number of prosecutions. Importantly, however, the former approach clearly aims to offer children protection while in their homes, without formal legal intervention. The extent to which the other system shelters children abused at home remains unknown.

The nature of the reasons for the paucity of prosecutions is actually most pronounced and best reflected in locales without systems. In these "systems," families are assumed to know what is best for their children, who belong to their families rather than being independent agents. The veil of family privacy and parental rights obstructs intervention. These factors clearly play important roles in other legal approaches to child sexual abuse: the inquisitorial systems aim to protect families and children from legal/criminal intervention, and the accusatorial systems must necessarily balance familial interests and defendants' rights with their attempt to uncover and react to instances of abuse.

Where progress seems to have been made to uncover abuses, the outcome of reforms remains to be determined. Laudable attempts aim to make systems more child-friendly, such as changes in competency and corroboration requirements of children's evidence, use of television links in courts, acceptance of videotaped evidence, and reduction of the waiting time for court hearings. Although impressive for their rapidity and exhaustive reach, several of the reforms have yet to be fully investigated, let alone enacted and actually used.

Whether inaction or reaction results from the recognition of child sexual abuse, all of the approaches necessarily rely on legal actors torn between conflicting roles: to protect children, to provide therapy, to maintain family structure, to investigate, and/or to punish offenders. For example, all the models seem to express antagonistic feelings toward direct state intervention into family life: the inquisitorial models deal with the antagonism by providing broad family support and voluntary services; the accusatorial models aim to provide strict legal rules for managing intervention into family life. The need to balance roles at implementation levels reflects what needs to be done at the larger policy level. The nature of the allocation of scarce resources importantly plays a key role in determining the response to child sexual abuse. If anything, our investigation thus far demonstrates that the allocation remains difficult; all systems leave entire groups of children at risk. These difficulties and seemingly inherent failures increase the urgency of considering alternative approaches, such as the one offered by international human rights law.

International Law's Formal Approach to Child Sexual Abuse

Given international law's venerable focus on inter-state behavior and state action, it is no surprise to find that child sexual abuse traditionally has not been a concern of international treaties. Yet, recent innovative treaties explicitly attempt to alleviate the plight of sexually abused children, even when those who maltreat admittedly do not act under state auspices. The international innovations aim to revision the role of states and individuals in the protection of children, all in an effort to re-image notions of childhood and child protection.

The international community offers its most explicit and innovative response to child sexual abuse in the Children's Convention. The Convention's Article 19 centers on the protection of children from sexual abuse while in the care of others, including parents and legal guardians.[175] The procedure Article 19 adopts to ensure protection from sexual abuse exemplifies well the international perspective. The international approach aims to protect children from sexual abuse by remedying familial and other problems that may contribute to abuse. To accomplish this goal, Article 19 places a duty on States Parties to establish, as appropriate, social programs that aim to prevent, identify, report, refer, and investigate cases of child sexual abuse. Article 19 also specifies that the programs for dealing with offenders are to be neither predominantly punitive nor the responsibility of any one state agency; e.g., judicial involvement is to be resorted to only "as appropriate."

Other important articles supplement Article 19. Most particularly, the Convention's Articles 34 and 35 mandate that States Parties "shall take all appropriate national, bilateral and multilateral measures to prevent" the inducement or coercion of a child to engage in any unlawful sexual activity and child abduction.[176] Equally important, Article 39 mandates that States Parties take all appropriate measures to promote the physical and psychological recovery and social reintegration of child victims.[177]

Taken at face value, the provisions provide very forceful statements that demand countries address child sexual abuse. Yet, the statements have not attracted commentaries. Exactly how countries are to piece together the provisions and interpret them in light of the Convention and other human rights principles remains to be determined. Although the Convention does remain flexible and somewhat vague, it still addresses important concerns and makes significant demands. Two mandates are particularly important to consider. The first demand moves international law beyond the focus on public, inter-nation action into more private intra-state action and seeks to influence the manner in which states treat individuals who maltreat others. The second demand involves the creation of child-centered systems.

Beyond the public/private divide

Full recognition of child sexual abuse as a denial of human rights faces a rather strong challenge. The recognition requires acceptance that a government can be made internationally accountable for the acts of private individuals within the home and community. This is not necessarily the role of international law. Traditional human rights law and norms assume imputability for *public* acts; violations of human rights law occur in the public arena and involve state action. In addition, international law clearly concerns itself with inter-nation actions, not necessarily national actions and the actions of individuals within those nations.[178] Yet, recent developments as well as commentaries about the proper role and nature of human rights law reveal a burgeoning redefinition of human rights. The developments both in the span of human rights and also in the methods of enforcing those rights already have been investigated in Chapter 2. It is important to move beyond that investigation to examine contentions that human rights law *may* reach private actions; for separation between private and public spheres remains problematic in terms of child protection: pervasive harms against children occur in the private sphere.[179] The recognition of the usual site of violence has led to increasing demands to invade that sphere, as reflected in the initiatives reviewed in the previous part of this chapter and in international human rights law initiatives discussed below.[180]

It would be difficult to argue that international law provides directly enforceable mandates that regulate private behavior. Although international law does remain concerned mostly with inter-state actions, several commentators have shown how international law expands its coverage to individuals, even to include the protection of individuals from family members.[181] These proposals rest on modern developments and reinterpretations of laws that actually do enhance prospects for state accountability for the actions of non-state actors.[182] Attempts to extend the reach of international law have come in several forms.[183]

The most common approach to reaching private actions focuses on theories of government agency and finds states responsible for violating explicit international duties. Interpretations of these obligations often point to *Velasquez-Rodriguez v. Honduras*.[184] In that case, the Inter-American Court commented on state tolerance of human rights violations in the form of torture, and stressed that illegal acts that breach human rights laws can lead to a *state's* international responsibility. According to the Court, the treaty in question imposed on ratifying States Parties two distinct obligations beyond abstention from violating guaranteed human rights: (1) prevention of violations by state and non-state actors, and (2) investigation and punishment of both state and private human rights infringements.[185] Such obligations derived from the text of the ratified treaty that required parties "to respect" the rights guaranteed in the document and to "ensure" to all persons their full and free exercise.[186] Importantly, though, a precondition that must be met before the *Velasquez-Rodriguez* principles can begin to bite involves the attribution to the state of some conduct that implies the nonperformance or active violation of an international duty; in this instance, it was an international treaty to which the country was a ratifying party. Despite that important limitation, the development reflects a move from concern with restraints on the exercise of state power, with limited affirmative duties for the protections, to a more generalized obligation of ensuring respect for human rights.[187]

It would seem imprudent to venture that *Velasquez-Rodriguez* sets a clear and broad principle that leads to the ready assumption of state responsibility for private acts. The case clearly is distinguishable from others that deal with purely domestic issues; it involved the torture of citizens from another country. It would be equally hazardous to conclude that the narrow approach to state action is inherent in international law and that governments cannot be held accountable by their failure to act. A notable case found that a country's development of a legal system that ignores part of violence against children may be held accountable. In the case of *X and Y v. Netherlands*, the European Court of Human Rights ruled Dutch criminal law inadequate in its failure to provide a remedy for a sixteen-year-old mentally retarded child who had been sexually abused. The failure to protect involved the denial of parents' right to initiate criminal proceedings. The court held that respect for family life includes positive obligations upon states and may require the adoption of measures designed to secure respect for private life, even in the sphere of individual relations.[188] Again, however, the facts and principles remain limited; yet the decisions by the oldest and most effective international human rights courts has led commentators to propose that the case holds major implications for the protection of individuals from each other, particularly from family members.[189]

Another important approach proposes that international law recognizes that *individuals* or private parties are capable of committing violations of human rights and that they can be held accountable. These proposals actually have considerable merit. Even the most traditionally recognized international human rights treaties note the duty of private individuals.[190] Although these attempts to hold individuals accountable face enormous challenges,[191] persons acting as agents of non-state entities can be held criminally accountable before courts of national and international jurisdictions if they have perpetrated serious violations of international humanitarian law.[192] These arguments are buttressed by the straightforward language of the Universal Declaration of Human Rights' preamble, which finds that individuals have duties to the community,[193] and by the recognition that various jurisdictions exist to prevent, punish, or compensate these violations. In this regard, even traditional international law recognizes that states have the obligation to take such steps as examining and adapting their policies at all levels, including legislation, case law and policy directives within the public and private sectors, educational curricula, media representations, etc. The extent to which international human rights law seeks to set standards for how Nation States treat persons within national jurisdictions is highlighted by the constant questioning of international law's legitimacy to interfere with individual nations' sovereignty through limiting the ways in which nations can act domestically.

Another approach to dealing with the distinction between private and public focuses less on the need to challenge the traditional conceptions concerning international human rights law and more on the contention that it no longer remains viable to cling to the traditional view that human rights violations only exist in terms of public state action. These commentaries suggest that human rights problems require private intervention and mandate holding individuals accountable. International documents increasingly and more explicitly point to the need to reach private action. These developments provide evidence of the future direction of international law, as exemplified in the more recent Children's Convention,[194] Women's Convention,[195] and Convention against Racial Discrimination.[196] The developments are even more explicit in recent declarations that formally deal with violence. For example, the definition of violence in article 1 of the 1993 Declaration on Violence Against Women explicitly covers violence "in public or private life" and under article 4(c) States must punish acts of violence against women whether perpetrated by the State or by private persons.[197] These developments represent a forward-thinking conceptualization and stress the crucial importance of collapsing the private/public boundaries in human rights law.[198]

The issue that remains, then, is not whether international rights apply in the private sphere, but rather which rights apply, when they apply, and to what extent.[199] The Children's Convention and other international documents clearly indicate that child sexual abuse falls within the rights that could be protected. As in the case of other forms of violence, states' duties seem two-pronged. States are firstly under a duty to prevent such violations and further, if such violations occur, then they are obliged to investigate and punish them.[200] In states which do not investigate a persistent pattern of more severe forms of violence and do not have adequate civil remedies and criminal prosecutions, victims of such violence may have a cause of action under human rights treaties which allow individuals to petition either for breaches of inhuman and degrading treatment or for breaches in their private life.[201] Importantly, the Children's Convention arguably reinforces states' responsibility for intra-familial abuse both by clearly bringing intra-familial child abuse into the public sphere through Article 19 and also by extending the state's duty beyond identification, investigation, and prosecution to prevention. As a matter of international law, states have a duty to put in place an effective legal system that does not tolerate child sexual abuse. This approach moves away from the search for state actors toward protection and reparation for those who suffer human rights violations. The approach recognizes the changes in conceptions of "state" and addresses private threats from individuals and private structures, and the climates private actors create and help facilitate. In the end, the issue becomes not whether sexual abuse falls under the power of international law, but rather what kind of system international law mandates.

The international mandate to create child-centered systems

Although commentators have discussed how international law prescribes changes in the way countries approach cultural practices deemed maltreating and those that relate to sexual exploitation, commentators have failed to explore more precisely what international law mandates in terms of protections from sexual abuse as conceptualized and more commonly experienced in the West.[202] Likewise, even commentators who explore sexual abuse from the more traditional domestic perspectives generally fail to address how legal systems could be created to better respond to child sexual abuse.[203] Yet, commentators on both international and domestic laws champion the development of "child-centered" systems.[204] Such systems actually are not difficult to imagine. Systems would consist of the following qualities, all of which emphasize the primary needs of the child victim as articulated in the Children's Convention. First, child-oriented child protection efforts would place priority on the prevention, treatment, remediation, and support needs of children. Second, systems would respect the child's family and recognize the importance of even abusive ties.[205] Lastly, when prosecution would be deemed necessary, systems would provide supportive services to children throughout the various phases: investigation, prosecution, treatment, and remediation.

The apparent simplicity and attractiveness of a child-centered approach to child sexual abuse is somewhat deceptive. Taken seriously, it involves taking a rather radical stance. Most fundamentally, it means rethinking the investigative, prosecutorial zeitgeist that currently preoccupies several child protection systems, especially in their approaches to sexual abuse.[206] Likewise, it means reconsidering how efforts that focus mainly on treatment tend to ignore the potential role of the criminal justice system and may leave children at risk in families, even when officials know that parents are sexually abusive.[207] Given the above discussion about different countries' efforts, the balance appears rather difficult. But broad social policy could be more responsive to the silent ecology of child sexual abuse and could better address what we know about the causes, prevention, and outcomes of sexual abuse.

An important step would be to move toward both recognizing other social ills and appropriately reacting to all forms of sexual maltreatment. In terms of reacting to sexual abuse, our review suggests that focusing on sexual maltreatment and sleuthing underemphasizes the social construction of children's problems.[208] The narrow focus leads to the public misperception that children's problems do not run deeper and wider than sexual maltreatment. The broader focus on children assists in efforts to rethink intervention and would allow us to merge the consideration of child sexual abuse with that of other childhood problems. Research indicates that the sexually abusive experience is only one event that requires treatment;[209] sexual abuse seldom appears without some other mistreatment, especially physical neglect or abuse, and these combinations have more problematic outcomes.[210] Likewise, given what we know about the very wide range of outcomes, it is not surprising that some forms of sexual abuse may even have a less negative impact on children than other forms of abuse, particularly physical abuse and verbal abuse.[211] In terms of recognizing abuse, social policy could better allow for recognition of abuses that do not fit into recognized offense stereotypes. This is particularly significant in that abusive experiences that do not fit into such stereotypes receive little attention; they are invisible.[212] Indeed, this often encourages victims to mold their reports of abuse into stereotypically abusive behaviors,[213] which results in discrediting their abuse. In short, the proposed child-centered approach focuses on individual needs and allows for effectively recognizing and dealing with the complex nature of child maltreatment.

Another necessary step would be to challenge current moral attitudes attached to sexual maltreatment. For example, if the goal is to protect children, there should, in some circumstances, be more flexibility in prosecutorial and offender punishment goals. This approach should reach beyond innovative diversion and treatment programs already in existence[214] and move toward proposals for much-needed prevention efforts[215] and innovative intervention techniques championed by professionals who deal with child sexual abuse.[216] Given the difficulty of helping children protect themselves, other primary and secondary intervention programs offer considerable promise. These efforts begin by altering the "normative standards that create an environment in [which] child sexual abuse can flourish."[217] It would, for example, move beyond abhorrence that leads to the denial, under-reporting, and underdetection of abuse, particularly in cases of mothers and fathers abusing their sons.[218]

It would also make sense to reconsider how to deal with offenders. Given the emerging societal and legal responses, it increasingly does not make sense for offenders and potential offenders to seek assistance. A person must first commit an offense, be identified, and be labeled as an offender before assistance can be offered or, more likely, mandated.[219] Proposals for more flexible interventions are not without empirical support. Recent studies examining offender diversion programs report that, at least for intra-family abuse, avoiding legal intervention altogether leads to better outcomes for both offenders and victims.[220] Offender recidivism research also reveals that community-based programs tend to be more successful than those run within institutions,[221] and that communities are not at greater risk for sexual offenses when selected sexual offenders are permitted to remain in the community and participate in treatment.[222] In addition, research suggests that involuntary treatment does not seem to be effective with sex offenders, although it does tend to be successful with other forms of child maltreatment.[223] Although the approaches to therapy remain controversial, recent reports reject confrontational techniques because they may be antitherapeutic and push offenders further away from contemplating and taking responsibility for potential changes in their own behavior.[224] Other research also reveals that involuntary treatment tends to be counterproductive: Therapists in a widely cited study about a sex offender treatment program found that clients' revelations of incidents of sexual abuse stopped after a mandatory reporting law went into effect.[225] This has led commentators to suggest a return to somewhat more flexible standards for reporting past abuse and for involving the criminal justice system.[226] Proposals for more flexibility receive support from studies from other countries: jurisdictions which have adopted flexible approaches to cooperating with police report that *self* referrals for child sexual abuse perpetration have increased dramatically.[227] In further support for reconsidering approaches that ignore therapeutic efforts, evidence suggests that programs that provide support for parents who seek to protect children in confidence gain increasing popularity. Such programs provide children immediate protection, do not disrupt the child's relationships with nonabusing individuals, and, more importantly, support nonabusing parents—the factor most often identified as critical to positive outcomes for abused children.[228] Lastly, dire need for reform that moves toward therapeutic models arises from the simple fact that even the most aggressive criminal justice approach tends to be *lenient*. In the U.S., research indicates that those actually convicted of child sex offenses have low incarceration rates[229] and, on average, get sentences that do not average more than four years, while relevant statutes specify sentences of twenty years or more.[230]

Even without changes in attitudes toward offenders and without taking a broader view of child welfare, progress could be made to ensure that child services could make a difference. It is difficult to argue that victims receive their fair share of services, particularly in accusatorial systems. First, almost half of the *substantiated* cases of abuse receive no formal intervention.[231] Indeed, the amount of appropriate treatment offered has been so minimal that, in a recent review of the literature, leading researchers concluded that most children essentially treat themselves![232] Second, the children who do end up in treatment *and* subsequently have their abuse reported tend to suffer for it: evidence suggests that reporting suspected abuse both disrupts treatment and increases the risks to children. This contention finds support from research finding negative effects of disclosing sexual abuse, both for children[233] and adults.[234] It is further supported by the high number of mandated reporters who, when confronted with some abusive situations, question the utility of official intervention and refuse to report.[235] Third, research concerning what actually happens to children when allegations of child sexual abuse are made reveals that systems do not necessarily work in children's interests. For example, one important analysis revealed that (1) it remains almost impossible to determine whether abuse occurred or not; (2) evidence suggesting that abuse had occurred does not predict whether prosecution or other services are provided; and (3) the factors that do predict service provision were simply whether services were available and the "safe parent" suggested such services.[236] This type of research suggests that conclusions or findings about abuse may actually be based on decision-making practices rather than on actual cases of maltreatment.[237] The policy-oriented literature reveals repeated attempts to design and implement intervention strategies that do not necessarily reflect recipients' needs.[238] Fourth, to the extent to which resource-led organizational decisions are made, they vary considerably in different systems. The filtering process is perhaps more obvious and extreme in the criminal justice system. In terms of prosecution, the evidence clearly indicates that prosecutors rely heavily on whether victims make "good witnesses" and whether prosecutions could be obtained on the strength of the evidence.[239] The results of all these studies and commentaries support an increasing number of proposals charging that systems, except in a minority of cases, work on detection and prediction, rather than responding to children's actual harms and injuries.[240]

In the final analysis, child protection from the child-centered approach means envisioning a child protection movement that accomplishes its goals by fostering a community that educates itself in the diverse ways it can protect its children. The most effective way this can be accomplished is through focusing on the moral responsibility of every adult to protect children. Recognizing community responsibility in child protection is far from a novel suggestion: it is what the children's rights movement asks of us.

To be sure, adopting a child-centered child protection system poses considerable legal challenges, regardless of the country that seeks to adopt it. At its core, any child protection system necessarily must resolve fundamental tensions between individual freedom and the efforts of the state to protect its young citizens by setting standards for acceptable behavior that all citizens legitimately expect.[241] The rights most often in conflict in child sexual abuse cases are those of parents or caretakers versus those of the abused child, coupled with the state's *parens patriae* power to intervene in families to protect children.[242] The general rule currently used by countries that tend to be most reticent about direct, coercive family intervention mediates this conflict to the advantage of children. The United States Supreme Court highlighted children's rights rather well: Although parents may become martyrs if they like, they are not "free . . . to make martyrs of their children."[243] The state's delegation of responsibility to parents is conditional. Thus, parental rights and powers are concomitants of public duties and obligations; all aim to ensure children's interests.

Despite its clarity, the general rule leaves considerable and important discretion in cases not involving extremes of abuse. In light of the children's rights movement, this is a rather significant concern for several reasons. First, intervention could be encouraged since family jurisprudence could give less weight to the right to family privacy. Second, it could be less difficult to take a child's perspective if both legisprudence and jurisprudence would bestowed rights upon children, rather than giving family rights to parents.[244] Third and far from complete, the recognition of socioeconomic rights would begin to ensure more comprehensive support for children, families, and communities.[245] These three changes would reflect well the new significance attached to ensuring greater respect for children's self-determination and supporting greater awareness of the need to increase children's participation in cultural life; the changes also parallel suggestions for dealing with forms of maltreatment identified in previous chapters.

Admittedly, the above proposals ask for dramatic shifts in child welfare policy-making, regardless of whether legal systems follow accusatorial or inquisitorial approaches. Yet, even without these possible changes, it is important to recall that child protection always will remain fraught with discretionary action, principally because policies are implemented by individuals who vary significantly in their underlying assumptions and interpretations of policy.[246] Ensuring that street-level implementation takes children's perspectives more seriously would be an important step. Although legislatures, courts, and other law-making and law-interpreting bodies may promulgate minimal standards, it is clear that policy responses are free to offer greater protections and to move beyond providing minimal services.[247] All street-level implementors possess discretion and can help recognize and push children's agendas.

Limits of international law's child-centered systems

Although it is easy to become impassioned with possibilities, it is important to recognize that enormous obstacles limit responses to child welfare issues. Despite comprehensive plans endorsed by the international community and despite expanded private duties, it would be unwise to play down the enormous obstacles to proper implementation. Although necessary, comprehensive and flexible programs remain difficult to implement. Given the lack of important findings and the controversial nature of some programs, it would be unwise to embark on an immediate exportation of U.S. and other Western countries' approaches to combatting sexual abuse, whether they are based on accusatorial or inquisitorial models. Precisely where and how to place resources and emphases largely remain empirically and morally contested issues that only have begun to be addressed.[248] The extent to which controversies remain, high rates of abuse continue, and reform efforts meet resistance reveals two important points: the need for societal transformations and the demands international human rights law places on the West. These points significantly highlight how the human rights movement seeks to transform all societies, and underscore the difficulty of doing so.

If there are any lessons to be learned from the West, it undoubtedly is the difficulty of enacting more comprehensive reforms. As we have seen, existing legal approaches to assisting child victims of sexual abuse all necessarily have costs and leave children unprotected. Although both legal models investigated above have been criticized, the problems inherent in the accusatorial model have been the most documented. For example, the United States' accusatorial approach to sexual abuse has been criticized for its excessively reactive and prosecutorial focus. The U.S. Advisory Board on Child Abuse and Neglect[249] recently reinforced the criticism by noting how a reactive ethos reverberates throughout the child protection system and ultimately affects research and policy alternatives. The criticisms have considerable merit. Research efforts intended to shape future policies to prevent child sexual maltreatment remain narrowly focused. Instead of more appropriately focusing on the effects of interventions on children, extensive research focuses on child witnesses and on whether reporters comply with legal mandates.[250] Likewise, the narrow focus results in the considerable lack of research examining the effects of child sexual abuse: the short- and long-term effects of maltreatment are only now being made the focus of large-scale research programs.[251] Lastly, the deleterious effects of a narrow focus are felt most profoundly in preventative research: research concerned with prevention is only starting to move beyond focusing solely on children to focusing on offenders, families, and other community members.[252] Although research points to the need for more proactive policies and comprehensive approaches, it remains unclear how they could be adapted to accusatorial models characteristic of the U.S. system. In addition, it remains unclear how comprehensive approaches can assist children in countries that use inquisitorial models: their rates of child sexual abuse seemingly are as high and it is unclear how they actually protect children by focusing on limiting the role of direct, coercive interventions in families.

To exacerbate matters, leading commentators suggest that legalism and proceduralism do not necessarily have their intended impact. For example, as procedures become more complex, detailed, and wide-ranging, the chance of making procedural mistakes increases. The result is that attention shifts away from making the *right* decision to taking a *defensible* action.[253] The observation is particularly accurate in light of a series of incidents in which the methods of medical and social services authorities have been fiercely criticized for inappropriate investigations of child sexual maltreatment.[254] The criticism also is accurate in light of the use of reforms. For example, the use of videotaped investigations means that investigations aim toward production of videos even though it remains far from clear that videos spare children from getting therapeutic support prior to proceedings, prevent children from having to give evidence-in-chief in person, or increase the possibility that prosecutions will actually be made.[255] Likewise, the highly touted focus on having professionals who have the most contact with children—school personnel—report suspicions of abuse results in a relatively small portion of reports and in only limited compliance.[256]

In addition to the difficulty of enacting more comprehensive reforms, it remains to be seen how broad social development and family support policies can be implemented. Indeed, it is disappointing to note that the focus on broad social supports has yet to result in the implementation of more comprehensive policies in individual Nation States. Although reports from other countries reveal similar experiences,[257] trends in the United States are again illustrative. For instance, while the 1980s were characterized by a strong concern for child sexual abuse,[258] that decade (and the one following) also has been characterized by an unprecedented erosion of social services for children, particularly in the areas of health care, economic supports, and social services.[259] To exacerbate matters, the erosion of services continues at a time in which traditional supports for families continue to erode.[260] Importantly, critics of the movement to support and serve children in families propose that the effort actually is designed to legitimize resource rationing.[261] Trends toward undermining family supports stand in direct opposition to the international approach's focus on preventing abuse by, for example, supporting families and communities.

In addition to the continued need to generate enough societal will to enact appropriately comprehensive reforms, the international approaches are not without limitations themselves. These limitations act as barriers to implementing human rights. Arguably the most serious weakness in the international approach to child sexual abuse concerns its failure to state explicitly the nature of the rights of children *vis à vis* other rights, particularly those of adults. Although it is true that no adult has the right to mistreat children, other rights conflict to the extent that they make it difficult to uncover abuse, hamper the recognition of some forms of abuses, and result in the failure to provide resources to help prevent and alleviate abuse. The conflicts between emerging rights is important to emphasize. Rhetorically, the notion of rights is appealing. Yet, it can be misleading: no sensible right can be indifferent to other rights.

Perhaps the most critical legal analysis that still remains absent relates to the child's right to protection from sexual abuse as it conflicts with the firmly established family right to privacy.[262] Programs aimed at family intrusion and child protection indelibly affect a family's right to privacy, especially since the best protection against child sexual abuse arguably is to make families more public and to allow increased community monitoring of families.[263] Yet the intervention can become precarious and can lead to societal backlash against child protection efforts.[264] Regardless of the validity of either approach to child protection (inquisitorial versus accusatorial intrusion in families), Nation States only have begun to disentangle the relevant rights. For example, although the U.S. is known for its investigative focus, its constitutionally based procedural rules that govern child abuse investigations actually remain unsettled.[265] Likewise, other countries, most notably New Zealand,[266] recently have refused to mandate reporting suspicions of child maltreatment largely on the grounds that it may lead to excessive intrusion into the private domain of family life. Although research does reveal the danger that vague reporting mandates pose for family integrity,[267] it is difficult to imagine how firmly prohibiting intrusions into family life will ultimately benefit children.

Relatedly, even the more therapeutic approaches are not immune from criticisms. Despite more intensive research and growing number of allegations, professionals around the world lack reliable and accepted techniques for evaluating children's allegations.[268] Yet, intervention and labelling continues and actually becomes critical to determining the eventual outcomes of instances of abuse. Researchers note how victimization that becomes recognized by professionals makes children the target of mental health labelling and "special needs" designations. One leading critic appropriately expresses frustration and suggests how these efforts threaten to lead to iatrogenic effects. She notes that the act of incest leads to heightened scrutiny of children for any nonconformity, rebelliousness, or dispute with the system. The child then comes under surveillance for symptoms, and even normal responses to childhood upheaval may be interpreted as clinical symptoms of the child's pathologies.[269] Although there is no question that an understanding presence offers some children benefit, the commentator still proposes that "the dominant emphasis on the language of pathology, treatment, and therapy as the primary social response to incest, actually isolates and marginalizes victims—even while announcing that 'you are not alone.' "[270] The language transforms efforts to help into "an emphasis on pacification, on deflecting attention from all larger social meanings."[271] The lack of focus on larger social meanings and influences is rather critical to consider. It runs the danger of isolating the family from broader influences. These attitudes are becoming especially prominent in the re-privatization of family life.[272]

The therapeutic model that focuses on voluntary action also poses significant disadvantages. Without investigations, for example, it is likely that cases will remain undiscovered and children will be denied protection.[273] Importantly, it is not only the fear of compulsory state action that hampers disclosure of abuse; abuse remains uncovered because of the nature of abusive relationships, particularly the fear instilled in victims and the normalization of abuse. Equally critical is the concern that a strategy based on confidentiality and without recourse to criminal law does not provide protection for other children who may be abused. Yet, although insufficient evidence justifies a complete shift to other services, it does not negate the proposal that a self-referral-based system could play a role alongside more prosecutorial approaches.

Lastly, the focus on private families as the source of problem behavior and as the site for intervention, prevention, and policing tends to ignore what recent commentators emphasize as heterosexist and ethnocentric assumptions of family life. Any family's definition and boundaries inevitably connect with wider institutions and practices, such as images of the state. What becomes problematic in the positioning of families as the primary site for the socialization of children is that it works to exonerate the state from its responsibilities. The sociocultural influences that construct the family unit remain largely ignored. The failure results in the inability to recognize how family organization connects with cultural, economic, and political issues.

In addition to problems inherent in focusing on private families, there remains the problem of recognizing the extent of child sexuality. Struggles in sex education and conflicting beliefs about child sexuality best indicate the reluctance to accept child sexuality. Recent initiatives have had doubtful success.[274] After studying children aged five to fifteen years in four cultures, one study concluded that "One fact is abundantly clear. Children perceive it is the adults who have hang-ups about sex, and adults who deliberately or unconsciously withhold the information and knowledge the children seek."[275] Surprisingly, the adults are not necessarily withholding information; they may not have the information. Our understanding of the development of inappropriate sexual age preferences remains limited, despite the well-documented interest children have in sexual activities[276] and emerging research indicating how basic knowledge about sexuality enhances children's development and self-image.[277] The failed understanding is intensified by the inability to transform public preference for punitive approaches to sexual abuse,[278] and by the difficulty of establishing intervention priorities between professional groups who have direct contact with offenders and victims.[279]

Conclusions

The international statement addressing child sexual abuse is remarkable for its lack of specificity. Yet, the new mandates are rather significant. The international community actually seeks to ensure that states develop programs to deal with sexual abuse. This mandate presents a rather radical departure from traditional international law that regulated how nations behaved, not individuals' private behaviors. Equally remarkable is the way the protections actually complement well our current understanding of ways to deal with sexual abuse. The international approach appropriately reinforces the need to refocus on broad-based efforts that reinforce the number of institutions and people responsible for child protection and focus on diverse sources and forms of maltreatment. Only by increasing broader accountability can we understand, prevent, and appropriately deal with the negative effects of sexual maltreatment. The focus on encouraging a more flexible approach to victims' and perpetrators' needs is one of the most promising aspects of international efforts to combat sexual abuse. Viewed in this light, the Convention and recent international developments appear to be rather exceptional statements regarding children's right to be protected from sexual abuse.

Although international law has taken decisive steps, the extent to which it can be integrated with current systems presents unique challenges. For example, inquisitorial systems greatly emphasize the protection of families from criminal and other formal legal intervention, and focus on protecting children from judicial and criminal justice processes, even to the extent that children simply will be excluded or will be given the option to exclude themselves. Likewise, in those systems, children's best interests relate firmly to family preservation, whether it is formally stated or simply the practical outcome of systems that do not criminally pursue the prosecution of sex crimes against children. In the accusatorial model, efforts increasingly are aimed at uncovering instances of abuse and prosecuting offenders, as revealed by several reforms devised to accommodate child witnesses in court proceedings; yet the innovations and their use remain limited by defendants' rights, family rights, and the lack of resources.[280] In countries that have yet to legally address the sexual abuse of children, the obstacles are equally great. Although these countries may have taken strides toward ensuring justice for children, profound difficulties in providing even basic life necessities largely override concerns about sexual abuse. Despite truly remarkable and rapid developments aimed at responding to child sexual abuse, then, efforts remain constrained and limited. The extent to which child sexual maltreatment research leads to the conclusion that sleuthing and criminalization efforts, including the procedural reforms they have generated, remain somewhat misguided; efforts that focus on therapeutic, limited intervention are not necessarily child-friendly either. The conundrum continues: increased societal concern and legal reforms matched by continued failure to protect children.

Forging a strategy that respects children's rights requires societies to rethink their basic concern: protecting children from sexual abuse. In efforts to rethink societal attempts to protect children, it would be fruitful to recall what the broader human rights movement is all about. The movement attempts to rebuild a sense of moral and social obligation, of mutuality, of citizenship, and of community. In terms of children's rights, the effort simply aims to promote a greater sense of collective responsibility as the basis for welfare provisions by rebuilding common interests in cooperative social relations that are based on reciprocity, trust, and democratic principles. These developments project a rather different image of state action than that of the different existing legal approaches to child sexual abuse. The state is not only in the business of providing goods and services that the market undersupplies within a scheme that specifies citizen's entitlements and enforcement agencies. The state seeks to promote a sense of valued membership, sharing, and protection from all forms of harms. The vision for approaching the sexual abuse of children, then, asks that *all* societies transform their approach to children and their maltreatment; human rights laws demand universal reform and no society is immune to their reach.

7 | Abuse by Young Offenders

Although young offenders actually commit some of the most frequent forms of child maltreatment, their behaviors have yet to be fully recognized by domestic legal systems and international law. Despite that failure, children's human rights law may be marshalled to assist child victims and human rights law may help better address offending behavior. The following discussion suggests that international law now mandates that societies address a broad variety of practices perpetrated by children and suggests that even the most radical conceptions of children's rights have yet to recognize the need for transformations in laws regulating children's access to legal systems and social service delivery. Although the aspects of sexual maltreatment presented in this chapter undoubtedly remain the least recognized and most controversial, attempts to address the practices provide the greatest hope for the alleviation of child sexual maltreatment as experienced and conceived in the West.

Introduction

Children and adolescents can commit sexually abusive acts similar to those perpetrated by adults against children and other adults. Commentators and researchers who examine sexual offending by children generally describe three types of offenses.[1] The first involves passive or noncontact offenses, such as obscene phone calls, exhibitionism, and voyeurism. The second group of offenses includes contacts and some degree of force, aggression, or coercion, such as rape, fondling, and attempted rape. Pedophiliac offenses constitute the last form, which are sexual acts perpetrated against younger victims. Although offenders' actions tend not to be limited to one category, and although all categories have been the subject of research, research dealing with young sex offenders generally pays most attention to the third category. Youth who offend against younger children are the ones most likely to be identified and apprehended through juvenile justice or social service systems.[2] Although the acts included in the young pedophiliac category have long been identified and treated as sexually abusive,[3] there has been a burgeoning interest in other forms of abusive acts that do not fit neatly into the first two categories, yet still are sexual in nature and control victim's sexuality and sexual behavior. Although discussions of juvenile sex offending and discussions of child sexual abuse generally do not deal with these other practices, offenses committed by juveniles may include peer sexual harassment, dating violence, and sexual assault by acquaintances. Despite the general failure to include these practices as part of the abuses children suffer, responses to these forms of maltreatment are rapidly changing and reflect a move toward greater recognition of their nature, extent, and consequences. This chapter includes these practices for four practical reasons. The three forms of maltreatment involve a significant amount of abuse, present developmental precursors to later victimization, provide an opportune time for intervention, and involve practices that still tend to be deemed part of normative development by victims, perpetrators, and society.

In addition to practical reasons for adopting a broad approach to the forms of sexually abusive acts perpetrated by juveniles, the approach makes sense from a human rights perspective. Three major developments support the interpretation that international law demands that societies address practices involving offending against peers and younger children. First, as we have seen, the international movement to respect children's rights no longer permits the inappropriate and coercive control of children's sexuality and sexual behavior. As the discussion will suggest, the failure to address offending against children by juveniles results in a failure to respect each individual's inherent dignity and self-determination—the foundational rights of modern human rights law. Second, practices that support, tolerate, or ignore a broad range of sexual offenses committed by young offenders structure social relationships that eventually will produce adults who perpetrate violence toward children and other adults. Since addressing these forms of violence is necessary in the eventual reduction of sexual maltreatment rates, international law's new mandates that aim to prevent and respond to child sexual maltreatment require societies to take all appropriate steps to respond, even to the "maximum extent of their resources."[4] Third, developments in young offenders' rights mandate not only that offenders receive protection from arbitrary interference with their rights, but also that societies assist in these offenders' reintegration into society and help prevent the development of conditions that lead to victimization.

To address the human rights involved in child sexual maltreatment perpetrated by young offenders, the chapter first delineates the nature of the various forms of abuses, starting with the least recognized and ending with the most researched and accepted as problematic by society. Thereafter, the discussion focuses on the extent to which sociolegal systems have responded appropriately to the existence and nature of the various forms of abuse. Given that the practices involve new areas of policy-making, the analysis focuses on the United States, with few references to recent research and legal recognition in other countries. The analysis reveals a general failure to respond and appropriately recognize the varieties of maltreatment. The forms that have been addressed reveal that the responses to youth sexual offending are uneven; this requires the chapter to provide some technically specific analyses in some instances and simply broad analyses in others. In addition, the discussion indicates that these forms of violence have not been addressed directly by commentaries or instruments dealing with international human rights. Given these failures, the chapter concludes with an analysis of how the international movement to ensure children's rights can serve to guide future responses to peer maltreatment and juvenile pedophiliac offending. It is important to emphasize that the analysis remains exploratory and moves considerably beyond the current purview and even discussions of international law. Despite that caution, the presentation highlights how the international children's rights movement demands that societies address these forms of maltreatment.

Varieties of Sexual Abuse Perpetrated by Adolescents and Children

Adolescents and young children perpetrate a wide range of sexually abusive behaviors. This section presents the nature of some of the most common forms of abuse and general trends in sociolegal responses. The analysis highlights how victims, perpetrators, and society tend to view the abusive and coercive acts as normative, part of a "normal" pattern of gender role formation and child sexual behavior. The misperception contributes to the pervasively invisible nature of peer abuse and the harms suffered by child victims. Although the forms of abuse presented generally are not recognized as abusive events,[5] available research suggests that there is a move toward greater recognition, a need to reconsider the place of coercive experiences in child development, and a need to rethink the nature of intervention and prevention in order to face the challenges presented by abusive experiences that occur in children's everyday rela-tionships and which have significant developmental influences.[6]

Adolescent dating violence

THE NATURE OF DATING VIOLENCE

Juveniles suffer physical, psychological, and sexual abuse in their sexual relationships that constitute what others label domestic violence or spousal battering when perpetrated by adults.[7] Unlike other analyses of sexual abuse, this presentation includes these practices for four rea-sons. The first reason for inclusion is the extent to which this form of violence constitutes a significant part of several adolescent relationships. Approximately one out of ten high school students experiences physical violence in his or her romantic relationships.[8] This is a high number, par-ticularly when analyzed from the perspective of those who are involved in relationships: between 20 and 30 percent of adolescents who are dating report violence in their current relationships[9] and over 35 percent of adult men *and* women who recall their dating experiences report that they have inflicted *and* sustained physical violence.[10] The second reason dating violence is critical to consider in analyses of sexual abuse derives from the major finding that battering in relationships controls children's sexual behavior and their sexuality. The control is so extensive that vic-tims often profess "love" for abusers, defend abusers even after severe beatings, blame themselves for the abuse done to them, and deny or minimize the threatening nature of the abuse.[11] For example, almost half of dating violence victims report that their partner's violence was at least "somewhat justified,"[12] a similarly high percentage take responsibility for initiating violence,[13] and an equal number expect the relationship to continue.[14] The third reason is that victims of dating violence report high rates of injury. In a comprehensive study of dating violence across North Carolina, for example, researchers found that nearly 70 percent of girls and over half of the boys who said they had been in violent relationships had also sustained injuries.[15] The last major reason to consider dating violence relates to the issue of control, but emphasizes that the control poses special risks for juvenile victims and contributes to the develop-ment of maladaptive patterns that allow victimization and offending to continue, even into other relationships. The nature of control and the special vulnerability of children are worthy of elaboration, for they but-tress proposals for treating these practices as significant rights violations.

Control has long been identified as the major area of concern in dealing with violent relationships. Researchers argue that the tendency of battered victims to blame themselves, protect abusers, and remain in violent relationships reflects the building of traumatic bonds to abusers.[16] The concept of traumatic bonding is particularly important in considerations of juvenile relationships. Some adolescent victims, like individuals in psychologically comparable "hostage" situations (abused children, battered women, cult members, prisoners of war, etc.) adopt a survival strategy that further commits them to abusive relationships.[17] Evidence suggests that adolescents may be at higher risk for traumatic bonding: adolescence is marked by extreme conformity to gender roles, dependency on relationships, and conformity to peer pressure to be involved in relationships.[18] Social dependency and emotional attachment cement the hold to batterers, a pattern similar to those of adult victims who are emotionally and financially dependent on abusers.[19] Importantly, during adolescence, boys cling as much to relationships as girls do, even though, unlike adult women, girls perpetrate more mild, moderate, and severe violence, even when researchers control for self-defense.[20]

In addition to the nature of abusive relationships, what we know about the adolescent period indicates that it provides an environment conducive to maltreatment. First, adolescent life involves testing limits of self-control and risk-taking, which leads to experimentation with alcohol and other practices that increase the risk of relationship violence.[21] Second, adolescence is characterized by a general detaching from families;[22] this places youth in precarious positions. Victims may be unable or unwilling to ask for assistance from their families, even when relationships take abusive turns.[23] Even if adolescents do seek assistance, they may not be taken seriously. Adults typically minimize the bonding of adolescent relationships, expect that youth can break bonds and date others, and fail to realize that youth could be involved in violent relationships.[24]

In addition to the nature of the adolescent period, the nature of adolescent relationships also places youth at risk. Romantic relationships tend to be highly passionate, exciting, and possessive.[25] Because adolescents are necessarily inexperienced in these relationships, they may not possess the ability to handle the intense feelings. For example, the intensity of feelings may lead to interpreting jealousy as a normal way to express love and to the failure to recognize problems. Adolescents are particularly prone to experiencing "normative confusion": what happens in their relationships establishes what is normal, and their abusive relationships are experienced as neither problematic nor intolerable.[26] Proneness to normative confusion suggests that adolescents may not possess the "maturity" to deal with complex problems that may arise in relationships.[27] In addition, courtships actually may be inherently violent: studies of "normal" high school dating relationships, for example, find that over 50 percent report physical violence, over 95 percent report psychological violence, and over 15 percent report forced sexual activity.[28] Researchers attribute much of the process of courtship violence to the normal working out of relationship difficulties such as jealousy, rejection, and breaking up.[29]

Although the nature of adolescent relationships may increase youth's vulnerability to relationship violence, certain types of relationships may compound the risk. For example, research indicates that gay and lesbian youth report difficulty in obtaining assistance.[30] Likewise, researchers have long noted that the risk of violence to both adult and adolescent women either begins or intensifies when boyfriends learn of pregnancy.[31] Pregnancy, motherhood, and homosexual orientations exacerbate risks for maltreatment simply because adolescents experiencing them have fewer resources than adults, and the judgments and blaming received from adults and peers increase these youths' reluctance to seek assistance. Given the lack of support, the circumstances contribute to these adolescent victims' sense of helplessness and isolation, and increase their dependency on abusing partners.

Research that examines reasons young batterers offend also highlights factors that warrant concern for violence in juvenile relationships. Three areas of research are especially informative. The first area of research focuses on social influences that particularly impact adolescents, such as the encouragement and approval adolescent batterers receive from the media and friends. These researchers argue that peers and the media instill the belief that men should dominate women in relationships and that men have the right to use aggressive behavior.[32] The second research area suggests that adolescent relationship violence simply results from learned, maladaptive behavior. This research indicates that parental abusive behavior and domestic violence place youth at risk for perpetrating domestic violence, both as adolescent victims and as victimizers.[33] The last general form of research centers more on relationships themselves and highlights how the dynamics of abuse lead abusers to define and experience violence as rewarding. For example, being in control increases one's self-esteem and allows for the use of revenge for real or imagined wrongs. Likewise, repeated emotional and physical violence tends to ensure that victims will comply with demands. This self-reinforcing pattern is likely to continue, especially since adolescent batterers may not experience negative consequences that might motivate them to alter their behavior.[34]

Emerging approaches to understanding the perpetration of adolescent battering are significant. The vulnerability of youth to particular social influences, the developmental roots of antisocial behavior, the dynamics of violent relationships, and the failed societal recognition of adolescent relationship violence all contribute to the perpetuation of battering. These factors complement the previously discussed literature on factors that contribute to the victimization of adolescents: lack of dating experience, increase in peer pressure, need to conform to gender role expectations, the vicissitudes of normal adolescence, and the nature of romantic relationships. These approaches importantly locate personal violence in a larger social context. The structure of emotional relationships and violence between intimates relates to the structure of social arrangements. Broad social forces that impact child and adolescent development also influence intimate relationships and the emergence of violence.

RESPONSES TO ADOLESCENT DATING VIOLENCE

The response to adolescent relationships that become violent is best understood in the general context of the general domestic violence movement. The recent recognition of domestic violence as an important social problem fueled the enactment of an impressive series of federal and state domestic violence statutes.[35] Although several components of these statutes remain controversial, the movement reflects the recognition that victims need increased protection and that the legal system could play a decisive role in intervention and prevention. Thus, although all statutes and policies vary in actual content and emphasis, the response has been to confront relationship violence in essentially all relevant legal and social service arenas. In terms of adolescent violence, however, the proliferation of policies essentially remains unhelpful; policies generally exclude adolescents.

Domestic violence statutes have been tailored to deal with the effects of violence between *adults*. Thus, despite similarities in the social dynamics of adult battering and adolescent dating violence, considerable differences remain in the availability and utilization of legal remedies. Minors must overcome numerous, often insurmountable, obstacles in order to receive protection from new domestic violence policies. The most difficult of these obstacles is the number of ways statutes operate to exclude dating adolescents from coverage. These restrictions are important. If adolescent victims and perpetrators are in relationships that are not statutorily recognized, the statutes simply do not apply. When statutes do not apply, adolescents are left without legal recourse and without mandated or otherwise available services.[36]

Numerous examples of exclusion emerge from a close statutory examination.[37] Several states restrict "domestic violence" to relationships between individuals who possess adult qualities; i.e., individuals must have reached the age of majority or be married before they can receive protection and benefit from resources available to adult victims of domestic violence. The great majority of adolescents in abusive relationships cannot receive protections simply because they are dating or are not old enough. Yet another exclusionary mechanism is the requirement that victims be current or former cohabitants or spouses. The aim of these restrictions is straightforward: to protect live-in relationships. Residency and marital requirements make it unlikely that the domestic violence protections offered in these states could protect adolescent dating couples. Although some adolescents fit into these categories, many do not. Again, these statutes do not aim to protect teens who are simply dating. Yet another common mechanism that excludes dating adolescents is the requirement that victims be either current or former spouses, current or former cohabitants, or coparents. This approach at least does protect a very distinct group of adolescents at risk for maltreatment: teen mothers. Only thirteen states allow for the *possibility* of including dating adolescents in their definitions of domestic violence.[38] Only one state has seen fit to confirm explicitly that the minority of an individual does not exclude them from domestic violence program service provisions.[39]

In addition to allowing or prohibiting minors to petition for relief, states also restrict the extent to which minors can be the subject of civil actions brought under the umbrella of domestic violence statutes. One-fifth of the states expressly *allow* civil protection orders to be brought *against* minors. Although laudable, even these states limit their expansion of protection. Even in states that allow orders to be brought against minors, the statutory remedies still remain underdeveloped.[40] For example, it is not clear whether adolescent perpetrators would be subject to civil or criminal sanctions.[41]

The current lack of services available to youth through either social service or justice systems reveals a heightened need for recognition. Adolescents' needs essentially go unrecognized as the legal system fails to confront adolescent relationship violence. A primary example of the consequences of this failed recognition is the finding that lack of victim advocacy and understanding of adolescent relationships increases the likelihood that state officials will not appropriately understand adolescent violence and thus not respond appropriately.[42] It is important to emphasize that those who arguably are in most need have the least legal recourse; and those who will become abusers as adults are setting their patterns in adolescent relationships.

Sexual harassment

THE NATURE OF JUVENILE SEXUAL HARASSMENT

What precisely constitutes child sexual harassment remains a contested issue. As with other forms of sexual maltreatment, researchers, policy-makers, and the courts have yet to agree on a single working definition. Despite controversies, commentators generally posit that sexually harassing behaviors encompass many types of *unwanted* or *unwelcomed* behaviors that range from bullying, both physical and verbal, to sexual aggression committed against individuals because of their gender, sexuality, and vulnerable position.[43] Although the focus on unwanted or unwelcomed behaviors considerably narrows the scope of behaviors that may fall inappropriately under the rubric of sexual harassment, others opt for an even narrower approach that limits the focus and emphasizes the problematic behaviors' persistency and impact, and the harasser's explicit power over victims.[44]

Regardless of definitional controversies, it is important to emphasize that more agreement exists than disagreement. It is fairly well established that isolated incidents of name-calling or touching do not constitute peer harassment. Although some believe that cases of stolen kisses constitute sexual harassment and inappropriately attempt to censure youth for innocent, normative behaviors, the majority of commentators who urge reform center on serious, unwelcomed violations of a person's physical and emotional self.[45] This very high threshold comports with two recent developments in societal responses to sexual harassment. First, the definition reflects the series of important cases in which children's actionable harms included persistent, pervasive, and intrusive sexualized behaviors.[46] Second, the definition corresponds with the Office for Civil Rights' recent guidelines that include peer sexual harassment. These guidelines, issued only in 1997, view peer harassment as activities that would be "sufficiently severe, persistent, or pervasive to limit a student's ability to participate in or benefit from an education program or activity, or to create a hostile or abusive educational environment."[47] These two developments are significant to emphasize for the simple reason that, although commentators and society may quibble about definitional issues, they tend to concur on when harassment occurs. Where they disagree is in determinations of when schools or others should be held responsible for the harassing behaviors.

Although the narrow approach increasingly dominates analyses, it is important to emphasize that the approach leaves unaddressed numerous forms of problematic behavior. A helpful way to understand the extent to which several forms of harassing behaviors are ignored is to compare children's experiences with those of adults. For example, children and youth regularly tolerate sexually demeaning insults, lewd gestures, demeaning attitudes, and cruel jokes. These events are rarely viewed as inappropriate behavior; yet, such invasive sexual comments, questions, and demands clearly could qualify as sexual harassment if the victims were adults. Likewise, if young victims were adults, physical forms of sexual harassment, such as roughing and grabbing, would be considered abusive.[48] In addition, adults would not be expected to engage in the "servicing" some youth do for others, such as "lending" money, doing homework, shopping, and other services children must do to maintain a certain image and reputation. Comparing harassing behaviors children must endure to those that would be inappropriate if acted upon adults helps illustrate two points. First, the comparison reveals the extent to which we hold children to a different standard, even though society generally believes that children deserve more protections from harm because they are especially vulnerable. Second, the comparison reveals how behaviors may inappropriately control children because of their gender or sexual behavior. As we have seen with relationship violence, harassment by youth involves controlling behavior that remains essentially invisible. Even this comparative approach, though, remains limited; for it leaves some behaviors unchallenged. Not all forms of adult harassment are easily recognizable and not all are condemned equally, such as those committed against individuals of homosexual orientations and those that involve visual harassment.[49]

Difficulties encountered in attempts to imagine the extent of peer sexual harassment reveal why peer sexual harassment research often is viewed as groundbreaking, for they all find harassing behaviors pervasive in junior high and high schools. Large surveys in Canada,[50] Britain,[51] and the United States[52] report high rates of sexual harassment, of unwanted and unwelcomed sexual behaviors that interfere with students' lives. Estimates from the leading survey indicate that 75 percent of boys and 85 percent of girls report being the targets of sexually harassing behaviors.[53] Although these findings may overemphasize minor or infrequent events, it is important to note that a high number report that they are harassed more than once: 58 percent of students report being sexually harassed often or occasionally, and boys comprise almost half of that group.[54] The extent to which it occurs is highlighted by the finding that over half of girls *and* boys admit that they have harassed another student.[55] The most comprehensive research reveals that over half of boys and girls report being both victims *and* offenders, even though they report finding their own victimization upsetting.[56] These findings are significant; sexual harassment is widespread, it impacts both sexes, and victims are likely to offend.[57]

In addition to high prevalence rates, sexual harassment has significant consequences; all of which reflect how harassment inappropriately controls victims' lives. Results from the leading study again reveal several important findings. First, students who have experienced sexual harassment report being embarrassed or self-conscious about incidents: 64 percent of girls and 36 percent of boys have felt embarrassed.[58] Second, the harassing behavior results in changing victims' daily routines. To avoid harassers, 69 percent of girls and 27 percent of boys alter their routines.[59] Up to a third of the students report that they did not want to attend, let alone participate in, classes because of the harassment.[60] Third, both boys and girls fear harassment: 78 percent of girls, and 30 percent of boys, report being afraid of being sexually harassed.[61] Although these outcomes are significant and commonplace enough that some researchers even have conceptualized a "sexual harassment syndrome,"[62] these findings are highlighted by arguments that explicit, easily measured changes in behavior do not index the extent to which sexual harassment endangers more than individual victims. Several researchers appropriately describe sexual harassment as part of the hidden curriculum that links harassment to unequal access to education and more general problems relating to sexuality and gender inequity in social opportunities.[63]

Despite links to negative outcomes, many forms of sexually harassing behavior are normalized and unconsciously accepted as part of the reality of adolescent life. Those who admit that they harass justify their behavior on the grounds that it is just part of school life and a lot of students do it.[64] The apparent normalness helps explain why not only observers but also victims remain silent. The failure to disclose unwanted sexual and/or gendered attention is multi-determined. It is clear that a number of social pressures and expectations placed on girl and boy victims militate against disclosure. One often identified factor that inhibits disclosure relates to issues of intentionality. Perceptions of the harasser's intent often are determinative. For example, if victims feel the behaviors are intended to flatter, or were done "by mistake," they are not likely to report.[65] Harassing behavior results in victim's confusion as to what is genuine and wanted attention and what is unwanted sexual attention. A second factor involves victims' lack of personal interpretations of the nature of harassment. Victims are at a loss to describe the behavior; children have no name for annoying, teasing, and even abusive behaviors and would be exceptional if they knew that the law requires them to expressly reject the harassment in order to invoke its protection. The language deficiency, and the inability to communicate and recognize the existence of such problems, prevents victims from sharing the experience with others, forcing them to be isolated, vulnerable, and silent.[66] A third factor involves the difficulty of finding others to confide in, especially when the abusers are heterosexist and both genders are either involved in the perpetration or remain silent as the abusive behavior continues unchecked. A fourth factor simply relates to expectations of harassment: girls may struggle with a desire to be noticed and accept uncomfortable overtures,[67] and gay or feminine boys who are at increased risk of harassment simply expect to be subject to homophobic harassment.[68] These reasons for failed recognition of victimization highlight the need to understand the diverse ways peers may have unequal relationships that may lead to unrecognized coercive behavior, such as when one child has authority over another as president of a club, as parent or hero in play situations, or when some children have disparate self-images due to popularity, talents, competence, or relationships to certain adults.

The result of the failure to recognize and respond to negative outcomes is that those who perpetrate sexually harassing behaviors do not always realize that such abuses are actually offensive and hurtful. The toleration continues because of the prevailing attitude that "boys will be boys," that "girls will be girls," and that behaviors are part of normal courtship and heterosexual sex role socialization. The abusive behaviors go unchallenged, even behaviors that occur in front of individuals who could offer assistance.[69] Perpetrators and their victims may not see troubling behavior as abusive simply because they have become inured to it.

The current understanding of sexual harassment contributes three points to our understanding of adolescent development and the maltreatment youth suffer. First, there is a need for heightened awareness and reaction to the link between gender role socialization, perceptions of heterosexuality, harassing behavior, and adolescent life. During adolescence, gender roles are intensified and result in exaggerated and accepted extremes in how boys and girls interact with one another. Images of how boys and girls operate become embedded and form stereotypes which, if not followed, have important consequences: being labelled as having the opposite sex's characteristics is a common form of sexual harassment, just as adopting sex role extremes may lead to harassing behavior and its acceptance. Again, in recognizing the links, it is critical to appreciate how society broadly determines the nature of femininity and masculinity and largely influences what boys and girls can do. Second, although gender plays an important role, it is critical to emphasize that harassing behavior involves how adolescents treat each other sexually and how they attempt to control those over whom they may have power, regardless of their gender. That is, the continued finding that both boys and girls occupy victim and perpetrator roles challenges the current form of framing the problem in gendered terms, around a victim/perpetrator model.[70] Harassing behavior permeates adolescent life and remains largely ignored. Third, an important part of the societal silencing involves the way the failure of recognition separates adults from children and ignores parallels between the abusive events. For example, peer abuse links to adult forms of harassing behaviors to the extent that those who hold dominant relationships structure relationships to maintain both personal and group power.[71] Just as adult sexual harassment serves to maintain power imbalances between individuals, so the sexual harassment of children serves to maintain the adult-dominated society by devaluing and mistreating children. The problem is far from being one in which adults actively maltreat children.[72] Rather, the problem is that adults largely ignore children's coercive sexual behaviors and allow the victimization of vulnerable youth to continue.

Arguably, then, sexual harassment forms part of a continuum of sexual violence against children. Likewise, it seems that the consequences of sexual harassment are numerous and varied. Sexual harassment impacts girls' and boys' emotional and physical well-being. Victims are frequently burdened with feelings of humiliation, guilt, and frustration. The cumulative effects can be as devastating and harmful as sexual assault. Yet, society has yet to address this form of maltreatment as fully as might have been expected.

RESPONDING TO CHILD SEXUAL HARASSMENT

Although the identification of adult sexual harassment has been part of public consciousness for the past two decades, the recognition has yet to filter down to the level of policy-making for children.[73] Children and adolescents who wish to seek redress for sexually harassing behaviors face enormous obstacles.

Since most of the sexually harassing incidents are perpetrated in school or are related to school activities, the first avenue of redress tends to involve in-school sexual harassment policies. Only once existing internal school procedures are exhausted can formal legal remedies be sought. The extent to which victims will use available procedures remains debatable, for four reasons. First, schools generally do not have sexual harassment polices; and if they do, the policies are pervasively ignored.[74] Second, many students properly perceive that complaints to school authorities will not be treated confidentially and fear retaliation from alleged perpetrators or their friends and/or families.[75] Third, without school awareness and school programs, children and their parents may not even know of other avenues for redress.[76] Fourth, parents may not find the behavior disturbing and may contribute to the harassment.[77] Given these limitations in avenues of redress, it is not surprising that parents increasingly try to pursue legal actions to help their children deal with peer harassment.

Several important issues emerge once students, through their parents, do seek legal redress. The first is whether legal systems even allow for such challenges. In the U.S., there generally are no direct prohibitions against sexual harassment. Victims' rights fall under certain statutory titles dealing with discrimination; and through those statutes school boards may be held liable for harassment by other students.[78] Existing legal challenges reveal that two arguments may be made. The first line of cases are brought under Title IX of the Education Amendments of 1972, which prohibits discrimination on the basis of sex in any federally funded education program.[79] The second line of cases involves proposals that a special relationship exists between school officials and school children which creates an affirmative duty to protect students from sexual harassment.[80] The law, however, still remains somewhat unsettled. The Supreme Court makes it unclear whether courts generally will be prepared to apply existing legal mechanisms to cases of student-to-student harassment.[81] This is exacerbated by the failure of Title IX to explicitly prohibit sexual harassment[82] and by numerous cases that do not find a "special relationship" between schools and their students to the extent that an affirmative obligation to protect would arise.[83] Reviews, for example, find the possibility of students' succeeding in their legal challenges to stop sexually harassing behavior by other students as "remote."[84]

In jurisdictions that may allow suits to be pursued, other problems arise. The burden of proof that must be met by the complainant undoubtedly constitutes an enormous challenge; what would constitute a proper standard and how it could be met remain highly controversial. Typically, victims must show that the "reasonable person" would view the acts as unwelcomed. Such standards are actually quite tricky to determine; i.e., whether conduct constitutes sexual harassment can be approached in terms of whether the reasonable person is a reasonable girl, reasonable boy, simply a reasonable child, or an expert in the field of child sexual harassment.[85] To complicate matters, it remains unclear how victims' actions should be considered. The "normal" reaction tends to include laughing off such behavior or responding in kind; if the victim experiences the behavior from a vulnerable position, she may blame herself and not express disapproval of certain behavior. A focus on conduct may also be problematic if the victim has had previous relationships with the harasser or has had amicable relationships in which teasing was not originally unwelcome but later became problematic. In these situations, emphasis placed on the past conduct of complainants can be troubling. In addition, there may need to be a focus on overt violence and persistence, a requirement that leaves children unprotected. The focus on "repeated" behavior leaves several forms of harassment unaddressed, and actions need not be overtly violent to be harmful. These issues reflect the extent to which harassment law has yet to be properly adapted to children's lives and show how attempts to equate the practices may enable the behavior to continue and allow cases involving children to go unrecognized and unremarked.

Although important controversies remain, cases of sexual harassment are not always so problematic. Cases involving physical harassment may be less difficult than the more ambiguous forms of harassment such as leering, sexual gestures, or inappropriate graffiti. Likewise, there are other forms of legal protections. When harassment escalates into more extreme physical and sexual violence, criminal codes may come into effect. These alternatives, however, also are limited. First, they are available only if the abuse is recognized appropriately in the first place. Second, the high burden of proof needed for criminal convictions makes harassing behavior even more difficult to prove. Lastly, the criminal justice system still focuses on punishing offenders rather than on offering victims assistance.

Once legal obstacles to obtaining legal redress are met, remedies become important to consider. Remedies can take several forms: compensatory awards, proactive remedies, or actual punishment of offenders. Again, however, several obstacles block such redress. For example, compensations for pain and suffering are difficult to determine; some simply want to ensure that school boards take more active stances. Legally, it also remains to be determined whether schools can actually take effective proactive measures to address the problem of sexual harassment within schools. Likewise, there is also the important consideration that behaviors may be occurring outside of school grounds; and if so, protections are rather slim. Again, though, for extreme cases, the criminal justice system offers another, albeit limited, route.

Regardless of the avenues sought, more practical considerations come into play. Time and financial investment necessary to launch legal actions for sexual harassment make such efforts problematic. If those factors are problematic for adults, they are even more so for children. Again, however, legal avenues may be more appropriate for extreme cases. For students who only attend certain classes or schools for short spans, legal avenues are likely to be ineffective. Likewise, the sluggish process of legal action does not stop the behavior immediately: justice is not swift. These difficulties are reflected in a plethora of important precedent-setting cases. Currently, these cases indicate that attempts to obtain redress are fraught with obstacles even though the right to proceed legally *may* be recognized.[86]

Beyond practical and legal considerations, existing research questions the adequacy of current responses. Since over half of all high school students identify themselves as perpetrators and victims,[87] policies that aim to punish and protect victims make improbable that sexual harassment may be abolished and properly addressed. The pervasiveness of harassing behavior and the infrequency of litigated cases has led researchers to propose accepting the forms of difficulties students confront and expanding the "public" agenda of schools to confront and hotly debate issues of violence, sexuality, and ethics.[88]

Efforts to have schools act more proactively and address violence in a more systematic fashion have yet to spur systematic and appropriate reform, as evidenced in recent statutory developments. Five states now require school districts to instate sexual harassment polices that govern students' behavior toward one another.[89] Minnesota, for example, was the first state to enact legislation prohibiting sexual harassment in schools, and actually provided a model curriculum for use in junior and senior high schools.[90] In terms of legal relief, Washington arguably has the most comprehensive policy of sexual harassment in the country. Washington's statute mimics the guarantees of sexual educational access embodied in adult sexual harassment law and defines sexual harassment in a way that encompasses both the quid pro quo and hostile environment standards.[91] Nonetheless, even the few states that have laws requiring policies are not immune to criticism. States generally offer no guidance for the development of new sexual harassment policies and remain punitive: they aim to expel, suspend, or otherwise discipline individual offenders.[92] Just as importantly, states do not provide provisions for staff training or curricular development that would help students define the boundaries of appropriate behavior and recognize power relations.[93] Even if legislation addresses issues of peer harassment, it does not necessarily do so appropriately or constructively.

Despite increased societal recognition and some legal developments, then, enormous obstacles block efforts to reform sociolegal arrangements that could assist in the alleviation of sexual harassment rates. Importantly, though, obstacles to responding more effectively to harassing behaviors reveal significant points. First, they reflect the extent to which statutes designed for adult behaviors are not readily adaptable to children's actions. Second, they indicate the extent to which gender plays an important role, and how there may be a need to move beyond gendered analyses. Third, they highlight the significance of addressing numerous societal forces that contribute to maltreating behaviors. Fourth, they reinforce the need to recognize and focus on adolescents' own voices and priorities. Lastly, they reveal how some jurisdictions actually are responding and attempting to recognize harms children suffer.

Peer sexual assault

THE NATURE OF PEER ASSAULT

Although numerous definitions of sexual assault exist, all emphasize the notion of nonconsensual sexual conduct, and researchers tend to include a broad range of behaviors that may be regarded as threats to victims. Behaviors included in research mainly involve unwanted sexual contact, sexual coercion, and unwanted sexual intercourse.[94] The focus on coercive and unwanted contact makes the form of abuse important to consider. Particularly when acquaintances are involved, investigations reveal that victims, perpetrators, and others who may have knowledge of the behavior, fail to understand the actions' coerciveness. Coercive behavior is interpreted as normal, as part of sexual relationships and sex role development. As with the previous practices, then, it is important to consider the extent and nature of peer sexual assault and the role it plays in the sexual maltreatment of youth.

The general finding that emerges from national and local samples continues to be that approximately one-quarter of women report having been victims of rape or attempted rape, over 80 percent of them by acquaintances.[95] These are important findings that particularly relate to young victims. Estimates reveal that adolescent victims may account for over 50 percent of rapes.[96] The vast majority of these assaults take place in acquaintance or dating situations. One recent national project found that 92 percent of adolescent sexual assault victims were assaulted by someone they knew, and that more than half actually were raped while on a date.[97] Although these findings confirm previous research estimates derived from smaller samples,[98] several challenge the finding of high assault rates.[99] Yet, given that the inability of victims themselves to define assaults as rape is a critical part of the phenomenon of acquaintance rape, it is understandable that researchers have sought to use measures that include instances in which even victims fail to recognize the violence. Broader definitions of sexual assaults by acquaintances, for example, allow for considering boys' experiences, which, when investigated, reveal rates of coerced sexual activity similar to those experienced by girls.[100]

Despite controversies, researchers generally do not doubt the significance of sexual assault and do support the conclusion that many assaults go undetected simply because victims remain silent about their abuse. Approximately half of the victims who identify themselves as victimized by sexually coercive acts ever tell anyone.[101] A major reason for the silence is that youth tolerate coercive behavior. High school students find coercive sexual intercourse permissible in a variety of situations, most notably if the partners had previously engaged in sexual activity, if the girls wore revealing clothing, or if the girls were otherwise responsible for sexually exciting the perpetrator.[102] These perceptions are highlighted by one study's finding that one-quarter of female subjects agreed that a woman who refuses a date's advances has not been raped and that only one-fifth of the subjects strongly believed that she has been raped.[103] In addition to research about perceptions of rape, a large body of research relating to "rape myths" reveals how youth adhere to rape myths even without understanding the meaning of rape.[104] This research is supported by recent investigations that reveal how slightly over one-quarter of rape victims view their victimizations as rapes even when their experiences fall under the legal category of rape[105] and how half of rape victims who are physically coerced blame themselves for the rape.[106] Given that the potential victims would not view *coerced sex* as sexual assault, it is not surprising that the same forces influence offenders and allow those who have raped to believe that they have neither been sexually coercive nor committed a crime.[107]

Researchers attribute the silence about abuse, failure to recognize the actual experience of assault, and the broader culture of acceptance to social stereotypes that govern gendered social relationships. The major stereotype that arguably forms the basis of the abuse holds that males dominate, control, and use power, while women do the opposite. Each gender expects disparate levels of aggressiveness and victimization and conditions those involved in violence to not even notice coercion.[108] Emerging literature suggests that the extent to which victims view themselves as assault victims depends on whether or not they have supportive friends who reassure them that they were not to blame and who help define the victimization as rape; those whose friends interpret the experience as loving unanimously find that they were not rape victims.[109]

Research investigating the culture of acceptance and gender relations reports important findings that go beyond highlighting how assaultive acts are silenced. First, although the main research focus stresses the significance of gender and power dynamics, it is important to consider that males can be coerced by females. One study reported 35 percent of females and 21 percent of males reported being victims of sexual coercion.[110] These findings do more than simply contradict popular perceptions; they urge us to rethink the nature of sexual coercion and consent, let alone the causes and consequences of rape. The second major finding involves the rampant distortion of nonverbal, sexual cues. Perceptions of those cues vary, particularly by age, ethnicity, attitudes toward sex, education, socioeconomic status, and other important variables.[111] The significance of variations in nonverbal contexts implicit in sexual courting operates at several points in response to sexual assault, beginning with dates' misinterpretations[112] and ending with juries that may misinterpret the significance of the nonverbal context of the situation when attempting to discern the parties' intentions.[113] This has led commentators to propose that, although individuals operate as though rape is readily identifiable, mythic and stereotypical images of rape guide reactions to coercive situations and interpretations of those reactions.

RESPONSES TO PEER SEXUAL ASSAULT

The current sociolegal response to acquaintance sexual assault can be viewed in the context of the rapid reforms that have occurred in rape law. Viewed in that light, the response can be characterized as nonfeasance. Laws have failed to respond appropriately in efforts to protect children from their peers.

Two major waves of reform have had a significant impact on the current character of rape law.[114] The first wave aimed to reform difficulties in proving the occurrence of the crime. Reforms sought to counter the prevailing belief that complainants' credibility in rape cases was inherently more suspect and subject to greater fabrication than in other cases. Reforms entailed removing from consideration several actions that had been deemed relevant to determining credibility or consent to the sexual acts. Limits now have been placed on the need to prove resistance, the need for corroboration of the victim's testimony, the need for "fresh complaints" that immediately follow the rape, and the need to admit evidence of victims' prior sexual histories. For example, some jurisdictions have addressed issues of consent by ignoring physical force and proposing that the force inherent in sexual penetration meets the threshold requirement absent consent. Thus, sexual assault occurs when the act of penetration was made without affirmative and freely given permission of the victim.[115] This makes for an important move; traditionally, courts have required that victims resist, even when resistance or force are not elements of the crime.[116] These reforms reflect the need to rethink burdens of proof and facilitate the ability to bring actions, particularly when parties are acquaintances.[117]

Rather than focusing on reform to prove rape, the second wave questioned the very nature of rape itself. A most notable move has been to essentially abolish the crime of "rape" and to graduate offenses into different degrees of sexual assault including, for example, a focus on force, age differentials, nature of sexual acts, and the relationship between offender and victim. This move helped expand the popular view of rape as solely acts perpetrated by strangers.[118] Although the focus particularly helped include protections from spousal rape, the focus also placed interest on acquaintances. When dealing with adults, sexual assault involved sexual acts and coercion, no matter who the perpetrator was.[119]

Although it is important not to minimize the importance of reform efforts, it is also important to note that their impact still remains debatable.[120] Three findings support propositions that reforms have not been as fruitful as anticipated. First, despite reforms, acquaintance rape and sexual assault have very low arrest rates and even lower conviction rates.[121] Researchers and commentators reveal how sexual assault perpetrated by acquaintances, although the most common, is viewed with suspicion and remains resistant to legal mandates aimed at reform.[122] These assaults often do not involve weapons or forceful struggle; the result is that victims are assumed to be able to prevent the attack and are thought to "want" or to "deserve" it.[123] Familiarity or prior intimacy with the accused leads to the conclusion that victims implied consent, and therefore could not have been raped.[124] The second reason for the apparent limits of rape law reform is that despite progress, several jurisdictions have not embraced developments. For example, despite efforts to rethink the nature of rape and coercion, several states in the U.S. still do not criminalize nonconsensual sexual assault without force.[125] The third reason for the limited success is that the reforms that have been made attempt to eliminate the most overt biases. The removal of biases leads to the misleading and superficial appearance that rape laws are now administered in a neutral and fair manner, an appearance that makes the legal system fail to confront the deeper problems created by the culture of acceptance. The culture of acceptance continues to color the manner in which rape laws are understood and implemented.[126]

When it comes to minors, the failure to protect is even greater, even though it is generally thought that laws automatically protect children from all forms of rape. Statutory rape laws that do impose strict liability on those who would engage in sexual relations with minors provide a particularly powerful example of the failure to protect. Despite popular perceptions that these laws protect well, they fail simply because they essentially *exclude* peers from liability when those involved are within statutory age limits.[127] For example, if the victim and perpetrator are both fourteen, or the perpetrator is two years older, their sexual interactions tend to be permissible when there has been no sign of overt coercion. The rationale for excluding peers is that it properly allows for sexual encounters and avoids the difficulties that would arise if there were attempts to control voluntary sexual relationships of all children. Admittedly, it often is difficult for victims and perpetrators, let alone legal systems, to distinguish among assault, aggression, seduction, and passion.[128] Despite the apparent need for such flexibility, three arguments challenge the statutes that exclude peer liability. First, adolescents' peer relationships may involve coercion that goes undetected. Peer pressure, the desire to be accepted, and other reasons for sexual interactions have been challenged as inappropriate.[129] Second, the existence of statutory rape law may result in the failure to recognize even overt coercion; coercion may be tolerated and seen as normal to adolescent sexual relationships.[130] Researchers convincingly propose that issues of coerciveness still are interpreted along prevailing myths, such as the belief that girls are sexually provocative, that provocative behavior generates consent, that females are naturally passive, and that girls are not to be trusted.[131] Third, the existence of special laws for children has led to the failure to enact reforms that protect victims to the same degree as those that protect adults. A prime example is the continued existence of the promiscuity defense, which, in some jurisdictions, applies to juveniles but generally not to adults.[132]

Sociolegal responses reflect the difficulty of responding to abuses suffered from acquaintances and young offenders. It remains difficult to respond to the variety of ways children may be coerced into unwanted sexual activity. Even when the coerciveness could be recognized, there remains the difficulty of addressing the prevailing culture of acceptance. Unlike developments that have dealt with sexual abuse perpetrated by adults, this area of law generally has not proposed and enacted efforts to protect children by minimizing or negating biases. Unaddressed cultural attitudes toward coercive sexuality perpetuate misconceptions of children's lives and allow the practices to continue. Particularly problematic is the failure to respond more properly to consensual sexual activity: efforts now criminalize sexual activity devoid of aggression[133] when there is increasing recognition that minors have a right to privacy in intimate relations and that mature minors may be capable of consent to medical procedures related to their sexual activity.[134] The failure to respond appropriately continues despite rapid and extensive law reform relating to rape.

Juvenile sex-offending against younger children

THE NATURE OF JUVENILE SEX OFFENDING

Researchers generally define juvenile sex offenses as involving coercion, force, or threats; sexual behavior that violates conventional norms; and (usually) a younger child.[135] Using this definition, available evidence indicates that young perpetrators are an important source of child sexual abuse. Researchers reveal that juvenile sexual offenses actually are as common as those committed by adult offenders. Reports estimate that adolescents commit over 50 percent of sexual offenses perpetrated against children under twelve years of age.[136] Research from other countries reports similar results: adolescents and preadolescents commit sexual offenses against children at rates similar or higher than other age groups.[137] Although these rates may appear relatively high, even these numbers may be underestimates of the magnitude of the problem. Research relating to abusive adolescents relies mainly on official reports of abuse, which often classify sexual offenses as assaults and ignore non-contact offenses; and, as with other offenses, many simply are not reported to authorities.[138] In addition, other evidence indicates that up to 80 percent of adult offenders commit their first acts of sexual assault during their adolescent years.[139] Regardless of the statistical and methodological controversies, all findings point to the need to consider the role young offenders play in the sexual abuse of children.

Juvenile sex offending involves a wide variety of relationships and ages. The general belief is that boys in their early teens are at higher risk for offending. Offenders who have been identified have reached their early teens, their modal age is 14,[140] and about 95 percent are male.[141]

The modal victim—the one most likely to be encountered in research and the one most described in commentaries—is likely to be a seven- or eight-year-old girl. Studies indicate that victims do tend to be prepubescent—over 60 percent are under twelve years of age and over 40 percent of these are younger than six.[142] A large number of victims, however, are male; estimates range from 45 to 63 percent.[143] Importantly, evidence reveals that victims tend to know their offenders, who are likely to be siblings, babysitters, or children who live in close proximity.[144]

In addition to findings relating to age and relationship differences, other important trends emerge from research that reports on the abusive events. The abusive behaviors that have been identified are neither isolated events nor the result of curious exploration. Young offenders already have explored sexuality in nondeviant ways before they proceed to illegal behavior.[145] Offenders also have repeated their offenses: the average number of victims of juvenile offenders is seven.[146] Young child offenders tend to use verbal threats and bribes and other coercive measures;[147] much like their adult counterparts, they do not predominantly use physical force.[148] These findings reveal that the behaviors tend to be difficult to uncover, again much like sexual abuse perpetrated by adults.

Several important themes emerge from research that reports the characteristics of young offenders. First, social characteristics of young offenders range considerably, from tough delinquent, social outcast, and popular star athlete to honor-roll student. The heterogeneity is further reflected in the failure to find mental illness in up to 95 percent of child offenders.[149] Second, although studies consistently reveal that adolescent offenders are a heterogeneous population, differences may exist between offenders who offend against peers and those who offend against young children: the latter tend to be more dependent, passive, avoidant, and more deviant than the former.[150] Third, a history of family violence has been found to contribute to sexual deviance. Young sex offenders are more likely to come from families that expose them to aggressive and sexually deviant models. For example, young sex offenders's familial experiences are more likely to include child abuse, spousal abuse, and sexual molestation than those of other juvenile offenders.[151] Fourth, offenders have poor relationship skills and few peer relations, with significant numbers reporting no friends at all.[152] Indicators of shyness, timidity, withdrawal, and sexual isolation continue to be more frequent in adolescent offenders than in other delinquents and other control groups.[153] These findings relate to clinical research that emphasizes the contribution to offending of the lack of empathic experiences and sexualized patterns of coping.[154] These findings are significant in that they suggest that abused offenders have an earlier onset of offending, an increased number of victims, a tendency to also abuse males, and a greater likelihood of exhibiting deviant sexual arousal.[155]

As with adult offending, many hypotheses have been put forth to explain the etiology of sexually abusive behaviors.[156] However, given the present knowledge of adolescent sex offenders, their characteristics do not contribute markedly to the debate about the etiology of offending while in childhood. The genesis of deviant sexual behavior in childhood and adolescence is still obscure despite a wide range of studies. Existing research does suggest, however, that offenders move beyond mere sexual curiosity and seemingly offend as part of coercive interactions, such as bullying.[157] This theme coincides with the belief that sexual deviancy is secondary to the abusive nature of the problem[158] and with research that highlights how beliefs, attitudes, and sexual interests of many nonoffenders are not so different from those of many abusive youth.[159] The finding that a common behavior pattern may be coercion and manipulation reveals a need to consider the developmental roots of what leads to young sex offenders' distorted cognitions about the effects of the offense, lack of empathy with others' needs, and pattern of making demands on others. Despite these findings, two points still generally remain clear: we do not know what mechanisms lead to child sex offending as opposed to other forms of delinquent acts; nor do we know how the mechanisms may be related to the eventual development of older individuals who offend against children.

RESPONSES TO JUVENILE SEX OFFENDING

The array of potential dispositions for documented cases of sexual offending by juveniles falls along a continuum from no legal response to extreme legal consequences. Until recent years, juveniles who engaged in behaviors that were both sexual and criminal were often ignored.[160] The pendulum has swung with the growth of public awareness that adult offenders begin abuse in their early teens, as highlighted by estimates that, without intervention, an adolescent sex offender will go on to commit 380 sexual crimes during his lifetime.[161] Two trends have emerged in responses to public concern about sexually abusive juveniles. The first focuses on treatment while the other centers on a more aggressive use of the juvenile and criminal justice systems. The two responses reflect the tension between treating youth with the hope that they can be rehabilitated and holding youth accountable as adults for committing criminal acts; the responses also reflect the general trend toward increasing community protection by enacting more punitive and repressive responses to youth violence.

Many states now label sexually abusive youth as "special offenders" and encourage rigorous prosecutorial efforts that most notably include tougher sentencing, registration, and public notification.[162] The trend toward holding youth accountable, although increasingly part of juvenile justice systems, is contrary to the philosophy of focusing on delinquent youths' treatment, privacy, confidentiality, and reintegration.[163] For example, a New Jersey appellate court recently upheld the application of notification statutes applied to juveniles.[164] In that case, a twelve-year-old was adjudicated delinquent for the sexual assault of his eight-year-old stepbrother. The court sentenced the delinquent to three years of probation, sixty days of incarceration, and registration with local officials upon release to the community.[165] These developments conflict with two fundamental concerns of the rehabilitative model: confidentiality and stigmatization. Under New Jersey law, juveniles who perpetrate sex crimes are increasingly treated the same as adults: their only opportunity to terminate the registration requirement comes after fifteen years.[166] Although New Jersey's sex offender registration laws currently are the most severe, they do reflect two trends. First, concern for public protection fuels the enactment of laws, not concern for the best interests of those who have been adjudicated sex offenders.[167] Second, states simply are following strict federal mandates. For example, the Jacob Wetterling Crimes Against Children Act requires every state to enact laws governing the registration of sexually violent offenders by September 13, 1997.[168] Of the forty-nine states that have sex offender registration laws, only five specifically exclude juveniles from their coverage.[169] The use of laws for crimes committed by juveniles poses important problems. Although juveniles are subject to harsh provisions of the law, they may still be tried as delinquents and thus not be entitled to the same constitutional protections in procedures that are afforded adult offenders. The trend reveals a shift from rehabilitation to retribution and deterrence, and from guidance to punishment.

Despite the general move away from rehabilitation, there is still a notable focus on treatment that reflects the long history of the juvenile court's focus on rehabilitation and reintegration.[170] In fact, the recognition of the existence of young offenders led to the rapid development of sex offender programs, even to the extent that programs treating child and juvenile sex offenders have surpassed those aimed at treating adults.[171] It is important to emphasize, however, that courts disagree on whether juveniles actually have a right to treatment,[172] and several legislatures have redefined the purpose of their juvenile courts to play down the role of rehabilitation and highlight the role of safety, punishment, and individual accountability.[173] Although commentators propose that the better view is that juveniles should have a right to treatment and rehabilitative services,[174] the effectiveness of programs developed to treat sex offenders actually remains unknown.

The majority of published articles examining treatment alternatives for juvenile sex offenders reveal that childhood and early adolescence offers an opportune time to intervene if society hopes to allow offenders to return to a more normative course of development and to avoid further sexually abusive behaviors.[175] Although that proposition undoubtedly seems true, outcome studies of treatment efforts have yet to support claims that the therapeutic and rehabilitative community has the technology to help rehabilitate youth. Numerous forms of therapeutic approaches exist, although most efforts use group therapy, familial therapy, and a host of psycho-socioeducational modalities.[176] All of these approaches increasingly emphasize that problems are multidimensional and that interventions should focus on altering the offender's systemic contexts in support of behavioral changes. Although theoretically sound, few outcome studies exist to date. Studies tend to simply describe treatment modalities, rely on very small samples, have short-term follow-ups, use outcome measures that do not necessarily indicate change, or use self-reports of aggressive acts after treatment.[177] For example, one groundbreaking therapeutic outcome study that has received considerable attention compared young sex offenders and a comparison group.[178] Although the results showed the importance of taking multisystemic approaches, the study involved only sixteen sex offenders. Another example deals with high rates of therapeutic success; e.g., two robust studies reported that only 6 and 7.5 percent of released juveniles committed other sex crimes during long-term follow-ups.[179] In context, however, the findings are less striking: adolescent sex offenders, like adult offenders, have very low recidivism rates, seemingly regardless of the form of therapy or intervention.[180] These findings do not mean that attempts to treat sexually aggressive youth are necessarily unsuccessful; they simply mean that the clinical utility of interventions with these juveniles remains largely theoretical.

In considering responses to young sex offenders, it is important to highlight that little research has focused on preventing the development of young offenders.[181] The major preventative efforts, as with efforts to prevent child sexual abuse, focus on potential victims. Although a focus on self-protection, reporting, and prosecution undoubtedly plays an important role, confronting the development of new offenders remains the ultimate solution. Despite the general lack of research and efforts to tackle the development of offending, some programs have been designed to teach adolescents who are at risk of abusing children about the nature and causes of child sexual abuse and to help adolescents develop skills that relate to empathy, anger management, problem-solving, decision-making, and impulse control.[182] However, a recent review of primary prevention of perpetration reports that few efforts address primary prevention in community and family life, in relation to childhood sexuality, or intervention for high-risk groups.[183] Importantly, commentators emphasize the need to also reform societal attitudes about children, male-female relationships, and sexuality.[184] Although few programs may exist, it is critical to note that, since sexually abusive children exhibit other problems that contribute to offending, the current general targeting of delinquent behavior may help alleviate the extent to which youth sexually offend.

Although sexual offending by youth against children has become the most recognized form of child sexual abuse perpetrated by young offenders, it is important to recognize that the recognition and response remain limited. First, the offenses still remain largely hidden. Recall that offenders, on average, committ seven offenses before there are official reactions and identifications of abusive acts. Second, efforts to rehabilitate, even though they would be consistent with the original mission of juvenile justice provisions, remain limited. Third, efforts to prevent the development of young offenders essentially do not exist. Fourth, the failures exist despite the recognition that abuse by children and youth provides an opportune time, if not the only hope, to intervene and thwart the development of future sex offenders.

International Law's Approach to Youth Offending

International law's mandate to fight child sexual maltreatment does not exempt violations perpetrated by children and youth. Three important international children's rights developments have emerged that may be used to better address sexual violence perpetrated by young offenders. The first involves attempts to revision juvenile justice systems' treatment of offenders. The second considers increasing children's access to legal systems and legal services. The third involves the manner in which key socialization systems—family, education, and health systems—may be reformed in light of the movement to recognize children's voices, consider their best interests, and balance their protection and autonomy.

These important moves reflect the way international law aims to control how countries treat their citizens, rather than limiting itself to how nations treat one another. In addition, the new mandates offer rather innovative, and in several ways radical, departures for current domestic practices, points of departure that are neither entirely unimaginable nor impracticable.

RESPONSES TO YOUNG ABUSERS

International law directs countries to deal with young sex offenders through the development of the rights of children accused of offenses or who have been found to have committed offenses. Although children's juvenile justice rights as articulated in international law have been the subject of only a few commentaries,[185] three significant trends have emerged. The importance of these trends cannot be underestimated, for they highlight the extent to which international law has moved toward regulating intra-state behavior and how the developments allow for adopting the most cutting-edge developments in dealing with young offenders.

The first trend applicable to young sex offenders reflects the concern for controlling state infringement of individual's rights. These developments include rather extensive due process protections found in numerous international documents.[186] These documents generally require states to adopt different trial procedures for juveniles, consider the juvenile's age, and promote rehabilitation. The provisions also provide important substantive rights, such as an explicit statement that deprivations of liberty are to "be used only as a measure of last resort."[187]

The second trend involves moving beyond procedural rights and extra protections toward developing social policies and practices that avoid criminalizing and penalizing behaviors.[188] Although it remains to be determined how these rights could impact responses to violent sexual offenders, it does seem that less violent sexual acts could fall under the purview of these mandates.[189] Regardless of the acts, however, it is clear that all would be affected by the mandate to rechannel resources in order to *prevent* antisocial behavior. For example, international instruments urge countries to strengthen families, reform educational programs, and reorient community resources toward supporting healthier developmental paths for children and families.[190] This development in human rights law is critical beyond the obvious and important focus on prevention; the development highlights how international law seeks to entitle families and children to resources.[191]

The third trend involves reliance on children themselves and emphasizes the need to protect youth while also bestowing upon them a "voice" in decisions that ultimately affect them.[192] Although, again, the extent to which these provisions are meant for young sex offenders remains unknown, they do reflect a general reconception of youth who offend. For example, commentators suggest that the efforts seek to hold children accountable for their actions by giving youth the power to influence dispositional decision-making. Thus, unlike the traditional focus on either rehabilitation or punishment to deal with problem youth, commentators highlight how international law offers a third alternative. That alternative balances rehabilitation and punishment, as exemplified by restorative justice and reintegrative justice models that hold youth accountable by involving them in deciding the outcome of their cases and the nature of their punishment.[193] Research has found the new approaches more than promising,[194] and as we have seen, they may be useful in attempts to deal with young sex offenders.[195] Despite this development, however, numerous countries recently have enacted important reforms that focus more on according youth procedural rights and protections from governmental intrusions rather than on providing services that would foster reintegrative and preventive efforts.[196]

These three developments seek to ensure that offending youth and their victims receive appropriate messages about justice and interpersonal relations. Intervention can facilitate confrontation of the offender, demonstrate that conduct is socially unacceptable, and communicate that the state does not sanction abusive behavior. Efforts to make intervention less arbitrary helps further socialize youth into proper societal roles and helps them recognize the importance of maintaining healthier relationships. State recognition of these behaviors as violent also plays an important psychological function for victims and may, for example, help assuage feelings of guilt, inadequacy, and shame that inhibit positive recovery. Equally critical for victims is the belief that legal recognition would help combat fears that prevent youth from seeking assistance. Both of these points suggest that recognition, even in the context of the current move toward using adult, criminal sanctions and decreasing the focus on therapeutic services for troubled youth, is critical to uncovering and preventing future abuse.

VICTIMS' ACCESS TO LEGAL SYSTEMS

Although important sources of international rights form the basis of a substantial policy framework designed to address the rights of youth who offend, the rights of victims remain undeveloped. Indeed, this is one of the areas of international children's rights that reflect how the movement has not fully recognized the juridical personhood of youth.

Despite claims that children have a legal personhood and the existence of explicit protections against child sexual maltreatment, it is difficult to find authority to support arguments that children have direct access to legal systems. It is especially difficult given that offenders explicitly have been given direct access to legal and other appropriate assistance while victims have not, suggesting that the rights would have been bestowed if thought necessary.[197] Yet, three arguments support efforts to expand young victims' access to legal protection. The first is that children have both the right to express their views freely if they are capable of doing so and also the right to an "opportunity to be heard" in judicial and administrative proceedings affecting them.[198] Second, nations are under the obligation to take "all appropriate measures" to protect children from sexual maltreatment;[199] if it could be shown that legal access would be appropriate or necessary, children might be granted the right. The third proposes that, to the extent laws provide access to services for adults, they must not discriminate against youth, as reflected in the Children's Convention's prohibition against "discrimination of any kind irrespective of the child's . . . status."[200] In brief, these developments reflect the general change in children's legal personhood from passive object of measures of protection to active subjects able to exercise their rights.

Although the above arguments may be found in international instruments, proposals that aim to give youth greater access to legal protections undoubtedly would generate considerable resistance. It is not difficult to imagine the nature of the opposition. Traditionally, efforts to offer children greater legal autonomy and to advance their civil rights have been challenged on grounds that increasing a minor's legal autonomy may intrude impermissibly upon parental rights to protect, control, and guide their own children's lives, or may lead to an outburst of false accusations that will overburden social service systems and lead to the false conviction of innocent individuals.[201] Although these arguments are persuasive in several contexts, a close look at arguments against offering youth greater access to sexual violence protections reveals the unpersuasiveness of these common objections and highlights the need for increasing access.

The concern that the inclusion of children in judicial efforts to prevent sexual violence would grant youth unfettered autonomy is significant to consider, since even the Children's Convention still seeks to protect the rights of parents to guide and largely determine the upbringing of their children.[202] Yet, the Children's Convention importantly limits that parental right in at least two ways. First, the extent "of the child's evolving capacities" dictates the power of parental rights.[203] It could be argued that, in the context of obtaining court protection, children could have a right to access. Even those who are less capable may have access. Children's autonomy would not go unchecked; e.g., protection orders require judicial review, and legally permissible social services involve other adults who may be in a position to safeguard parental rights. The second important limitation on parental rights involves the extent to which parental rights are appropriate in the exercise of the child's rights.[204] One instance in which it may no longer be appropriate to respect parental rights is when youth are subjected to violence. The public's interest in protecting children and preventing escalating injury arguably outweighs parental rights. Just as states may intrude in children's lives to protect them from unwise parental decision-making, so states have an obligation to infringe upon parental rights in the name of protecting their children, especially when parents fail to do so. Unquestionably, allowing for intrusion does not mean that parental rights should be ignored. The intervention, however, does mean that, like the judicial bypass needed to protect adolescents' rights in other areas,[205] legal systems should afford protection to those minors in danger and those minors not willing to seek assistance if it involves informing certain people. This would address the consistent finding that, while adolescents caught in violent relationships, subject to harassing behavior, or victimized by acquaintance rape could benefit from adult guidance, young victims remain reluctant to involve adults.[206]

The fear that false accusations will increase if legal systems offer victims greater access is not supported by evidence. Although several challenge child abuse laws on the grounds that they have led to unjust interventions,[207] available research suggests that children do not fabricate stories of abuse more than adults do and, if anything, they have more difficulty maintaining lies.[208] Likewise, the perception that rape victims will file false reports continues despite strong evidence that false rape accusations are no higher than false accusations for other crimes—five percent—and the traumas inflicted by the judicial system guard against frivolous accusations.[209] In addition, the perception that certain groups may have vested interests in accusing also is not supported by evidence. For example, the belief that teenagers who become pregnant will be more prone to "cry rape" is not supported by evidence; those who do accuse actually tell prosecutors the acts were consensual.[210] This does not mean, of course, that the sexual interactions were free of coercion. It does mean, though, that victims do not necessarily fit the myth that they are pathologically disturbed and motivated by greed to falsely report and lead prosecutors to convict.

It is important to emphasize that providing minors an explicit right to bring actions against other minors or adults would actually involve a radical turn in current implementation of adolescent jurisprudence and children's rights. Children still are considered legally incompetent. In the context of domestic violence, for example, only two states in the U.S. that *explicitly* allow teenagers sixteen and older to initiate actions on their own also have domestic violence statutes. Victims in other states and those below sixteen in some innovative states remain essentially legally invisible. Given the extent to which a radical move would be needed, it is also important to note an important alternative. Jurisdictions that remain unwilling to grant minors direct legal protection could allow courts to appoint guardians ad litem or attorneys to bring or defend actions, as may be done under some domestic violence statutes.[211] Although the alternative would be a positive move, it still would remain limited; the extent to which adults may not support youth is highlighted by the currently ignored rate of adolescent relationship violence and harassing behavior.

REVISIONING THE ROLE OF SOCIALIZING INSTITUTIONS

Although pivotal, legal recognition should not be seen as a panacea: the inherent limits of legal access to courts remain. Policies that simply aim to expand rights do not always change the nature of private and public relationships.[212] Nonlegal institutions that impact youth's lives—families, schools, and mental health systems—necessarily must be involved in efforts to combat sexual violence perpetrated by youth. In fact, international law now mandates that these institutions be involved, a move that makes sense from the current understanding of the varieties of sexual abuse perpetrated by juveniles against children.

As we have seen above, an important development in ways to deal with offenders is to move toward primary prevention, particularly in the form of support for families and communities. International law also now has extensive provisions that reflect the need to prevent abuse.[213] Intervention in family life provides a powerful source of hope. Family violence clearly increases the risk of victimization and perpetration inside and outside the home. Unlike other developments in international law, the mandate already tends to be part of the role played by domestic legal systems. International law could encourage states to make more vigorous use of existing laws. For example, child abuse and neglect laws could be enforced more strictly, parents could be offered services, and destructive relationships could be severed.[214] Likewise, domestic violence statutes which enable parents to seek assistance, stop domestic violence, and protect children from witnessing abuse undoubtedly could play a critical role.[215] In addition to more traditional methods of intervening in families, family intervention could also mean "intervening" to bolster family supports and transform social environments in which violent behaviors are learned, reinforced, or ignored. The extent to which families do not necessarily respond to abusive peer behavior highlights the significance of this move.

International law provides two important mandates for schools. International children's rights explicitly protect children in the care of others, such as school officials.[216] Perhaps more importantly, international law has explicit mandates for the development of educational programs that aim to respect human rights and fundamental freedoms, particularly tolerance and equality of the sexes.[217] To comply with international developments to combat violence perpetrated by youth, for example, schools could enhance awareness among students, teachers, and school officials; provide students with adequate complaint or reporting mechanisms; take appropriate steps to react to reports of violence; and, at a minimum, report suspected child maltreatment.

Some of these educational efforts undoubtedly would be difficult, for legal considerations may limit schools' approaches to dealing with adolescent sexuality[218] and violent youth.[219] However, innovative programs suggest that several approaches can be taken to address violence. For example, successful relationship violence programs may be developed to increase nonviolent management of interpersonal conflict; develop means of coping with anger, jealousy, and possessiveness; and alter attitudes that verbal and physical violence are acceptable means of conflict resolution.[220] In addition to improving basic interpersonal skills, some programs have helped reduce the incidence of dating violence by altering social norms associated with partner violence and by decreasing gender stereotyping.[221] Likewise, several programs have been developed to help students identify and deal with sexually harassing behavior.[222] Schools that are unable to develop intensive programs still could adopt a proactive stance aimed at broad prevention, much as several schools have done with drug abuse, "normal" sexual behavior, and general violence.[223] Critical to these developments is a focus on new forms of sexuality education that relate more closely to children's lives and that incorporate power relations.[224] These innovative programs reinforce claims that there is clearly enough known about some forms of sexual violence to guide intervention efforts. Schools undoubtedly must play a role in combatting sexual and gendered violence.

In addition to school and family services, international law recognizes children's right to the "highest standard of health," and places an obligation on countries to create facilities for treatment and rehabilitation[225] and to promote the recovery of child victims of abuse.[226] Although programs do exist for children who have been sexually abused, few counseling and treatment services are available to help adolescents who are experiencing or perpetrating relationship violence, harassing behavior, or acquaintance rape.[227] The major reason for the current failure of professionals to offer appropriate assistance is that adolescents tend to underutilize professional support services that do exist.[228] Victims fail to seek formal support simply because they may be unaware of available opportunities for assistance, they may rely on informal social networks, or, as we have seen, they may define their violence as normative, requiring no intervention.

The international movement finds significance in more than its encouragement of efforts to prevent and deal with violence in educational, mental health, and familial environments. It is the manner in which the international movement does so that provides considerable hope. The focus on children's own rights means that there must be an attempt to alter social arrangements that overtly or subtly support violence against children. To change social policies that perpetuate violence, legal rules and policy-making must challenge children toward social change. International law seeks to include children and youth in matters that affect them, either through encouraging more direct access to legal services or through creating family environments and offering social services that foster their involvement. This challenge highlights the most devastating aspect of current domestic legislation and jurisprudence: it largely ignores the power of children in determining their own lives. This perspective suggests that youth must be supported with the information, resources, and skills needed to work toward prosocial change in their own lives, in the youth subculture, and in broader society.[229] Clearly, the active agent in social change is participation by those who would benefit most by personal and societal reform. They can only be involved if societies adopt a more enlightened and realistic view of children's lives. Children are social actors who coproduce their own development and actively create their own environments and their own cultures within and outside of adults' lives.[230]

Conclusions

By bestowing legal personhood upon children, international developments allow for transforming conceptions of children and of the way they are mistreated. Given that little attention has been paid to these developments in light of the sexual abuse committed by youth, it remains debatable that their impact will be felt any time soon. Yet, the developments are rather significant and consistent with current knowledge of more appropriate responses to the extent, nature, and consequences of abuse perpetrated by young offenders.

Research suggests a need to reconsider children's roles in their own development and in the exercise of their own rights. Children's capacity to influence themselves, let alone abuse their peers, suggests that adults and legal systems still largely underestimate children's capacity for self-determination and their powerful sense of agency. International law helps recognize the sense of agency and seeks to revision societies so that they respond more appropriately to children's self-determination. The development is significant: abusive relationships can be addressed only by recognizing children's capacities for victimization and perpetration. The recognition is the first step needed to combat "normative confusion" and to react more appropriately to the destructiveness of some young peoples' interactions. International developments allow for the recognition of this self-determination in the form of the rights it bestows on young offenders and victims and in the form of mandates to revision institutions that may foster or more appropriately react to victimization.

The mandates that could be used to address violence perpetrated by youth involve a rather new role for international human rights law—one which likely will encounter resistance. Yet, the currently ignored behaviors profoundly violate children's rights. Even the least physically intrusive behaviors have the effect of controlling victims through intimidation, embarrassment, or humiliation to the extent that they give in, tolerate, and try to ignore sexually maltreating acts. The legal recognition of the entire continuum of acts that constitute sexual abuse indicates an important and necessary shift from defining these experiences as personal or relational problems that are tolerated, to recognizing them as violent social problems and as broader human rights issues.

8 | Reconstructing the Law of Childhood, Cultural Life, and Sexual Maltreatment

International human rights law seeks to transform the regulation of childhood and the internal workings of all the world's cultures. The ongoing international developments provide a momentous opportunity to rethink the dimensions of and responses to child sexual maltreatment. This closing chapter delineates the thematic reconceptions international law offers for children's rights, details the implications those themes provide for sexually maltreated children, and highlights why children's rights and human rights law matter and can make a difference.

Introduction

Recent global developments mark a sweeping approval of human rights instruments and unprecedented advances in human rights law. Whether reluctantly or eagerly, all nations aim to accept, understand, and respect the moral aspirations of modern notions of human rights. The result is that the notion of human rights expresses the norms of the *international* community and no longer is reducible to any single state's interpretation. Ultimately, *national* laws and practices increasingly will become accountable and subordinate to norms embodied in international law. In the process, states increasingly will accept criteria by which to judge the treatment of everyone within their jurisdictions. This is international law's radical vision. At no other time has international law aimed to be so extensive. Individuals as well as states and nongovernmental organizations are asked to identify, respect, and actively ensure human rights that the international community has made part of its laws regulating human relations.

The broadening acceptance of the power of international law, its expanding moral vision, and its novel approaches to ensuring that societies respect the rule of human rights law make the accompanying formulations of children's human rights principles momentous. In light of invigorating developments in international law, emerging conceptualizations of children's rights attain unprecedented significance. Children's international human rights mandate fundamental transformations in laws and policies that regulate childhood and its cultural life. The following concluding sections review the potential contributions that these transformations offer to efforts to address sexual maltreatment. The analyses revisit the major transformations in conceptions of children's human rights, highlight obstacles and rationales for applying broad human rights principles to even broader conceptions of sexual maltreatment, and detail directions that could be taken in efforts to conceptualize and respond to child sexual maltreatment.

International Law and the Regulation of Childhood

Previous chapters proposed that international law provides a useful basis upon which to transform conceptions of childhood. Possible reconceptions, in turn, reveal how international law offers opportunities to rethink sexual maltreatment. Before detailing the nature of these opportunities, it is necessary to revisit international law's approach to children's rights and the regulation of childhood. At the risk of doing an injustice to the intricacies and complexities explored in previous chapters, it seems fair to conclude that four basic developments in human rights law may serve as a springboard to rethinking responses to child sexual maltreatment.

The primary transformation in legal approaches to childhood is the simple fact that the modern human rights movement actually includes children. International law now recognizes children's inherent sense of personhood and human dignity. This recognition markedly departs from traditional human rights law that had recognized that children needed protection but refused to recognize them as individual human persons. International law now recognizes that children no longer need to earn their status as persons: children have become subjects of rights, not mere objects of parental or other caretakers' rights. This development, fostered by other legal and social science developments, allows for bestowing upon children their own legal personhood and necessarily translates into the obligation, at a minimum, to realize that children's legal rights are critical to more effective child protection and liberation.

The second critical metamorphosis involves changing perceptions of the interactions children have with family members and members of other societal institutions. The movement appreciates how children are *individual* human persons inseparable from their social fabric and assumes diversity among societies and individuals. Assuming the existence of differences in children and their social conditions has two important implications. First, the focus attempts to ensure and recognize rights without inappropriately discriminating against children based on their social position, particularly as reflected in their social class, gender, abilities, nationalities, and locations. Second, it places emphasis on legally protecting and fostering the development of all children as well as their social conditions. At their core, then, human rights principles establish the inseparability of all children from their collective, even global, condition.

The third revolutionary development follows from the recognition of the important place children occupy in society, the diverse situations in which children find themselves, and the need to foster children's individual personhoods. This recognition dictates a new approach to the legal standards used to address children's needs. The standards championed by international law mandate that nations, societies, families, and individuals act in children's best interests. This approach differs considerably from traditional notions of best interests. What constitutes children's best interests must now be interpreted in light of the need to recognize, respect, foster, and ensure children's right to self-determination. This constitutes the foundation of the children's rights movement's most radical development. The foundational nature of this reconceptualization requires special elaboration of its implications for both individual children and their cultures.

In terms of individual development, children's self-determination, coupled with the mandate that societies act in children's best interests, switches the current starting points in thinking of children in societies and the law. This conception of children's rights radically departs from the adult-centered conceptions of rights. The widespread adult-centered approach to childhood and children's rights manifests itself in all institutions: in families and their ways of treating children, in laws and their enactment, in governments and their policies, in societies and their socialization practices, and in the global community and its traditional concerns. For example, sweepingly stated, the adult-centered approach equates children's familial interests with those of adults, ignores the need to ensure children's own access to courts and legal services, places societal priorities on economic interests rather than on children's needs, and plays down concern for the manner in which individual societies treat their children in favor of nations' treatment of each other. The international conceptual revolution seeks to rebalance concerns toward children's best interests and to rethink the nature and the influence these cultural institutions have on children. This development gives children greater voice and control in determining how all institutions will impact their lives.

Reconceptualization of self-determination also provides support and a primary mechanism for another emerging development in international human rights law—cultural self-determination. At cultural levels, the developments allow for rethinking the diverse institutions that constitute cultures. Prior to these developments, conceptions and proposals for cultural self-determination often were charged with allowing traditional practices to control vulnerable individuals and with allowing repressive regimes to oppress their vulnerable constituencies. Although these charges still remain, modern conceptions of cultural self-determination and of "culture" itself address these problems. Modern conceptions counter these criticisms through a focus that aims to respect difference and engage in exchanges. The belief is that cultures recursively impact upon one another and that the nature of imperialism has changed even to the extent that some global forces operate largely independently of individual cultures. Although recent developments in international human rights recognize the power of global, exogenous forces that impact cultural life, they still appreciate the power of endogenous forces that operate to transform and challenge deeply ingrained social institutions, and assume the need for local revolutions in the way children are treated. Simply put, modern international law moves away from focusing solely on how nations and the cultures within them must behave toward one another, and moves toward taking greater advantage of the natural involvement cultures have with one another and toward making greater use of indigenous beliefs to develop and foster human rights.

The fourth development encapsulates the previous three and serves to energize them. This development rests on the simple proposition that international rights are fundamental, "human" rights. As such, the international documents that recognize rights do more than reflect a demand for technical adherence to justice and equality. The international instruments express the moral outrage against dehumanization of both human persons *and* the human condition. Since children's rights are inalienable to both their human personhood and the human condition, responsibility for protecting children's rights rests both on individuals and states. All must be enlisted to recognize, respect, and ensure children's fundamental rights. This conception of rights and obligations takes a very expansive view of law. Law is much more than what courts and lawyers do; law fundamentally involves the manner in which people treat one another.

The four basic developments, summarized only in skeletal form at this point, highlight how it would be difficult to overemphasize the extent of the transformation in the way international law conceives of children and their rights. The global community now agrees that children have rights, that children's rights adhere to children themselves, and that an urgent need exists for greater commitment to developing and ensuring those rights. The development and investigation of diverse practices that may be construed as violating children's right to protection from sexual maltreatment grow from these recognitions and demands international law places on everyone.

International law, then, calls for investigations like the one offered in previous chapters. Despite that obligation derived from international mandates, studies that adopt a broad, human rights approach still readily face serious obstacles. These obstacles challenge the potential impact children's human rights may have on responses to child sexual maltreatment. Although basic obstacles complicate analyses and question the eventual impact of the four major transformations in children's human rights, a close reading of the nature of these obstacles reveals that they do not vitiate the need for analyses. Obstacles make studies even more critical. The following section delineates the nature of these obstacles in an effort to lay the groundwork for the concluding analysis of the potential impact of children's human rights on responses to child sexual maltreatment.

Child Sexual Maltreatment from a Human Rights and Global Perspective: Obstacles and Rationales

International children's rights law most fundamentally seeks to rethink how institutions interact with children. This goal makes it unsurprising that international law and the conceptualizations it spurs readily face significant obstacles. Although our previous analyses revealed numerous obstacles, it is useful to highlight three particularly fundamental ones. These obstacles concern the way basic social institutions render invisible the beliefs that foster maltreatment, rationalize problematic practices that do become visible, and remain highly immune from efforts to protect children from recognized forms of maltreatment. As we will see, these obstacles do much more than make practical applications of children's human rights difficult. These obstacles reinforce and provide rationales for considering how other countries approach child sexual maltreatment, for further developing children's human right to protection from sexual maltreatment, and for adopting a broad human rights approach.

Obstacles to a global, human rights approach

The first obstacle faced by a human rights approach involves the diverse manner in which institutions foster sexual maltreatment and the extent to which institutionalized beliefs and practices remain largely invisible. Indeed, we have seen how numerous institutions render some forms of maltreatment invisible and how some forms of maltreatment thrive because of their relative invisibility. The invisibility emerged at essentially all points in our review of the way societies treat children. Some societies attempt to view children as nonsexual beings and thus fail to accept their potential sexual aggressiveness, as revealed in our investigation of young child perpetrators of rape and sexual harassment. Other societies hold to the ideal of family privacy that guards against intrusion to protect children from sexual maltreatment—a family ideal that takes different forms and leads to different responses to sexual maltreatment that still leave children at risk. Yet other societies simply hasten the period of adulthood and thus remove children from the category of "childhood" and from the protections those children would otherwise receive; e.g., societies that allow child marriages generally provide a cultural framework that condones the negative effects of early sexual activity. Other societies do the converse; they refuse to recognize the extent to which some children have been forced to become independent and deny children benefits they could receive if they were adults. For example, Western societies place youth at risk for sexual victimization when they fail to recognize youth as possibly independent from their parents, such as when laws forbid youth shelters and even neighbors from providing shelter, services, and general assistance to homeless and runaway youth who do not have parental permission to obtain such supports. Likewise, some societies do not view children as individuals in their own right; instead, they view children as exchangeable, familial property. This makes it difficult to accept that children should not be married, sold, or rented to profit others. We also have seen how problematic practices often coincide with efforts to buffer children from certain harms; for example, commentators report that female genital operations, early marriage, virginity exams, and the pervasive "double standard" girls face regarding their sexual activity all seem to protect children as they reduce their availability to certain sexual partners. These examples underscore how cultural practices unwittingly condone or foster maltreatment.

The first obstacle, then, essentially deals with the invisibility of potentially problematic beliefs and practices. Examples of this obstacle reveal how the complexity, cultural embeddedness, and utility of practices and beliefs render cultural institutions unable to see how certain forms of interactions with children and certain perceptions of childhood contribute to maltreatment. The inability, in turn, makes suspect efforts to include practices in conceptions of what violates basic human rights. This obstacle lays the foundation for the other two obstacles.

The second obstacle derives from the way cultures maintain problematic practices by simply not recognizing how their belief systems place children at risk. This obstacle involves the way societies can marshal locally legitimate arguments that allow them to view practices as unproblematic. Our investigation revealed numerous examples of arguments and rationalizations, many of which appear reasonable, that challenge efforts to conceptualize practices as sexual maltreatment. These arguments were especially strong in defense of female genital operations, child marriages, indigenous rituals that involve sexual interactions with children, sex tourism, and sexual harassment by young children. Some of the major arguments against including these practices as potential violations of children's fundamental human rights included the proposal that cultures simply do not necessarily view the practices as sexual. For example, some propose that the practices simply involve permissible child labor or involve proper gender role socialization into adulthood. Other major arguments against conceiving these practices as sexual maltreatment rested on the proposition that the practices were in fact sexual, but that the experience of such sexuality remained critical to healthy development; e.g., some fear that viewing some forms of sexually aggressive behavior by children as problematic will lead to the criminalization of sexuality and warp children's sexual development. These are important arguments that constitute powerful obstacles against defining many of the reviewed practices as sexual maltreatment. As we have seen, local arguments remain difficult to counter, largely because local arguments appear most reasonable, and because outsiders' conceptions and intrusive efforts are easily construable as impermissibly imperialistic.

The third obstacle to human rights analyses also relates to the first. This obstacle relates to the difficulty of pressing for changes in culturally embedded practices even though the practices may be recognized as problematic and worthy of response. As we have seen, several practices continue despite condemnation from outside and inside the observed societies. Child sexual abuse, as conceptualized in Western countries, provides a powerful example of a form of maltreatment that has been the subject of numerous legal and policy responses fueled by intense public concern. Yet, the sexual abuse of children continues essentially unabated in every Western country studied by researchers. Two examples illustrate the difficulties cultural practices and beliefs pose for efforts to combat child sexual abuse. The first difficulty derives from the failure to reconsider how to make the internal workings of families more public and how to offer greater protection to individual members. We have seen how family privacy hinders intervention efforts to help individual children and to offer services. The second difficulty emerges from the manner in which the conceptualization of sexual abuse leaves entire groups of children at risk. For example, policy-makers have failed to recognize the extent to which boys may be abused, particularly by other boys, and how their socialization makes it difficult for them to disclose, seek assistance, or simply acquire skills to avoid maltreatment. As we have seen, conceptions of masculinity, views of homosexuality, and impressions of the way the sexes interact hinder attempts to assist boys. Properly addressing the abuses boys suffer necessitates confronting traditional views and values. These two examples reveal how pervasive forms of maltreatment remain difficult to combat even though the relevant societies exhibit a sincere public commitment to address all forms of child sexual maltreatment. Thus, the "practice" of sexual abuse continues largely because certain sex role socializations and familial patterns leave children vulnerable. The failure to combat this and other forms of maltreatment relates to the inability to accept how certain cultural beliefs place children at risk and to the fear that addressing the problems will intrude impermissibly upon deeply rooted cultural values.

The three closely related obstacles are fundamental, yet often are ignored by commentaries that delineate obstacles to combatting child maltreatment. The basic obstacles identified by this study are even more fundamental than the often-noted failure to provide adequate resources to combat sexual maltreatment. As we have seen, even massive resources in the form of antipoverty programs do not suffice to alter or respond to practices that place children at risk. The obstacles are also more fundamental than the belief that maltreatment continues due to the failure to criminalize certain relationships with children. As we have seen, criminalization often fails to alter matters and can even exacerbate them; and many practices legitimately may be viewed as part of a continuum of violence against children that requires a variety of responses making variable use of fiscal, educational, therapeutic, and criminal justice resources. Likewise, the obstacles are even more fundamental than the lack of political will to foster reform. Several recent legislative efforts consider aspects of the reviewed practices; local and customary laws also often recognize aspects of the problematic practices and aim for ideals that often diverge from everyday reality. Although addressing obstacles identified by commentaries certainly could alleviate some maltreatment rates, it would not necessarily address root causes of sexual maltreatment. As we have seen, root causes have more to do with the problematic cultural beliefs and practices that remain invisible, the culturally salient beliefs that rationalize problematic practices, and the culturally ingrained socialization patterns that leave children vulnerable to forms of abuses societies mark for eradication. Although commentaries often play down these root causes in favor of a push for resources, tougher law enforcement, and an increase in political will, our review highlights what researchers and child advocates know: the desire to help children, strict legal sanctions, and the infusion of resources remain far from enough.

Our analyses of obstacles suggest two conclusions that gain significance from our earlier analyses of children's human rights law. First, to highlight a major theme from previous chapters, the manner in which problematic practices are situated in cultural life restricts attempts to envision and propose different approaches. Many of the cultural forces that support the practices are not well-suited for, or do not even make it onto, the sociopolitical agenda. Second, responses to the central obstacles identified by existing commentaries may be necessary, but they remain insufficient to protect children from sexual maltreatment. Rampant failures to protect children do not necessarily rest on failed efforts to provide resources, the inability to enact specific responses to maltreatment, or a general lack of political will to address maltreating practices. Instead, our analyses suggest that the basic obstacles to child protection deal more with the cultural saliency of the practices and the contributing forces that remain culturally condoned. These two conclusions acquire importance when considered in light of our often-repeated proposal that failures in child protection generally arise from the inability to take seriously children's rights and to recognize the importance of the human rights framework. Given that our analyses rest on the need to overcome the inability to adopt a children's human rights perspective, the next section revisits reasons the children's rights movement provides an opportunity to rethink cultural frameworks that leave children vulnerable to child sexual maltreatment.

Rationales for a global, human rights approach

As we have seen, the major obstacles to attempts to reconceptualize sexual maltreatment from a global perspective do not invalidate efforts to do so. On the contrary, the obstacles underscore the importance of a careful examination of practices not readily perceived as sexual maltreatment and of societal beliefs that support maltreatment. The obstacles also reinforce the need for a broad, human rights approach that responds appropriately to these diverse culturally embedded conceptions of what constitutes harm. The remainder of this section highlights the fundamental reasons for a broad, human rights analysis and serves as a prologue to conclusions regarding the implications of the human rights approach to child sexual maltreatment.

International law mandates that societies confront practices deemed maltreating. This mandate provides a primary reason for a comprehensive approach and investigation of the way children may be sexually maltreated. For example, international law explicitly finds that children have a right to protection from sexual abuse, exploitation, and harmful traditional practices. The failure to address what falls under these broad categories threatens to weaken the power of the international mandate. As we have seen, international developments reflect the increasing need not necessarily to categorize the practices as maltreating, but to use global principles to help determine whether they may constitute maltreatment. The principles to be used in conceptualizing and responding to sexual maltreatment, presented in Chapters 4, 5, 6, and 7, largely deal with providing voice to those who could be harmed and with re-envisioning different ways to offer assistance. The design of better ways to offer assistance and determine harms will become more feasible only with fuller, nuanced analyses of the contours of child sexuality and of the way children's interests may be involved in reform efforts to protect children from inappropriate sexual activities and beliefs.

Beyond the obvious international mandate, the investigation of very diverse practices gains significance in that, without doubt, the practices profoundly relate to children's current sexual life or their future lives as sexual beings. Given that the practices as developed and explained within practicing cultures fundamentally relate to human sexuality, the practices implicate children's right to sexual self-determination. The implications of that right continue regardless of how particular communities narrowly define the right. A primary example of such implications involves the institutionalization of child marriages and the way both developed and developing countries have difficulty recognizing child sexuality. In developing countries, such marriages determine children's sexual partners and generally put children at risk for early sexual activity and pregnancy, and for their negative outcomes; in developed countries, laws vacillate between condoning the practice and charging fathers with statutory rape. Thus, even this practice, which arguably remains the only one that reaches legitimacy among all cultures, still involves conditions that may be viewed as sexually maltreating in the form of a basic failure to recognize children's right to sexual self-determination.

World migration trends provide a third reason to approach sexual maltreatment from a broad human rights perspective that includes practices that some societies do not view as maltreating. Emerging global trends reveal that practices condoned in one culture, such as male and female genital alterations, become problematic when practiced in different societies. The proper way to respond to these imported practices rests on a deeper understanding of the broad manner in which children are treated across societies. For example, simply criminalizing circumcision that occurs in countries where such rituals are not indigenous may simply exacerbate the problems that were the subject of concern; i.e., medical complications, discrimination, and death of young girls may increase when practices are driven underground by efforts to criminalize practices. Proper responses to the migration of practices that become problematic require broad analyses of human relationships and cultural systems.

The way modernization actually exacerbates the difficult circumstances in which some children find themselves also undergirds the need for a focus on other countries' potential conceptions of child sexual maltreatment. The way international forces contribute to increases in sex tourism and the inter-state trafficking of child pornography provides examples of the need for domestic as well as international regulation. As we have seen in the contexts of these two forms of sexual maltreatment, taking a more forceful stance against some forms of maltreatment in one country may simply mean that offenders will find victims in other countries. Relatedly, global conditions contribute to child maltreatment in that they play a critical role in fostering private relationship patterns that place children at risk, a process made most obvious by the way global patterns increase poverty in some countries, thus raising the rates of child sexual exploitation by leaving children and families without resources. The context of modernization also serves to highlight challenges faced by international law and the need for some concordance in approaches to child victimization. As we have seen, modernization and moves to other areas to find children become most obvious and bizarre with the development of technology that allows individuals to slip into body suits and physically simulate sexual interactions with children. It remains to be imagined how societies will deal with this and other new technology that makes use of child pornography. Currently, the United

States stands alone in making the possession of some forms of child pornography worthy of any response, even though current research reveals that traditional and computerized pornography places children at risk for sexual maltreatment and increases the need for a coordinated international response. Challenges prompted by modernization signal the need to consider how societies will cooperate and coordinate efforts to protect vulnerable children.

It is also important to consider the wide variety of practices from a human rights perspective because they tend to reveal fundamental, underlying themes of how children are viewed and treated. For example, all the reviewed practices demonstrate how the failure to see children as individuals in their own right results in the inability to respond appropriately to their needs. One increasingly obvious but still largely ignored example is the Western failure to assume that adolescents are not victims of battering in their own sexual relationships. The failed recognition leaves victims without legal assistance and access to social services adult victims enjoy. Again, reasonable arguments could be made that the crime involves assault and battery, not sexual maltreatment. Yet, upon close scrutiny, sexual dimensions emerge: battering serves as an index for what some would label sexual maltreatment and would associate with its primary causes. For example, our analysis revealed how adolescent battering closely relates to gender role socialization, rape, pregnancy, child sexual abuse, and the failure to recognize that youth may be sexual beings involved in serious sexual relationships. Thus, although there may be disagreement that battering or any other practice may not be seen as sexual maltreatment, the investigation reveals the need to consider the root and nature of violence that remains highly sexual and gendered.

In addition to the above reasons for a broad, human rights approach, it is important to return to another significant theme. Recall, as explored most fully in Chapter 5, that a major contribution of the human rights movement derives from the way violence becomes public and the way individuals perceive violence. This contribution serves to highlight the need for a globalized approach to sexual maltreatment and for an approach anchored in human rights law. As we have seen, the extent to which some individuals and cultures view certain practices as problematic actually fosters children's rights and increases protection from child maltreatment by promoting discussion, participation, and change. A particularly important yet generally dismissed example is the growing recognition that male circumcision must be questioned not only to address boys' own rights but also to address the underlying structure of systems that allow female circumcision to continue. Thus, although those who view male circumcision as maltreatment may remain in the minority, an analysis of prevailing reasons for including this practice in conceptions of maltreatment reveals that the same arguments tend to be made to support both male and female circumcision, and that addressing either practice necessitates confronting their common, underlying rationales.

To recapitulate, the review thus far consists of three important points. The first point involves resistance to human rights analyses. The resistance to a global, human rights approach essentially concerns the failure to realize that such an approach may have local legitimacy. That failure derives from the inability to view one's deeply held cultural convictions as problematic or in need of reform. The inability is unsurprising; societies necessarily attach significance to their own traditions and resist intrusion. The second point concerns the way the current globalization of cultures and the rapid transformation of all societies increasingly defy efforts to maintain traditions and to resist intrusion. Sociolegal changes accompanying global transformations provide rationales for looking to human rights law and for reconsidering the manner in which societies view children; they provide reasons the major obstacles to human rights approaches must be overcome. The third point relates more specifically to child sexual maltreatment. The wide variety of ways children are sexually maltreated illustrates how the apparent globalization and rapid sociolegal transformations inevitably will challenge resistance to global approaches. The convergence of these three points provides an unusual opportunity to rethink responses to child sexual maltreatment. We now turn to detailing implications offered by these transformations and by the international children's rights movement.

Implications for Addressing Child Sexual Maltreatment

Given the need to consider children's human rights law and the diverse ways societies treat children, it is important to highlight the benefits of an international children's human rights approach and to provide concrete examples of potential contributions. Although international law offers an expansive, if not idealistic, vision that may remain far from reach and subject to constant refinement, the international movement does spur forward some minimal reconceptions that may play central roles in efforts to combat child sexual maltreatment. The previous chapters framed these considerations as the need to make more visible children's circumstances and the forces that lead to sexual maltreatment. Previous chapters also proposed that the need to increase the visibility of problematic cultural beliefs and practices complemented emerging principles in children's human rights law. A reasonable way to continue that discussion and present the children's rights movement's potential contributions is to return to the four major developments delineated at the beginning of this chapter and pinpoint how they may contribute to uncovering and dealing with sexual maltreatment, and how the envisioned approach diverges from prevailing responses to sexual maltreatment.

The first contribution involves the manner in which the human rights movement seeks to make children subjects of their own rights. Children own their rights. This development significantly departs from traditional law, which holds that parents and society control the limited rights children have as well as the nature of those rights. For example, current law generally defers to parental rights when issues arise concerning whether children should have access to certain educational resources, or whether children will be provided social services and supports. In terms of sexual maltreatment, the recent developments mean that children's own primary interests, not those of their parents, would dictate whether children have access to family planning services. Children's own interests would also dictate the content of sexuality education; parents would not possess nearly unilateral control over the information children receive. In addition to programs that address child sexuality, the rethinking would impact sexual maltreatment prevention programs. At a minimum, the switch would result in concern about the inadequate and scarce amount of available information, in terms of both professional knowledge and also the information societies seem willing to convey to children and youth. The development conceivably could go quite further. Recognizing that children are legally independent entities with a need for and right to individual consideration in all matters concerning their treatment by others would lead to a reconfiguration of family life, particularly of family privacy, and could allow for greater "intrusion" into family life in order to protect children. As we have seen in Chapter 6, legal systems that have recognized sexual interactions with children as abusive still have difficulty protecting children, and much of that difficulty derives from concern to protect family privacy. Unlike current approaches to child protection, then, the international approach bestows upon children their own legal personhood that must be considered in the design of policies that affect children. Legal systems must acknowledge and address children's own claims and not render them invisible by allowing parents or other caretakers to control rights that the global community recognizes as belonging to children.

The second contribution emphasizes two important points of focus in thinking about ensuring children's rights. The first focus seeks to increase recognition that children are individuals and that their needs are inseparable from their social conditions. The second focus emphasizes that children, like adults, are not socially autonomous; they thrive only in and through relationships. Although numerous implications arise from these two related developments, previous chapters centered on the way the developments support the need to consider various ecological dimensions of sexual maltreatment if societies are ever to secure children's rights. From this perspective, the transformation in approaches to children's rights offers important avenues for reform in the current understanding of, and in responses to, the full complexity of victimization. Three examples illustrate the perspective's significance. The first example highlights the recognition that a broad range of sources contribute to maltreatment. Teen pregnancy and child prostitution, among other difficult circumstances children face, provided clear examples of the need for such approaches. Both teen pregnancy and child prostitution are associated with early child sexual maltreatment and later coercive sexual activity that places teens at risk for behaviors that are seen as problems, rather than as symptoms. Recognizing these behaviors as symptoms makes for a rather different approach. The recognition leads to considering the need to bolster family supports and the willingness to intervene in family life rather than, for example, focusing efforts on punishing young prostitutes's clients, fathers of young girls' children, or the girls themselves. Although room still exists for the development of punitive laws, the development in international human rights emphasizes that legal systems can play an even greater, preventive role in ensuring children's right to protection. The second example follows from the recognition that personal relationships provide important buffers against maltreatment and from the need to rethink the nature of those relationships and their ecological contexts. For example, the movement urges societies to rethink how children in families may differently enjoy familial rights, privileges, and protections. The seemingly global discrimination against girls in families' efforts to educate children provides a recurring example: girls receive fewer educational opportunities, which contributes to numerous other negative outcomes, such as early marriage, decreased economic opportunities, and lack of resources. These consequences, in turn, all increase girls' vulnerability to traditional practices deemed harmful to their health. The third example relates to the above examples and emphasizes the need to recognize diverse ways to protect children. The proposal suggests that protection must remain flexible and comprehensive, and must be placed within a larger social context. This development, supported by recent conceptions of children's rights, translates into approaches to child protection that accept the duties of parents and community members and offer them requisite support to help prevent sexual maltreatment. The current understanding of how to prevent the sexual abuse of children in the West provides an important example. Recent prevention efforts make greater use of parental education and community awareness. These developments arise from the recognition that placing the burden for prevention on children themselves remains inadequate and ignores what has been called the silent ecology of child sexual abuse; i.e., the manner in which children are "seduced" into sexual relationships and remain trapped in them exemplifies the need to focus beyond children as the source of prevention. At its core, then, the second transformation in approaches to children's rights recognizes that prevailing conceptions of childhood are ideological artifacts that hinder ways to assist maltreated children and that may foster maltreatment. The ecological focus realizes that societal imperatives structure children's lives and highlights how demands for children's rights can achieve their goals only if they consider and aim to restructure these imperatives.

The third contribution dealt with the important focus on self-determination, both at individual and cultural levels. Both levels are important to consider. We already have seen the significance attached to increasing children's legal independence in the form, for example, of ensuring their right of access to information and social services. Issues of children's individual self-determination, however, are omnipresent in child protection laws, as reflected in the subtle ways laws perceive children. Although children's sense of independence may be obvious to those not versed in law, perceptions of children's incapacities and dependencies primarily guide current legal approaches to children's lives. The international development in this area requires that children's sense of agency be made more visible and that it actually be harnessed in efforts to assist. As we have seen, the past decade's reforms in Western sexual abuse laws largely focused on protecting children who became involved in legal processes that attempted to punish offenders, or, in the alternative, focused on not prosecuting offenders for fear that children were suspect witnesses. These concerns with children's ability to make decisions ignored the reality children face. Victims make numerous decisions, such as whether they should tell about abuse. Indeed, the majority of children, like adults in comparable situations, decide not to disclose. Yet, the law uses children's reticence to exclude their testimony. Given the psychological and social complexities involved in disclosure, legal reconceptions could, for example, rethink the role of disclosure in prosecutorial efforts. An obvious possible reform would respect children's sense of self-determination and seek to treat child victims more like self-determining adult victims. At a minimum, prosecutors and parents would be unable to manipulate victims to have them participate in prosecutions. In addition, concern for children's self-determination could be used to question whether there should be greater respect for those who would prefer not to disclose, or at least greater respect for children's own determination of the outcome of their cases. If the proposal for reform were taken seriously, it could mean that, as for adults, the law would not mandate children's therapists to disclose their clients' sexual victimization and violate patient-therapist confidentiality. Instead, for example, the law simply could mandate therapists to take appropriate steps to determine whether abuse has stopped or to protect the child from further abuse, much as the law requires therapists to take action with other forms of abuse. These reforms would ensure that the law acts therapeutically and places greater emphasis on children's interests. Clearly, reforms that increase children's self-determination would be controversial. However, controversiality should not bar efforts to imagine reform; it is only in considering such possibilities that more effective means will emerge to deal with disclosure, treatment, and prevention. In fact, we already have seen how mandatory reporting laws have been subjected to increasing criticisms, not the least of which have been the observations that such laws may stifle therapeutic efforts for both children and offenders and that many professionals simply refuse to report for fear they will do more harm than good. Likewise, children in some jurisdictions already essentially possess the power to veto prosecutors' decisions. The proposal is not as radical as it may appear; several states in the U.S., and several countries systematically forego some prosecutions and mandate services for offenders, child victims, and families. Again, although perhaps initially outrageous, thinking of how else to treat children helps further their rights and leads to more enlightened reform.

The third contribution also involves the need to consider cultural self-determination, a point related to rethinking children's individual self-determination. This development suggests a need to resist the conclusion that children must be saved from their cultures. Currently, massive efforts are made to save Third World children and offer modernization in hopes that it will alleviate maltreatment. These efforts are problematic for several reasons. First, more "advanced" countries do not necessarily protect their own children. Second, forces of modernization actually may exacerbate existing maltreatment rates and place more children at risk for other forms of sexual maltreatment. Third, such imperialism simply does not work and contravenes basic democratic, international principles. As revealed in Chapter 5, when it is applied in different cultures that resist the imposition of alien standards, international law is to provide principles of deliberation and respect diversity. Instead of saving children from cultures, international developments allow for using indigenous concepts and basic values to foster children's rights. As we have seen, child protective strategies reach effectiveness when they connect basic children's rights themes with localized and widely shared values. For example, the universal recognition that children should not be exploited offers an important opportunity. The goal would be to delineate more precisely what constitutes exploitation and the conditions under which it will be tolerated. Efforts to characterize practices as torturous also reflect this approach's effectiveness, most obviously seen in efforts to catalyze responses against genital alterations and sexual slavery. Reform attempts that frame practices such as virginity exams as violations of basic human dignity also increase the likelihood of reform simply because human rights policy-making places strong emphasis on the concept of human dignity. By linking international values with local values, human rights law provides a common language that serves as a stepping stone for changing approaches to child protection.

The approach that aims to protect cultural self-determination by linking global to local standards also offers important lessons and opportunities for developed countries to ensure children's rights. Two examples serve to highlight the potential effectiveness of such efforts. The first example involves the way links can be made between children's basic rights and the highly touted concept of family values. The approach is useful to the extent that the latter may help address the former. That is, when the rationale that families exist to protect children serves to decrease intrusion into family life, the failure to protect children erodes the power of the rationale to resist intervention. The difference in stance toward child protection is significant. The approach suggests that concern for child protection would increase willingness to intervene prior to discovery of abuse, even though societies generally wait to intervene after the discovery of problems. Again, such approaches may be controversial. But, as we have seen, some societies readily intervene in families to support children even without proof or allegations of abuse; these societies simply use nonintrusive techniques, such as offering social services and community support programs, instead of waiting until coercive and punitive measures become the only available response. The second example deals with links that may be made between ideals of self-sufficiency and democratic life, on the one hand, and what may be done to reduce rates of sexual maltreatment, on the other. Developed countries grant educational institutions the task of furthering democratic ideals, particularly with regard to individuals' economic self-sufficiency. The role played by education in fostering democratic principles has been so effective that it also plays a major role in moving other countries toward democracy. Regardless of the society, we have seen that the basic democratic commitment to providing children with educational opportunities coincides with protecting them from sexual maltreatment. Ensuring children's own educational rights means, for example, providing resources to poor families so they will allow children to be ready for schooling, securing access to quality education that prepares children for rapidly changing societal mores, and increasing the availability of social services, including therapeutic and family planning services, to children who come from disruptive homes and to children who have become sexually active. In brief, education that takes children's interests seriously fosters the full range of children's rights and prepares children for living in the kind of world envisioned by modern human rights law. These examples reveal the potential effectiveness of strategically connecting children's needs to widely shared values and means of achieving culturally settled ideals consistent with global conceptions of children's rights.

The fourth contribution provided children's human rights with a sense of energy and urgency. The belief that children's rights could impact children's lives is not obvious from existing commentaries, particularly those that examine sexual abuse as conceptualized by Western societies. Commentators generally fail to consider the potential role of international law in examinations of child sexual maltreatment. That failure reveals how it may be questionable whether human rights law offers a fruitful arena for renegotiating models of human development, family life, culture, and civil society. Admittedly, international law does not provide all the answers; nor are its answers clear-cut. As we have seen, for example, even the most radical approaches to children's human rights remain limited. Much more work still needs to be done to rethink ways to protect youth from sexual victimization while not inappropriately infringing on their other rights—such as the right to sexual expression, the right to certain sexual information, the right to determine the use of their own bodies, and the right to participate in their own cultures. Despite these important limitations, the response to concerns about the role of human rights law remains quite simple and even more basic than the rationales addressed earlier. The continued failure of traditional efforts mandates a consideration of new visions of childhood and the law.

Given the void in proposals for rethinking how to protect children, it is important to emphasize two points about human rights law and the significance of those points. First, human rights advocates often find themselves with little in the way of legislation and litigation tactics to aid them in their causes; indeed, their causes often find hostility in existing law. Second, despite hostility, the progress in efforts to conceptualize, foster, and globally negotiate human rights reaches beyond any historical precedent. These two points reaffirm that human rights law actually remains especially well-suited to assist in efforts to fundamentally restructure society and the place of children in it. The conviction derives from the manner in which international human rights law provides an important, supportive source for conceptualizing and enacting reforms. Much of the discussion found in previous chapters highlighted how international law does not necessarily resolve disputes; more important, it provides methods of deliberation and accommodation. For example, as with other human rights advocacy, published reports, use of the media, and international law's usual methods can be used to cajole, push, threaten, and punish actors who fail to make progress in attempts to address the needs of sexually maltreated children. These methods of advocacy are important not only for action at Nation State levels, but also for action directed toward individual actors who have discretion in the implementation of laws, as well as toward those subject to that discretion. Existing evidence suggests that such efforts are far from futile. For example, the development of a documentary record of maltreating experiences already contributes to a deeper understanding of the difficulties children face; recall that documentary records effectively have placed several forms of violence against children on the public agenda, such as the sexual violence involved in organized sex tourism, genital mutilation, rape, and harassment. Put into the perspective of our analyses, these efforts work simply because they appropriately aim to make maltreating experiences, and their sustaining forces, visible. As we have seen, children's human rights law will work because it offers principles and mechanisms that ensure consideration of children's own interests and that capitalize on the natural transformation of cultural life.

The last point captures the significance of our investigation. Our analyses underscore how human rights law increasingly becomes well-suited for the task of combatting the visible and invisible forms of maltreatment in a rapidly changing world. Efforts guided by universal principles that aim to respect children and ensure their inherent sense of human dignity breathe life into existing sociolegal frameworks. At its core, human rights law challenges the tendency to narrowly define and isolate practices from broader issues of violence against children and children's personhood. Such tendencies severely limit analyses of children's problems and possible responses, even where current laws and societies roundly condemn maltreating practices. As we have seen, traditional conceptualizations of maltreating practices too narrowly filter our capacity to imagine solutions and alternative visions. Expanding and reconceptualizing visions of maltreatment and human rights law can promote a questioning of the legitimacy of existing social institutions and practices. The extent to which the international questioning, challenging, and reconceptualization of prevailing notions of childhood and maltreatment will follow from the new right to protection from sexual maltreatment will reveal how the spectacular international commitment to children can become even more dramatic in practice.

Notes

1. Invisible Acts

1. James P. Grant (1994). *The State of the World's Children*. NY: Oxford University Press.

2. Robert Desjarlais, Leon Eisenberg, Byron Good & Arthur Kleinman (1995). *World Mental Health: Problems and Priorities in Low-Income Countries*. NY: Oxford; Cristina Szanton Blanc (1994). *Urban Children in Distress: Global Predicaments and Innovative Strategies*. Longhorne, PA: Gordon and Breach.

3. James Garborino (1995). *Socially Toxic Environments*. San Francisco: Jossey-Bass.

4. Patricia D. Levan (1994). Curtailing Thailand's child prostitution through an international conscience, *American University Journal of International Law and Policy* 9, 869–912.

5. Kelly D. Weisberg (1984). Children of the night: The adequacy of statutory treatment of juvenile prostitution, *American Journal of Criminal Law* 12, 1–67.

6. Eric Thomas Berkman (1996). Responses to the international child sex tourism trade, *Boston College International and Comparative Law Review* 19(2), 397–422.

7. Julia Foreman (1990). Can we end the shame?—Recent multilateral efforts to address the world child pornography market, *Vanderbilt Journal of International Law* 23, 435–468 at 449.

8. Although child pornography estimates are difficult to obtain, some reports indicate the extent of the problem. In Los Angeles alone, for example, an estimated 30,000 children are exploited through prostitution and pornography every year. R. Barrie Flowers (1994). *The Victimization and Exploitation of Women and Children*. Jefferson, NC: McFarland.

9. Parker Rossman (1976). *Sexual Experience between Men and Boys*. Wilton, CT: Association Press.

10. Emily Benedek (1996). Unkindest cut? How circumcision came full circle, *New York Times* May 19, E3; George C. Denniston & Marilyn Fayre Milos (Eds.) (1997). *Sexual Mutilations: A Human Tragedy*. NY: Plenum.

11. Sarah Y. Lai & Regan E. Ralph (1995). Female sexual autonomy and human rights, *Harvard Human Rights Journal* 8, 201–227.

12. Human Rights Watch/Women's Rights Project (1994). *A Matter of Power: State Control of Women's Virginity in Turkey*. NY: Human Rights Watch; Sarah Y. Lai & Regan E. Ralph (1995). Female sexual autonomy and human rights, *Harvard Human Rights Journal* 8, 201–227; Sriani Basnayake (1990). The virginity test—A bridal nightmare, *The Journal of Family Welfare* 36(2), 50–59.

13. Gilbert H. Herdt (Ed.) (1993). *Ritualized Homosexuality in Melanesia*. Berkeley: University of California Press.

14. Suzanne G. Frayser (1994). Defining normal childhood sexuality: An anthropological approach, *Annual Review of Sex Research* 5, 173–217; Lloyd DeMause (1991). The universality of incest, *The Journal of Psychohistory* 19(2), 123–164.

15. For example, Chasnoff and his colleagues have shown how similar maternal-neonatal behaviors have powerful sexualizing effects on the boy's behavior at a very young age. M. D. Chasnoff et al. (1986). Maternal-neonatal incest, *American Journal of Orthopsychiatry* 56, 577–580.

16. For example, DeMause and Frayser, cited above, come to dramatically different conclusions regarding the abusiveness of the behavior.

17. See Thomas G. Weiss, David P. Forsythe & Roger A. Coate (1994). *The United Nations and Changing World Politics.* Boulder, CO: Westview; Ervin Laszlo (1993). *The Multicultural Planet.* Chatham, NY: Oneworld.

18. David Finkelhor (1994). The international epidemiology of child sexual abuse, *Child Abuse & Neglect* 18, 409–417.

19. Gary B. Melton (1992). The improbability of prevention of sexual abuse. In D. J. Willis, W. E. Holden & M. S. Rosenberg (Eds.) *Prevention of Child Maltreatment,* (168–189). NY: Wiley; Leslie M. Tutty (1993). Are child sexual abuse prevention programs effective? A review of research, *Sexological Review* 1(2), 93–114.

20. Monica L. Oberman (1994). Turning girls into women: Re-evaluating modern statutory rape law, *Journal of Criminal Law & Criminology* 85, 15–79; Julie M. Guggino & James J. Ponzetti, Jr. (1997). Gender differences in affective reactions to first coitus, *Journal of Adolescence* 20, 189–200.

21. Susan Sprecher, Elaine Hatfield, Anthony Cortese, Elena Ptapova & Anna Levitskaya (1994). Token resistance to sexual intercourse and consent to unwanted sexual intercourse: College students' dating experiences in three countries, *Journal of Sex Research* 31, 125–132.

22. Gail Ryan, Thomas J. Miyoshi, Jeffrey L. Metzner, Richard D. Krugman & George Fryer (1996). Trends in a national sample of sexually abusive youths, *Journal of the American Academy of Child and Adolescent Psychiatry* 35(1), 17–25.

23. Nan Stein (1995). Sexual harassment in school: The public performance of gendered violence, *Harvard Educational Review* 65, 145–162.

24. Kelley L. Armstrong (1994). The silent minority within a minority: Focusing on the needs of gay youths in our public schools, *Golden Gate University Law Review* 24, 67–97.

25. Dirk Johnson (1996). Students still sweat, they just don't shower, *New York Times* April 22, 1, A12.

26. Id.

27. Commentators and researchers, however, tend to focus on either influence to the exclusion of the other; see, e.g., David B. Sugarman & Gerald T. Hotaling (1989). Dating violence: Prevalence, context, and risk markers. In Maureen A. Pirog-Good & Jan E. Stets (Eds.) *Violence in Dating Relationships: Emerging Social Issues* (3–32). NY: Praeger.

28. Roger J. R. Levesque (1997). Dating violence, adolescents and the law, *Virginia Journal of Social Policy and Law* 4, 339–379.

29. A. A. Rosenfeld, et al. (1986). Determining contact between parent and child: Frequency of children touching parents' genitals in a non-clinical population, *Journal of the American Academy of Child Psychiatry* 25, 224–229.

30. It is important to recognize, however, that societies are far from monolithic

and that practices are often encouraged and sustained by select groups within societies.

31. Roger J. R. Levesque (1994). The sexual use, abuse and exploitation of children: Challenges in implementing children's human rights, *Brooklyn Law Review* 60, 959–998; Geraldine Van Bueren (1995). *The International Law on the Rights of the Child*. Boston: Martinus Nijhoff Publishers.

32. For example, Article 1 of the Draft Optimal Protocol to the Convention on the Rights of the Child Concerning the Elimination of Sexual Exploitation and Trafficking of Children, E/CN.4/1995/95, reiterates the significant breakthrough in proclaiming that "States Parties recognize that crimes of sexual exploitation of, or trafficking in, children represent crimes against humanity."

33. Although it still ignores issues of sexual maltreatment, the only book-length analysis of the concept importantly demonstrates the new challenges *erga omnes* obligations place on international law. Maurizio Ragazzi (1997). *The Concept of International Obligations* Erga Omnes. NY: Oxford University Press.

34. Under Article 2(a) of The Draft Optional Protocol to the United Nations Convention on the Rights of the Child Concerning the Elimination of Sexual Exploitation and Trafficking of Children, E/CN.4/1995/95, States Parties agree to give effect in their national legislation to the principle of universal criminal jurisdiction concerning sex crimes against children. This form of jurisdiction is most commonly exercised in relation to crimes of piracy and war crimes under the Geneva Convention of August 12, 1949. See Joseph Gabriel Starke (1989). *Introduction to International Law* (10th ed.). (234). St. Paul, MN: Butterworths.

35. The only exception is states which consistently objected to a specific customary norm as it has emerged. See Ann Bayefsky & Joan Fitzpatrick (1992). International human rights law in United States courts: A comparative perspective, *Michigan Journal of International Law* 14, 1–89.

36. Failure to recognize human rights violations is part of the problem with all children's issues. Roger J. R. Levesque (1996). International children's rights: Can it make a difference in American family policy? *American Psychologist* 51, 1251–1256.

37. John E. B. Myers (1994). Definitions and origins of the backlash against child protection. In John E. B. Myers (Ed.) *The Backlash: Child Protection Under Fire* (17–30). Thousand Oaks, CA: Sage.

38. Philip Jenkins (1993). *Intimate Enemies: Moral Panics in Contemporary Great Britain*. NY: Aldine De Gruyter.

39. The arguments are similar to those found in the recent commentaries that problematize poverty and the manner in which it led to the making and unmaking of the Third World. Arturo Escobar (1995). *Encountering Development: The Making and Unmaking of the Third World*. Princeton: Princeton University Press.

40. Several propose that those arguing for cultural relativism and respect for state and cultural sovereignty are motivated by the freedom to practice intolerance without external criticism. Anne F. Bayefsky (1996). Cultural sovereignty, relativism, and international human rights: New excuses for old strategies, *Ratio Juris* 9(1), 42–59.

41. Roger J. R. Levesque (1995). Prosecuting sex crimes against children: Time for "outrageous" proposals? *Law & Psychology Review* 19, 59–91.

42. Detlev W. Belling & Christina Eberl (1996). Teenage abortion in Germany: With reference to the legal system in the United States, *Journal of Contemporary Health Law and Policy* 12, 475–502.

43. For analyses of gay youths' right to sexually explicit information, see Donna I. Dennis & Ruth E. Harlow (1986). Gay youth and the right to education, *Yale Law & Policy Review* 4, 446–478. Nancy Tenney (1995). The constitutional imperative of reality in public school curricula: Untruths about homosexuality as a violation of the First Amendment, *Brooklyn Law Review* 69, 1599–1651. For a review of the significance of pornography to gay males' sexual development, see Jeffrey G. Sherman (1995). Love speech: The social utility of pornography, *Stanford Law Review* 47, 661–705.

44. A. Mark Liddle (1995). Child sexual abuse and age of consent laws: A response to some libertarian arguments for "sexual liberty." In R. Emerson Dobash, Russell P. Dobash & Lesley Boaks (Eds.) *Gender and Crime* (313–339). Cardiff: University of Wales Press.

45. The only exception, of course, involves maltreatment conducted "under color of law."

46. The best example is the notion of family privacy. Roger J. R. Levesque (1994). The failures of foster care reform: Revolutionizing the most radical blueprint, *Maryland Journal of Contemporary Legal Issues* 6, 1–35.

47. Liz Kelly (1992). Pornography and child abuse. In Catherine Itzin (Ed.) *Pornography: Women, Violence & Civil Liberties* (113–123). NY: Oxford University Press.

48. Maryanne Lyons (1992). Adolescents in jeopardy: An analysis of Texas' promiscuity defense for sexual assault, *Houston Law Review* 29, 583–632.

49. Kelley L. Armstrong, (1994). The silent minority within a minority: Focusing on the needs of gay youths in our public schools, *Golden Gate University Law Review* 24, 67–97.

50. Roger J. R. Levesque (1996). The peculiar place of adolescents in the HIV-AIDS epidemic: Unusual progress & usual inadequacies in "adolescent jurisprudence," *Loyola Chicago Law Journal* 27, 701–739.

51. Nora V. Demleitner (1994). Forced prostitution: Naming an international offense, *Fordham International Law Journal* 18, 163–197.

52. See Volkmar Gessner (1994). Global legal interaction and legal culture, *Ratio Juris* 7(2), 132–145. See also Anthony Giddens (1990). *The Consequences of Modernity*. Stanford: Stanford University Press.

53. Considerable research has long revealed that, as children near adolescence, they increase sex play, even to the extent that by twelve, one in every four boys has tried to have intercourse with a female. The most famous of this research is, of course, that reported by Kinsey and his colleagues. Alfred C. Kinsey, Wardell B. Pomeroy & Clyde E. Martin (1948). *Sexual Behavior in the Human Male*. Philadelphia: W. B. Saunders. Researchers continue to show even higher levels of sexual actvitity before children reach twelve; see Jeffrey J. Haugaard (1996). Sexual behaviors between children: Professionals' opinions and undergraduates' recollections, *Families in Society* 77, 81–89.

54. Important studies now attempt to determine the epidemiology of early sexual socialization, the extent to which early sexual play and games involve coercion, and professionals' reactions to and perceptions of child sexual activity. For important studies of these issues, see, respectively, Frank Lindbald, Per A. Gustafsson, Ingbeth Larsson & Bjorn Lundin (1995). Preschoolers' sexual behavior at daycare centers: An epidemiological study, *Child Abuse & Neglect* 19, 569–577; Sharon Lamb & Mary Coakley (1993). "Normal" childhood sexual play and games: Differentiating play

from abuse, *Child Abuse & Neglect* 17, 515–526; Marsha L. Heiman, Sandra Leiblum, Susan Cohen Esquilin, Laura Melendez Pallitto (1998). A comparative survey of beliefs about "normal" childhood sexual behaviors, *Child Abuse & Neglect* 22, 289–304.

2. Transforming Legal Conceptions of Childhood

1. Carrington, for example, argues that the international human rights movement proclaims that "the whole world community should resemble as nearly as possible suburban middle-class America." Paul D. Carrington (1991). Aftermath. In Peter Cane and Jane Stapleton (Eds.) *Essays for Patrick Atiyah* (113–149). Oxford: Clarendon Press. For other challenges, see Rhoda Howard (1993). Cultural absolutism and the nostalgia of community, *Human Rights Quarterly* 15, 315–38; Richard Rorty (1989). *Contingency, Irony and Solidarity.* Cambridge: Harvard University Press. Others embrace universality and the notion that human rights norms transcend cultural location; contemporary defenses of universalism range from natural rights arguments to positivism, utilitarianism, and contract theories. See Tracy E. Higgins (1996). Anti-essentialism, relativism, and human rights, *Harvard Women's Law Journal* 19, 89–126. The extent to which power should be bestowed upon the U. N. has been the subject of numerous commentaries; for a review of controversies, see Karin L. Swisher (Ed.) (1997). *The United Nations.* San Diego: Greenhaven Press.

2. The most forceful argument is that it introduces an adversarial quality to the discourse surrounding children. Katherine O'Donovan (1993). *Family Law Matters.* London: Pluto Press; Michael King & Judith Trowell (1992). *Children's Welfare and the Law: The Limits of Legal Intervention.* London: Sage.

3. For an analysis of criticisms, see Roger J. R. Levesque (1994). International children's rights grow up: Implications for American jurisprudence and domestic policy, *California Western International Law Journal* 24, 193–240.

4. See Winfried Brugger (1996). The image of the person in the human rights concept, *Human Rights Quarterly* 18, 594–611.

5. International human rights law is codified in multilateral treaties that may be called charters, covenants, conventions, or protocols. These treaties are adopted by states as members of international governmental organizations to promote and protect human rights. In essence, a treaty is the equivalent of a contract among states. Those states that decide to take part in a treaty and agree to be bound by its provisions are called "States Parties." Other sources of human rights law are declarations of states' representatives issued at international conferences or meetings of international organizations. These declarations do not create legal obligations for the states and are therefore not enforceable in international or domestic courts, nor are they enforceable by other methods. Roger J. R. Levesque (1996). International children's rights: Can they make a difference in American family policy? *American Psychologist* 51, 1251–1256.

6. GA Res 217A, UN GAOR, 3d Sess (Part I. Resolutions), UN Doc A/810 (1948).

7. GA Res 2200, UN GAOR, 21st Sess (Supp No 16 at 52), UN Doc A/6316; 999 UNTS 171; 6 ILM 368 (1966).

8. GA Res 2200 Annex, UN GAOR, 21st Sess (Supp No 16 at 49), UN Doc A/6316; 993 UNTS 3; 6 ILM 360 (1966).

9. John P. Humphrey (1976). The International Bill of Rights: Scope and implementation, *William and Mary Law Review* 17, 527–541.

10. GA Res 44/25. UN GAOR, 44th Sess (Supp No 49 at 166), UN Doc A/44/49; 28 ILM 1448 (1989).

11. Again, it is important to note the focus on international human rights. Clearly, as human rights, these rights have a deeper history. They were declared in the great democratic revolutions at the end of the eighteenth century in the United States and France.

12. The controversial nature of the first and second generation rights is reflected in the protracted negotiations, drawn-out drafting, and the extended time needed for formal adoption by the United Nations: almost twenty years.

13. Howard Tolley (1987). *The U. N. Commission on Human Rights.* Boulder, CO: Westview Press.

14. The phrase made its debut in American constitutional law in the late 1800s; see Samuel D. Warren & Louis D. Brandeis (1890). The right to privacy, *Harvard Law Review* 4, 193–220.

15. The terms North and South have become widely used to refer to colonial and imperialist legacies and actualities that, broadly speaking, characterize the historical and current relations between countries of the northern hemisphere and those of the South. Other terms in circulation include the polarities First/Third World, West/Third World, developed/developing countries, and rich/poor. Although I adopt these terms here, it is important to recognize that there are many national and regional norths and souths within the northern and southern hemispheres, and that this practice homogenizes and totalizes complete and multiple political, economic, and geographical conditions.

16. Some nations have not welcomed this approach. For example, in 1986, when the U. N. General Assembly adopted the Declaration of the Right to Development, the United States cast the only negative vote. United Nations (1986). Declaration of the Right to Development, A/41/153 (December 4, 1986).

17. S. James Anaya (1996). *Indigenous Peoples in International Law.* NY: Oxford University Press.

18. The International Labor Organization (ILO) is at the forefront of the practical enumeration of these fourth generation rights. Interestingly, the ILO is also in the forefront of engaging and enacting protections against child sexual exploitation. Roger J. R. Levesque (1994). The sexual use, abuse and exploitation of children: Challenges in implementing children's human rights, *Brooklyn Law Review* 60, 959–998.

19. Will Kymlicka (1995). *The Rights of Minority Cultures.* NY: Oxford University Press.

20. James Crawford (1992). *The Rights of People.* NY: Oxford University Press; S. James Anaya (1996). *Indigenous Peoples in International Law.* NY: Oxford University Press.

21. See Philip Alston (1994). The best interests principle: Towards a reconciliation of culture and human rights. In Philip Alston (Ed.) *The Best Interests of the Child: Reconciling Cultural and Human Rights* (1–25). Oxford: Clarendon Press.

22. Roger J. R. Levesque (1997). *Adolescents, Society and Law: A Comprehensive Guide to Social Science Research.* Chicago: American Bar Association.

23. Alston (1994) *supra.*

24. Michael Longford (1996). NGOs and the rights of the child. In Peter Wil-

letts (Ed.) *"The Conscience of the World": The Influence of Non-Governmental Organizations in the UN System* (214–240). Washington, DC: Brookings.

25. See Roger J. R. Levesque (1994). International children's rights grow up: Implications for American jurisprudence and domestic policy, *California Western International Law Journal* 24, 193–240.

26. Id.

27. World Declaration on the Survival, Protection and Development of Children and Plan of Action for Implementing the World Declaration on the Survival, Protection and Development of Children in the 1990s, UN Doc E/CN.4/1991/59 (1990) para 22.

28. As of March 10, 1995, the convention had been ratified by 170 states, and it has been signed but not been ratified by eight states. CRC/C/39 (1995).

29. Levesque (1996) *supra.*

30. For a review, see Levesque (1994). International children's rights, *supra.*

31. Elizabeth M. Calciano (1992). United Nations Convention on the Rights of the Child: Will it help children in the United States? *Hastings International & Comparative Law Review* 15, 515–534; Kerri Ann Law (1994). Hope for the future: Overcoming jurisdictional concerns to achieve United States ratification of the Convention on the Rights of the Child, *Fordham Law Review* 62, 1851–1876.

32. See, e.g., Bruce C. Hafen & Jonathan O. Hafen (1996). Abandoning children to their autonomy: The United Nations Convention on the Rights of the Child, *Harvard International Law Journal* 37, 449–491.

33. See, e.g., Gary B. Melton (1993). Is there a place for children in the New World Order? *Notre Dame Journal of Law, Ethics & Public Policy* 7, 491–529.

34. Levesque (1996) *supra*; Allison Dundes Renteln (1997). Who's afraid of the CRC: Objections to the Convention on the Rights of the Child, *ILSA Journal of International & Comparative Law* 3, 629–640.

35. Susan P. Limber & Brian L. Wilcox (1996). The application of the UN Convention on the Rights of the Child to the United States, *American Psychologist* 51, 1246–50; Gary B. Melton (1996). The right to a family environment: Why children's rights and family values are compatible, *American Psychologist* 51, 1234–38; Bruce C. Hafen & Jonathan O. Hafen (1996). Abandoning children to their autonomy: The United Nations Convention on the Rights of the Child, *Harvard International Law Journal* 37, 449–491; Roger J. R. Levesque (1996). Children's rights: Can they make a difference in American family policy? *American Psychologist* 51, 1251–1256; Roger J. R. Levesque (1994). The internationalization of children's human rights: Too radical for American adolescents? *Connecticut Journal of International Law* 9, 237–293.

36. Renteln (1997) *supra.*

37. Melton (1993) *supra.*

38. Attempts to eliminate child marriage in India, and the more recent campaigns against rape and dowry, offer a powerful case in point. See Ranta Kapur & Brenda Cossman (1996). *Subversive Sites: Feminist Engagement With Law in India.* Thousand Oaks, CA: Sage.

39. Carol Smart (1986). Feminism and law: Some problems of analysis and strategy, *International Journal of Sociology of Law* 14, 109–123; Chris Weedon (1987). *Feminist Practice and Poststructural Theory.* Oxford: Basil Blackwell.

40. Ronald Dworkin (1978). *Taking Rights Seriously.* London: Duckworth.

41. As the Human Rights Commission noted, the Convention's articles and principles are to be interpreted holistically, all together. Philip Alston (1994) *supra.*

42. American Bar Association (ABA) (1993). *Report of the American Bar Association Working Group on the United Nations Convention on the Rights of the Child.* Washington, DC: American Bar Association.

43. Louis Henkin (1990). *Constitutionalism, Democracy and Foreign Affairs.* NY: Columbia University Press.

44. Preambles of Universal Declaration of Human Rights, Covenant on Economic, Social and Cultural Rights, Covenant on Civil and Political Rights & Children's Convention (emphasis added).

45. Children's Convention, Article 3.

46. Children's Convention, Article 3.

47. Children's Convention, Article 18(1).

48. GA Res. 34/180, UN GAOR, 34th Sess (Supp No 46) (1979). For a similar analysis, see Douglas Hodgson (1994). The international legal recognition and protection of the family, *Australian Journal of Family Law* 8, 219–236.

49. Philip Alston (1994) *supra.*

50. For example, Children's Convention, Article 12.

51. Leonard P. Edwards & Inger J. Sagatun (1995). Who speaks for the child? *University of Chicago Law School Roundtable* 2, 67–95.

52. Roger J. R. Levesque (1995). Prosecuting sex crimes against children: Time for "outrageous" proposals? *Law & Psychology Review* 19, 59–91.

53. Id.

54. The abortion issue is a clear case in point. See Levesque (1994). The internationalization of children's rights, *supra.*

55. Cynthia Price Cohen (1993). The developing jurisprudence of the rights of the child, *Saint Thomas Law Review* 6, 1–96.

56. Levesque (1996) *supra.*

57. The Women's Convention and numerous other women's rights documents aim to equalize women's and men's roles in family life; they ignore children. Winston E. Langley (1991). *Women's Rights in International Documents: A Sourcebook with Commentary.* Jefferson, NC: McFarland & Company.

58. Stuart N. Hart (1991). From property to person status: Historical perspective on children's rights, *American Psychologist* 46, 53–59.

59. See Levesque (1996) *supra.*

60. Alston (1994) *supra.*

61. Dorothy Q. Thomas & Michele E. Beasley (1993). Domestic violence as a human rights issue, *Human Rights Quarterly* 15, 36–62.

62. Jo Boyden (1990). Childhood and the policy makers: A comparative perspective on the globalization of childhood. In Alison James & Alan Prout (Eds.) *Constructing and Reconstructing Childhood* (184–215). London: Falmer Press.

63. Roger J. R. Levesque (1996). Future visions of juvenile justice: Lessons from international and comparative law, *Creighton Law Review* 29, 1563–1585.

64. Roger J. R. Levesque (1998). Educating American youth: Lessons from human rights law, *Journal of Law and Education* 27, 173–209.

65. The most universally accepted manner in which the law accomplishes this goal is to bestow considerable power upon parents, families, and communities in determining what is best for children. When those institutions fail, the law intervenes and attempts to impose agreed-upon standards of how caretakers should behave. This

is the United State's Supreme Court's approach, which has been extremely influential internationally.

66. Hafen & Hafen (1996) *supra.*

67. The argument that children are likely to make mistakes and bad choices, because they lack experience in decision-making, is tautological. If children are not allowed to make decisions because they have no experience in decision-making, how do they ever get started? Likewise, mistakes are not necessarily negative; they provide opportunities to learn. And again, adults make mistakes! Likewise, we should not confuse the right to do something with doing the right thing. We often accept that adults have the right to do something which is wrong for them, e.g., smoke or engage in risky behavior. Ronald Dworkin (1977). *Taking Rights Seriously.* London: Duckwoth. The inadequacy of adult decision-making is little more than a catalogue of blunders: war, inequality, famine, racism, and injustice are some fruits of adult deliberation and choice. It is hard to imagine a worse track record.

68. Levesque (1994). The internationalization of children's rights, *supra.*

69. Daniel Stern (1985). *The Interpersonal World of the Infant: A View from Psychoanalysis and Developmental Psychology.* NY: Basic Books.

70. Levesque (1994). The internationalization of chilren's rights, *supra.*

71. A. Mark Liddle (1995). Child sexual abuse and age of consent laws: A response to some libertarian arguments for "sexual liberty." In R. Emerson Dobash, Russell P. Dobash & Lesley Noaks (Eds.) *Gender and Crime* (313–339). Cardiff: University of Wales Press.

72. Levesque (1994). Prosecuting sex crimes, *supra.*

73. In the United States, the debate essentially revolves around the right to abortion. Groundbreaking cases outside the United States also narrowly have recognized children's choice rights. For example, the House of Lords in 1985 upheld the right of a child under the age of sixteen to obtain confidential medical services regarding contraception, contrary to the wishes of her parents, so long as the child has "sufficient understanding and intelligence." *Gillick v. West Norfolk and Wisbech Area Health Auth.* 3 All. E. R. 402, 409–410 (H. L. 1985).

74. Hyman Rodman (1991). Should parental involvement be required for minors' abortions? *Family Relations* 40, 155–160; Suellyn Scarnecchia & Julie Kunce Field (1995). Judging girls: Decision making in parental consent to abortion cases, *Michigan Journal of Gender and Law* 3, 75–123.

75. Roger J. R. Levesque (1994). Sex differences in the experience of child sexual victimization, *Journal of Family Violence* 9, 357–369.

76. Donna Eder, Catherine Evans & Stephen Parker (1996). *School Talk: Gender and Adolescent Culture.* New Brunswick: Rutgers University Press.

77. Roger J. R. Levesque (1997). Dating violence, adolescents and the law, *Virginia Journal of Social Policy and Law* 4, 339–379.

78. Levesque (1996). Future vision of juvenile justice, *supra.*

79. Levesque (1996). International children's rights, *supra.*

80. Roger J. R. Levesque (1995). Combatting child sexual maltreatment: Advances and obstacles in international progress, *Law & Policy* 17, 441–469.

81. This argument is very akin to the feminist perspective which holds that defining rights in terms of restrictions on states may actually disable the state from intervening to reallocate private power within the family. See Charlotte Bunch (1995). Transforming human rights from a feminist perspective. In Julie Peters & Andrea Wolper (Eds.) *Women's Rights, Human Rights: International Feminist Perspectives*

(11–17). NY: Routledge. See also Catherine A. McKinnon (1989). *Towards a Feminist Theory of State*. Cambridge: Harvard University Press.

82. Alison Dundes Renteln (1990). *International Human Rights: Universalism Versus Relativism*. Newbury Park, CA: Sage; David P. Forsythe (1991). *The Internationalization of Human Rights*. Lexington, MA: Lexington Books; Jack Donnelly (1993). *International Human Rights: Dilemmas in World Politics*. Boulder, CO: Westview Press.

83. The much-touted distinction between collectivist and individualist cultures has been the subject of considerable scholarly attention. Virginia Murphy-Berman, Helen LaCrosse Levesque & John J. Berman (1996). U. N. Convention on the Rights of the Child: A cross-cultural view, *American Psychologist* 51, 1257–1261.

84. African conceptions do not know such individualism. Issa G. Shivji (1989). *The Concept of Human Rights in Africa*. London: Colesria Book Series.

85. Tracy E. Higgins (1996). Anti-essentialism, relativism, and human rights, *Harvard Women's Law Journal* 19, 89–126.

86. Josiah A. M. Cobbah (1987). African values and the human rights debate: An African perspective, *Human Rights Quarterly* 9, 309–331.

87. Rhoda E. Howard (1986). *Human Rights in Commonwealth Africa*. Totowa, NJ: Rowan & Littlefield; Philip Alston (1982). *The International Dimensions of Human Rights*. Westport, CT: Greenwood Press.

88. Ronald Cohen (1993). Endless teardrops: Prolegomena to the study of human rights in Africa. In Ronald Cohen, Goran Hyden & Winston Nagen (Eds.) *Human Rights and Governance in Africa* (3–38). Gainesville: University of Florida Press (14).

89. Ebow Bondzie-Simpson (1988). A critique of the African Charter on Human Rights and Peoples, *Howard Law Journal* 31, 643–665 (656).

90. Timothy Fernyhough (1994). Human rights and precolonial Africa. In Ronald Cohen, Goran Hyden & Winston Nagen (Eds.) *Human Rights and Governance in Africa* (39–73). Gainseville: University of Florida Press.

91. Latif O. Adegbite (1968). African attitudes to the intentional protection of human rights. In Asbjorne Eide & Aygyst Shou (Eds.) *International Protection of Human Rights* (68–81). NY: Interscience.

92. Levesque (1996). International children's rights, *supra*.

93. Accusations ensued between West and Asian countries at the World Conference on Human Rights held in Vienna in June 1993. The Asian countries, while recognizing universalism, argued that rights must be considered in the context of a dynamic and evolving process of international norm-setting, and that those who wish to intervene must bear in mind the significance of national and regional particularities and cultural, historical, and religious backgrounds. United Nations World Conference on Human Rights, UN Doc A/CONF.157/PC/59 (1993). The U.S. strenuously objected and argued that cultural relativism leads to repression. See Elaine Sciolino (1993). US rejects notion that human rights vary with culture, *New York Times* June 15, A1.

94. Robert Bellah and his colleagues have most recently popularized the role of individualism in modern American life and character. They demonstrated well the American emphasis placed on individual freedom and the tendency toward isolation from the community in American culture. However, they also pointed to "countervailing tendencies that pull people back from their isolation into social communion. . . . The habits and practices of religion and democratic participation educate the citizen

to a larger view than his private world would allow." Robert H. Bellah, William M. Sullivan, Ann Swindler & Steven M. Tipton (1985). *Habits of the Heart: Individualism and Commitment in American life.* NY: Harper and Row. 65.

95. Once certain statutory benefits are granted, they cannot be withdrawn without due process of law, nor can they be distributed in a way that denies equal protection.

96. Carol Gilligan (1982). *In a Different Voice.* Cambridge: Harvard University Press; Susan H. Williams (1997). A feminist reassessment of civil society, *Indiana Law Journal* 72, 416–447.

97. Robert M. Galatzer-Levy & Bertram J. Cohler (1993). *The Essential Other: a Developmental Psychology of Self.* NY: Basic Books.

98. Rhoda E. Howard (1986). Evaluating rights in Africa: Some problems of implicit comparisons, *Human Rights Quarterly* 6, 160–179.

99. Harold J. Berman (1989). Toward an integrative jurisprudence: Politics, morality, history, *California Law Review* 76, 779–801.

100. Lawrence M. Friedman (1994). Is there a modern legal culture? *Ratio Juris* 7, 117–131. Lawrence M. Friedman (1996). Borders: On the emerging sociology of transnational law, *Stanford Journal of International Law* 32, 65–90.

101. James N. Rosenau & Ernst-Otto Czempiel (Eds.) (1992). *Governance Without Government: Order and Change in World Politics.* NY: Cambridge University Press; John Macmillan & Andrew Linklater (Eds.) *Boundaries in Question: New Directions in International Relations.* NY: Pinter.

102. Yoshikazu Sakamoto (Ed.) (1994). *Global Transformation: Challenges to the State System.* NY: United Nations University Press.

103. Michael G. Wyness (1996). Policy, protectionism and the competent child, *Childhood: A Global Journal of Child Research* 3, 431–447.

104. The prevailing tendency in writings on women's international human rights is to strongly oppose cultural relativism. See Eva Brems (1997). Enemies or allies? Feminism and cultural relativism as dissident voices in human rights discourse, *Human Rights Quarterly* 19, 136–167.

105. Jill Korbin (1995). Social networks and family violence in cross-cultural perspective. In Gary B. Melton (Ed). *The Individual, the Family, and Social Good: Personal Fulfillment in Times of Change* (107–134). Lincoln: University of Nebraska Press.

106. U.S. Advisory Board on Child Abuse and Neglect (1993). *Neighbors Helping Neighbors: A New National Strategy for the Protection of Children.* Department of Health and Human Services, Washington, D.C: U.S. Government Printing Office.

107. Cohen (1993). Endless teardrops, *supra.*

108. Adamantia Pollis (1996). Cultural relativism revisited: Through a state prism, *Human Rights Quarterly* 18, 316–344.

109. Margaret A. Healy (1995). Prosecuting child sex tourists at home: Do laws in Sweden, Australia, and the United States safeguard the rights of children as mandated by international law? *Fordham International Law Journal* 18, 1852–1923.

110. Philip Leroy Kilbride & Janet Capriotti Kilbride (1990). *Changing Family Life in East Africa: Women and Children at Risk.* University Park, PA: State University Press; R. E. Downs, Donna O. Kerner & Stephen P. Reyna (Eds.) (1991). *The Political Economy of African Famine.* Philadelphia: Gordon & Breach; M. Vaughn (1987). *The Story of an African Famine: Gender and Famine in Twentieth Century Malawi.* Cambridge: Cambridge University Press.

111. The theme has been highlighted by the International Year of the Family. See Levesque (1994). Children's rights grow up, *supra*; Douglas Hodgson (1994). The international legal recognition and protection of the family, *Australian Journal of Family Law* 8, 219–236.

112. William A. Schabas (1996). Reservations to the Convention on the Rights of the Child, *Human Rights Quarterly* 18, 472–491. The actual extent to which nations appropriately may limit the scope of the instrument remains contentious. Traditional solutions proposed by international law and the guidance provided by legal scholars arguably remain woefully inadequate to deal with the variety of ways states seek to limit their obligations. Thus, although the broad endorsement of the Convention provides a major step toward the eventual recognition of children's rights, the support does not remove complications that may arise in progress toward the internationalization of children's rights.

113. Articles 42 & 44 (6).

114. Article 43 established the Committee on the Rights of the Child and Article 44 requires States Parties to submit reports to the Committee.

115. For a discussion of these standards, see Cynthia Price Cohen, Stuart N. Hart & Susan M. Kosloske (1996). Monitoring the United Nations Convention on the Rights of the Child: The challenge of information management, *Human Rights Quarterly* 18, 439–71.

116. Kevin T. Jackson (1994). *Charting Global Responsibilities: Legal philosophy*. Lanham, MD: University Press of America; Ann Fagan Ginger (1993). The energizing effect of enforcing a human rights treaty, *Depaul Law Review* 42, 1341–1404.

117. James W. Nickel (1993). How human rights generate duties to protect and provide, *Human Rights Quarterly* 15, 77–86.

118. Ann Marrie Clark (1995). Non-governmental organizations and their influence on international society, *Journal of International Affairs* 48, 507–525 (514).

119. The 1993 United Nations Conference on Human rights acknowledged the important role of nongovernmental organizations in increasing public awareness of human rights issues and effectively implementing the Convention on the Rights of the Child. It is often through their expertise, recommendations, and lobbying that the United Nations and governments have become motivated to correct injustices. Part I, para 38 and Part II, para 52, respectively, of the Vienna Declaration and Programme of Action. Stuart N. Hart & Laura Thetaz-Berman (1996). The role of nongovernmental organizations in implementing the Convention on the Rights of the Child, *Transnational Law & Contemporary Problems* 6, 373–392.

120. Chadwick F. Alger (1994). Citizens and the UN System in a changing world. In Yoshikazu Sakamoto (Ed.) *Global Transformation: Challenges to the State System* (301–329). NY: United Nations University Press.

121. Ian Brownlie (1990). *Principles of Public International Law* (4th ed). NY: Oxford University Press.

122. American Bar Association (ABA) (1993). *Report of the American Bar Association Working Group on the United Nations Convention on the Rights of the Child*. Washington, DC: American Bar Association.

123. Levesque (1996). International children's rights, *supra*.

124. Id.

125. Roger J. R. Levesque (1994). The failures of foster care reform: Revolutionizing the most radical blueprint, *Maryland Journal of Contemporary Legal Issues* 9, 1–39.

126. *Suter v. Artist*, 112 Supreme Court 1360 (1992).

127. See Levesque (1994). International children's rights, *supra*.

128. Richard H. Gaskins (1994). Default presumptions in legislation: Implementing children's services, *Harvard Journal of Law & Public Policy* 17, 779–800.

129. For further discussion, see Chapter 7.

130. More recently, the formal representatives to the United Nations and regional organizations have been supplemented by a small army of nongovernmental organizations. These organizations lobby nations and the U. N. to ensure that human rights remain an active part of the international community's agenda. Increasingly, these organizations have proven to be critical to ensuring children's rights and championing children's agendas. See Diane Goodman (1990). Recent United Nations actions to reduce sexual exploitation of children, *Response* 13(2), 9–13.

131. A growing number of nongovernmental organizations, such as ECPAT (End Child Prostitution in Asian Tourism), have embarked on combatting child sexual maltreatment. Indeed, ECPAT recently has broadened its agenda and initiatives, as exemplified by its new name: End Child Prostitution, Child Pornography, and Trafficking of Children for Sexual Purposes; see ECPAT (1997). *ECPAT-USA NEWS* 2(2), 4. For descriptions of their work, see Ron O'Grady (1992). *The Child and the Tourist: The Story behind the Escalation of Child Prostitution in Asia*. Auckland, New Zealand: Pace Publishing. The problem has become a concern of highly regarded organizations that have an international reach, such as INTERPOL; see Vitit Muntarbhorn (1994). *Sale of Children, Child Prostitution and Child Pornography*, E/CN.4/1994/84.

132. The commitment to ending the sexual maltreatment of children identified in the Convention has been reaffirmed by several world conferences on human rights; see United Nations (1993). *Report of the World Conference on Human Rights*. NY: Author; Stephanie Farrior (1997). The international law on trafficking in women and children for prostitution: Making it live up to its potential, *Harvard Human Rights Journal* 10, 213–255.

133. Article 34.

134. Muntarbhorn (1994) *supra*.

135. Most notably the *Program of Action for the Prevention of the Sale of Children, Child Prostitution, and Child Pornography* (1992), and the more recent *Draft Program of Action for the Prevention of Traffic in Persons and the Exploitation of the Prostitution of Others* (1994), E/CN.4/1994/71 Annex.

136. Part II, para 48.

137. Stephanie Farrior (1997). The international law on trafficking in women and children for prostitution: Making it live up to its potential, *Harvard Human Rights Journal* 10, 213–255.

3. Deconstructing Childhood and Sexual Maltreatment

1. On the social construction of social problems, see Malcolm Spector and John I. Kitsuse (1977). *Constructing Social Problems*. Menlo Park, CA: Cummings.

2. Richard Shweder (1991). *Thinking through Cultures: Expeditions in Cultural Psychology*. Cambridge: Harvard University Press.

3. For a review of these theories and their relevance to social policy-making, see Roger J. R. Levesque (1997). Evolving beyond evolutionary psychology: A look at family violence. In Nancy L. Segal, Glenn E. Weisfeld & Carol C. Weisfeld (Eds.)

Genetic, Ethological and Evolutionary Perspectives on Human Development (502-513). Washington, DC: American Psychological Association. See also Owen D. Jones (1997). Evolutionary analysis in law: An introduction and application to child abuse, *North Carolina Law Review* 75, 1117-1242.

4. Helen E. Fisher (1992). *Anatomy of Love: The Natural History of Monogamy, Adultery, and Divorce.* NY: Norton; Mary Batten (1992). *Sexual Strategies: How Females Choose Their Mates.* NY: Putnam; David M. Buss (1994). *The Evolution of Desire: Strategies of Human Mating.* NY: Basic Books.

5. Xinhua Steve Ren (1996). Regional variation in infant survival in China, *Social Biology* 43, 1-19.

6. Thus, it is no surprise that factors which arguably have had the most impact on conceptions of childhood, both as a set of ideas and as a phase of life, have been primarily economic, demographic, and political. The potency of these ecological factors vary. In the West, it has been economic development which has allowed for both the shift in the experience of childhood from work to school, and for the emergence of the idea that childhood should be a time of dependency. Likewise, political concerns for safety and future needs of the state have provided the impulse for public action concerning children, as seen in efforts to combat child maltreatment and to control child sexuality. See Margaret K. Rosenheim & Mark F. Testa (Eds.) (1992). *Early Parenthood and Coming of Age in the 1990s.* New Brunswick: Rutgers University Press.

7. Nancy Scheper-Hughes (1984). Infant mortality and infant care: Cultural and economic constraints on nurturing in Northeast Brazil, *Social Science and Medicine* 19, 535-546. See also Marvin Harris & Eric B. Ross (1987). *Death, Sex, and Fertility: Population Regulation in Preindustrial and Developing Societies.* NY: Columbia University Press.

8. See, e.g., Maris A. Vinovskis (1987). Historical perspectives on the development of the family and parent-child interactions. In Jan B. Lancaster et al. (Eds.) *Parenting across the Life Span* (299-312). NY: De Gruyter.

9. The differentials are particularly pronounced, for example, with the switch from traditional modes of agricultural production to urbanization and industrialization, which favors males; see Sheila Johansson (1984). Delayed infanticide. In Glenn Hausfater and Sara Hrdy (Eds.) *Infanticide: Comparative and Evolutionary Perspectives* (463-485). NY: Aldine.

10. Lauris McKee (1984). Sex differentials in survivorship and the customary treatment of infants and children, *Medical Anthropology* 8, 91-108; Jo Boyden (1993). *Families: A Celebration and Hope for World Change.* London: Faine & UNESCO.

11. Vitit Muntarbhorn (1991). *United Nations Special Rapporteur on the Sale of Children, Child Prostitution and Child Pornography, Preliminary Report on the Sale of Children,* UN Doc No E/CN.4/1991/51 (January 28, 1991) para 34.

12. Human Rights Watch/Asia (1996). *Death by Default: A Policy of Fatal Neglect in China's State Orphanages.* New Haven: Yale University Press; Sharon K. Hom (1991-92). Female infanticide in China: The human rights specter and thoughts towards (an)other vision, *Columbia Human Rights Law Review* 23, 249-314.

13. Christopher Colgough & Kevin Lewin (1993). *Educating all the Children: Strategies for Primary Schooling in the South.* Oxford: Clarendon Press.

14. Males are also discriminated against under certain circumstances. Lee Cronk (1993). Parental favoritism toward daughters, *American Scientist* 81, 272-279;

Lee Cronk (1991). Preferential parental investment in daughters over sons, *Human Nature* 2, 387–417.

15. See the AAUW Report (1992). *How Schools Shortchange Girls: The AAUW Report*. Washington, DC: American Association of University Women Educational Foundation.

16. The Convention, for example, envisions adulthood as a state of peace and mutual understanding. See Children's Convention, Preamble, and Articles 28 and 29.

17. This move already has strong historical roots. For example, several have noted how the introduction of child labor laws and compulsory education transformed the wage-earning nonchild into the category of the economically worthless child-scholar. As one leading commentator put it, these forces at the end of the nineteenth century defined the majority of children into a romantic middle-class ideal of childhood in which children became emotionally "priceless." Viviana Zelizer (1985). *Pricing the Priceless Child: The Changing Social Value of Children*. NY: Basic Books. The general rule continues to be simple: as children lose their economic value to parents and become economic burdens, they become increasingly emotionally valued. Ironically, as proponents of the demographic "value of children" approach propose, it is no mistake that, at the same time that children are experiencing an emotional valuation with adults, the proportion of children in the total population has undergone an unprecedented decline. Rodolfo A. Bulatao (1982). The transition in the value of children and the fertility transition. In Charlotte Hohn & Rainer Mackensen (Eds.) *Determinants of Fertility Trends: Theories Re-examined* (95–122). Liege: Ordina Editions.

18. Judith Ennew & Brian Milne (1989). *The Next Generation: The Lives of Third World Children*. London: Zed Books.

19. The many forms of child sexual maltreatment challenge the Western fiction that childhood is a time to play and a time of innocence, a time of asexual and peaceful existence. Jenny Kitzinger (1988). Defending innocence: Ideologies of childhood, in family secrets: Child sexual abuse, *Feminist Review* 28, 78–87.

20. Anuradha Vittachi (1989). *Stolen Childhood: In Search of the Rights of the Child*. Oxford: Polity Blackwell; Jean Renvoize (1993). *Innocence Destroyed: A Study of Child Sexual Abuse*. New York: Routledge.

21. Arnon Bar-on (1997). Criminalizing survival: Images and reality of street children, *Journal of Social Policy* 26, 63–78.

22. Id.

23. Dona Schneider (1995). *American Childhood: Risks and Realities*. New Brunswick: Rutgers University Press.

24. Ruth Frankenberg (1993). Growing up white: Feminism, racism and the social geography of childhood, *Feminist Review* 45, 51–84.

25. Ennew & Milne (1989) (*supra* note).

26. Olga Nieuwenhuys (1994). *Children's Lifeworlds: Gender, Welfare and Labour in the Developing World*. NY: Routledge.

27. For example, books dealing with sexual maltreatment or with the general maltreatment of children do not have boys on their front covers. The extent to which even popular culture makes use of images of the "girl child" has become an important area of commentary; see Calerie Walkerdine (1997). *Daddy's Girl: Young Girls and Popular Culture*. Cambridge: Harvard University Press.

28. Barbara Crossette (1996). U. N. is urged to combat sex abuse of children, *New York Times* September 25, A7.

29. Kenneth Crimaldi (1996). "Megan's Law": Election-year politics and constitutional rights, *Rutgers Law Journal* 27, 169–204.

30. Images of children as innocent victims are without markers of culture, history, community, or even family ties. Their plight suggests that these common markers—families, communities, and cultures—are directly responsible for children's fate. Although detrimental environmental and societal conditions contribute powerfully to the incidence of several forms of maltreatment, societies may contribute unwittingly to children's "abuse." Ironically, the view of children as passive, susceptible recipients of experience detracts from children's own rights to cultural membership and participation in communal and familial struggles, struggles that result in unwarranted yet well-intentioned separations of children from their families and cultures. See Jo Boyden (1994). Children's experience of conflict related emergencies: Some implications for relief policy and practice, *Disasters: The Journal of Disaster Studies and Management* 18, 254–267.

31. The representation of childhood has been abstracted and sentimentalized away from history and culture in a manner that suppresses cultural, gender, and age inequalities. Patricia Holland (1992). *What is a Child? Popular Images of Childhood.* London: Virago Press.

32. The process constitutes a rather insidious variety of cultural chauvinism and colonial paternalism: as the South is infantilized, the North becomes adult and mature. See Erica Burman (1994). Innocents abroad: Western fantasies of childhood and the iconography of emergencies, *Disasters: The Journal of Disaster Studies and Management* 18, 238–253; Erica Burman (1994). Poor children: Ideologies of childhood and charity appeals, *Changes: Journal of Psychology and Psychotherapy* 12(1) 29–36.

Highly cultural and class-specific human development models (from the white middle class of the northern hemisphere) give rise to a globalization of development that is reinscribed within international aid and development policies. Despite rhetoric of cultural sensitivity and specificity, it is difficult to move away from a developmental psychology committed to prescriptions for child care and development that are assumed to transcend cultural variation. See Erica Burman (1995). The abnormal distribution of development: Policies for Southern women and children, *Gender, Place and Culture* 2(1), 21–36. As ardent critics of the United Nations trenchantly suggest, the U. N. globalizes what are, in fact, middle-class, Northern models of childhood. The most trenchant attacks come from Jo Boyden (1990). Childhood and the policymakers: A comparative perspective on the globalization of childhood. In A. James and A. Prout (Eds.) *Constructing and Reconstructing Childhood* (299–312). Lewes: Falmer Press. Although the U. N. does attempt to counter the exportation of Northern images of childhood, it remains important not only to emphasize the difficulty of doing so but also to stress that the U. N. is far from alone in the globalization of childhood. For example, the increasingly discontinuous and fluid global consumer market which has challenged many perceptions about the role of Nation States, traditional identities, and nationalism, also exports Northern images of childhood. Several document the massive toy promotions that go deeper than the influence of children's preferences for particular brands of toys. Children have now been observed in many countries utilizing and taking on the characters and themes of promotional television programs such as *Sesame Street, Ninja Turtles, Mortal Kombat* and *Batman.* Children's use of these themes in their pretended play and in their stories and conversations impacts their socialization and the "internationalization of children's culture." The images gain a reality of their own. Nancy Carlsson-Paige and Diane E. Levin

(1987). *The War Play Dilemma: Children's Needs and Society's Future.* NY: Teachers College Press. Anthropologists have long identified the importance of play in the inculcation of cultural sensibilities; see Helen B. Schwartzman (1979). *Transformations: The Anthropology of Children's Play.* NY: Plenum. See Stephen Kline (1995). The play of the market: On the internationalization of children's culture, *Theory, Culture & Society* 12, 103–129. See also Stephen Kline (1993). *Out of the Garden: Children's Toys and Television in the Age of Marketing.* London: Verso. Historians also now document the significant changes in children's toys and how they reflect and change cultural life; see Gary Cross (1997). *Kid's Stuff: Toys and the Changing World of American Childhood.* Cambridge: Harvard University Press.

33. The distinctions between private and public have been appropriately challenged in family law, domestic violence law, and, more recently, international law. See Frances Olsen (1985). The myth of state intervention in the family, *University of Michigan Journal of Law Reform* 18, 835–864. Martha Albertson Fineman (Ed.) (1994). *The Public Nature of Private Violence.* NY: Routledge; Hilary Charlesworth (1995). Worlds apart: Public/private distinctions in international law. In Margaret Thornton (Ed.). *Public and Private: Feminist Legal Debates* (243–260). NY: Oxford University Press.

34. Children's Convention, Article 1.

35. Id.

36. Monica L. Oberman (1994). Turning girls into women: Re-evaluating modern statutory rape law, *Journal of Criminal Law & Criminology* 85, 15–79.

37. J. S. LaFontaine (1978). *Sex and Age as Principles of Social Differentiation.* London: Academic Press.

38. Jeffrey Jensen Arnett & Susan Taber (1994). Adolescence terminable and interminable: When does adolescence end? *Journal of Youth and Adolescence* 23, 517–537.

39. John Y. Luluaki (1997). Customary marriage laws in the commonwealth: A comparison between Papua New Guinea and Anglophonic Africa, *International Journal of Law, Policy, and the Family* 11, 1–35.

40. Id.

41. Sudhir Kakar (1981). *The Inner World: A Psycho-analytic Study of Childhood and Society in India.* NY: Oxford University Press.

42. For example, Robert A. LeVine reports that among the Gussi of West Africa, the marriage of a young man "depends on his family's wealth, his patriarch's willingness to permit him the use of cattle. . . . Wealthy and fortunate young men may be married by age twenty, whereas unfortunates must postpone it until they are able to raise the bridewealth inside the family or through their own efforts—often until thirty or later." Robert A. LeVine (1979). Adulthood among the Gusii. In N. Smelser and E. Erikson (Eds.) *Themes of Work and Love* (77–104). Cambridge: Harvard University Press. See also S. P. Malhotra & H. S. Trivedi (1981). Child population and attitudes towards children in an Arid village, *Man in India* 61, 356–71.

43. Tamar Rapaport (1992). Two patterns of girlhood: Inconsistent sexually-laden experiences across institutions of socialization and socio-cultural milieux, *International Sociology* 7, 329–346.

44. Id.

45. Even the document most directly on point skirted the issue and simply recognized that it was "in the interests of States Parties to harmonize, as far as possible, their national legislation on sexual exploitation of children in order to improve

the co-ordination and effectiveness of action taken at both national and international levels." *Draft Optional Protocol to the United Nations Convention on the Rights of the Child Concerning the Elimination of Sexual Exploitation and Trafficking of Children*, E/CN.4/1995/95 last Preambular paragraph.

46. There have, though, been important steps in terms of child labor. The International Labor Organization has prescribed in its Minimum Age Convention 1973 (No. 138) that the basic minimum age shall not be less than fifteen years except for countries "whose economy and educational facilities are insufficiently developed," which may instead initially specify a minimum age of fourteen years. Article 2. See International Labor Organization (1996). *Child Labour: Targeting the Intolerable.* Geneva, Switzerland: International Labor Office.

47. Commentators too often focus too much on children's liberation rights; see, e.g., David Archard (1993). *Children: Rights and Childhood*. NY: Routledge.

48. Such a strategy is not entirely without precedent. The concept of "intersectionality" in innovative discrimination law reflects well how individuals may be discriminated against on multiple, simultaneous grounds. See Kimberle Crenshaw (1993). *Words that Wound: Critical Race Theory, Assaultive Speech, and the First Amendment.* Boulder, CO: Westview Press.

49. Deborah Daro, Genevieve Migely, David Wiese & Sara Salmon-Cox (1996). *World Perspectives on Child Abuse: The Second International Resource Book.* Chicago: International Society for Prevention of Child Abuse and Neglect.

50. Roger J. R. Levesque (1995). Combatting child sexual maltreatment: Advances and obstacles in international progress, *Law & Policy* 17, 441–469.

51. Gilbert H. Herdt (Ed.) (1993). *Ritualized Homosexuality in Melanesia.* Berkeley: University of California Press.

52. Jill Korbin (1995). Social networks and family violence in cross-cultural perspective. In Gary B. Melton (Ed.) *The Individual, the Family, and Social Good: Personal Fulfillment in Times of Change* (107–134). Lincoln: University of Nebraska Press.

53. David Finkelhor (1979). *Sexually Victimized Children.* NY: Free Press.

54. Ann Wolbert Burgess, A. Nicholas Groth, Lynda Lytle Holsmtrom & Suzanne M. Sgori (1978). *Sexual Assault of Children and Adolescents.* Lexington, MA: Lexington Books.

55. Florence Rush (1980). *The Best Kept Secret.* NY: McGraw-Hill.

56. Cynthia Crosson Tower (1996). *Understanding Child Abuse and Neglect.* Boston: Allyn and Bacon.

57. Douglas Hodgson (1994). Sex tourism and child prostitution in Asia: Legal responses and strategies, *Melbourne University Law Review* 19, 512–544.

58. Deepak Kumar Behera (1995). Review of "In Search of the Girl: A Critical Review of Literature on Girlhood in the South," *International Journal of Children's Rights* 3, 485–487.

59. Jan Faust, Melissa K. Runyon & Maureen C. Kenny (1995). Familial variables associated with the onset and impact of intrafamilial childhood sexual abuse, *Clinical Psychology Review* 15, 443–456.

60. Geraldine Van Bueren (1994). Child sexual abuse and exploitation: A suggested human rights approach, *The International Journal of Children's Rights* 2, 45–59.

61. Roger J. R. Levesque (1996). The peculiar place of adolescents in the HIV-AIDS epidemic: Unusual progress & usual inadequacies in "Adolescent Jurispru-

dence," *Loyola Chicago Law Journal* (Special Inaugural Issue on Child Law) 27, 701–739.

62. Vicki F. Li (1995). Child sex tourism in Thailand: The role of the United States as a consumer country, *Pacific Rim Law & Policy Journal* 4, 505–542.

63. Thomas G. Eschweiler (1995). Educational malpractice in sex education, *Southern Methodist University Law Review* 49, 101–132.

64. This realization by Michel Foucault broke new ground for social scientists. Michel Foucault (1977). *Discipline and Punish: The Birth of the Prison*. NY: Pantheon. Pierre Bourdieu's (1977) concept of habitus explains well how structures of violence may be socially reproduced. A society may internalize a "habitus" for violence—e.g., systems of racial segregation, gender based discrimination, and age oppression—that structures social interactions in coercive ways reproducing the cultural divisions on which those very same forcible practices are based. Pierre Bourdieu (1977). *Outline of a Theory of Practice*. Cambridge: Cambridge University Press.

65. As Urie Bronfenbrenner suggests in his important book on the ecology of child development, Urie Bronfenbrenner (1979). *The Ecology of Human Development*. Cambridge: Harvard University Press.

4. The Sexual Exploitation of Children

1. For recent reviews, see Dany Lacombe (1994). *Blue Politics: Pornography and the Law in the Age of Feminism*. Toronto: University of Toronto Press; Susan Dwyer (Ed.) (1995). *The Problem of Pornography*. NY: Wadsworth; Brian McNair (1996). *Mediated Sex: Pornography and Postmodern Culture*. NY: Arnold; Lynn Hunt (Ed.) (1993). *The Invention of Pornography: Obscenity and the Origins of Modernity, 1500–1800*. NY: Zone Books; Gordon G. Hawkins & Frank E. Zimring (1991). *Pornography in a Free Society*. Cambridge: Cambridge University Press; L. Segal & M. McIntosh (Eds.) (1992). *Sex Exposed: Sexuality and the Pornography Debate*. NY: Routledge; Robert Stoller (1991). *Porn: Myths of the Twentieth Century*. New Haven: Yale University Press; Susan M. Easton (1994). *The Problem of Pornography: Regulation and the Right to Free Speech*. NY: Routledge; Barbara Sullican (1997). *The Politics of Sex: Prostitution and Pornography in Australia Since 1945*. NY: Cambridge University Press.

2. For an analysis of the debate, see Deborah L. Rhode (1997). *Speaking of Sex: The Denial of Gender Inequality*. Cambridge: Harvard University Press. Chap. 5.

3. In fact, some show a decrease in use of pornography and rise in sexual assaults and other sexual crimes. See Michale S. Kimmel & Annulla Linders (1996). Does censorship make a difference? An aggregate empirical analysis of pornography and rape, *Journal of Psychology & Human Sexuality* 8(3), 1–20.

4. Easton (1994) *supra*, Chapters 1 and 2.

5. Reports from China and Japan reveal that the sexual development and awareness most often involve viewing erotic pictures, as opposed to dating, talking about sex, or seeing individuals nude. Dalin Liu, Man Lun Ng, Li Ping Zhou & Erwin J. Haeberle (1997). *Sexual Behavior in Modern China: Report on the Nationwide Survey of 20,000 Men and Women*. NY: Continuum Publishing.

6. Children are viewed as unable to consent and therefore as unable to participate in pornography. The second reason is that the reality of child pornography involves more than simple pictures. Pornographic materials are actual evidence of child sexual assaults.

Tim Tate (1992). The child pornography industry: International trade in sexual abuse. In Catherine Itzin (Ed.) *Pornography: Women, Violence and Civil Liberties: A Radical New View* (201–216). NY: Oxford University Press. Tate notes that child pornography is a misleading term. The empirical disinterest reflects the most powerful obstacle that hinders efforts to alleviate the plight of children exploited by child pornography: the prevailing belief that pornography does not necessarily harm children. Arguably, much of the predicament derives from the prevailing tendency to confuse child pornography with the "glamor" of *Playboy* and other erotic forms of adult entertainment. Given this tamer image, it is not surprising that some commentators erroneously conclude that simply photographing children does not exploit them. In addition, child pornography has remained empirically invisible partly because it seems so straightforward; child pornography seems quite understandable, even to the extent that it seems readily obvious and easy to prohibit and control.

7. The average age of exposure is eleven and nearly half of girls and 60 percent of boys report having learned some or much from pornography. Gloria Cowan & Robin R. Campbell (1995). Rape causal attitudes among adolescents, *The Journal of Sex Research* 32, 145–153.

8. Catherine Itzin (1996). Pornography and the organization of child sexual abuse. In Peter C. Biggy (Ed.) *Organized Abuse: The Current Debate* (167–196). Brookfield, Vermont: Ashgate Publishing.

9. See 18 U.S. C. Sec. 2256(2) (1996).

10. Larry A. DiMatteo (1995). Deconstructing the myth of the "Infancy Law Doctrine": From incapacity to accountability, *Ohio Northern University Law Review* 21, 481–525.

11. See Tate (1992) *supra*.

12. U.S. Department of Justice (1986). *Attorney General's Commission on Pornography: Final Report.* 649.

13. U.S. Department of Justice (1986). *Attorney General's Commission on Pornography: Final Report.* See pages 649–650.

14. Ray Wyer (1992). Pornography and sexual violence: Working with sex offenders. In Catherine Itzin (Ed.) *Pornography: Women, Violence and Civil Liberties: A Radical New View* (236–248). NY: Oxford University Press.

15. W. L. Marshall (1988). The use of sexually explicit stimuli by rapists, child molesters, and non offenders, *The Journal of Sex Research* 26, 267–88. See also Daniel Lee Carter, Robert Alan Prentky, Raymond A. Knight, Penny L. Vanderveer & Richard J. Boucher (1987). Pornography in the criminal and developmental histories of sexual offenders, *Journal of Interpersonal Violence* 2, 196–211.

16. Mimi Silbert & Ayala Pines (1984). Pornography and sexual abuse of women, *Sex Roles* 11/12, 857–68.

17. Berl Kutchinsky (1983). The effect of easy availability of pornography on the incidence of sex crimes: The Danish experience. Cited in Tim Tate (1990). *Child Pornography*. London: Methuen.

18. For a recent review, see Catherine Itzin (1997). Pornography and the organizaiton of intrafamilial and extrafamilial child sexual abuse: Developing a conceptual model, *Child Abuse Review* 6, 94–106.

19. Tate (1992) *supra*.

20. Partly because of uproar and rediscovery of child abuse, several countries quickly prohibited the distribution of child pornography. Statutes that prohibited the distribution are linked to the dramatic changes in the nature and eventual production

of child pornography; collectors of child pornography essentially became the industry's new producers.

21. Tate (1992) *supra.*

22. These careers are often well-documented. A Pennsylvania engineer recently was arrested with pornographic pictures of children; in his home, police found 700 index cards with names of boys and girls as young as seven, detailing what he had done to them.

23. Catherine Itzin (Ed.) (1992). *Pornography: Women, Violence and Civil Liberties: A Radical New View* (236–48). NY: Oxford University Press.

24. Tate (1992) *supra.*

25. Michael S. Serrill (1993). Defiling Children, *Time* June 21, 52–55.

26. Id.

27. Kelly (1992) *supra.*

28. Vitit Muntarbhorn (1994). *Sale of Children, Child Prostitution and Child Pornography*, E/CN.4/1994/84.

29. Tim Golden (1996). 16 indicted on charges of internet pornography, *New York Times* July 17, A8.

30. Gitta Sereny (1986). *Invisible Children: The Shattering Tragedy of Runaways on Our Streets.* London: Pan.

31. Mimi Silbert & Ayala Pines (1984). Pornography and sexual abuse of women, *Sex Roles* 11/12, 857–68.

32. Kelly (1992) *supra.*

33. Id.

34. Shirley O'Brien (1992). *Child Pornography* (2nd ed.). Dubuque, IO: Kendall/Hunt Publishing Co.

35. Joshua Quittner (1993). Computers Customize Porn, *Newsday* March 6.

36. Keith F. Durkin & Clifton D. Bryant (1995). "Log on to sex": Some notes on the carnal computer and erotic cyberspace as an emerging research frontier, *Deviant Behavior: An Interdisciplinary Journal* 16, 179–200.

37. See Jason Kay (1995). Sexuality, live without a net: Regulating obscenity and indecency on the global network, *Southern California Interdisciplinary Law Journal* 4, 355–389.

38. Just as a state has an interest in seizing foreign-made child pornography to protect potential child victims, not necessarily foreign children.

39. 458 U.S. 747 (1982).

40. *New York v. Ferber*, 458 U.S. 747, 753 (1982).

41. Pornography involving adults is not explicitly regulated; it tends to be addressed under the rubric of obscenity. In determinations of obscenity, courts place considerable emphasis on involving local communties and local laws in determining contemporary community standards. To determine obscenity, local courts or juries focus on (1) whether the materials lack serious literary, artistic, political, or scientific value; (2) whether a community would find that the materials apply primarily to prurient interests; and (3) whether applicable state law specifically defines the sexual conduct that is depicted or described as patently offensive. See *Miller v. California*, 413 U.S. 5 (1973); for a discussion, see Susan Dwyer (1995). Legal Appendix. In Susan Dwyer (Ed.) *The Problem of Pornography* (233–247). NY: Wadsworth. Other countries have adopted lower thresholds. For example, Britain moved away from the common law rule that took the most vulnerable member of the community as the baseline, to a focus on respecting community standards through targeting those who are likely

to obtain the information and addressing the potential effect on those persons. Yaman Akdeniz (1996). Computer pornography: A comparative study of the US and UK obscenity laws and child pornography laws in relation to the internet, *International Review of Law, Computers & Technology* 10, 235–261.

42. See generally, Lisa S. Smith (1991). Private possession of child pornography: Narrowing at-home privacy rights, *Annual Survey of American Law* 1991, 1011–1045; John Quigley (1991). Child pornography and the right to privacy, *Florida State Law Review* 43, 347–404.

43. Howard A. Davidson & Gregory A. Loken (1987). *Pornography and Prostitution: Background and Legal Analysis.* Washington, DC: National Center for Missing & Exploited Children. 11. For a review and critique of laws, see T. Christopher Donnelly (1979). Protection of children from use in pornography: Toward constitutional and enforceable legislation, *Journal of Law Reform* 12, 295–337; Jeffrey J. Kent & Scott D. Truesdell (1989). Spare the child: The constitutionality of criminalizing possession of child pornography, *Oregon Law Review* 68, 363–392.

44. 495 U.S. 103 (1990).

45. For a list of statutes, see Edward E. Cavazos & Gavino Morin (1994). *Cyberspace and the Law: Your Rights and Duties in the On-line World.* Boston: MIT Press.

46. See David B. Johnson (1994). Why the possession of computer-generated child pornography can be constitutionally prohibited, *Albany Law Journal of Science & Technology* 4, 311–331.

47. Section 18 USCS 371 and 2252 penalize mailing or receiving, or conspiring to mail or receive, child pornography. See also Section 2251, which makes it illegal to advertise child pornography.

48. See Akdeniz (1996) *supra.*

49. Id.

50. Id.

51. See note 47.

52. See note 47.

53. Vitit Muntarbhorn (1994). *Sale of Children, Child Prostitution and Child Pornography,* E/CN.4/1994/84.

54. Julia Foreman (1990). Can we end the shame?—Recent multilateral efforts to address the world child pornography market, *Vanderbilt Journal of International Law* 23, 435–468.

55. Cavazos & Morin (1994) *supra.*

56. 1995 5th Circuit.

57. Under 18 U.S. C. 2252.

58. See Akdeniz (1996) *supra.*

59. R. Barri Flowers, (1994). *The Victimization and Exploitation of Women and Children.* Jefferson, NC: McFarland & Company.

60. Cavazos & Morin (1994) *supra.*

61. Patricia N. Chock (1987). The use of computers in the sexual exploitation of children and child pornography, *Computer Law Journal* 7, 383–407.

62. For a discussion, see Akdeniz (1996) *supra.*

63. William S. Byassee (1995). Jurisdiction of cyberspace: Applying real world precedent to the virtual community, *Wake Forest Law Review* 30, 197–220; David J. Loundy (1993). E-Law: Legal issues affecting computer information systems and systems operator liability, *Albany Law Journal of Science and Technology* 3, 79–163;

Sean Selin (1996). Governing cyberspace: The need for an international solution, *Gonzaga Law Review* 32, 365–388; Patrick T. Egan (1996). Virtual community standards: Should obscenity law recognize the contemporary community standard of cyberspace? *Suffolk University Law Review* 30, 117–152; J. Allan Cobb (1997). An examination of venue issues concerning online crimes against children: What happens when cyberspace is used to lure children into sexual relations—A look at federal venue provisions, *Journal of Family Law* 35, 537–554.

64. This focus is permissible because the Supreme Court has found that the government has a right to regulate broadcasts if necessary to keep indecent materials away from minors. Thus, although adults may have a right to receive indecent messages, broadcasts may be limited when they pose a reasonable risk that children may be in the audience. *FCC v. Pacifica Foundation*, 438 U.S. 726 (1978); *Sable Communications of California v. FCC*, 492 U.S. 115 (1989).

65. To be codified at 47 U.S. C. Sec. 23 (a)–(h).

66. Telecommunications Competition and Deregulation Act of 1996, S. 652, 104th Cong., 2nd Sess. Sections 501 et seq. The Act criminalizes the knowing use of "any comment, request, suggestion, proposal, image, or other communication that, in context, depicts or describes, in terms patently offensive as measured by contemporary community standards, sexual or excretory activities or organs . . . " Id. Sec 502(e).

67. The current focus aims to regulate children's access to sexually explicit information on the Internet. Fred H. Cate (1996). Cybersex: Regulating sexually explicit expression on the internet, *Behavioral Sciences and the Law* 14, 145–166.

68. *Reno v. American Civil Liberties Union*, S. Ct. No. 96–511 (1997). The Court found that the statute impermissibly abridged the freedom of speech protected by the First Amendment. The Court reiterated the long-standing precedent that sexual expression that is indecent but not obscene is protected by the Constitution. The Court did recognize the important governmental interest in protecting children from harmful materials, but it found that the restrictions would reduce the level of discourse available to the adult population to what is fit for children.

69. Akdeniz (1996) *supra*. Terry Palfrey (1996). Policing the transmission of pornographic materials, *Information & Communications Technology Law* 5, 197–213.

70. For an example of arguments supporting the proposition, see Melanie A. Kennedy (1997). Information superhighway: Parental regulation—the best alternative, *Journal of Family law* 35, 575–593.

71. This was Compuserve's response—an individual control system that provides subscribers with software for selectively blocking any material the user or user's parents find offensive. For a discussion, see Akdeniz (1996) *supra*.

72. The U.S. Supreme Court struck down that relevant provision of the 1996 Act. See *Reno v. American Civil Liberties Union*, S. Ct. No. 96–511 (1997).

73. The government or the Internet Service Providers (ISPs) may limit access to Usenet discussion groups. But, because of the nature of the Internet, they remain unable to control some World Wide Web (WWW) pages, file transfer protocols, and Internet relay chat. ISPs may limit access to Usenet groups because they store news in their own servers; but that is not the case with the other parts of the Internet. Likewise, because gateway technology is not ubiquitous in cyberspace, it remains unable to verify who obtains the information, which leaves several to conclude that those who use it are the ones most likely to be regulated. Palfrey (1996) *supra*; Keth A. Ditthavong (1996). Paving the way for women on the information superhighway:

Curbing sexism not freedoms, *The American University Journal of Gender & the Law* 4, 455–510.

74. Arizona Rev. Stat. Ann. Section 13-3554 (West 1978 & Supp. 1987). For a review of statutes, see Cavanos & Morin (1994) *supra*.

75. See Johnson (1994) *supra*.

76. The Child Pornography Prevention Act of 1995 aimed to address and criminalize such materials. It has yet to pass. See Akdeniz (1996) *supra*.

77. Denmark is a prime example. See Economic and Social Council (1996). *Comments on the Guidelines for a Possible Draft Optional Protocol,* E/CN.4/1996/WG.14/2.

78. See Colin Manchester (1995). Criminal Justice and Public Order Act of 1994: Obscenity, pornography and videos, *Criminal Law Review* 1995, 123–131; Colin Manchester (1995). Computer pornography, *Criminal Law Review* 1995, 546–555.

79. The Canadian Supreme Court unanimously ruled in 1992 that certain types of pornography are obscene if they depict explicit sex with violence or depict nonviolent sex that still subjects people to degrading or dehumanizing treatment. The rationale focused on equality, not necessarily harm to participants. The Court conceded the indeterminacy of the empirical evidence linking pornography to violence. *R. v. Butler,* 1 S. C. R. 452 (1992). The Canadian Court was concerned more with the infringement of other rights found in the Canadian Charter, such as equality. It did not need a conclusive link to harm. For a review and discussion of the case, see Lee Lacombe (1994) *supra*. Swiss law focuses on whether the overall impression of the item or work causes "moral offense to a person of ordinary sensitivity." The approach was met with approval by the European Court of Human Rights, for it kept pace with prevailing views of society. See *Müller v. Switzerland* (1988). Series A, Vol 133; (1991) 13 EHRR 1665.

80. Geraldine Van Bueren (1995). *The International Law on the Rights of the Child.* Boston: Martinus Nijhoff Publishers.

81. For a review of cooperation efforts, see Roger S. Clark (1994). *The United Nations Crime Prevention and Criminal Justice Program: Formulation of Standards and Efforts at Their Implementation.* Philadelphia: University of Pennsylvania Press.

82. Sheila Davey (1988). *Children and Pornography: A Survey of the Protection of Minors against Pornography.* Geneva: International Catholic Children's Bureau.

83. As expected, actual community standards vary when dealing with pornographic materials. For example, the problems encountered throughout individual countries are exacerbated at the international level. For example, Britain bans the U.S. edition of *Penthouse* on the grounds that it is considered obscene. Akdeniz (1996) *supra.* Note that visual representations of sexual activity cannot under British law extend to depictions of an erect penis or to penetration (vaginal, oral, or anal). See Bill Thompson (1994). *Soft core.* London: Cassell.

84. Josephine Steiner (1995). *Enforcing E. C. Law.* London: Blackstone Press.

85. Heike Jung (1993). Criminal justice—A European perspective, *Criminal Law Review* 1993, 237–245; Janet Dine (1993). European community criminal law, *Criminal Law Review* 1993, 246–254.

86. Palfrey (1996) *supra*.

87. Antipoverty and educational programs can help alleviate the need for some children to be involved in exploitative, money-making enterprises. See Roger J. R. Levesque (1994). The sexual use, abuse and exploitation of children: Challenges in

implementing children's human rights, *Brooklyn Law Review* 60, 959–998. Although there are undoubtedly other reasons children become involved in sexually exploitative situations, such as excitement and curiosity, these are all too often ignored; it seems clear that comprehensive programs would go a long way toward alleviating this form of maltreatment. Id.

88. The sexualization in advertising is a clear case in point and is often referred to as accepted and mirrored of child pornography. Itzin (1992) *supra.*

89. The extent to which children are sexualized through various media is made more obvious by the media directed to children: comics have a long history of portraying sensuous and sexual activity. See Maurice Horn (1985). *Sex in Comics.* NY: Chealsea House Publishers. Likewise, there is a large market for "comic" books for older youth and adults. For example, in Japan, a new genre of sexually oriented literature has emerged; "Little eros" frequently portrays gang rape of young girls and sadistic scenes in which girls are bound and beaten. Kuniko Funabashi (1995). Pornographic culture and sexual violence. In Kimiko Fujimura-Fanselow & Atsuko Kameda (Eds.) *Japanese Women: New Feminist Perspectives on the Past, Present and Future* (255–263). NY: CUNY. Several authors now analyze how children and images of youth are idealized, fetishized, and eroticized in everyday culture; see James R. Kincaid (1998). *Erotic Innocence: The Culture of Child Molesting.* Durham, NC: Duke University Press.

90. Recent research has highlighted how the failure of recognition works. For example, children are actually part of the appeal of adult pornography: adult pornography unquestionably includes massive amounts of kiddie porn. Judith Reisman's research is illustrative. Judith Reisman (1986). Children in *Playboy, Penthouse* and *Hustler*—Research report, *Preventing Child Abuse* (Summer 1986), 4. Cited in Kelly, *Pornography* (1992). *supra.* She interestingly details how issues of *Playboy, Penthouse,* and *Hustler* contain, on average, ten illustrations and cartoons depicting children. Thus, over a ten year period, these adult, mainstream sources of pornography actually contain hundreds of images of children involved in sexual associations with adults. Reisman also documents the astonishingly creative ways women are "childified." The magazines publish pictures of children, for example, through the inclusion of pictures of "Playmates" as children and as young girls developing toward sexual maturity.

91. Article 34(c).

92. Arguably, access to sexually charged materials could benefit youth as they deal with the challenging issues of sexuality and sexual relationships. For example, current attempts to acknowledge and respect different sexualities necessarily increase the need to also respect their development. Gay youth, for instance, often suffer from harassment, ridicule, and lack of role models; they arguably could benefit from access to pornographic materials. These discussions raise highly controversial issues, yet they are obvious and much-needed points of discussion if societies are to move toward tolerance and respect children's individual right to self-determination. For a review of the significance of pornography to gay males' sexual development, see Jeffrey G. Sherman (1995). "Love speech: The social utility of pornography," *Stanford Law Review* 47: 661–705.

93. United Nations (1993). *Report of the Working Group on Contemporary Forms of Slavery on its Eighteenth Session,* E/CN.4/Sub.2/1993/30.

94. Id.

95. Ron O'Grady (1992). *The Child and the Tourist: The Story behind the Escalation of Child Prostitution in Asia.* Auckland, New Zealand: Pace Publishing.

96. Prawase Wasi (1990). Tourism and child prostitution. In International Campaign to End Child Prostitution in Asian Tourism (ECPAT) *Caught in Modern Slavery: Tourism and Child Prostitution in Asia* (26–28). The Ecumenical Coalition on Third World Tourism.

97. Susan O'Rourke von Struensee (1995). Violence, exploitation and children: Highlights of the United Nations children's convention and international response to children's human rights, *Suffolk Transnational Law Review* 18, 589–627.

98. Sudarat S. Srisang (1990). Tourism and child prostitution in Thailand. In ECPAT (1990) *supra* (37–46).

99. Maureen Seneviratne & Shirley J. S. Peiris (1990). Tourism and child prostitution in Sri Lanka. ECPAT (1990) *supra* (47–52). Chok C. Hiew (1992). Endangered children in Thailand: Third World families affected by socioeconomic changes. In George W. Albee, Lynne A. Bond & Toni V. Cook Monsey (Eds.) *Improving Children's Lives: Global Perspectives on Prevention* (129–145). Newbury Park, CA: Sage.

100. George Kent (1995). *Children in the International Political Economy.* NY: St. Martin's Press.

101. International trafficking for the purposes of prostitution has a long, well-documented history. In the middle of the nineteenth century, there was trafficking of young children from England to the continent—especially to Belgium, France, and Holland—for the purposes of prostitution. At the turn of the century, girls were purchased in China, taken to the United States, and sold in open markets or directly to individuals. Kathleen Barry (1984). *Female Sexual Slavery.* NY: New York University Press. Chinese girls were also trafficked to Singapore. In 1884, at least 2,000 out of 6,600 Chinese women in Singapore were prostitutes, most of whom were between the ages of thirteen and sixteen. Kent (1995) *supra* (58).

102. United Nations Economic and Social Council, Report of the Working Group on Contemporary Forms of Slavery on its Fourteenth Session, UN Doc No E/CN.4/Sub.2/1990/39 (August 28, 1989) para 29.

103. K. T. Suresh (1990). Child prostitution and tourism in India. In ECPAT *supra* (63–67).

104. Asia Watch (1993). *A Modern Form of Slavery: Trafficking of Burmese Women and Girls into Brothels in Thailand.* NY: Author.

105. United Nations Commission on Human Rights (1996). Rights of the child: Report of the Special Rapporteur on the Sale of Children, Child Prostitution and Child Pornography, UN Doc No E/CN.4/1996/100 (Jan. 17, 1996), 7.

106. International Labor Organization (1996). *Child Labour: Targeting the Intolerable.* Geneva, Switzerland: International Labor Office.

107. United Nations Economic and Social Council, Written Statement Submitted by the United Nations Children's Fund on the Exploitation of Child Labor, Doc No E/CN.4/Sub.2/1990/52 (August 22, 1990) para 3.

108. A. Bouhdiba (1982). *Special Rapporteur of the Sub-Commission on Prevention of Discrimination and Protection of Minorities, Exploitation of Child Labor* (Final Report), UN Doc No E/CN.4/Sub/2/479/Rev 1 (1982), para 122.

109. Kenneth J. Herrman, Jr. & Michale Jupp (1986). International sex trade. In Daniel S. Campagna & Donald L. Poffenderger (Eds.) *The Sexual Trafficking in Children: An Investigation of the Child Sex Trade.* Dover, Massachusetts: Auburn House. Investigative reporters for the National Broadcasting Company were surprised

to find the ease with which they located travel agencies in West Germany and England willing to offer child sex-tours to Thailand. Kent (1995) *supra.*

110. Robert W. Peters (1997). There is a need to regulate indecency on the internet, *Cornell Journal of Law and Public Policy* 6, 363–381.

111. Margaret A. Healy (1995). Prosecuting child sex tourists at home: Do laws in Sweden, Australia, and the United States safeguard the rights of children as mandated by international law? *Fordham International Law Journal* 18, 1852–1923.

112. Fourth preambular paragraph of the *Draft Optional Protocol to the United Nations Convention on the Rights of the Child Concerning the Elimination of Sexual Exploitation and Trafficking of Children, E/CN.4/1995/95.*

113. Michael S. Serrill (1993). Defiling Children, *Time* June 21, 52–55.

114. Healy (1995) *supra.*

115. These sexually abused children are extremely vulnerable and at great risk of being directly infected with AIDS. Because child prostitutes have sexual contact with men who belong to high-risk groups, such as homosexuals, drug addicts, and laborers, they have become the highest risk group. Studies indicate that prostitutes have become a major source of HIV transmission (exceeding even IV drug users). Healy (1995) *supra.* In other surveys, the youngest age group (those up to nineteen years of age) had the highest proportion of HIV positive members (44 percent). Id.

116. See Douglas Hodgson (1995). Combating the organized exploitation of Asian children: Recent developments and prospects, *International Journal of Law and the Family* 9, 23–53.

117. Serrill (1993) *supra.*

118. K. T. Suresh (1990). Child prostitution and tourism in India. In ECPAT (1990) *supra* (63–67).

119. Id.

120. Vickie F. Li (1995). Child sex tourism in Thailand: The role of the United States as a consumer country, *Pacific Rim Law & Policy Journal* 4, 505–542.

121. Patricia D. Levan (1994). Curtailing Thailand's child prostitution through an international conscience, *American University Journal of International Law and Policy* 9, 869–912; Thanh-Dam Truong (1990). *Sex, Money & Morality: Prostitution and Tourism in Southeast Asia.* London: Zed Books; Kathleen Barry (1995). *The Prostitution of Sexuality.* NY: New York University Press; Sandra Pollock Sturdevant & Brenda Stoltzfus (Eds.) (1992). *Let the Good Times Roll: Prostitution and the U.S. Military in Asia.* NY: New Press.

122. Kent (1995) *supra.*

123. Eva Arnvig (1993). Child prostitution in Cambodia: Did the UN look away? *International Children's Rights Monitor* 10(3) (3rd Quarter, 1993), 4–6.

124. Vitit Muntarbhorn (1994). *Rights of the Child: Special Rapporteur Appointed in Accordance with the Commission on Human Rights, Commission on Human Rights,* 50th Sess., UN Doc E/CN.4/1994/84, para 157.

125. Also in other areas, such as the Philippines. See Adule de Leon, Emma Contor & Amihan Abueva (1990). Tourism and child prostitution in the Philippines. In ECPAT *supra* (53–59).

126. Violation of children's rights in El Salvador, 1989–91. *Children's Rights International* 1991, 26.

127. See Vitit Muntarbhorn (1990). Trafficking and sale of children, *International Review of Penal Law* 62, 747–754.

128. Kenneth J. Herrman, Jr. & Michale Jupp (1986) *supra* (143). See also Susann M. Bisignaro (1994). Intercountry adoption today and the implications of the 1993 Hague Convention on tomorrow, *Dickinson Journal of International Law* 13, 123–149.

129. The size of the countries where the phenomenon occurs, the difficulties facing the military and the federal police, pressures exerted upon the parents who sell their babies, and the colluding among certain social sectors all contribute to making the investigation and prevention of trafficking difficult. Maria Josefina Becker (1990). Trafficking and sale of children: The two sides of the question, *International Review of Penal Law* 62, 799–818.

130. Reports reveal that children have been stolen from streets, stolen from hospitals by paid agents, and sold by impoverished women. See Milton Jimenez (1993). Trafficking in Central America: The case of the Honduras, *International Children's Rights Monitor* 10(1&2), 6–7; Jorge L. Carro (1994). Regulation of intercountry adoption: Can the abuses come to an end? *Hastings International & Comparative Law Review* 18, 121–155.

131. The German ambassador to Thailand reports the "terrifying" number of marriages of German men in Thailand designed only to bring young Thai women to Germany in order to force them into prostitution. Kent (1995) *supra* (60).

132. Herrman & Jupp (1986) *supra*.

133. See Vitit Muntarbhorn (1990). Trafficking and sale of children, *International Review of Penal Law* 62, 747–754.

134. Bisignara (1994) *supra*.

135. Forced marriage, prostitution, and rape related to warfare recently have been reported in Burma, the Philippines, and Uganda. Judy el Bushra & Eugenia Piza-Lopez (1994). Gender, war and food. In Joanna MacRae & Anthony Zwi (Eds.) *War & Hunger: Rethinking International Responses to Complex Emergencies* (180–193). London: Zed Books.

136. For an important analysis of these issues, see Ryan Bishop & Lillian S. Robinson (1997). *Night Market: Sexual Cultures and the Thai Economic Miracle.* NY: Routledge. Although the authors focus on adult prostitution, their work readily applies to children as it traces the historical, cultural, material, and textual traditions that have combined in unique and complex ways to establish sex tourism as an integral part of the developing "Thai Economic Miracle."

137. Li (1995) *supra* (508). See also Wasi (1990) and Srisang (1990). Tourism and Child Prostitution in Thailand. In ECPAT (1990) *supra* (37–46).

138. Srisang (1990) *supra* (44).

139. Also in other areas, such as the Philippines. See Adule de Leon, Emma Contor & Amihan Abueva (1990). Tourism and Child Prostitution in the Philippines. In ECPAT *supra* (53–59).

140. Indeed, tourism has been viewed as a less overt form of colonialism and as a symptomatic manifestation of the pervasive economic imperialism practiced by the rich developed nations. Srisang (1990) *supra*.

141. Levesque reports a study in which 63 percent of the girls below the age of sixteen were brought to brothels by their parents, and 21 percent were brought by neighbors or friends who also sold their daughters to brothels. Levesque (1994) *supra*.

142. Levan (1994) *supra*.

143. Again, popular press accounts highlight well the extent of the practice. Children have been discovered chained to their beds, bruised from being whipped

with clothes hangers, and imprisoned by barbed wire and live electrical lines. Paul Ehrlich (1993). Asia's Shocking Secret, *Reader's Digest* October, 69–74. In some brothels, girls are presented in cages or windows so men may contemplate their choices and select sexual partners based on the color-coded price tags pinned to their blouses: "yellow $4; blue $8; red $12; clear $20." Steven Erlanger (1991). A plague awaits, *New York Times Magazine* July 14.

144. Kenneth L. Klothen (1994). *Human Rights Abuses against Women, 1994,* Hearings Before the Subcomm. on International Security, International Organizations and Human Rights of the House Committee on Foreign Affairs, 103rd Cong. 2nd Sess.

145. O'Grady (1993) *supra;* United Nations (1993). *Report of the Working Group on Contemporary Forms of Slavery on its eighteen session,* E/CN.4/Sub.2/-1993/30, para 32.

146. Carol Bellamy (1997). *The State of the World's Children 1997.* NY: Oxford University Press.

147. Florence Bruce (1990). The International Catholic Child Bureau (ICCB). In ECPAT (1990) *supra* (29–36).

148. These rights are recognized not only in the Children's Convention, but also in the Universal Declaration of Human Rights, and the International Covenants.

149. Even the regimes that have been most egregious in their reaction to child prostitution agree that it is a violation of children's basic human rights. See Levesque (1994) *supra.*

150. For a review, see Susan Jeanne Toepfer & Bryan Stuart Wells (1994). The worldwide market for sex: A review of international and regional legal prohibitions regarding trafficking in women, *Michigan Journal of Gender and Law* 2, 83–128; Nora V. Demleitner (1994). Forced prostitution: Naming an international offense, *Fordham International Law Journal* 18, 163–197.

151. Marie-Francoise Lucker-Babel (1990). Inter-country adoption and trafficking in children: An initial assessment of the adequacy of the international protection of children and their rights, *International Review of Penal Law* 62, 799–818.

152. UN Doc A/1251 (1949). Reprinted in *International Human Rights Instruments.* NY: United Ntions.

153. Article 1.

154. UN Doc A/Res/34/180 (1980). Reprinted in *International Instruments.*

155. Panudda Boopala (1996). The role of the International Labor Organization. In Maureen Jaffee & Sonia Rosen (Eds.) *Forced Labor: The prostitution of Children* (53–62). Washington, DC: Department of Labor. 55. The Conventions include the Forced Labor Convention 1930 (No. 29), 39 U. N. T. S. 55 and the Forced Labor Convention 1957 (No. 105), 320 U. N. T. S. 291. Importantly, these are two of the most ratified Conventions; for a list of ratifying parties, see International Labor Organization (1996). *Child Labour: Targeting the Intolerable.* Geneva, Switzerland: International Labor Office.

156. International Covenant on Civil and Political Rights, G. A. Res 2200A(XXI), UN GAOR, 21st Sess. Sup. No. 16, at 52, UN Doc A/6316 (1966). Article 8(1).

157. Eric Thomas Berkman (1996). Responses to the international child sex tourism trade, *Boston College International and Comparative Law Review* 19, 397–422; Healy (1995) *supra.*

158. Eric Thomas Berkman (1996) *supra.*

159. Vickie F. Li (1995) *supra*; Rupert Ticehurst (1996). Jurisdiction in "sex tourism" cases, *New Law Journal* 46, 1826-27.

160. Patricia D. Levan (1994). Curtailing Thailand's child prostitution through an international conscience, *American University Journal of International Law and Policy* 9, 869-912.

161. Healy (1995) *supra*.

162. See Hodgson (1995) *supra*.

163. Id.

164. For a review of those laws, see Levan (1994) *supra*.

165. Senevirante & Peiris (1990) *supra*.

166. Id; Michael Perry (1995). Asian crackdown on pedophiles has little impact, Reuters Ltd. Mar. 21, available in LEXIS, NEWS Library, CURNWS File.

167. Asia Watch (1993) *supra* condemned those police and government officials who are allegedly profiting from the forcible recruitment of thousands of Burmese women and girls into Thai prostitution.

168. Levesque (1994) *supra*.

169. UNICEF statement at para 6 and Working Group Report at para 34 (*supra* note).

170. Joint Study of Research and Development Division of the Police Department and the Population Institute of Chulalongkorn University, Bangkok Post, January 3, 1993, cited in Kathleen Barry (1995). *The Prostitution of Sexuality*. NY: New York University Press.

171. This is not to say, however, that the practice should not be condemned. If, for example, consent and absence of physical force had been the criteria for determining whether slavery was or was not a violation of human dignity and human rights, slavery would not have been recognized as a violation, because an important element of all forms of slavery is acceptance of their condition by many slaves. Just like slaves, many prostitutes accept their fate, which makes rendering them assistance exceedingly difficult.

172. O'Grady (1992) *supra* (132).

173. Saisuree Chutikul (1990). Psychological Perspectives on Child Prostitution. In ECPAT (83-86) *supra*.

174. Senevirante & Peiris (1990) *supra*.

175. Id.

176. Paul Ehrlich (1993) *supra*.

177. See Bruce (1990) *supra*.

178. Articles 6(2) and 27.

179. Children's Convention (1990) *supra*.

180. Declaration on the Right to Development, GA Res 41/128, Dec. 4 1986.

181. Id. Article 1(1).

182. Covenant on Economic, Social and Cultural Rights, Article 11.

183. Covenant on Economic, Social and Cultural Rights, Article 10.

184. Steven Erlanger (1992). A plague awaits, *New York Times* July 14, 49. A Thai minister argues that poverty is merely an accelerator of prostitution, not the primary cause; the main causes are culture and demand, which are exacerbated by boredom and the media. Parker Rossman (1976). *Sexual Experience between Men and Boys*. Wilton, CT: Association Press.

185. Levan (1994) *supra*.

186. Seneviratne & Peiris (1990) *supra*.

187. Levesque (1994) *supra*.

188. Hodgson (1995) *supra*; Healy (1995) *supra*.

189. Siriporn Skrobanek (1990). *Child Prostitution in Thailand*. First National Assembly on Child Development, Government House, Thailand, August 30–31, 1990, Report, UNICEF; Ove Narvesen (1989). *The Sexual Exploitation of Children in Developing Countries*. Oslo, Norway: Redd Barna.

190. Kent (1995) *supra*.

191. For the higher estimates, see R. Barri Flowers (1994). *The Victimization and Exploitation of Women and Children*. Jefferson, NC: McFarland & Company; D. Kelly Weisberg (1984). Children of the night: The adequacy of statutory treatment of juvenile prostitution, *American Journal of Criminal Law* 12, 1–67.

192. Carol Bellamy (1997). *The State of the World's Children 1997*. NY: Oxford University Press.

193. Roger Sawyer (1988). *Children Enslaved*. NY: Routledge.

194. David Finkelhor, Gerald Hotaling & Anreas Sedlak (1990). *Missing, Abducted, Runaway, and Thrownaway Children in America, First Report: Numbers and Characteristics National Incidence Studies, Executive Summary*. Washington, DC: U.S. Department of Justice, Office of Juvenile Justice and Delinquency Prevention.

195. See James Collins, Pamela M. Messerschmidt, Mary Ellen McCalla, Ronaldo Iachan & Michael L. Hubbard (1994). *Planning the Second National Incidence Studies of Missing, Abducted, Runaway, and Thrownaway Children: Final Report*. Washington, DC: U.S. Department of Justice, Office of Juvenile Justice and Delinquency Prevention; Gregory A. Loken (1995). "Thrownaway" children and throwaway parenthood, *Temple Law Review* 68, 1715–1762.

196. See, for example, Gary L. Yates, R. G. Mackensie & A. Swafford (1991). A risk profile comparison of homeless youth involved in prostitution and homeless youth not involved, *Journal of Adolescent Health* 12, 545–549.

197. The most notable research has been conducted by Weisberg and Snell. See D. Kelly Weisberg (1985). *Children of the Night: A Study of Adolescent Prostitution*. Lexington, MA: Lexington Books; Cudore L. Snell (1995). *Young Men in the Street, Help-seeking Behavior of Young Male Prostitutes*. Westport, CT: Praeger.

198. The example of gay adolescents provides an important illustration. Kelli Kristine Armstrong (1994). The silent minority within a minority: Focusing on the needs of gay youth in our public schools, *Golden Gate University Law Review* 41, 67–97; Michael Radkowsky & Lawrence J. Siegel (1997). The gay adolescent: Stressors, adaptations, and psychosocial interventions, *Clinical Psychology Review* 17, 191–216.

199. Lesley A. Welsh, Francis X. Archambault, Mark-David Janus & Scott W. Brown (1995). *Running for Their Lives: Physical and Sexual Abuse of Runaway Adolescents*. NY: Garland.

200. Mimi Silbert & Ayala Pines (1984). Pornography and sexual abuse of women, *Sex Roles* 11/12: 857–868.

201. Mark-David Janus, Arlene McCormack, Anne Wolbert Burgess & Carol Hartman (1987). *Adolescent Runaways: Causes and Consequences*. Lexington, MA: Lexington Books.

202. Debra Boyer (1989). Male prostitution and homosexual identity, *Journal of Homosexuality* 17, 151–184; D. Kelly Weisberg (1985). *Children of the Night: A Study of Adolescent Prostitution*. Lexington, MA: Lexington Books; Flowers (1994) *supra*; Welsh et al. (1995) *supra*.

203. Edward D. Farber & Jack A. Joseph (1985). The maltreated adolescent: Patterns of physical abuse, *Child Abuse and Neglect* 9, 201–206; T. Houghten & M Golembiewski (1976). *A Study of Runaway Youth and Their Families.* Washington, DC: Youth Alternatives Project.

204. Augustine Brannigan & Erin Givvs Van Brunschot (1997). Youthful prostitution and child sexual trauma, *International Journal of Law and Psychiatry* 20, 337–354. See also Les B. Whitbeck, Danny R. Hoyt & Keven Ackley (1997). Abusive family backgrounds and late victimization among runaway and homeless adolescents, *Journal of Research on Adolescence* 7, 375–392.

205. Nathaniel Eugene Terrell (1997). Street life: Aggravated and sexual assaults among homeless and runaway adolescents, *Youth & Society* 28, 267–290.

206. Welsh et al. (1995). *supra*; Terrell (1997) *supra*; Les B. Whitbeck, Danny R. Hoyt & Kevin A. Ackley (1997). Families of homeless and runaway adolescents: A comparison of parent/caretaker and adolescent perspectives on parenting, family violence, and adolescent conduct, *Child Abuse & Neglect* 21, 517–528.

207. Welsh et al. (1995) *supra*.

208. Bill McCarthy & John Hagan (1992). Mean streets: The theoretical significance of situational delinquency among homeless youth, *American Journal of Sociology* 98, 567–627; James Garbarino, Cynthia J. Schellbach, Janet M. Sebes & Associates (Eds.) (1986). *Troubled Youth, Troubled Families.* NY: Aldine Publishing.

209. See Johan C. Gonsiorek, Walter H. Bera & Donal Le Touorneay (1994). *Male Sexual Abuse: A Trilogy of Intervention Strategies.* Thousand Oaks, CA: Sage.

210. Id.

211. James Garbarino, Janis Wilson & Anne C. Garbarino (1986). The adolescent runaway. In James Garbarino, Cynthia J. Schellbach, Janet M. Sebes & Associates (Eds.) *Troubled Youth, Troubled Families* (41–56). NY: Aldine Publishing.

212. Arlene McCormack, Mark-David Janus & Ann Wolbert Burgess (1986). Runaway youths and sexual victimization: Gender differences in an adolescent runaway population, *Child Abuse and Neglect* 10, 387–395.

213. Terrell (1997) *supra*.

214. Mimi H. Silbert (1980). *Sexual Assault of Prostitutes: Phase One.* Washington, DC: National Institute of Mental Health.

215. Ellen Hale (1981). Center studies causes of juvenile prostitution, Gannett News Service, May 21.

216. Jennifer James (1980). *Entrance into Juvenile Prostitution.* Washington, DC: National Institute of Mental Health. 18. Cited in Flowers (1994) *supra*.

217. House Committee on Education and Labor, Subcommittee of Human Resources (1984). *Juvenile Justice, Runaway Youth and Missing Children's Acts.* Amendments, 98th Congress, 2nd Sess, 7, March.

218. Julia M. Robertson (1992). Homeless and runaway youths: A review of the literature. In Marjorie J. Robertson & Milton Greenblatt (Eds.) *Homelessness: A National Perspective* (287–297). NY: Plenum.

219. Welsh et al. (1995) *supra*. The only exception is that boys are more likely to be assaulted with a gun or weapon on the street than at home.

220. Robert W. Deisher & William M. Rogers II. (1991). The medical care of street youth, *Journal of Adolescent Health* 12, 500–503; Yates et al. (1991); Crowley and Patel (1997).

221. McCarthy & Hagan (1992) *supra*. For a more thorough analysis of youth

homelessness and crime, see John Hagan & Bill McCarthy (1997). *Mean Streets: Youth Crime and Homelessness.* NY: Cambridge University Press.

222. Walsh et al. (1995) *supra.*

223. Weisberg (1985) *supra.*

224. Davidson & Loken (1987) *supra.*

225. Robertson (1992) *supra.*

226. Anne Crowley & Gera Patel (1997). Accounting for "child prostitution." In Ian Butler & Ian Shaw (Eds.) *A Case of Neglect? Children's Experiences and the Sociology of Childhood* (125–141). Brookfield, VT: Avebury.

227. Id.

228. Weisberg (1984) *supra.*

229. James Christopherson (1989). European child-abuse management systems. In Olive Stevenson (Ed.) *Child Abuse: Professional Practice and Public Policy* (74–87). NY: Harvester Wheatsheaf.

230. Weisberg (1984) *supra.*

231. Codified at 42 U.S. C. A. Sec. Sec. 5701, 5702, 5731, 5751 (West 1995).

232. For a list, see Loken (1995) *supra.*

233. Deborah Bass (1992). *Helping Vulnerable Youths: Runaway and Homeless Adolescents in the United States.* Washing DC: NASW Press.

234. For a list, see Loken (1995) *supra.*

235. Jody Greene et al. (1995). *Youth with Runaway, Throwaway, and Homeless Experiences: Prevalence, Drug Use, and Other Risk Behaviors, Vol I: Final Report.* Washington, DC: U.S. Department of Health & Human Services. See also Loken (1995) *supra.*

236. Shiela A. Pires & Judith Tolmach Silber (1991). *On Their Own: Runaway and Homeless Youth and Programs that Serve Them.* Washington, DC: CASSP Technical Assistance Center, Gerorgetown University Child Development Center.

237. See Jeanne Kalinoski & Caitlin Rothermel (1995). Lessons from the Street: Outreach to Inner-city Youth, *SEICUS Report* 23(2), 14–17.

238. Finkelhor et al. (1990) *supra.*

239. Loken (1995) *supra.*

240. Universal Declaration of Human Rights, GA Res 217 (III), art 25(1), UN Doc A/810 (1948).

241. Children's Convention (1990), Article 27 (1) and (3).

242. Dorothy L. Miller, D. Miller & F. Hofman et al. (1980). *Runaways—Illegal Aliens in Their Own Land.* NY: Praeger.

243. Covenant (1966), Article 11.

244. Id.

245. U. N. Commission on Human Rights, Sub-Commission on Prevention of Discrimination and Protection of Minorities (1993). *The Right to Adequate Housing: Progress Report Submitted by Mr. Rajindar Sachar, Special Rapporteur.* UN Doc E/CN.4/Sub.2/15 (1993).

246. See Marc-Olivier Herman (1994). Fighting homelessness: Can international human rights law make a difference? *Georgetown Journal on Fighting Poverty* 2, 59–82.

247. Kelli Kristine Armstrong (1994). The silent minority within a minority: Focusing on the needs of gay youth in our public schools, *Golden Gate University Law Review* 41, 67–97.

248. Cudore L. Snell (1995). *Young Men in the Street, Help-Seeking Behavior of Young Male Prostitutes.* Westport, CT: Praeger; Welsh et al. (1995) *supra.*

5. The Sexual Use of Children

1. For an important cross-cultural analysis of normative child sexuality, see Suzanne G. Frayser (1994). Defining normal childhood sexuality: An anthropological approach, *Annual Review of Sex Research* 5, 173–217. For analyses of *indigenous* concepts of maltreatment, see the work of leading commentators compiled in Jill E. Korbin (Ed.) (1981). *Child Abuse and Neglect: Cross-cultural Perspectives.* Berkeley: University of California Press; Laura L. O'Toole & Jessica R. Schiffman (Eds.) (1997). *Gender Violence: Interdisciplinary Perspectives.* NY: New York University Press.

2. It is not only important to recognize people as cultural beings, but also to recognize the complexities of children's lives and circumstances. In addition to variations in children's lives, it is critical to keep in mind intra-cultural variation; just as there are defenders of traditional practices who are active members of their families, communities, and cultures, so there are campaigners for the abolition of cultural practices who are also inside their cultures. Isabelle R. Gunning (1991–92). Arrogant perception, world-travelling and multicultural feminism: The case of female genital surgeries, *Columbia Human Rights Law Review* 23, 189–248; Kay Boulware-Miller (1985). Female circumcision: Challenges to the practice as a human rights violation, *Harvard Women's Law Journal* 8, 155–177.

3. See Deborah A. Elliston (1995). Erotic anthropology: "Ritualized homosexuality" in Melanesia and beyond, *American Anthropologist* 22, 848–867. Elliston charges that examinations of same-sex ritualized relationships improperly focuse on erotics and sexuality as pancultural and precultural universals.

4. Efforts to reconcile individual and cultural interests must keep in mind the way in which notions of "cultural values" are constituted. Ideologies, power relations, and disparities in access to information and communications all affect the degree to which "community values" really reflect the values held by members of that community. Community values may seem strong, homogeneous, and uncontroversial simply because persons or groups of persons have been excluded from the debate, or have had their interests discounted or devalued. The human rights movement seeks to protect the interests of all persons in a community.

5. Jack Donnelly (1989). *Universal Human Rights in Theory and Practice.* Ithaca, NY: Cornell University Press.

6. Clitoridectomies and excision of women have been studied by anthropologists and feminists for decades. Mary Daly and Charlotte Bunch call the practices torture; see Mary Daly (1979). *Gyn/ecology: The Metaethics of Radical Feminism.* Boston: Beacon Press. Charlotte Bunch and others label them "genital mutilation." Charlotte Bunch (1990). Women's rights as human rights, *Human Rights Quarterly* 12, 489–498.

7. Anna Funder (1993). De minimis non curat lex: The clitoris, culture and the law, *Transnational Law and Contemporary Problems* 3, 417–467.

8. American Anthropological Association, "Statement on Human Rights," submitted to the Commission on Human Rights, United Nations, by the Executive Board, American Anthropological Association, June 24, 1947, *American Anthropologist* 49, 539–543.

9. For an analysis of international documents devoted to minority, cultural,

and indigenous rights, see Roger J. R. Levesque (1994). The sexual use, abuse and exploitation of children: Challenges in implementing children's human rights, *Brooklyn Law Review* 60, 959–998.

10. For important essays arguing same, see Robert Borofsky (Ed.) (1994). *Assessing Cultural Anthropology.* NY: McGraw-Hill; Renato Rosaldo (1989). *Culture and Truth: The Remaking of Social Analysis.* Boston: Beacon Press; Joan Comaroff & Jean Comaroff (1992). *Ethnography and the Historical Imagination.* Boulder, CO: Westview Press. It is important to reiterate that "Western" society is not homogenous and unitary. There are multifarious cultural realities in the West, each with its own set of precepts and customs. Clearly, there are only generalizations of Western society, as there are only generalizations of other broadly categorized cultures.

11. Arif Dirlik (1987). Culturalism as hegemonic ideology and liberating practice, *Cultural Critique: The Nature & Context of Minority Discourse* 6, 13–50.

12. Catherine Lutz & Lila Abue-Lughod (Eds.) (1990). *Language and the Politics of Emotion.* Cambridge: Cambridge University Press.

13. The reification of culture has helped form a new kind of right claimed on the basis of peoples' membership in a collective defined by their cultures. The primary example is the Civil Rights Movement in the United States that championed collective rights based on a shared culture and, in so doing, inspired and helped to shape many other ethnic liberation movements. See William J. Wilson (1987). *The Truly Disadvantaged: The Inner City, the Underclass, and Public Policy.* Chicago: University of Chicago Press; Gerd Baumann (1996). *Contesting Culture: Discourses of Identity in Multi-ethnic London.* NY: Cambridge University Press. For a critique of the use of culture, see Terence Turner (1993). Anthropology and multiculturalism: What is anthropology that multiculturalists should be mindful of it? *Cultural Anthropology* 8(4), 411–29.

14. There is actually a third view of culture. This widely held view regards culture as a process of artistic and scientific creation. In this view, individuals have the right to create their own cultures, without restrictions. Thus, there is a focus on "high" or elite culture and its preservation; culture is the product of the talents and labor of a small number of cultural creators.

15. Children's Convention (1990), Article 31.

16. Id. Article 28(3). See Roger J. R. Levesque (1998). The international human right to education: The lore and lure of law, *Annual Survey of International and Comparative Law* 5, 205–252.

17. Children's Convention (1990), Article 30.

18. See Asbjorn Eide (1995). Cultural rights as individual human rights. In Asbjorn Eide, Catarina Krause & Allan Rosas (Eds.) *Economic and Cultural Rights* (229–240). Boston: Martinus Nijhoff; Lyndel V. Prott (1988). Cultural rights as peoples' rights in international law. In James Crawford (Ed.) *The Rights of Peoples* (92–106). NY: Oxford University Press.

19. See Eric Hobsbawn & Terence Ranger (Eds.) (1992). *The Invention of Tradition.* NY: Cambridge University Press.

20. Rodolfo Stavenhagen (1995). Cultural rights and universal human rights. In Asbjorn Eide, Catarina Krause & Allan Rosas (Eds.) *Economic and Cultural Rights* (63–86). Boston: Martinus Nijhoff.

21. For informative discussions, see Jan Bertin et al. (Eds.) (1990). *Human Rights in a Pluralist World: Individuals and Collectives.* Westport, CT: Meckler.

22. Levesque (1994) *supra.*

23. For comprehensive discussions, see Christian Tomuschat (Ed.) (1993). *Modern Law of Self-determination.* Boston: Martinus Nijhoff.

24. See Allan Rosas (1995). The right to self-determination. In Asbjorn Eide, Catarina Krause & Allan Rosas (Eds.) *Economic and Cultural Rights* (79–86). Boston: Martinus Nijhoff.

25. Protections located in traditional international texts are fraught with difficulties not only in basic conceptualizations but also in their implementation. When cultural rights are at issue, a collective approach may be required, since some cultural rights can be enjoyed only in community with others. The community must have the possibility to preserve, protect, and develop what it has in common for individual children to enjoy it. That is, beneficiaries of rights may be individuals, but the rights evaporate without the collective rights of groups. Individuals who possess the right belong to specific cultures and are shaped by these cultures, engage in collective action, share common values, and can only be the bearers of these common values by joining with other members of their own group.

26. Children's Convention (1990), Article 30 protects the rights of ethnic, religious, or linguistic minorities or persons of indigenous origin.

27. Id.

28. Id. Article 30.

29. Levesque (1994) *supra.*

30. Several scholars argue that jurisprudence should focus on what lawyers and judges do; see Dennis Patterson (1993). The poverty of interpretive universalism: Toward the reconstruction of legal theory, *Texas Law Review* 72, 1–56.

31. Outi Korhonen (1996). New international law: Silence, defense or deliverance? *European Journal of International Law* 7, 1–28.

32. See Roger Colinvaux (1997). What is law? A search for legal meaning and good judging under a textualist lens, *Indiana Law Journal* 72, 1133–1163.

33. For example, states engage in international policy-making when they decide the terms to which they commit themselves. Joseph Frankel (1988). *International Relations in a Changing World* (4th ed.). NY: Oxford University Press.

34. As others have argued, there are good reasons why courts should be modest in their interpretations of legal texts and in their creation of new rights. See Cass R. Sunstein (1993). Liberal constitutionalism and liberal justice, *Texas Law Review* 72, 305–313; Robert George (1997). Law, democracy, and moral disagreement, *Harvard Law Review* 110, 1388–1406. For example, courts may lack the tools for successful implementation; their efforts may be futile or counterproductive. Likewise, courts can only effect significant social reform under a set of very narrow and special conditions. See Gerald N. Rosenberg (1992). *The Hollow Hope: Can Courts Bring about Social Change?* Chicago: University of Chicago Press.

35. Again, allowing for consciousness-raising may not ensure respect for human rights; knowledge of the existence of child sexual maltreatment despite well-articulated legal rules that prohibit maltreating behaviors has only just begun to have an impact.

36. See, e.g., Gary B. Melton (1995). The right to a family environment for "Children Living in Exceptionally Difficult Conditions," *Law & Policy* 17, 345–351.

37. Law is viewed as a system of meaning-making, a communicative system which produces norms of conduct both for its own operations and for society at large. The way it does so is actually quite theoretically controversial. See Michael King

(1993). The "truth" about autopoiesis, *Journal of Law and Society* 20, 218–236; Gunther Teubner (1993). *Law as an Autopoietic System.* Cambridge, MA: Blackwell.

38. This, of course, is an area of contentious debate. However, it is possible to acknowledge the impossibility of locating an objective source of justification while still arguing that efforts toward recognition and implementation should continue. See Jan Goerecki (1996). *Justifying Ethics: Human Rights and Human nature.* New Brunswick, NJ: Transaction Publishers.

39. Such protection is derived, for example, through protection of autonomy, privacy, freedom of association, and liberty of conscience. See Children's Convention (1990), Articles 12—16.

40. Several argue that courts must confine themselves to perfecting the process of representative democracy. See John Hart Ely (1980). *Democracy and Distrust.* Cambridge: Harvard University Press.

41. Mortimer Sellers (1994). Republican principles in international law, *Connecticut Journal of International Law* 11, 403–432.

42. Children's Convention (1990), 7th preambular paragraph (emphasis added).

43. Several propose that legal justification and legal reasoning is not confined to the realm of what lawyers ordinarily think of as legal reasoning. See Ronald Dworkin (1986). *Law's Empire.* Cambridge, MA: Belknap Press.

44. Clifford Geertz (1984). Distinguished lecture: Anti-anti-relativism, *American Anthropologist* 86, 263–278.

45. This is a rather benevolent view of international forces. For example, several countries ratify international treaties to receive foreign aid and take obligations upon themselves to act in certain ways. UNICEF's work in the Sudan provides a clear case in point: Sudan was required to prohibit female circumcision in order to obtain certain foreign humanitarian assistance. Paul Lewis (1997). A re-engineered Unicef wins points, and rights for children, *New York Times* April 27, A9.

46. For example, the Supreme Court of the United States is necessarily "conservative" in that it tends to affirm and reflect preexisting societal impulses, which provides a primary mechanism through which the Court gains legitimacy. See, for example, Thomas R. Marshall (1988). Public opinion, representation, and the moderate Supreme Court, *American Politics Quarterly* 16, 296–316.

47. See Robert Cover (1983). The Supreme Court, 1982 term—Forward: Nomos and narrative, *Harvard Law Review* 97, 44–68.

48. See Martha Minow (1987). Interpreting rights: An essay for Robert Cover, *Yale Law Journal* 96, 1860–1915.

49. Rights have served as a motivational source of hope for women. Patricia J. Williams put it as follows: "It is the magic world of visibility and invisibility, of inclusion and exclusion, or power and no-power. The concept of rights, both positive and negative, is the marker of our citizenship, our participatoriness, our relation to others." (431). Patricia J. Williams (1987). Alchemical notes: Reconstructing ideals from deconstructed rights, *Harvard Civil Rights—Civil Liberties Law Review* 22, 402–447.

50. John Rawls (1993). *Political Liberalism.* NY: Columbia University Press; Cass R. Sunstein (1993). *The Partial Constitution.* Cambridge: Harvard University Press.

51. See Ludwig Wittgenstein (1953). *Philosophical Investigations.* NY: Macmillan. 371–373.

52. For example, torture is wrong because it violates culture's celebration of the individual and a shared sense of the essential dignity and equality of human beings.

53. In the enforcement of human rights, the United Nations created the position of "High Commissioner for Human Rights." The High Commissioner was not charged by the international community to play the role of chief prosecutor, but rather to use political and diplomatic channels to ensure a continuous dialogue to enhance human rights. Jose Ayala-Lasso (1996). Making human rights a reality in the twenty-first century, *Emory International Law Review* 10, 497–508. The Commissioner's actions must be based on cooperative, inclusive, and comprehensive approaches.

54. Robert H. Mnookin (Ed.) (1996). *In the Interests of Children: Advocacy, Law Reform, and Public Policy.* Cambridge, MA: PON Books.

55. See, e.g., Bronwyn Winter (1994). Women, the law, and cultural relativism in France: The case of excision, *Signs* 19, 939–974.

56. Andrew Clapham (1993). *Human Rights in the Private Sphere.* NY: Oxford University Press.

57. Vladlen S. Vereshchetin (1996). New constitutions and the old problem of the relationship between international and national law, *European Journal of International Law* 7, 29–41.

58. This phenomenon involves the general disaggregation of sovereignty that recognizes the manner in which national judicial, executive, and legislative branches increasingly interact with one another and take account each other's approaches. For an analysis of international law's new focus on networks of transnational transactions by social and economic actors, the multiple channels of communication and actions that are both transgovernmental and transnational, and the blurring of the distinction between domestic and foreign issues, see Ann-Marie Slaughter (1995). International law in a world of liberal states, *European Journal of International Law* 6, 503–538.

59. Levesque (1998) *supra.*

60. This is part of the peculiar paradox of the Nation State system guiding international law: sovereignty is a claim to autonomy but is simultaneously dependent for its legitimacy on exogenous universal principles.

61. Robert I. Levy (1973). *Tahitians: Mind and Experience in the Society Islands.* Chicago: University of Chicago Press.

62. Fred R. Myers (1986). *Pintupe Country, Pintupe Self.* Washington, DC: Smithsonian Institution Press.

63. The major justification for the use of the phrase is to semantically convey a sense of horror and disgust about the practice and to distinguish it from male circumcision. For examples of anthropological investigations, see Janice Boddy (1982). Womb as oasis: The symbolic context of pharonic circumcision in rural Northern Sudan, *American Ethnologist* 9, 682–698; John G. Kennedy (1970). Circumcision and excision in Egyptian Nubia, *Man* 5, 175–191; Hamid Rushwan, Corry Slot, Asma El Dareer & Nadia Bushra (1983). *Female Circumcision in Sudan: Prevalence, Complications, Attitudes and Changes.* Sudan: University of Khrtoum; Janice Boddy (1989). *Wombs and Alien Spirits: Women, Men, and the Zar Cult in Northern Sudan.* Madison: University of Wisconsin Press; Daniel Gordon (1991). Female circumcision and genital operations in Egypt and the Sudan: A dilemma for medical anthropology, *Medical Anthropology Quarterly* 5, 3–14; Hanny Lightfoot-Klein (1989). *Prisoners of Ritual: An Odyssey into Female Genital Circumcision in Africa.* NY: Haworth Press. For major studies of female circumcision from a human rights perspective, see Katherine Brennan (1989). The influence of cultural relativism and international

human rights law: Female circumcision as a case study, *Law and Inequality* 8, 367–398; Alison T. Slack (1988). Female circumcision: A critical appraisal, *Human Rights Quarterly* 10, 437–486; Kay Boulware-Miller (1985). Female circumcision: Challenges to the practice as a human rights violation, *Harvard Women's Law Journal* 8, 155–177; Isabelle R. Gunning (1991–92). Arrogant perception, world-travelling and multicultural feminism: The case of female genital surgeries, *Columbia Human Rights Law Review* 23, 189–248; Stephen A. James (1994). Reconciling international human rights and cultural relativism: The case of female circumcision, *Bioethics* 8, 1–26. Several activists also have written impressive reports. See especially Nahid Toubia (1993). *Female Genital Mutilation: A Call for Global Action.* NY: Women, Ink; Fran P. Hosken (1982). *The Hosken Report: Genital and Sexual Mutilation of Females* (3rd ed.). Lexington, MA: Women's International Network News.

64. World Health Organization (1997). *Female gential mutilation: A joint WHO/UNICEF/UNFPA Statement.* Geneva: World Health Organization. For a report and review of these and other estimates, see Layli Miller Bashir (1996). Female genital mutilation in the United States: An examination of criminal and asylum law, *American University Journal of Gender and Law* 4, 415–454.

65. Roger Sawyer (1988). *Children Enslaved.* NY: Routledge; Robyn Cerny Smith (1992). Female circumcision: Bringing women's perspectives into the international debate, *Southern California Law Review* 65, 2449–2504; Catherine L. Annas (1996). Irreversible error: The power and prejudice of female genital mutilation, *Journal of Contemporary Health Law and Policy* 12, 325–353.

66. Nahid Toubia (1993). *Female Genital Mutilation: A Call for Global Action.* NY: Women, Ink.

67. Hope Lewis (1995). Between *Irua* and "female genital mutilation": Feminist human rights discourse and the cultural divide, *Harvard Human Rights Journal* 8, 1–55.

68. Andrea Rugh (1984). *Family in Contemporary Egypt.* Syracuse: Syracuse University Press.

69. See Winter (1994) *supra.*

70. Hamid Rushwan, Corry Slot, Asma El Dareer & Nadia Bushra (1983). *Female Circumcision in Sudan: Prevalence, Complications, Attitudes and Changes.* Sudan: University of Khrtoum.

71. Sawyer (1988) *supra.* See also Asma El Dareer (1982). *Women, Why Do You Weep?* London: Zed.

72. Alison T. Slack (1988). Female circumcision: A critical appraisal, *Human Rights Quarterly* 10, 437–486; Kristen Lee (1994). Female genital mutilation—medical aspects and rights of children, *The International Journal of Children's Rights* 2, 35–44.

73. The end of colonialism left a legacy of so-called plural legal systems in which family law derived from European law was applicable to non-Africans, while the majority of the African population remained subject to a legal regime labeled customary. See Martin Chanock (1989). Neither customary nor legal: African customary law in an era of family law reform, *International Journal of Law and the Family* 3, 72–88. It is important, though, to note that modern customary law is a product of the interaction between African customary law and colonial rule. Doing so makes it more difficult to invoke custom in opposition to reform. It is a problem arising out of the growth of the state and its modes of regulation everywhere, both where communities are relatively homogenous and where they are culturally and religiously diverse. See

Jerold S. Auerbach (1983). *Justice without Law.* NY: Oxford University Press. The disparity and possible conflict between different kinds of laws, those of custom and those of the modern state, is not unique to Africa, nor to colonialism. It is more marked where the pace of economic change has been more rapid, and where there are wide diversities between regions and classes. There is a disparity between different levels of law: law on the books and law in practice.

74. Contrary to popular commentaries, there is no homogenous African culture or customary law; and customary law differs from tribe to tribe and from ethnic group to ethnic group within the same tribe. Fitnat Naa-Adjely (1995). Reclaiming the African woman's individuality: The struggle between women's reproductive autonomy and African society and culture, *American University Law Review* 44, 1351–1381.

75. See Arthur Phillips & Henry F. Morris (1971). *Marriage Laws in Africa.* NY: Oxford University Press.

76. Ester K. Hicks (1996). *Infibulation: Female Mutilation in Islamic North-eastern Africa.* New Brunswick, NJ: Transaction Publishers.

77. Atoki (1995) *supra*; see also A traditional practice that threatens health—Female Circumcision (1986). *WHO Chronicle* 40, 31–32.

78. Id.

79. Otto Meinardus (1967). Mythological, historical, and sociological aspects of the practice of female circumcision among the Egyptians, *Acta Ethnographica* 16, 389–397.

80. James (1994) *supra*.

81. Alison Dundes Rentlin (1994). Is the cultural defense detrimental to the health of children? *Law and Anthropology* 7, 27–106.

82. Rushwan et al. (1983) *supra*.

83. For an informative review, see Jonathan P. Berkey (1996). Circumcision circumscribed: Female excision and cultural accommodation in the Medieval Near East, *International Journal of Middle East Studies* 28, 19–38.

84. Slack (1988) *supra* (458–459); Hamid Ruswan et al. (1983) *supra* report findings that over 70 percent of men and approximately 20 percent of women argue that the practice has religious significance.

85. Marnia Lazreg argues, in her critique of feminist scholarship on Algerian and North Africa, that the religious paradigm which dominates the social science and feminist approaches to women in the Middle East and North Africa effectively prevents Muslim women from expressing their own identity. Further, it leaves unexplained questions of the meaning of Islam for women. She argues that "[t]he overall effect of this paradigm is to deprive women of self-presence, of being. Because women are subsumed under religion presented in fundamental terms, they are inevitably seen as evolving in nonhistorical time. They have virtually no history. Any analysis of change is therefore foreclosed." Marina Lazreg (1990). Feminism and difference: The perils of writing as a woman in Algeria. In Marianne Hirsch & Evylen Fox Keller (Eds.). *Conflicts in Feminism* (326–348). NY: Routledge. 330.

86. Leila P. Sayeh & Adreien M. Morse, Jr. (1995). Islam and the treatment of women: An incomplete understanding of gradualism, *Texas International Law Journal* 30, 311–334.

87. Rushwan et al. (1983) *supra*.

88. Rentlin (1994) *supra*.

89. Gunning (1991–92) *supra*.

90. Fitnat Naa-Adjely (1995) *supra*.
91. Slack (1988) *supra*; Smith (1992) *supra*.
92. Kay Boulware-Miller (1985) *supra*.
93. Isabelle R. Gunning (1991–92) *supra*. (219).
94. See Slack (1988) *supra*; and Renteln (1994) *supra*.
95. See Blake M. Guy (1995). Female genital excision and the implications of federal prohibition, *William & Mary Journal of Women and the Law* 2, 125–169.
96. Brennan (1989) *supra*.
97. UN Doc E/CN.4/1986/42 at 21 (1986).
98. Sub-commission Res. 1988/34, UN Doc E/CN.4/Sub.2/1988/45, at 62 (1988).
99. Geraldine Van Bueren (1995). *The International Law on the Rights of the Child*. Boston: Martinus Nijhoff.
100. Declaration on the elimination of violence against women. UN GAOR, 48th Sess, Agenda Item 111 at 2, UN Doc A/RES/48/104 (1994).
101. See Boulware-Miller (1985) *supra*.
102. Slack (1988) *supra*.
103. Slack (1988) *supra* (450–455). See also, Olayinka Koso-Thomas (1987). *The Circumcision of Women: A Strategy for Eradication*. London: Zed Books.
104. Objective: Justice, A United Nations Review Dedicated to the Promotion of Justice Through the Self Determination of Peoples, the Elimination of Apartheid and Racial Discrimination, and the Advancement of Human Rights, United Nations, Secretariat, Vol. 23, No. 2 at 35, UN Doc [ST/]DPI/1182 (1991).
105. Id. Article 24(3).
106. Brennan (1990) *supra*; Sharon Detrick (Ed.) (1992). *The United Nations Convention on the Rights of the Child: A guide to the "Travaux Preparatoires."* Boston: Martinus Nijhoft.
107. Adam Lopatka (1996). An introduction to the United Nations Convention on the Rights of the Child, *Transnational Law & Contemporary Problems* 6, 251–262.
108. The Children's Convention (1990) *supra*. Article 25 states that "Everyone has the right to a standard of living adequate for the health and well-being of himself."
109. Audry R. Chapman (Ed.) (1994). *Health Care Reform: A Human Rights Approach*. Washington, DC: Georgetown University Press.
110. Brennan, Slack, Gunning, and Boulware-Miller all adopt this approach *supra*.
111. Renteln (1994) *supra*.
112. Shannon Brownlee et al. (1994). In the name of ritual, *U.S. News and World Report* Feb. 7, 56–58; Kriss Ann Balser Moussette (1996). Female genital mutilation and refugee status in the United States—A step in the right direction, *Boston College International and Comparative Law Review* 19(2), 353–395.
113. Van Beuren (1995) *supra*.
114. Boulware-Miller (1985) *supra* (164).
115. There is actually strong evidence for this claim. In the United States, for example, there is a recent case in which a doctor performed thousands of circumcisions on women after they had given birth. The operations enhanced the women's sexuality; the result was a flocking of more women to the doctor's practice. See Rosemary D. Welshe (1994). Casenote: Negligent credentialing: Ohio expands hospital

290 I Notes to Pages 118-120

liability in the wake of "Surgery of Love," *Browing v. Burt*, 613 N. E. 2d 993 (Ohio 1993), *University of Cincinnati Law Review* 63, 607–645.

116. See Atoki (1995) *supra*.

117. Id.

118. Id.

119. Janice Boddy (1991). Body politics: Continuing the anticircumcision crusade, *Medical Anthropology Quarterly* 5, 15–17, at 16. For example, between 200,000 and 1,000,000 American women had breast implants inserted into their bodies, until the manufacturing companies discontinued their sale and attempted to settle the potential legal claims of women who were injured. Mark Corriden (1996). Lawyers advise implant clients to reject offer, *American Bar Association Journal* Jan., at 18. Although some implants follow breast cancer surgery, 80 percent are undergone for purely cosmetic reasons. Marcia Angell (1992). Breast implants—Protection or paternalism, *New England Journal of Medicine* 326, 1695.

120. Laura Nader (1994). Comparative consciousness. In Robert Borosfsky (Ed.) *Assessing Cultural Anthropology* (84–94). N Y: McGraw-Hill.

121. Raven Rowanchilde (1996). Male genital modification: A sexual selection interpretation, *Human Nature* 7, 189–215.

122. James Myers (1992). Nonmainstream body modification, *Journal of Contemporary Ethnography* 21, 267–306.

123. Myers (1992) *supra*. Yet the practices differ: most traditional practices are performed on the very young, and arguably involve greater health risks. Lois S. Bibbings (1995). Female circumcision: Mutilation or modification? In Jo Bridgeman & Susan Millns (Eds.) *Law and Body Politics: Regulating the Female Body* (151–170). Brookfield, VT: Dartmouth.

124. Gordon (1991) *supra*. For example, in 1946, Sudanese law provided as follows: "Whoever voluntarily causes hurt to the external genital organs of a woman is said, save as hereafter excepted, to commit unlawful circumcision. Exception: It is not an offense under this section merely to remove the free and projecting part of the clitoris." Cited in Rushwan et al. (1983) *supra* (130).

125. Carolyn Bowra (1994). The debate on clitoridectomy: "Act of love" or Act of oppression, *Australian Yearbook of International Law* 15, 183–202.

126. Boulware-Miller (1985) *supra* and Slack (1988) *supra* both take this approach.

127. GA Res 46 UN GAOR, 39th Sess (Supp. No 51 at 197), UN Doc A/39/51; 23 ILM 1027, revised 24 ILM 535 (1984).

128. Geraldine Van Bueren (1994). Child sexual abuse and exploitation: A suggested human rights approach, *The International Journal of Children's Rights* 2, 45–59.

129. See *supra*.

130. African feminists disagree with Western feminists both about the characterization of the practices and about how to address them using human rights language. As Boulware-Miller discusses, when feminists advocate that such practices constitute mutilation and violate children's right to sexual and corporal integrity, in so describing an important part of African women's cultural identity, they offend all Africans. Awa Thiam reiterates: "People who understand nothing about ritual practices must beware attacking them, especially when they base their judgement on criteria which bear no relationship to the mentalities of people under consideration. The women of Black Africa have suffered enough from these colonial and neo-colonial

attitudes." A. Thiam 1986). Black sisters, speak out: Feminism and Oppression in Black Africa, 80. In Boulware-Miller (1985) *supra* (170); Karen Engle (1992). Female subjects of public international law: Human rights and the exotic other female, *New England Law Review* 26, 1509–1526.

131. See *infra*.

132. Gunning (1991) *supra* argues that the difficulties surgeries create for vaginal penetration serve as a physical armor against rape.

133. Rushwan et al. (1983) *supra*.

134. For example, see U.ii 'ersal Declaration of Human Rights, Article 3 ("Everyone has the right to life, liberty and the security of the person.") Id. Article 5. ("No one shall be subjected to torture or to cruel, inhuman or degrading treatment or punishment.") Banjul Charter, Article 4 ("Every human being shall be entitled to respect for his life and the integrity of the person.") and Article 5 ("All forms of torture and degradation . . . prohibited.")

135. James (1994) *supra*; see also Rushwan et al. (1983) *supra*.

136. Gunning (1991) *supra*.

137. Brownlee et al. (1994) *supra*, at 58.

138. The conundrum is rather great. One would have to be satisfied that the child had been adequately informed about the possible consequences and had not been subject to coercion. There are great social, family, and economic pressures to circumcision.

139. Levesque (1994). The sexual use, *supra*.

140. See Convention on Civil and Political Rights, Convention on Economic and Cultural Rights, and the new documents by ILO cited in Levesque (1994) *supra*.

141. See Bowra (1994) *supra*.

142. M. A. Ogbu (1997). Comment on Obiora's Bridges and Barricades, *Case Western Law Review* 47, 421–441.

143. There are many women's organizations in Africa actively opposing the practices, but they are doing so with language and strategies that differ from those of their Western counterparts. African women's movements are proceeding in a manner attuned to the sociopolitical cultures of their communities. Rather than arguing that these practices constitute mutilation and barbarism (which would not say much about the culture), some African opponents highlight the health risk involved for girls and women. They are actively engaged in struggles to define the meaning of their own cultural heritages and futures. Winter (1994) *supra*.

144. Some African countries, such as Cameroon, Dijbouti, Egypt, Ghana, and the Sudan have enacted legislation prohibiting the practice of FGM. Toubia (1993) *supra*.

145. See Winter (1994) *supra*, who notes that although countries pass laws against excision, there have not been any trials.

146. Female circumcision is documented to have occurred in the United States between 1890 and the late 1930s. Those practices were used for the treatment of psychological disorders, including nervousness and lesbianism. Slack (1988) *supra*; Gunning (1992) *supra*.

147. See Karen Hughes (1996). The criminalization of female genital mutilation in the United States, *Journal of Law and Policy* 4, 321–370.

148. Barrett A. Breitung (1996). Interpretation and Eradication: National and International responses to female circumcision, *Emory International Law Review* 10, 657–693.

149. Winter (1994) *supra*. The first trials followed a series of girls' deaths, which were related to their excision.

150. Defenses rely on two interlinked strategies. The first is the plea of ignorance, of not knowing that the practice is illegal. The second follows the notion that perpetrators are acting in accordance with a cultural tradition carrying the weight of higher law; individuals are thus not responsible, but are acting beyond their own free will. In the second approach, laws allow for the notion of intention and moral responsibility. It has become difficult to prove that there was intent to commit harm and that the perpetrator acted freely.

151. This has been an especially persuasive argument and has been used in campaigns against racism that stress the need to tolerate cultural diversity.

152. Winter (1994) *supra*.

153. Winter (1994) *supra*.

154. Breitung (1996) *supra*. Breitung excludes Sweden, even though it passed a law in 1982 that made all forms of female circumcision illegal; Bashir (1996) *supra*.

155. For an analysis of those statutes and the U.S. bill that eventually became law, see Breitung (1996) *supra*.

156. For example, Minnesota and North Dakota had passed laws making female circumcision a felony. See Minn. Stat Ann. Sec. 609.2245 (West 1996) and N. D. Cent. Code, Sec. 12.1–36–01 (1996).

157. Although there have yet to be challenges to this form of practice based on current child abuse laws, strong arguments could be made that the acts fall within the purview of such laws. Nancy I. Kellner (1993). Under the knife: Female genital mutilation as child abuse, *Journal of Juvenile Law* 14, 118–132.

158. Federal Prohibition of Female Genital Mutilation Act of 1995. Pub. L. No. 104–208, 100 Stat. 3009 (1996). For reviews of the Act's precursors, see Mary Ann James (1994). Federal prohibition of female genital mutilation: The Female Genital Mutilation Act of 1993, H. R. 3247, *Berkeley Women's Law Journal* 9, 206–208; Blake M. Guy (1995). Female genital excision and the implications of federal prohibition, *William & Mary Journal of Women and the Law* 2, 125–169. See also Robbie D. Steele (1995). Silencing the deadly ritual: Efforts to end female genital mutilation, *Georgetown Immigration Law Journal* 9, 105–135.

159. The law finds that " . . . whoever knowingly circumcises, excises or infibulates the whole or any part of the labia majora or clitoris of another person who has not attained the age of 18 years shall be fined under this title or imprisoned not more than 5 years, or both." 104th Congress H. R. 941 & S. 1030, Federal Prohibition of Female Genital Mutilation Act of 1995. The Act was enacted in September 1996 and went into effect March 1997. Pub. L. No. 104–208, 100 Stat. 3009 (1996); 18 U.S. C. Sections 116, 1, 3571(b)(3).

160. Hughes (1996) *supra*.

161. See the remarks of the bill's champion. Patricia Schroeder (1994). Female genital mutilation: A form of child abuse, *New England Journal of Medicine* 331, 739–40.

162. Judith S. Seddon (1993). Possible or impossible?: A tale of two worlds in one country, *Yale Journal of Law & Feminism* 5, 265–287. For the failure to prosecute, see Breitung (1996) *supra*.

163. Bashir (1996) *supra*.

164. David Fraser (1994). Heart of darkness: The criminalization of female genital mutilation, *Current Issues in Criminal Justice* 6, 148–160.

165. Ester K. Hicks (1996). *Infibulation: Female Mutilation in Islamic North-eastern Africa.* New Brunswick, NJ: Transaction Publishers.

166. Indeed, commentaries now call for rejection of express legislation that aims to eradicate the practice in favor of allocating existing resources to educational campaigns; see Mary-Jane Ierodiaconou (1995). "Listen to Us!" Female Genital Mutilation, Feminism and the Law in Australia, *Modern Law Review,* 20, 562–587.

167. 104th Congress, 2nd Session, House of Repreentatives Bill 3019(e)(1).

168. 104th Congress, 1st Session, House of Representaives Bill 2202.

169. For example, the Immigrant Responsibility Act of 1996 has been criticized on four fronts that arise from the failure to devote funding and specific provisions to enable states and localities to (1) pay proper attention to educating communities, (2) develop culturally sensitive outreach activities for victims, (3) involve community-based organizations and governmental agencies, and (4) address lack of attention to doctor-patient relationships. For an important analysis of these crticisms, see Khadijah F. Sharif (1997). Female Genital Mutilation: What Does the New Federal Law Really Mean? *Fordham Law Review* 24, 409–426.

170. The case of Lydia Oluloro (1994). In Timothy Egan (1994); An ancient ritual and a mother's asylum plea, *New York Times* March 4, A25; Patricia D. Rudloff (1995). *In Re Oluloro*: Risk of female genital mutilation as "extreme hardship" in immigration proceedings, *St. Mary's Law Journal* 26, 877–903. Canada dealt with the issue for quite some time. Canada already considers female genital circumcision a crime under its child abuse legislation in the Criminal Code. Hughes (1996) *supra.* It also has recently reformed its immigration guidelines for assessing whether women fearing gender related persecution qualify as refugees. Valerie Oosterveld (1993). Refugee status for female circumcision fugitives: Building a Canadian Precedent. *University of Toronto Faculty of Law Review* 51, 277–303. A result of the change was the recent grant of refugee status to a mother and her two children on the claim that her daughter would be subjected to female genital circumcision if she were forced to return to Somalia. Clyde H. Farnsworth (1994). Canada gives a Somali Mother Refugee Status, *New York Times* July 21, A14.

171. July, 28 1951, 189 U. N. T. S. 150.

172. Article 1 A(2).

173. Patricia A. Armstrong (1997). Female genital mutilation: The move toward the recognition of violence against women as a basis for asylum in the United States, *Maryland Journal of International Law and Trade* 21, 95–122.

174. United Nations High Commissioner, Report of the 39th Session, UN GAOR, 39th sess., UN Doc A/AC.96/673, para 115(4) at (k) (1985).

175. Report of the Forty-Fifth Session of the Executive Committee of the High Commissioner's Program, 44th Session, Agenda Item 21, UN Doc A/AC/96/821 (1993).

176. For a review of the cases, see Gregory A. Kelson (1995). Granting political asylum to potential victims of female circumcision, *Michigan Journal of Gender and Law* 3, 257–298.

177. L. Amede Obiorn (1997). Bridges and barricades: Rethinking polemics and intransigence in the campaign against female circumcision, *Case Western Law Review* 47, 275–378; Mary M. Sheridan (1997). *In Re Fauziya Kasinga*: The United States has opened its doors to victims of female genital mutilation, *St. John's Law Review* 71, 433–463.

178. Oosterveld (1993) *supra.*

179. Oosterveld (1993) *supra.*

180. J. Steven Svoboda (1997). Routine infant male circumcision: Examining the human rights and constitutional issues. In George C. Denniston & Marilyn Fayre Milos (Eds.) *Sexual Mutilations: A Human Tragedy* (205–214). NY: Plenum.

181. J. R. Taylor, A. P. Lockwood & A. J. Taylor (1996). The prepuce: Specialized mucosa of the penis and its loss to circumcision, *British Journal of Urology* 77, 291–95.

182. See Eugenie Anne Gifford (1994). "The courage to blaspheme": Confronting barriers to resisting female genital mutilation, *UCLA Women's Law Journal* 4, 329–364.

183. Frederick Hodges (1997). A short history of the institutionalization of involuntary sexual mutilation in the United States. In George C. Denniston & Marilyn Fayre Milos (Eds.) *Sexual Mutilations: A Human Tragedy* (17–40). NY: Plenum; Les Haberfield (1997). The law and male circumcision in Australia: Medical, legal and cultural issues, *Monash University Law Review* 23, 92–122.

184. Ester K. Hicks (1996). *Infibulation: Female Mutilation in Islamic Northeastern Africa.* New Brunswick, NJ: Transaction Publishers.

185. Alice Miller (1990). *Banished Knowledge* (135–140). London: Virago; Penelope Leach (1994). *Children First: What Our Society Must Do—and Is Not Doing—for Our Children Today.* London: Michael Joseph.

186. Hicks (1996) *supra.* In this regard, it may be argued that the practice actually deindividualizes and depersonalizes women, and formally subordinates young girls, as individuals, to the propagation of the family in the social system. It is a transfer to the "female adult collective" (85).

187. Children's Convention (1990), Article 2.

188. Children's Convention (1990), Article 7.

189. The extent to which international law may do so is exemplified by protections against child marriages.

190. Child brides are placed at risk not only for forced sex with their husbands but also for the high risks associated with early pregnancy. Sarah Y. Lai & Regan E. Ralph (1995). Female sexual autonomy and human rights, *Harvard Human Rights Journal* 8, 201–227.

191. See, e.g., Caroline H. Bledsoe & Barney Cohen (Eds.) (1993). *Social Dynamics of Adolescent Fertility in Sub-Saraban Africa.* Washington, DC: National Academy Press.

192. John Y. Luluaki (1997). Customary marriage laws in the commonwealth: A comparison between Papua New Guinea and Anglophonic Africa, *International Journal of Law, Policy, and the Family* 11, 1–35. Vitit Muntarbhorn (1994). *Sale of Children, Child Prostitution and Child Pornography,* E/CN.4/1994/84.

193. Jane C. Goodale (1971). *Tiwi Wives: A Study of the Women of Melville Island, North Australia.* Seattle: University of Washington Press.

194. See, e.g., Fay Gale (Ed.) (1970). Woman's role in Aboriginal society, *Australian Aboriginal Studies* 36, Social Anthropology Series 6. Canberra: Australian Institute of Aboriginal Studies; R. M. Berndt & C. H. Berndt (1951). *Sexual Behavior in Western Arnehm Land, Viking Publication in Anthropology* 16. NY: Viking Fund; Frederick G. G. Rose (1960). *Classification of Kin, Age Structure and Marriage amongst the Groote Eylandt Aborigines.* Berlin: Akadmie Verlag.

195. Rebecca Cook (1989). Reducing maternal mortality: A priority for human

rights law. In Sheila McLean (Ed.) *Legal Issues in Human Rights Reproduction* (185–212). Brookfield: Gower.

196. John L. Esposito (1982). *Women in Muslim Family Law.* Syracuse, NY: Syracuse University Press. 17.

197. Lai & Ralph (1995) *supra.*

198. It is important to consider, though, that divorces are prevalent. In a study of 500 women, more than half had been divorced twice and were thus able to flee the arranged marriage of childhood and take husbands of their own choosing. Sarah Levine & Robert Levine (1981). Child abuse and neglect in Sub-Saharan Africa. In Jill E. Korbin (Ed.) *Child Abuse and Neglect: Cross-cultural Perspectives* (35–55). Berkeley: University of California Press.

199. According to the World Health Organization, Nigerian girls aged fifteen have a maternal mortality rate seven times that of women aged twenty to twenty-four. Erica Royston & Sue Armstrong (Eds.) (1989). *Preventing Maternal Deaths.* Geneva: World Health Organization. 47.

200. Rebecca Cook (1989). Reducing maternal mortality: A priority for human rights law. In Sheila McLean (Ed.) *Legal Issues in Human Rights Reproduction* (185–212). Brookfield: Gower.

201. James Brook (1987). A Nigerian shame: The agony of the child bride, *New York Times* July 17, A4.

202. Lai & Ralph (1995) *supra.*

203. Sarah Levine & Robert Levine (1981). Child abuse and neglect in Sub-Saharan Africa. In Jill E. Korbin (Ed.) *Child Abuse and Neglect: Cross-cultural Perspectives* (35–55). Berkeley: University of California Press.

204. Lai & Ralph (1995) *supra.*

205. Morayo Atoki (1995). Should female circumcision continue to be banned? *Feminist Legal Studies* 3, 223–235.

206. John W. M. Whiting, Victoria K. Burbank, and Mitchell S. Ratner (1986). The duration of maidenhood across cultures. In Jane B. Lancaster & Beatrix A. Hamburg (Eds.) *School-aged Pregnancy and Parenthood: Biosocial Dimensions* (271–302). NY: Aldine de Gruyter.

207. Lai & Ralph (1995) *supra.*

208. Human Rights Watch (1995). In Lai & Ralph (1995) *supra.*

209. Thomas Poffenberger (1981). Child rearing and social structure in rural India: Toward a Cross-cultural definition of child abuse and neglect. In Jill E. Korbin (Ed.) (1981). *Child Abuse and Neglect: Cross-cultural Perspectives* (71–95). Berkeley: University of California Press.

210. Vitit Muntarbhorn (1994). *Sale of Children, Child Prostitution and Child Pornography,* E/CN.4/1994/84.

211. Vitit Muntarbhorn (1994). *Sale of Children, Child Prostitution and Child Pornography: Visit by the Special Rapporteur to Nepal,* E/CN.4/1994/84/Add.1. p. 13.

212. "Devadasi" means offering and dedicating girls to the goddess or the god. They are referred to by different names in different sates. See Jyotsna Bapat (1990). Devadasi rehabilitation programme: An empirical study, *Journal of Indian Anthropology* 25, 201–214.

213. Saskia C. Kersenboom-Story (1987). *Nityasumangali: Devadasi Tradition in South India.* Delhi, India: Motilal Banarsidass.

214. Kathleen Barry (1984). *Female Sexual Slavery* (22–35). NY: New York University Press.

215. Adjeley (1995) *supra*.

216. For a review of prosecutorial efforts, see Patricia Donovan (1997). Can statutory rape laws be effective in preventing adolescent pregnancy? *Family Planning Perspectives* 29, 30–34, 40; Sharon G. Elstein & Noy Davis (1997). *Sexual Relationships Between Adult Males and Young Teen Girls: Exploring the Legal and Social Responses*. Washington, DC: American Bar Association, Center on Children and the Law.

217. Mike Males and Kenneth S. Y. Chew (1996). The ages of fathers in California adolescent births, 1993, *Journal of Public Health* 86, 565–568; David J. Landry & Jacqueline D. Forrest (1995). How old are U.S. fathers? *Family Planning Perspectives* 27, 159–161.

218. Donovan (1997) *supra*.

219. Mireya Navarro (1996). Teen-aged mothers viewed as abused prey of older men, *New York Times* May 19, 1, 11. See also Margaret K. Rosenheim & Mark F. Testa (Eds.) (1992). *Early Parenthood and Coming of Age in the 1990s*. New Brunswick: Rutgers University Press; Frances Hudson & Bernard Ineichen (1991). *Taking it Lying Down: Sexuality and Teenage Motherhood*. London: Macmillan; Krisin Luker (1996). *Dubious Conceptions: The Politics of Teenage Pregnancy*. Cambridge: Harvard University Press; Sarah S. Brown & Leon Eisenberg (Eds.) (1995). *The Best Intentions: Unintended Pregnancy and the Well-being of Children and Families*. Washington, DC: Institute of Medicine.

220. Donovan (1997) *supra*.

221. In addition to being blamed for financial difficulties faced by welfare states, single mothers have been accused of being wedded to welfare and of contributing to increases in crime and delinquency through their lack of male partners. See, e.g., Peter Selman & Caroline Glendinning (1996). Teenage pregnancy: Do social polices make a difference? In Julia Branned & Margaret O'Brien (Eds.) *Children in families: Research and policy* (202–218). Washington, DC: Falmer Press. Annette Lawson & Deborah L. Rhode (Eds.) (1993). *The Politics of Pregnancy: Adolescent Sexuality and Public Policy*. New Haven: Yale University Press.

222. Report of the International Conference on Population and Development, UN Doc A/Conf.171/13 (1994) at paras 4.17, 4.21, 5.5, 6.7(c), and 6.11.

223. G. A. Res. 2018(XX), UN GAOR, 20th Sess, Supp. No. 14 at 36, UN Doc A/6014 (1965), princ. II. Note that the actual Convention only asks that each party set an "appropriate" minimum marriageable age. Convention on Consent to Marriage, Minimum Age for Marriage and Registration of Marriages, opened for signature Nov. 7, 1962, art. 2, 521 U. N. T. S. 231.

224. Id.

225. Convention on the Elimination of All Forms of Discrimination Against Women, opened for signature Mar. 1, 1980, 1249 U. N. T. S. 14. Art. 23(3).

226. Id. Art. 16.2.

227. International Covenant on Civil and Political Rights, opened for signature, Dec. 16, 1966, 999 U. N. T. S. 171 at art. 2(1).

228. Id. Art. 23(3).

229. Lai & Ralph (1995) *supra*.

230. 521 UNTS 231 (1962).

231. Judy Whitehead (1995). Modernizing the motherhood archetype: Public

health models and the Child Marriage Restraint Act of 1929, *Contributions to Indian Sociology* 29, 187–209.

232. The Children's Convention leaves open the question of whether sex with a minor in itself constitutes sexual abuse, even when no physical or mental violence is employed. Article 19 simply calls on governments to take "measures to protect the child from all forms of physical or mental violence, injury or abuse . . . maltreatment or exploitation, including sexual abuse."

233. Richard A. Posner & Katharine B. Silbaugh (1996). *A Guide to America's Sex Laws.* Chicago: University of Chicago Press.

234. Geraldine Van Bueren (1995). The international protection of family members' rights as the 21st century approaches, *Human Rights Quarterly* 17, 732–765.

235. Political Covenant, Art. 6.1. For a review of international documents, see Douglas Hodgson (1994). The child's right to life, survival and development, *The International Journal of Children's Rights* 2, 369–394.

236. The Covenant on Civil and Political Rights (1966), Article 6 (emphasis added).

237. Id., Article 12.1

238. Children's Convention (1990), Article 6(1)–(2) (emphases added.)

239. See B. G. Ramcharan (Ed.) (1985). *The Right to Life in International Law.* Boston: Martinus Nijhoff

240. Political Covenant (1966), Article 23.

241. Women's Convention (1980), 16(10(e)).

242. Rebecca J. Cook (1993). International human rights and women's reproductive health, *Studies in Family Planning* 24, 73–86.

243. For example, protections for physical security are found in the Universal Declaration of Human Rights, Art. 3, and the International Covenant on Civil and Political Rights, Art 9.1. Protections for human dignity are found in the Universal Declaration of Human Rights' preamble, the International Covenant on Civil and Political Rights, Art. 10.

244. The European Court of Human Rights, in *Dudgeon v. The United Kingdom*, App. No. 7525/76 3. Eur. H. R. Rep. 40 (1981) (commission report), noted that laws that punish consensual intercourse between males of an age, whether in public or private, constituted an unjustified interference with the right to privacy.

245. See, e.g., Peter Selman & Caroline Glendinning (1996). Teenage pregnancy: Do social polices make a difference? In Julia Branned & Margaret O'Brien (Eds.) *Children in Families: Research and Policy* (202–218). Washington, DC: Falmer Press.

246. Selamn & Glendinning (1996) *supra*; Hawkins & Meshesha (1994) *supra*.

247. Kirstan Hawkins & Bayeligne Meshesha (1994). Reaching young people: Ingredients to effective programs. In Gita Sen, Adrienne Germain & Lincoln C. Chen (Eds.) (1994). *Population Policies Reconsidered: Health, Empowerment, and Rights* (211–222). Boston: Harvard University Press; F. Scott Christopher (1995). Adolescent pregnancy prevention, *Family Relations* 44, 384–391.

248. Luluaki (1997) *supra*.

249. Bledsoe & Cohen (1993) *supra*.

250. Human Rights Watch. Women's Rights Project (1994). *A Matter of Power: State Control of Women's Virginity in Turkey.* N Y: Author.

251. Id.

252. Id.

253. Lai & Ralph (1995) *supra*.

254. Turkey: What Price Virginity? (1992). *Connexions: An International Women's Quarterly* 38, 12.

255. See Jack Goody (1976). *Production and Reproduction*. Cambridge: Cambridge University Press.

256. See Chapter 7.

257. Several women's rights conferences have, however, led to the development of a reproductive rights and health framework that aims to provide "conditions that would enable women to enjoy sexual relations safely and make autonomous, informed reproductive decisions." Sonnia Correa (1994). *Population and Reproductive Rights*. London: Zed Books (7–8).

258. The Convention against Torture and Other Cruel, Inhuman or Degrading Treatment or Punishment, opened for Signature Dec. 10, 1984, Annex G. A. Res. 46, 23 I. L. M. 1027 (1984), as modified, 24 I. L. M. 535 (1985).

259. Human Rights Watch (1994) *supra*.

260. See Alice Schlegel (1991). Status, property, and the value on virginity, *American Ethnologist* 18, 719–734.

261. E. G. UDHR: Art. 3 (Everyone has the right to life, liberty and the security of the person). Art. 5 (No one shall be subjected to torture or to cruel, inhuman or degrading treatment or punishment). Banjul Charter, Article 4 (Every human being shall be entitled to respect for his life and the integrity of the person). Art. 5 (All forms of torture and degradation . . . prohibited).

262. Levesque (1994) *supra*.

263. William H. Davenport (1965). Sexual patterns and their regulation in a society of the Southwest Pacific. In Frank A. Beach (Ed.) *Sex and Behavior* (164–297). N Y: Wiley.

264. Julia S. Brown (1959). A comparative study of deviations from sexual mores, *American Sociological Review* 17, 135–146; Randolph Trumback (1977). London's sodomites: Homosexual behavior and Western culture in the 18th century, *Journal of Social History* 11, 1–33.

265. J. R. Ungaretti (1978). Pederasty, heroism, and the family in classical Greece, *Journal of Homosexuality* 3, 291–300.

266. Vernon L. Quinsey (1986). Men who have sex with children. In David N. Weisstub (Ed.) *Law and Mental Health: International Perspectives* 2, 140–172. N Y: Permagon.

267. Nancy C. Lutkehaus & Paul B. Roscoe (Eds.) (1995). *Gender Rituals: Female Initiation in Melanesia*. New York: Routledge.

268. Gilbert H. Herdt (Ed.) (1984). *Ritualized Homosexuality in Melanesia*. Berkeley: University of California Press; Gilbert H. Herdt (1981). *Guardians of the Flutes: Idioms of Masculinity*. N Y: McGraw-Hill.

269. Id.

270. Herdt (1993) *supra*.

271. Gilbert H. Herdt (1982). *Rituals of Manhood: Male Initiation in Papua New Guinea*. Berkeley: University of California Press. 70–71.

272. Herdt (1981) *supra* (56).

273. For a vivid account, see Kenneth E. Read (1965). *The High Valley*. N Y: Charles Scribner's Sons. See also Kenneth E. Read (1984). The Nama Cult recalled. In Herdt (1984) *supra* (211–247).

274. Herdt (1981) *supra* (248).

275. Gilbert Herdt (1987). *The Sambia: Ritual and Gender in New Guinea*. New York: Holt, Rinehart and Winston.

276. Michael R. Allen (1984). Homosexuality, male power, and political organization in North Vanatu: A comparative analysis. In Herdt (1984) *supra* (83–126).

277. Laurent Serpenti (1984). The ritual meaning of homosexuality and pedophilia among the Kimam-Papuans of South Irian Jaya. In Herdt (1984) *supra* (292–317).

278. Id.

279. J. Van Baal (1984). The dialectics of sex in Marind-anim culture. In Herdt (1984) (128–166) *supra*.

280. Herdt is very careful to emphasize that Melanesian peoples who engage in ritualized homosexuality are not "homosexuals." See Gilbert H. Herdt (Ed.) (1993). *Ritualized Homosexuality in Melanesia*. Berkeley: University of California Press. See also Herdt's new introduction, in which he renames the practices as boy-inseminating rites (1993: ix) to avoid problems he now recognizes as endemic to his use of the term "homosexuality."

281. Arve Sorum (1984). Growth and decay: Bedamini notions of sexuality. In Herdt (1984) *supra* (318–336).

282. For a classic study, see Julia S. Brown (1959). A comparative study of deviations from sexual mores, *American Sociological Review* 17, 135–146.

283. For example, historically, children of high social status frequently escaped being subjected to erotic interactions with adults. In Ancient Rome, young boys of high status wore a gold ball around their necks so that adults would know not to approach them. Lloyd DeMause (1974). *The History of Childhood*. NY: Psychohistory Press. Likewise, the use of female children seems to have been restricted to girls of low social status. When outrage was expressed about the liaison, the relationship frequently involved men of low status and a child of high status. M. Ashley Ames and David A. Houston (1990). Legal, social, and biological definitions of pedophilia, *Archives of Sexual Behavior* 19, 333–342.

284. It would be difficult to argue that such practices as those examined above would be condoned in the West, as reflected in increasingly rapid attempts to criminalize the practices as they move with migrants and those seeking asylum.

285. Asmat boys are made to sit with decapitated human heads between their outspread legs. They do so because the heads' germinative powers are thought to transfer to the young boys' genitals and thus make the youth ready and able to reproduce. Gerald A. Zegwaard (1971). Headhunting practices of the Asmat of West New Guinea. In L. L. Langness & John Weschler (Eds.) *Melanesia: Reading on a Culture Area* (254–278). San Francisco: Chandler Publishing.

286. The Bena Bena reportedly allow these practices. L. L. Langness (1972). Violence in the New Guinea Highlands. In James F. Short, Jr. & Marvin E. Wolfgang (Eds.) *Collective Violence* (171–185). Chicago: Aldine.

287. Among the Polynesian Pukapukans, boys and girls freely engage in masturbation in public, without adult censure. Clellan S. Ford & Frank A. Beach (1951). *Patterns of Sexual Behavior*. NY: Harper & Row.

288. The Lepcha of India do not believe that girls will mature without sexual intercourse; sex play among boys and girls begins early, even to the extent that by the time they are eleven or twelve, most girls have engaged in sexual intercourse. The Chewa, Maori, and the Ila-speaking people of Africa believe that their children will

never have progeny unless they engage in early sexual activities: boys and girls, with their parents' approval, play at being husband and wife. Ford & Beach (1951) *supra.* Children among the Aymara in Bolivia and Peru have prepubertal sexual experiences that adults view with "amused tolerance." See Suzanne G. Frayser (1994). Defining normal childhood sexuality: An anthropological approach, *Annual Review of Sex Research 5,* 173–217.

289. Frayser (1994) *supra.*

290. Jill Korbin (1995). Social networks and family violence in cross-cultural perspective. In Gary B. Melton (Ed.) *The Individual, the Family, and Social Good: Personal Fulfillment in Times of Change* (107–134). Lincoln: University of Nebraska Press.

6. Abuse by Adult Offenders

1. C. Henry Kempe (1980). Incest and other forms of sexual abuse. In C. Henry Kempe & Ray E. Helfer (Eds.) *The Battered Child* (198–214). Chicago: University of Chicago Press. 198.

2. For a sampling of these definitions, see Sandra K. Wurtele & Cindy L. Miller-Perrin (1992). *Preventing Child Sexual Abuse: Sharing the Responsibility.* Lincoln: University of Nebraska Press.

3. Roger J. R. Levesque (1995). Prosecuting sex crimes against children: Time for "outrageous" proposals? *Law & Psychology Review 19,* 59–91.

4. David Finkelhor (1994). The international epidemiology of child sexual abuse, *Child Abuse & Neglect 18,* 409–417. The article cites research conducted in Australia, Austria, Belgium, Canada, Costa Rica, Denmark, Dominican Republic, Finland, France, Germany, Greece, Great Britain, Ireland, Netherlands, New Zealand, Norway, South Africa, Spain, Sweden, Switzerland, and the United States.

5. Id. There certainly are more countries that have served as sites for investigation. Regrettably, the studies are very weak and suffer from several limitations, including: anecdotal evidence, biased samples, small sample sizes, retrospective focus, and failure to consider gender analyses. Yet, if stringent criteria were used for inclusion within this review, the chapter would be very short. In a field that is only beginning to develop, it was decided that weak studies would be included, just as they were for previous chapters on the sexual use and exploitation of children.

6. Id. Austria and South Africa, respectively.

7. For example, Hong Kong reported only 134 cases of sexual abuse from 1986 to 1989. T. P. Ho & F. Lieh-Mak (1992). Sexual abuse in Chinese children in Hong Kong: A review of 134 cases, *Australian and New Zealand Journal of Psychiatry 26,* 639–643. Without even mandating reporting, the following shorter period from 1991 to 1993 revealed 2,243 reported cases. Indecent assault and unlawful sexual intercourse each ranked over 1,000 each, while over 130 rapes were reported. Thirty cases of indecent conduct toward a child, and nineteen cases of incest were reported. Ting-Pong Ho (1996). Children's Evidence: Mandating Change in the Legal System of Hong Kong. In Bette L. Bottoms & Gail S. Goodman (Eds.) *International Perspectives on Child Abuse and Children's Testimony* (182–200). Thousand Oaks, CA: Sage. Although the numbers are small relative to the 1.2 million people under the age of fifteen, the figures do highlight well the extent to which official reports do not necessarily reflect the realities of children's abusive experiences. Wurtele and Miller-Perrin outlined several reasons for underreporting in official estimates, such as failure to re-

port because the reporter feels there is insufficient evidence, reluctance by professionals to report when statutory provisions are vague, nondisclosure by victims because of ignorance, embarrassment, or threats of harm, and underreporting by social service providers due to lack of resources in managing cases. Sandra K. Wurtele & Cindy L. Miller-Perrin (1992). *Preventing Child Sexual Abuse: Sharing the Responsibility.* Lincoln: University of Nebraska Press.

   8. For example, some have noted that prevalence studies tend to use self-selected university students who do not represent the population as a whole; i.e., social misfits and unsatisfactory performers are not reached. See Freda Briggs & Russell M. F. Hawkins (1995). Protecting boys from the risk of sexual abuse, *Early Child Development and Care* 110, 19–32.

   9. David Finkelhor (1994). The international epidemiology of child sexual abuse, *Child Abuse & Neglect* 18, 409–417.

   10. See Kevin M. Gorey & Donald R. Leslie (1997). The prevalence of child sexual abuse: Integrative review adjustment for potential response and measurement biases, *Child Abuse & Neglect* 21, 391–398; Timothy F. Wynkoop, Steven C. Capps & Bobby J. Priest (1995). Incidence and prevalence of child sexual abuse: A critical review of data collection, *Journal of Child Sexual Abuse* 4, 49–66.

   11. Lloyd DeMause (1991). The universality of incest, *Journal of Psychohistory* 19, 123–164.

   12. David Finkelhor, Gerald Hotaling, I. A. Lewis & Christine Smith (1990). Sexual abuse in a national survey of adult men and women: Prevalence, characteristics, and risk factors, *Child Abuse & Neglect* 14, 19–28.

   13. Finkelhor, et al. (1990) *supra.*

   14. Carol R. Hartman & Ann W. Burgess (1989). Sexual abuse of children: Causes and consequences. In Dante Cicchetti & Vicki Carlson (Eds.) *Child Maltreatment: Theory and Research on the Causes and Consequences of Child Abuse and Neglect* (95–128). NY: Cambridge University Press; Karen McCurdy & Deborah A. Daro (1994). Child maltreatment: A national survey of reports and fatalities, *Journal of Interpersonal Violence* 9, 75–94.

   15. Roger J. R. Levesque (1994). Sex differences in the experience of child sexual victimization, *Journal of Family Violence* 9, 357–369.

   16. Vernon L. Quinsey (1986). Men who have sex with children, *Law and Mental Health* 2, 140–172.

   17. An important study reported that nearly 75 percent of sexual abuse victims initially deny abuse, and that nearly 25 percent recant allegations; T. Sorenson & B. Snow (1991). How children tell: The process of disclosure in child sexual abuse, *Child Welfare* 70, 3–15; for much lower estimates of cases that were eventually confirmed, see April R. Bradley & James M. Wood (1996). How do children tell? The disclosure process of child sexual abuse, *Child Abuse & Neglect* 20, 881–891.

   18. David Finkelhor (1994). The international epidemiology of child sexual abuse, *Child Abuse & Neglect* 18, 409–417. Kay Keary & Carol Fitzpatrick (1994). Children's disclosure of sexual abuse during formal investigation. *Child Abuse & Neglect* 18, 543–548.

   19. Catalina M. Arata (1998). To tell or not to tell: Current functioning of child sexual abuse survivors who disclosed their victimization, *Child Maltreatment* 3, 63–71.

   20. Levesque (1994) *supra.*

   21. Finkelhor (1994) *supra.* Some report closer estimates of 3F:2M; see Anthony

W. Baker & Sylvia P. Duncan (1985). Child sexual abuse: A study of prevalence in Great Britain, *Child Abuse & Neglect* 9, 457–476.

22. See Quinsey (1986) *supra*. Kathleen A. Kendall-Tackett, Linda Meyer Williams & David Finkelhor (1993). Impact of sexual abuse on children: A review and synthesis of recent empirical studies, *Psychological Bulletin* 113, 164–180.

23. Gurmeet K. Dhaliwal, Larry Gauzas, David H. Anonowicz & Robert R. Ross (1996). Adult male survivors of child sexual abuse: Prevalence, sexual abuse characteristics and long-term effects, *Clinical Psychology Review* 16, 619–639.

24. Several studies now report that the sexual abuse of boys is underrecognized and underreported, and that boys are not adequately protected by parents and current child protection curricula. The lack of response by those around boys has reverberating effects: lack of supervision in the community places boys at risk for extra-familial abuse; boys are blamed for their abuse because they are expected to protect themselves; women are not viewed as potential victimizers; and there is a denial of father-son as well as child-child abuse. Yet, it is undeniable that claims that male victimization is ignored have been met with an impressive amount of commentary to the contrary. See, e.g., Freda Briggs & Russell M. F. Hawkins (1995). Protecting boys from the risk of sexual abuse, *Early Child Development and Care* 110, 19–32; Bill Watkins & Arnon Bentovim (1992). The sexual abuse of male children and adolescents: A review of current research, *Journal of Child Psychology and Psychiatry* 33(1), 197–248; Carol S. Larson, Donna L. Terman, Deanna S. Gomby, Linda Sandham Quinn & Richard E. Behrman (1994). Sexual abuse of children: Recommendation and analysis, *Future of Children* 4, 4–30; Adrienne Crowder & Rob Hawkins (1995). *Opening the Door: A Treatment Model for Therapy with Male Survivors of Sexual Abuse.* NY: Brunner/Masel; John C. Gonsiorek, Walter H. Bera & Donald LeTourneau (1994). *Male Sexual Abuse: A Trilogy of Intervention Strategies.* Thousand Oaks, CA: Sage; William N. Friedrich (1995). *Psychotherapy with Sexually Abused Boys: An Integrated Approach.* Thousand Oaks, CA: Sage; Gillian C. Mezey & Michael B. King (Eds.) (1992). *Male Victims of Sexual Assault.* NY: Oxford University Press; Mathew Parynik Mendel (1995). *The Male Survivor: The Impact of Sexual Abuse.* Thousand Oaks, CA: Sage; Guy R. Holmes, Liz Offen & Glenn Waller (1997). See no evil, hear no evil, speak no evil: Why do relatively few male victims of childhood sexual abuse receive help for abuse-related issues in adulthood? *Clinical Psychology Review* 17, 69–88.

25. Finkelhor (1994) *supra*. For example, in the Epidemiological Catchment Area studies of Los Angeles, 93 percent of the perpetrators of child sexual abuse were male. J. M. Siegel, S. B. Sorenson, J. M. Golding, M. A. Burnam, J. A. Stein (1987). The prevalence of childhood sexual assault, *American Journal of Epidemiology* 126, 1141–1153.

26. Michele Elliott (Ed.) (1994). *Female Sexual Abuse of Children.* NY: Guilford; Liz Kelly (1990). Unspeakable Acts, *Trouble and Strife* 21 (Summer), 13–21. Kathleen Coulborn Faller (1987). Women who sexually abuse children, *Violence and Victims* 2, 263–276; Christine Lawson (1993). Mother-Son sexual abuse: Rare or underreported? A critique of research, *Child Abuse and Neglect* 17, 261–69.

27. Id.

28. One study found that 62 percent of offenders indicated being sexually abused by females; Elisa Romano & Rayleen V. De Luca (1997). Exploring the relationship between childhood sexual abuse and adult sexual perpetration, *Journal of Family Violence* 12, 85–98. Another study reported that nearly one-third of men on

a long-term sex offender program had experienced legally chargeable abuse by a woman. S. Carlson (1991). The victim/perpetrator. In Mic Hunger (Ed.) *The Sexually Abused Male: Prevalence, Impact, and Treatment* (Vol 2.) (249–266). Lexington, MA: Lexington Books.

29. Margaret M. Rudin, Christine Zalewski, & Jeffrey Bodmer-Turner (1995). Characteristics of child sexual abuse victims according to perpetrator gender, *Child Abuse & Neglect* 19, 963–973.

30. Quinsey (1986) *supra*. Quinsey reports results of a Gallop poll. See also the results of one of the most thorough studies of offender reports: W. D. Erickson, N. H. Walbek & R. K. Seely (1988). Behavior patterns of child molesters, *Archives of Sexual Behavior* 17, 77–86.

31. See also the Kinsey studies, which report that sexual behaviors seldom involved coitus (3 percent).

32. Vincent De Francis (1969). *Protecting the Child Victim of Sex Crimes Committed by Adults*. Denver, CO: American Humane Association, Children's Division.

33. Roland C. Summit (1983). The child sexual accommodation syndrome. *Child Abuse & Neglect* 7, 177–193.

34. Levesque (1995) *supra*.

35. Dennis Howitt (1995). *Paedophiles and Sexual Offenses against Children*. NY: Wiley. 38.

36. Gordon C. Nagayama Hall (1990). Prediction of sexual aggression, *Clinical Psychology Review* 10, 229–245.

37. This is the most frequent predictor in other areas as well; for the most comprehensive review of prediction research, see John Monahan & Henry J. Steadman (1994). *Violence and Mental Disorder: Developments in Risk Assessment*. Chicago: University of Chicago Press.

38. R. A. Lang & R. Langevin (1991). Parent-child relations in offenders who commit violent sexual crimes against children, *Behavioral Sciences and the Law* 9, 61–71. For similar attempts and findings, see James C. Overholser & Steven J. Beck (1989). The classification of rapists and child molesters, *Journal of Offender Counseling, Services & Rehabilitation* 13, 15–25; Kurt Freund & Michael Kuban (1994). The basis of the abused abuser theory of pedophilia: A further elaboration on an earlier study, *Archives of Sexual Behavior* 23, 553–563; Jackie Craissati & Grace McClurg (1996). The Challenge Project: Predictors of child sexual abuse in South East London, *Child Abuse & Neglect* 20, 1069–1077.

39. Psychometric data do not distinguish perpetrators well, nor predict recidivism. Jean Proulx, Bruno Pellevin, Yves Paradis, Andre McKibben, Jocelyn Aubut & Marc Ouimet (1997). Static and dynamic predictors of recidivism in sexual aggressors, *Sexual Abuse: A Journal of Research and Treatment* 9, 7–27. Linda M. Williams & David Finkelhor (1990). The characteristics of incestuous fathers: A review of recent studies. In W. L. Marshall, D. R. Laws & H. E. Barbaree (Eds.) *Handbook of Sexual Assault: Issues, Theories, and Treatment of the Offender* (231–255). NY: Plenum.

40. Earlier approaches distinguished between two categories—*fixated* and *regressed* offenders, which were distinguishable by the former being less likely to be married, being more likely to victimize strangers and acquaintances, and not exhibiting mature forms of sexual expression. A. Nicholas Groth & H. Jean Birnbaum (1978). Adult sexual orientation and attraction to underage persons, *Archives of Sexual Behavior* 7, 175–181. This research mirrors more recent efforts to focus on

distinguishing between abuse occurring either outside of or within families. Anne E. Pawlak, John R. Boulet & John M. W. Bradford (1991). Discriminant analysis of a sexual-functioning inventory with intrafamilial and extrafamilial child molesters, *Archives of Sexual Behavior* 20, 27–34. Despite the different focus and early belief that the abuses involved very different dynamics, research now finds increasing similarities: both commit similar sexual acts, use similar methods to obtain sexual gratification, and have similar reasons for offending. For an early critique of the differences, see Jon R. Conte (1985). Clinical dimensions of adult sexual abuse of children, *Behavioral Sciences and the Law* 3, 241–244.

41. Rudolph Alexander (1995). Employing the mental health system to control sex offenders after penal incarceration, *Law & Policy* 17, 111–130; Stuart A. Scheingold, Toska Olson & Jana Pershing (1994). Sexual violence, victim advocacy, and republican criminology: Washington State's Community Protection Act, *Law & Society Review* 28, 729–763.

42. W. L. Marshall (1996). The sexual offender: Monster, victim, or everyman? *Sexual Abuse: A Journal of Research and Therapy* 8, 317–335.

43. Despite current difficulties, research focusing on what distinguishes sex offenders from other perpetrators has the potential to offer valuable insight. For example, the finding that a previous history of victimization or aggressive behavior highlights the need for early intervention and provides areas that could be addressed in therapeutic settings. To obtain more robust and useful results, however, the sample base of these research efforts would need to expand: little or nothing is known about pedophiles who are not convicted or who never enter the criminal justice system. Researchers indicate that men who do enter the system constitute only a small percentage of those who sexually abuse children. Betty N. Gordon & Carolyn S. Schroeder (1995). *Sexuality: A Developmental Approach to Problems.* NY: Plenum.

44. For a review of current theories and their criticisms, see Gordon C. Nagayama Hall (1996). *Theory-based Assessment, Treatment, and Prevention of Sexual Aggression.* NY: Oxford University Press.

45. This work draws upon Finkelhor's seminal work. See David Finkelhor (1984). *Child Sexual Abuse: New Theory and Research.* NY: Free Press. David Finkelhor (1987). The sexual abuse of children: Current research reviewed, *Psychiatric Annals* 17, 233–41. For important efforts that also focus on inhibitors and motivators, see Gordon C. Nagayama Hall & Richard Hirschman (1992). Sexual aggression against children: A conceptual perspective of etiology, *Criminal Justice and Behavior* 19, 8–23; Dawn Fisher (1994). Adult sex offenders: Who are they? Why and how do they do it? In Tony Morrison, Marcus Erooga & Richard C. Beckett (Eds.) *Sexual Offending against Children: Assessment and Treatment of Male Abusers* (1–24). NY: Routledge.

46. Lucy Johnston & Tony Ward (1996). Social cognition and sexual offending: A theoretical framework, *Sexual Abuse: A Journal of Research and Treatment* 8, 55–88; Larry Neidgh & Harry Krop (1992). Cognitive distortion among child sexual offenders, *Journal of Sex Education and Therapy* 18, 208–215; Eileen Vizard, Elizabeth Monck & Peter Misch (1995). Child and adolescent sex abuse perpetrators: A review of the research literature, *Journal of Child Psychology and Psychiatry* 5, 731–756; Evelyn H. Yanagida & June W. Ching (1993). MMPI profiles of child abusers, *Journal of Clinical Psychology* 49, 569–576; Tony Ward, Stephen M. Hudson, Lucy Johnson & William L. Marshall (1997). Cognitive distortions in sex offenders: An integrative review, *Clinical Psychology Review* 17, 479–507.

47. Most experts agree that the therapeutic value of cognitive-behavioral approaches has been clearly demonstrated. W. L. Marshall & W. D. Pithers (1994). A reconsideration of treatment outcome with sex offenders, *Criminal Justice and Behavior* 21, 10–27. See also Mark Chaffin (1994). Research in action: Assessment and treatment of child sexual abusers, *Journal of Interpersonal Violence* 9, 224–237; Gordon C. Nagayama Hall (1995). Sexual offender recidivism revisited: A meta-analysis of recent treatment studies, *Journal of Consulting and Clinical Psychology* 63, 802–809; Lucy Johnson, Tony Ward & Stephen M. Hudson (1997). Deviant sexual thoughts: Mental control and the treatment of sexual offenders, *Journal of Sex Research* 34, 121–130.

48. R. K. Hanson, R. Gizzarelli & H. Scott (1994). The attitudes of incest offenders: Sexual entitlement and acceptance of sex with children, *Criminal Justice and Behavior* 21, 187–202; Lana E. Stermac & Zindel V. Segal (1989). Adult sexual contact with children: An examination of cognitive factors, *Behavior Therapy* 20, 573–584; Nathan L. Pollock & Judith M. Hashmall (1991). The excuses of child molesters, *Behavioral Sciences and the Law* 9, 53–59; Patricia Phelan (1995). Incest and its meaning: Perspectives of fathers and daughters, *Child Abuse & Neglect* 19, 7–24.

49. Research from therapeutic work reveals how the process works; see J. F. Gilgun & T. M. Connor (1989). How perpetrators view child sexual abuse, *Social Work* 29, 232–236.

50. Michael Gordon (1989). The family environment of sexual abuse: A comparison of natal and stepfather abuse, *Child Abuse & Neglect* 13, 121–130.

51. For example, female children in divorced families are at higher risk; see Rizwan Z. Shah, Paula W. Dail & Time Heinrichs (1995). Familial influences upon the occurrence of child sexual abuse, *Journal of Child Sexual Abuse* 4, 45–61. For a review of the role and perceptions of mothers, see Djenane Nakhle Tamaraz (1996). Nonoffending mothers of sexually abused children: Comparisons of opinions and research, *Journal of Child Sexual Abuse* 5, 75–104.

52. For example, mothers are often physically and emotionally abused by the perpetrator themselves. See Beverly Gomes-Schwarz, Jonathan M. Horowtiz & Albert P. Cardarelli (1990). *Child Sexual Abuse: The Initial Effects*. Newbury Park, CA: Sage. See also Kathlieen Coulborn Faller (1989). Why sexual abuse? An exploration of the intergenerational hypothesis, *Child Abuse & Neglect* 13, 543–548.

53. Howitt (1995) *supra.*

54. K. Marcellina Mian, Peter Marton, Deborah LeBaron & David Birtwistle (1994). Familial risk factors associated with intrafamilial and extrafamilial sexual abuse of three to five year old girls, *Canadian Journal of Psychiatry* 39, 348–353; Kelle Chandler Ray, Joan L. Jackson & Ruth M. Twonsley (1991). Family environments of victims of intrafamilial and extrafamilial child sexual abuse, *Journal of Family Violence* 6, 365–374. Kimberly Hoagwood (1989). Sexually abused children's perceptions of family functioning, *Child and Adolescent Social Work* 6, 139–149; Rochelle F. Hanson, Julie H. Lipovsky & Benjamin E. Saunders (1994). Characteristics of fathers in incest families, *Journal of Interpersonal Violence* 9, 155–169.

55. Rizwan Z. Shah, Paula W. Dail & Time Heinrichs (1995). Familial influences upon the occurrence of child sexual abuse, *Journal of Child Sexual Abuse* 4, 45–61.

56. Lee Eric Budin & Charles Felzen (1989). Sex abuse prevention programs: Offenders' attitudes about their efficacy, *Child Abuse & Neglect* 13, 77–87. Jon R. Conte, Steven Wolf & Tim Smith (1989). What sexual offenders tell us about preven-

tion strategies, *Child Abuse & Neglect* 13, 293–335; Michele Elliott, Kevin Browne & Jennifer Kilcoyne (1995). Child sexual abuse prevention: What sex offenders tell us, *Child Abuse & Neglect* 19, 579–594.

57. Budin and Johnson (1989) *supra*; Conte, Wolfe & Smith (1989) *supra*.

58. Lucy Berliner & Jon R. Conte (1990). The process of victimization: The victim's perspective, *Child Abuse & Neglect* 14, 29–40.

59. E. Alison Holamn & Daniel Stokols (1994). The environmental psychology of child sexual abuse, *Journal of Environmental Psychology* 14, 237–252.

60. Joan M. McDermott (1994). Criminology as peacemaking, feminist ethics and the victimization of women, *Women & Criminal Justice* 5, 21–44; Levesque (1995) *supra*.

61. Gary B. Melton (1992). The improbability of prevention of sexual abuse. In D. J. Willis, W. E. Holden & M. S. Rosenberg (Eds.) *Prevention of Child Maltreatment* (168–189). NY: Wiley.

62. For a review of programs, see Deborah J. Tharinger, Jame J. Krivacksa, Marsha Laye-McDonough, Linda Jamison, Gayle Vincent & Andrew D. Hedlund (1988). Prevention of child sexual abuse: An analysis of issues, educational programs, and research findings, *School Psychology Review* 17, 614–634; Jan Rispens, Andre Aleman & Paul P. Goudena (1997). Prevention of child sexual abuse victimization: A meta-analysis of school programs, *Child Abuse & Neglect* 21, 975–987.

63. Id. See also Sandy K. Wurtele & Julie Sarno Owens (1997). Teaching personal safety skills to young children: An investigation of age and gender across five studies, *Child Abuse & Neglect* 21, 805–814.

64. Freda Briggs (1987). South Australian parents want child protection programs to be offered in schools and preschools, *Australian Journal of Early Childhood* 12, 20–25.

65. For a comprehensive review, see Wurtele & Miller-Perrin (1992) *supra*.

66. Roberta A. Hibbard & Terrell W. Zollinger (1990). Patterns of child sexual abuse knowledge among professionals, *Child Abuse & Neglect* 14, 347–355; Deborah A. Daro (1994). Prevention of child sexual abuse, *Future of Children* 4, 198–223.

67. Jeffrey J. Haugaard & N. Dickon Reppucci (1988). *The Sexual Abuse of Children: A Comprehensive Guide to Current Knowledge and Intervention Strategies.* San Francisco: Jossey-Bass Publishers; N. Dickon Reppucci & Jeffrey J. Haugaard (1989). Prevention of child sexual abuse: Myth or reality? *American Psychologist* 44, 266–75.

68. Melton (1992) *supra*.

69. David Finkelhor & N. Strapko (1992). Sexual abuse prevention education: A review of evaluation studies, In D. J. Willis, E. W. Holden & M. Rosenberg (Eds.) *Child Abuse Prevention* (150–167). NY: Wiley. Margot Taal & Monique Edelaar (1997). Positive and negative effects of a child sexual abuse prevention program, *Child Abuse & Neglect* 21, 339–410.

70. Leslie M. Tutty (1994). Developmental issues in young children's learning of sexual abuse prevention concepts, *Child Abuse and Neglect* 18, 179–192.

71. Melton (1992) *supra*; Jill Duer Berrick & Neil Gilbert (1991). *With the Best of Intentions: The Child Sexual Abuse Prevention Movement.* NY: Guilford.

72. Lucy Sullivan (1990). Preventing Child Sexual Abuse: Whose Responsibility? *Australian Journal of Early Childhood* 15, 30–33.

73. Sandy K. Wurtele & Julie Sarno Owens (1997). Teaching personal safety

skills to young children: An investigation of age and gender across studies, *Child Abuse & Neglect* 21, 805–814. Leslie M. Tutty (1997). Child sexual abuse prevention programs: Evaluating *Who do you tell, Child Abuse & Neglect* 21, 869–881.

74. John E. B. Myers (1994). Adjudication of child sexual abuse cases, *Future of Children* 4, 84–101; Susan Janko (1994). *Vulnerable Children, Vulnerable Families: The Social Construction of Child Abuse.* N Y: Teachers College Press. These same criticisms have been echoed by international efforts, both in terms of formal international law and individual countries' responses. The Special Rapporteur for child sexual exploitation recently stepped down from his position: he found a lack of focus on preventive efforts and lack of commitment to abolishing sexual maltreatment. Margaret A. Healy (1995). Prosecuting child sex tourists at home: Do laws in Sweden, Australia, and the United States safeguard the rights of children as mandated by international law? *Fordham International Law Journal* 18, 1852–1923; Vitit Muntarbhorn (1994). *Sale of Children, Child Prostitution and Child Pornography,* E/CN.4/1994/84.

75. Levesque (1995) *supra.*

76. David A. Wolfe (1994). The role of intervention and treatment services in the prevention of child abuse and neglect. In Gary B. Melton & Frank D. Barry (Eds.) *Protecting Children from Abuse and Neglect: Foundations for a New National Strategy* (224–303). N Y: Guilford (280).

77. Judith V. Becker & John A. Hunter, Jr. (1992). Evaluation of treatment outcome for adult perpetrators of child sexual abuse, *Criminal Justice and Behavior* 19, 74–92; W. L. Marshall, Robin Jones, Tony Ward, Peter Johnson & H. E. Barbaree (1991). Treatment outcome with sex offenders, *Clinical Psychology Review* 11, 465–485. W. L. Marshall & W. D. Pithers (1994). A reconsideration of treatment outcome with sex offenders, *Criminal Justice and Behavior* 21, 10–27.

78. Several states, most recently Massachusetts, Virginia, and Florida, have moved toward eliminating therapeutic programs. See Levesque (1994) *supra.*

79. Charles M. Borduin, Scott W. Henggeler, David M. Blaske & Risa J. Stein (1990). Multisystemic treatment of adolescent sexual offenders, *International Journal of Offender Therapy and Comparative Criminology* 34, 105–113.

80. For a comprehensive review of efforts by a leading commentator, see Deborah Daro (1988). *Confronting Child Abuse: Research for Effective Program Design.* N Y: Free Press; Deborah Daro (1991). Prevention Programs. In Clive R. Hollin & Kevin Howells (Eds.) *Clinical Approaches to Sex Offenders and Their Victims* (285–305). N Y: Wiley. For example, Daro proposes that the following interventions are important in preventing child sexual abuse: increasing the parent's knowledge of child development and the demands of parenting; enhancing the parent's skill in coping with the stresses of infancy and child care; enhancing parent-child bonding, emotional ties, and communication; increasing parent's skills in coping with the stress of caring for children with special needs; increasing the parent's knowledge about home and child management; reducing the burden of child care; increasing access to social and health services for all family members.

81. Several pre-school and primary school programs report positive results in efforts to reduce delinquent behavior and deal with sexuality. See Joan McCord & Richard E. Tremblay (Eds.) (1992). *Preventing Antisocial Behavior: Intervention form Birth through Adolescence.* N Y: Guilford.

82. For the most recent meta-analysis, see Kendall-Tackett et al. (1993) *supra.*

83. Candice Fiering, Lynn Taska & Michael Lewis (1996). A process model for

understanding adaptation to sexual abuse: The role of shame in defining stigmatization, *Child Abuse & Neglect* 20, 767–782.

84. Feiring et al. (1996) *supra.*

85. Alice Mayall & Steven R. Gold (1995). Definitional issues and mediating variables in the sexual revictimization of women sexually abused as children, *Journal of Interpersonal Violence* 10, 26–42; Terri L. Messman & Patricia J. Long (1996). Child sexual abuse and its relationship to revictimization in adult women: A review, *Clinical Psychology Review* 16, 397–420; David M. Fergusson, L. John Horwood & Michael T. Lynskey (1997). Childhood sexual abuse, adolescent sexual behaviors and sexual revictimization, *Child Abuse & Neglect* 21, 789–803. See also Kendall-Tackett, et al. (1993) *supra.*

86. Gene G. Abel, Judith V. Becker & Jerry Cunningham-Rathner (1984). Complications, consent, and cognition in sex between children and adults, *International Journal of Law and Psychiatry* 7, 89–103; Haugaard & Reppucci (1988) *supra*, Chapter 4. For important reviews, see Joseph H. Beitchman, Kenneth J. Zucker, Jane E. Hood, G. A. DaCosta & Donna Akman (1991). A review of the short-term effects of child sexual abuse, *Child Abuse and Neglect* 15, 537–556. J. H. Beitchman, K. J. Zucker, J. E. Hood, G. A. DaCosta, D. Akman & E. Cassavia (1992). A review of the long-term effects of child sexual abuse, *Child Abuse and Neglect* 16, 101–118; B. Watkins & A. Bentovim (1992). Male children and adolescents as victims: A review of current knowledge. In G. C. Mezey & M. B. King (Eds.) *Male victims of sexual assault* (27–66). NY: Oxford University Press; Steven J. Collings (1995). The long-term effects of contact and noncontact forms of child sexual abuse in a sample of university men, *Child Abuse & Neglect* 19, 1–6; Shan A. Jumper (1995). A meta-analysis of the relationship of child sexual abuse on adult psychological adaptation, *Child Abuse & Neglect* 19, 715–728; Ferol E. Mennen & Diana Meadow (1995). The relationship of abuse characteristics to symptoms of sexually abused girls, *Journal of Interpersonal Violence* 10, 259–274; William R. Downs (1993). Developmental considerations for the effects of child sexual abuse, *Journal of Interpersonal Violence* 8, 331–345. Lynne Briggs & Peter R. Joyce (1997). What determines post-traumatic stress disorder symptomatology for survivors of child sexual abuse? *Child Abuse & Neglect* 21, 575–582.

87. Kendall-Tackett, et al. (1993) *supra.*

88. For example, the authoritative study by Kendall-Tackett et al. (1993) *supra* reviewed only studies of children and adolescents currently in sex abuse treatment programs.

89. Larry L. Constantine (1981). Early sexual experiences: A review and synthesis of research. In Larry L. Constantine & Floyd M. Martinson (Eds.) *Children and Sex: New Findings, New Perspectives.* Boston: Little Brown. For example, Kinsey's groundbreaking research indicates that worst and best case outcomes were related to the repeated exposure to aggression over time, a characteristic of incest. John H. Gagnon (1965). Female victims of sex offenses, *Social Problems* 13, 176–192. (Gagnon notes that about 80 percent of women who experienced repeated coerced sexual contact before puberty experienced serious difficulties in adult life, but fewer than 7 percent of women with lesser types of sexual contact before puberty experienced difficulty.

90. Robert Bauserman & Bruce Rind (1997). Psychological correlates of male child and adolescent sexual experiences with adults: A review of the nonclinical literature, *Archives of Sexual Behavior* 26, 105–141.

91. For a review, see Cecile Ernst, Jules Angst & Monika Foldenyi (1993). The

Zurich Study, *European Archives of Psychiatry and Clinical Neuroscience* 242, 293–300. See also Gomes-Schwarz, Horowtiz, & Cardarelli (1990) *supra*.

92. Marcellina Mian, Peter Maron & Deborah LeBaron (1996). The effects of sexual abuse on 3- to 5-year-old girls, *Child Abuse and Neglect* 20, 731–745; Daryl J. Higgins and Marita P. McCabe (1994). The relationship of child sexual abuse and family violence to adult adjustment: Toward an integrated risk-sequelae model, *Journal of Sex Research* 31, 255–266; Patricia J. Long & Joan L. Jackson (1994). Child sexual abuse: An examination of family functioning, *Journal of Interpersonal Violence* 9, 270–277.

93. Kendall-Tackett, et al. (1993) *supra*; Faust et al. (1995) *supra*. Indeed, research indicates that family dysfunction plays a large part in later adjustment for those who have not been abused; John F. Kinzl, Christian Traweyer & Wilfred Biebl (1995). Sexual Dysfunctions: Relationships to child sexual abuse and early family experiences in a nonclinical sample, *Child Abuse and Neglect* 19, 785–792.

94. Candice Fiering, Lynn Taska & Michael Lewis (1996). A process model for understanding adaptation to sexual abuse: The role of shame in defining stigmatization, *Child Abuse and Neglect* 20, 767–782.

95. M. E. Elwell and P. H. Ephross (1987). Initial reactions of sexually abused children, *Social Casework* 68, 109–116; see also Bruce Rind & Robert Bauserman (1993). Biased terminology effects and biased information processing in research on adult-nonadult sexual interactions: An empirical investigation, *Journal of Sex Research* 30, 260–269.

96. April R. Bradley & James M. Wood (1996). How do children tell? The disclosure process of child sexual abuse, *Child Abuse & Neglect* 20, 881–891.

97. John F. Tedesco & Steven V. Schnell (1987). Children's reactions to sex abuse investigation and litigation, *Child Abuse & Neglect* 11, 267–272; Desmond K. Runyan, Wanda M. Hunter, Mark D. Everson, Debra Whitcomb & Edward DeVos (1994). The intervention stressors inventory: A measure of the stress of intervention for sexually abused children, *Child Abuse & Neglect* 18, 319–329.

98. Unlike what may have been expected, older victims tend to have more negative reactions to testifying. Gail S. Goodman, Elizabeth Pyle Taub, David P. H. Jones, Patricia England, Linda K. Port, Leslie Rudy & Lydia Prado (1992). Testifying in criminal court: Emotional effects on child sexual assault victims, *Monographs of the Society for Research in Child Development* 57 (5, Serial No. 229). In addition, children who most likely would be negatively impacted also are often the ones who most want to testify. Gary B. Melton (1994). Doing justice and doing good: Conflicts for mental health professionals, *Future of Children* 4, 102–118. The results and utility of the child witness studies remain contentious. For example, some researchers have reported positive effects of involvement in the juvenile justice system. D. K. Runyan, (1993). The emotional impact of societal intervention into child abuse. In Gail S. Goodman & Bette L. Bottoms (Eds.) *Child Victims, Child Witnesses: Understanding and Improving Testimony* (263–77). NY: Guilford.

99. Joyce Plotnikoff & Richard Woolfson (1995). *Prosecuting Child Abuse: An Evaluation of the Government's Speedy Progress Policy.* London: Blackston Press.

100. Julie A. Lipovsky (1994). The impact of court on children: Research findings and practical recommendations, *Journal of Interpersonal Violence* 9, 238–257; Ellen Gray (1993). *Unequal Justice: The Prosecution of Child Sexual Abuse.* NY: Free Press; Patricia G. Tjaden & Nancy Thoennes (1992). Predictors of legal intervention in child maltreatment cases, *Child Abuse & Neglect* 16, 807–821.

101. Plotnikoff & Woolfson (1995) *supra*.

102. Melissa J. Himelein & Jo Ann V. McElrath (1996). Resilient child sexual abuse survivors: Cognitive coping and illusion, *Child Abuse and Neglect* 20, 747–758.

103. Mary Beth Williams (1993). Assessing the traumatic impact of child sexual abuse: What makes it more severe? *Journal of Child Sexual Abuse* 2, 41–59; Ann Hazzard (1993). Trauma-related beliefs as mediators of sexual abuse impact in adult women survivors: A pilot study, *Journal of Child Sexual Abuse* 2, 55–69. Terri L. Weaver & George A. Clum (1995). Psychological distress associated with interpersonal violence: A meta-analysis, *Clinical Psychology Review* 15, 115–140.

104. T. G. M. Sandfort (1992). The argument for adult-child sexual contract: A critical appraisal and new data. In William O'Donohue and John H. Geer (Eds.) *The Sexual Abuse of Children: Clinical Issues* (Vol 1) (38–48). Hillsdale, NJ: Lawrence Erlbaum.

105. Although the findings may be correct in reporting that children may have positive experiences, the findings do not necessarily challenge the deeply held values and principles about equality and self-determination, which, as a major figure in sexual abuse research reveals, may be the reason this type of research has had relatively little attention and relevance for policy. David Finkelhor (1991). Response to Bauserman, *Journal of Homosexuality* 20, 313–315.

106. John R. Spencer & Rhona Flin (1993). *The Evidence of Children: The Law and Psychology* (2nd ed.). London: Blackstone.

107. Common law countries follow the law of England, for they are former colonies: Australia, Canada, Scotland, South Africa, the U.S., New Zealand.

108. Most European countries, such as Germany and France, are traditionally classified as civil law systems.

109. Nigel Parton (1997). Child protection and family support: Current debates and future prospects. In Nigel Parton (Ed.) *Child Protection and Family Support: Tensions, Contradictions and Possibilities* (1–24). NY: Routledge.

110. Id.

111. Melton (1994) *supra*; Deborah A. Daro (1994). Prevention of child sexual abuse, *Future of Children* 4, 198–223.

112. John E. B. Myers (1996). A decade of international reforms to accommodate child witnesses: Steps toward a child witness code, *Criminal Justice and Behavior* 23, 402–422; Detlev Frehsee (1990). Children's evidence within the German legal system. In John R. Spencer, Gordon Nicholson, Rhona Flin & Ray Bull (Eds.) *Children's Evidence in Legal Proceedings: An International Perspective* (28–38). Cambridge, England: University of Cambridge Faculty of Law.

113. Myers (1996) *supra*.

114. Francien Lamers-Winkelman & Frank Buffing (1996). Children's testimony in the Netherlands: A study of Statement Validity Analysis, *Criminal Justice and Behavior* 23, 304–321.

115. When the cases are severe, they are recorded by different agencies, such as the Child Protection Board, which received close to 10,000 reports (5 percent of them were incest); Reported in 1992, cited in Lamers-Winkelman & Buffing (1996) *supra*. Over 90 percent of the cases investigated by police involve allegations of child sexual abuse. Id.

116. Beatrice Faust (1995). Child Sexuality and age of consent laws: the Netherlands model, *Australasian Gay and Lesbian Law Journal* 5, 78–85.

117. Adri van Montfoort (1996). Compassion versus control? Handling child abuse in the Netherlands. Detlev Frehsee, Wiebke Horn & Kai-D. Bussmann (Eds.)

Family Violence against Children: A Challenge for Society (149–159). NY: Walter de Gruyter.

118. Kathleen J. Sternberg, Michael E. Lamb & Irit Hershokowitz (1996). Child sexual abuse in Israel: Evaluating innovative practices, *Criminal Justice and Behavior* 23, 322–337.

119. Eliahu Harnon (1988). Examination of children in sexual offenses: The Israeli law and practice, *Criminal Law Review* 1988, 263–274.

120. The Israeli Knesset (Parliament) in 1955 passed the Law of Evidence Revision Protection of Children (LER-PC), which regulated the manner in which information was obtained from children under the age of fifteen who were alleged victims, witnesses, or perpetrators of sex crimes.

121. Eliahu Harnon (1990). Children's evidence in the Israeli criminal justice system with special emphasis on sexual offenses. In John R. Spencer, Gordon Nicholson, Rhona Flin & Ray Bull (Eds.) *Children's Evidence in Legal Proceedings: An International Perspective* (81–98). Cambridge, England: University of Cambridge Faculty of Law; Hava David (1990). The role of the youth interrogator. In Spencer, Nicholson, Flin & Bull (1990) *supra* (99–110).

122. Statistics cited in Kathleen J. Sternberg, Michael E. Lamb & Irit Hershokowitz (1996). Child sexual abuse in Israel: Evaluating innovative practices, *Criminal Justice and Behavior* 23, 322–337.

123. Harnon (1990) *supra.*

124. Proposals to reform the process through videotaping the investigators' interviews or interviews by judges.

125. Id.

126. The following summary derives from Johannes Andenaes (1990). The Scandinavian countries. In Spencer, Nicholson, Flin & Bull (1990) *supra* (9–16).

127. This is the case in Denmark; see Id.

128. Detlev Frehsee (1990). Children's evidence within the German legal system. In Spencer, Nicholson, Flin & Bull (1990) *supra* (28–38); Edward Ross Dickinson (1996). *The Politics of German Child Welfare from the Empire to the Federal Republic.* Cambridge: Harvard University Press.

129. Id. The law only provides for physical examination.

130. Wiebke Horn (1996). Sexual and physical abuse of children: Public attitudes and legal issues. Detlev Frehsee, Wiebke Horn & Kai-D. Bussmann (Eds.) *Family Violence against Children: A Challenge for Society* (121–132). NY: Walter de Gruyter.

131. Id.

132. Id.

133. Nigel Parton (1997). Child protection and family support: Current debates and future prospects. In Nigel Parton (Ed.) *Child Protection and Family Support: Tensions, Contradictions and Possibilities* (1–24). NY: Routledge.

134. An approach which other forms of child maltreatment have yet to evoke; see Margaret A. Berger (1992). The deconstitutionalization of the Confrontation Clause: A proposal for prosecutorial restraint model, *Minnesota Law Review* 76, 557–613; Douglas J. Besharov (1987). Child abuse: Arrest and prosecution decision-making, *American Criminal Law Review* 24, 315–377.

135. Steve J. Ceci (1994). Cognitive and social factors in children's testimony. In Bruce D. Sales, & G. R. VandenBos (Eds.) *Psychology in Litigation and Legislation.* Washington, DC: American Psychological Association; Steve J. Ceci & Maggie Bruck

(1993). Suggestibility of the child witness: A historical review and synthesis, *Psychological Bulletin* 113, 403–439.

136. John R. Spencer (1990). Children's evidence in legal proceedings in England. In Spencer, Nicholson, Flin & Bull (1990) *supra* (113–125).

137. Louise Dezwirek Sas, David A. Wolfe & Kevin Gowdey (1996). Children and the courts in Canada, *Criminal Justice and Behavior* 23, 337–338.

138. Id.

139. David A. Wolfe, Louise Sas & Christine Wekerle (1994). Factors associated with the development of posttraumatic stress disorder among child victims of sexual abuse, *Child Abuse & Neglect* 18, 37–50.

140. Until as recently as 1990, children below the age of six were incompetent. Ray Bull & Graham Davies (1996). The effect of child witness research on legislation in Great Britain. In Bette L. Bottoms & Gail S. Goodman (Eds.) *International Perspectives on Child Abuse and Children's Testimony* (96–113). Thousand Oaks, CA: Sage.

141. Joyce Plotnikoff & Richard Woolfson (1995). *Prosecuting Child Abuse: An Evaluation of the Government's Speedy Progress Policy.* London: Blackstone Press.

142. Cathy Colby (1991). Child victims of sexual abuse and the criminal justice system in England and Wales, *Journal of Social Welfare and Family Law* 13, 362–374.

143. A two-year study revealed that only 3 percent of applications for using live-link facilities were granted. Bull & Davies (1996) *supra.* In Scotland, on the other hand, a two-year period revealed that all sex related trials actually made use of reforms, the cases were heard by closed court, and, in the majority of cases, the trial judge and legal counsel took the unusual step of removing their wigs. Rhona Flin, Brian Kearney & Kathleen Murray (1996). Children's evidence: Scottish research and law, *Criminal Justice and Behavior* 23, 358–376.

144. How many prosecutions do not take place because the principle witness is a child is not known; yet, the theoretical trauma due to delays ostensibly spurred the reforms. For a discussion of lack of statistics and what has led to reform, see Plotnikoff & Woolfson (1995) *supra.*

145. Two hundred cases of child abuse, most of which involved sexual abuse, were monitored for over a period of two years. One hundred and eighty-six cases had reached plea or trial by the end of two years. Far from receiving priority, the cases actually took longer than the national average to reach disposition. Likewise, new statutory procedures to expedite cases were little used; those that were used actually were not effective in time reduction. Cases that used the new procedures actually took longer than others in the study sample. Id.

146. Judges have noted their inability to stop attorneys from intimidating child witnesses by looming up close on the TV screen or by rigorous cross-examinations. Id.

147. For example, the admissibility of videotaped interviews has been accepted, but only to replace evidence-in-chief. Thus, children are still required to be present for cross-examination at trial. Id. In addition, it is defendants who have a right to speedy trials, not victims and witnesses. The laws simply offer little more than encouraging statements for greater judicial and prosecutorial vigilance against unwarranted continuances. Id. The highly visible "solutions" seem barely to have impinged on the underlying problem of secondary abuse of children by the criminal justice system. The same is true in the U.S. Deborah Whitcomb (1992). *When the Victim is a Child* (2nd ed.). Washington, DC: National Institute of Justice.

148. Robert Van Krieken (1992). *Children and the State: Social Control and the Formation of Australian Child Welfare.* North Sydney, Australia: Allen & Unwin.

149. For over one hundred years, Australia recognized such crimes as child stealing and indecent assault on girls under twelve years of age. Sandra Shrimpton, Kim Oates & Susan Hayes (1996). The child witness and legal reforms in Australia. In Bette L. Bottoms & Gail S. Goodman (Eds.) *International Perspectives on Child Abuse and Children's Testimony* (132–144). Thousand Oaks, CA: Sage.

150. Recent research demonstrates that the emotional distress of victimization relates to the extent of delays (over a year between police interview and the trial) and difficulty with the court process. R. Kim Oates, Deborah L. Lynch, Anne E. Stern, Brian I. O'Toole & George Cooney (1995). The criminal justice system and the sexually abused child—Help or hinderance? *Medical Journal of Australia* 162, 126–130.

151. Patrick Parkinson (1991). The future of competency testing for child witnesses, *Criminal Law Journal* 15, 186–192.

152. Shrimpton, Oates & Hayes (1996) *supra.*

153. Although two still have not adopted mandatory notification; Id.

154. The most recent reports number almost 50,000 per year, for a population of almost 17 million. Amazingly, few reports are substantiated, about 4.2 per 1,000 children. Id.

155. Research from the U.S. reports that other forms of maltreatment may be more devastating, yet sexual abuse receives the most interest.

156. For example, on December 20, 1993, President Clinton signed into law the National Child Protection Act of 1993 (National Child Protection Act of 1993). United States Code, 42, 5119. The only purpose of the act was to enhance the criminal history record keeping system of the Federal Bureau of Investigation (House Report, 1993). House Report (1993). National Child Protection Act of 1993. House Rep. No. 103–393, 103rd Cong., 1st Sess. At the state level, Washington's impressive series of statutes is illustrative of the prevailing ethos. In 1990, a new law permitted offenders to be institutionalized for long-term treatment after their prison term ended, an approach which Washington's highest court found constitutionally permissible. *In re Young,* 1993; *State v. Ward,* 869 P.2d 1062 (Wash. 1994); *In re Young,* 857 P.2d 989 (Wash. 1993). The approach was deemed constitutional by the Supreme Court in *Kansas v. Hendricks,* 95–1649 (1997). In addition, Washington, and now over half the states, require convicted sex offenders to register with local law enforcement agencies. Myers (1994) *supra.* Some states have taken registration one step further: they require registered sex offenders to submit specimens of body fluids which are then available for comparison with specimens from future victims; see Myers (1994) *supra.* Although the subject of intense litigation, these new statutes also have been found to be constitutional. See, e.g., *State v. Olivas,* 856 P.2d 1076 (Wash. 1993). In addition to registration laws, one state (California) has enacted mandatory castration laws for some offenders and others are considering adding the procedure to their laws. See G. L. Stelzer (1997). Chemical castration and the right to generate ideas: Does the First Amendment protect the fantasies of convicted pedophiles? *Minnesota Law Review* 81, 1675–1709.

157. The Supreme Court has recognized the significance of the state interest and has decided not to "second-guess" states' efforts to protect their children (*Maryland v. Craig,* 1990, 838). *Maryland v. Craig,* 497 US 836 (1990). For an analysis of the case and reasons children need special protections, see Gail S. Goodman, Murray

Levine, Gary B. Melton & David W. Ogden (1991). Child witnesses and the confrontation clause: The American Psychological Association Brief in *Maryland v. Craig, Law and Human Behavior* 15, 13–29. Although the finding was carefully circumscribed, commentators note that legislatures now may craft legislation and enact legal reforms which provide for even more sleuthing and criminalization than current laws; cf. John E. B. Myers (1994). Adjudication of child sexual abuse cases, *Future of Children* 4, 84–101. Kenneth Crimaldi (1996). "Megan's Law": Election-year politics and constitutional rights, *Rutgers Law Journal* 27, 169–204.

158. Julie A. Lipovsky. (1994). The impact of court on children: Research findings and practical recommendations, *Journal of Interpersonal Violence* 9, 238–257.

159. Murray Levine & Lori Battistoni (1991). The corroboration requirement in child sexual abuse cases, *Behavioral Sciences & the Law* 9, 3–20.

160. For a review of these changes, see Chapters 11 and 12 of Inger J. Sagatun & Leonard P. Edwards (1995). *Child Abuse and the Legal System.* Chicago: Nelson-Hall Publishers.

161. Graham Davies & Helen Westcott (1995). The child witness: Empowerment or protection. In Maria S. Zaragiza, John R. Graham, Gordon C. N. Hall, Richard Hirschman & Yossef S. Ben-Porath (Eds.) *Memory and Testimony in the Child Witness* (199–213). Thousand Oaks, CA: Sage; Jean Montoya (1992). On truth seeking and shielding in child abuse trials, see *Hastings Law Review* 43, 1259–1319; Jean Montoya (1993). Something not so funny happened on the way to conviction: The pretrial interrogation of child witnesses, *Arizona Law Review* 35, 927–987; Julie A. Anderson (1997). The Sixth Amendment: Protecting defendants' rights at the expense of child victims, *The John Marshall Law Review* 30, 767–802.

162. Gail Goodman et al. (1922) *supra.*

163. Lynne Henerson (1997). Without narrative: Child sexual abuse, *Virginia Journal of Social Policy & the Law* 4, 479–544.

164. Others, on the other hand, may remain more skeptical about children's testimonies and focus on ways children's testimony may be unreliable and thus focus on tainting hearings in which attorneys may challenge the way the children were interviewed. The most famous case is *State of New Jersey v. Michaels*, 642 A.2d 1372 (1994). See Robert Rosenthal (1995). *State of New Jersey v. Margaret Kelly Michaels:* An Overview, *Psychology, Public Policy, and Law* 1, 246–271.

165. See Jane Morgan & Lucia Zedner (1992). *Child Victims: Crime, Impact and Criminal Justice.* NY: Clarendon Press.

166. Morgan & Zedner (1992) *supra.*

167. For example, although child rape is reported in Nigerian newspapers, it remains "ignored by the social systems: Nigerians choose to remain mute about rape." Francisca Isi Omorodion (1994). Child sexual abuse in Benin City, Edo State, Nigeria: A sociological analysis, *Issues in Comprehensive Pediatric Nursing* 17, 29–36 (29).

168. Uma A. Segal (1996). Children as witness: India is not ready. In Bette L. Bottoms & Gail S. Goodman (Eds.) *International Perspectives on Child Abuse and Children's Testimony* (266–282). Thousand Oaks, CA: Sage; Uma A. Segal (1995). Child abuse by the middle class? A study of professionals in India, *Child Abuse & Neglect* 19, 213–227; Uma A. Segal (1991). Child abuse in India: A theoretical overview, *Indian Journal of Social Work* 52, 293–302.

169. Segal (1996) *supra* (274).

170. Unpublished study conducted by Castelino, 1985, reported in Segal (1996) *supra.*

171. James P. Grant (1994). *The State of the World's Children* NY: Oxford University Press.

172. Segal (1996) *supra* (277).

173. Canada provides a prime example; see Karen J. Swift (1997). Canada: Trends and issues in child welfare. In Neil Gilbert (Ed.) (1997). *Combatting Child Abuse: International Perspectives and Trends* (38–71). NY: Oxford University Press.

174. For a review of countries' child welfare systems that focuses on reporting approaches, see Neil Gilbert (Ed.) (1997). *Combatting Child Abuse: International Perspectives and Trends.* NY: Oxford University Press.

175. Children's Convention (1990) *supra.*

176. Id.

177. Id.

178. For example, the United Nations Charter distinguishes between the public domain of international law and the private sphere of domestic jurisdiction, and protects the latter from international intrusion. Article 2(7) finds that "Nothing contained in the present Charter shall authorize the United Nations to intervene in matters which are essentially within the domestic jurisdiction of any states or shall require the Members to submit such matters to settlement under the present Charter. . . . " Even recent international human rights law replicates the division between public and private as it targets state-sanctioned or public actions. That development means that, to the extent national governments are accountable for actions within their domestic jurisdictions, they are accountable for "state actions." For example, the right to life and bodily integrity is applicable mainly as a protection of individuals from arbitrary deprivation of life through execution or arbitrary torture by government officials.

179. The recognition that abuse and danger can exist in the private sphere has perhaps been the major insight offered by family law scholars in the twentieth century. Frances E. Olsen (1985). The myth of state intervention in the family, *University of Michigan Journal of Law Reform* 18, 835–864; Jody Young Jakosa (1984). Parsing public from private: The failure of differential state action analysis, *Harvard Civil Rights-Civil Law Review* 19, 193–233; Duncan Kennedy (1982). The status of the decline of the public/private distinction, *University of Pennsylvania Law Review* 130, 1349–1357.

180. The distinction between private and public accounts for the long failure of international human rights doctrine to accommodate children's rights. The same public/private divide has been identified by feminists as especially detrimental to women. There is an enormous literature in this area. See J. Bethke Elshtain (1993). *Public Man, Private Women* (2nd ed.). Princeton: Princeton University Press. See also Rebecca J. Cook (Ed.) (1994). *Human Rights of Women: National and International Perspectives.* Philadelphia: University of Pennsylvania Press; Julie Stone Peters & Andrea Wolper (Eds.) (1995). *Women's Rights, Human Rights.* NY: Routledge; D. Dallmeyer (Ed.) (1993). *Reconceiving Reality: Women and International Law.* American Society of International Law; Hillary Charlesworth, Carol Chinkin & S. Wright (1991). Feminist approaches to international law, *American Journal of International Law* 85, 613–45; Hillary Charlesworth (1992). The public/private distinction and the right to development in international law, *Australian Yearbook of International Law* 12, 190–204; C. M. Chinkin (1989). The challenge of soft law: Development and change in

international law, *International and Comparative Law Quarterly* 38, 850–66. That is, international law typically excludes from its ambit matters within domestic jurisdiction, and a state's treatment of its children is still widely regarded as falling within its domestic jurisdiction.

181. The most notable commentator who has done so in light of developments in children's rights argues for an interpretation of international obligations that will inevitably pass into the private terrain of family life and interpersonal actions. Geraldine Van Bueren (1996). Crossing the frontier—The international protection of family life in the 21st century. In Nigel Lowe & Gillian Douglas (Eds.) *Families across Frontiers* (811–830). Netherlands: Kluwer Academic. See also Geraldine Van Bueren (1996). Deconstructing the mythologies of international human rights law. In Conor Gearty & Adam Tomkins (Eds.) *Understanding Human Rights* (596–610). London: Mansell; Geraldine Van Bueren (1995). The international protection of family members' rights as the 21st century approaches, *Human Rights Quarterly* 17, 732–765.

182. For a comprehensive review, see Andrew Clapham (1993). *Human Rights in the Private Sphere.* NY: Oxford University Press.

183. Rebecca J. Cook (1993). Women's international human rights law: The way forward, *Human Rights Quarterly* 15, 230–261.

184. Inter-American Court of Human Rights (Cer C) No. 4 (1988).

185. Responsibility is imputable to the state even though the alleged act is not directly imputable to the state; e.g., private persons committed the acts or responsible parties cannot be identified. The state can be responsible not because of the act itself, but because of the failure to "prevent the violation or to respond to it as required by the Convention" (Para 172). The Court also found that the prevention obligation on states included all means of a "legal, political, administrative and cultural nature" (Para 175). The court even further found that where human rights violations by private parties are not seriously investigated the parties are in a sense aided by the government, making the state responsible on the international level. Dinah Shelton (1990). Private violence, public wrongs and the responsibility of states, *Fordham Journal of International Law* 13, 1–34.

186. The court found that states are required to exercise "due diligence" to prevent human rights violations. See Shelton (1990) *supra.*

187. For example, the Human Rights Committee, in its general comments on the right to life, has affirmed that states must ensure individuals' protection against acts of torture whether inflicted by people in their official capacity, outside their official capacity, or in a private capacity. For an analysis of these comments, see Dominic McGoldrick (1991). *The Human Rights Committee.* NY: Oxford University Press.

188. The Court was explicit: Rights found in the European Convention create obligations for States which involve "the adoption of measures designed to secure respect for private life *even in the sphere of the relations of individuals between themselves.*" Case of X and Y v. The Netherlands (1985). Series A, Vol. 91, para. 23 (emphasis added).

189. The case involved a rape inside a private institution, which leads commentators to propose that other private institutions, particularly the family, may be a site for intervention and protection through international law. Van Bueren (1996) *supra.*

190. For example, international law fixes duties upon individuals for "crimes against humanity" and recognizes that private individuals can be tried and punished in any court for the crime of genocide. Convention on the Prevention of Punishment of the Crime of Genocide, Article IV. International attention has been directed to-

wards the widespread rapes, torture, and forced pregnancies in the former Yugoslavia. The recent establishment by the Security Council of the International Criminal Tribunal for the Former Yugoslavia (SC Res 827, May 25, 1993) and of the International Tribunal for Rwanda (SC Res 955, November 8, 1994) are breakthroughs with regard to the enforcement of international humanitarian law. Christine Chinkin (1994). Rape and sexual abuse of women in international law, *European Journal of International Law* 5, 326–41. Rape has long been prohibited by the law of war and has been incorporated into various modern Codes of Military Conduct. Theodore Meron (1993). Rape as a crime under international humanitarian law, *American Journal of International Law* 87, 42–428; Daniel B. Pickard (1995). Security Council Resolution 808: A step toward a permanent International Court for the Prosecution of International Crimes and Human Rights Violations, *Golden Gate University Law Review* 25, 435–462; Arden B. Levy (1994). International prosection of rape in warfare: Nondiscriminatory recognition and enforcement, *UCLA Women's Law Journal* 4, 255–297.

191. The identification, arrest, and detention of accused persons, the collection and presentation of evidence, the rules of evidence, and the procedure to be followed must be resolved.

192. Van Boven put it as follows:

> In the history of the United Nations there is a notable trend from standard-setting toward implementation and from non-conflictual monitoring towards inquiry into violations of human rights involving State responsibility. State practices and State responsibility are usually the central focus. Recent developments now hint in the direction of focusing not only on States and on State practices but also on individual persons and criminal acts committed by them. These developments are in line with the recognition of individuals as emerging subjects of international law. Theo van Boven (1995). Human rights and rights of peoples, *European Journal of International Law* 6, 461–476.

In this regard, it is important to note the International Law Commission's efforts to create an international criminal court that would prosecute individuals who breach treaty crimes of an "exceptionally serious" and international nature, such as war crimes, torture, highjacking, and, more controversially, drug trafficking. See Timothy L. H. McCormack & Gerry J. Simpson (1995). A new international criminal law regime? *Netherlands International Law Review* 42, 177–206. Paul D. Maraquardt (1995). Law without borders: The constitutionality of an international criminal court, *Columbia Journal of Transnational Law* 33, 73–148; Barbara M. Arnold (1994). Doctrinal basis for the international criminalization process, *Temple International & Comparative Law Journal* 8, 85–115; Roy Godson & William J. Olson (1995). International organized crime, *Society* 32, 18–29; Jimmy Gurule (1994). Terrorism, territorial sovereignty, and the forcible apprehension of international criminals abroad, *Hastings International & Comparative Law Review* 17, 457–495.

193. The Declaration reads as follows: "The General Assembly proclaims this Universal Declaration of Human Rights as a common standard of achievement for all peoples of all nations, to the end that *every individual and every organ of society*, keeping this Declaration constantly in mind, shall strive by teaching and education to promote respect for these rights and freedoms and by progressive measures, national and international, to secure their universal recognition and observance." Universal Declaration of Human Rights.

194. For example, Article 7 reads as follows:

(1) No child shall be subjected to arbitrary or unlawful interference with his or her privacy, family, home or correspondence, nor to unlawful attacks on her honor or reputation.
(2) The child has the right to the protection of the law against such interference or attacks.

It is important to note the absence of any reference to public authorities. A leading commentator on children's rights who took part in the actual development of the convention notes the changes in international laws' approach to family life. Traditional international law aimed to safeguard against intrusion into family life, rather than attempt to regulate the quality of the relationship within the family. This is no longer the case; for example, international law now moves into "unfamiliar areas in which the effect of a human rights tribunal decision is tantamount to deciding the role of family members." Van Bueren (1996) *supra* (818). One such decision might involve allowing children to participate in decisions within families. Van Bueren notes that the development implies a loss of adult power which has been associated with childhood. Child-oriented expression implies shifting the focus from what children cannot do to what they can do and to what decisions and parts of decisions they can make. She also correctly argues that States Parties are obliged to ensure children who are capable of forming views of the rights to express those views "in all matters affecting the child" and to give those views "due weight in accordance with the age and maturity of the child"; "there is no longer a traditional area of exclusive parental or family decisionmaking." (819–20). Because they are bound to address two criteria of equal value, the age and maturity of the child, States Parties do not have an unfettered discretion as to when to consider and when to ignore the views of children who disagree with the traditional family decision-makers. This participation right of the child within family life amounts to supported and active participation.

195. For example, the expert committee responsible for the Convention found that the Convention covers public and private acts. The recommendation examined private activity such as family violence, forced marriages, and female circumcision. See Committee on the Elimination of Discrimination against Women, General Rec. 19, CEDAW/C/1992/L.1/Add.15, Jan. 19, 1992.

196. Convention on the Elimination of All Forms of Racial Discrimination, Article 5(b), guarantees the right to "security of the person . . . against violence . . . whether inflicted by government officials or by any individual, group or institution." Theodore Meron finds that the Convention clearly extends prohibitions of discrimination to private life. Theodore Meron (1986). *Human Rights Law-making in the United Nations.* Oxford: Clarendon Press.

197. GA Res 48/104 (1993).

198. For an analysis of how the advances seek to transcend public/private divisions, see Hilary Charlesworth (1995). Worlds apart: Public/private distinctions in international law. In Margaret Thornton (Ed.) *Public and Private: Feminist Legal Debates* (242–260). NY: Oxford University Press.

199. The work of a leading commentator on international law, Louis Henkin, underscores the development. In the late 1970s Henkin argued that human rights "are rights against society as represented by government officials." In the late 1980s, Henkin proposed that state parties were obligated "to ensure" the recognized rights; this, he argued, "seems to imply that rights recognized are not merely rights against governments (as are rights under the U.S. Constitution for example), but also against

other persons." See Louis Henkin (1979). *The Rights of Man Today*. London: Stevens & Sons. 2. Louis Henkin (1987). The international bill of rights. In R. Bernhardt & J. A. Jolowicz (Eds.) *International Enforcement of Human Rights*. Berlin: Springer-Verlag. 10.

200. For a similar argument, see Van Bueren (1996) *supra* (827–828).

201. Van Bueren (1996) *supra* (828).

202. Roger J. R. Levesque (1995). Combatting child sexual maltreatment: Advances and obstacles in international progress, *Law & Policy* 17, 441–469.

203. The best we have had have been very general blueprints; see Roger J. R. Levesque (1995). Prosecuting sex crimes, *supra*.

204. See, for example, Ron Davie, Graham Upton & Ved Varma (1996). *The Voice of the Child: A Handbook for Professionals*. Washington, DC: Falmer Press; U.S. Advisory Board on Child Abuse and Neglect (ABCAN) (1993). *Neighbors Helping Neighbors: A New National Strategy for the Protection of Children*. U.S. Department of Health and Human Services, Washington, DC: U.S. Government Printing Office.

205. David A. Wolfe (1993). Child abuse intervention research: Implications for policy. In Dante Cicchetti, Sheree L. Toth & I. E. Sigel (Eds.) *Child Abuse, Child Development, and Social Policy, Advances in Applied Developmental Psychology* (369–397). Norwood, NJ: Ablex Publishing.

206. U.S. Advisory Board on Child Abuse and Neglect (ABCAN) (1993). *Neighbors Helping Neighbors: A New National Strategy for the Protection of Children*. U.S. Department of Health and Human Services, Washington, DC: U.S. Government Printing Office.

207. See notes 109–132 and accompanying test, *supra*.

208. Roger J. R. Levesque (1995) Combatting child sexual maltreatment, *supra*.

209. Researchers have long established that many children experience several forms of maltreatment that need intervention; Jay Belsky (1993). Etiology of child maltreatment: A developmental-ecological analysis, *Psychological Bulletin* 114, 413–434; Larry E. Beutler, Rebecca A. Williams & Heidi A. Zetzer (1994). Efficacy of treatment for victims of child sexual abuse, *Future of Children* 4, 156–175.

210. Philip G. Ney, Tak Fung & Adele Rose Wickett (1994). The worst combinations of child abuse and neglect, *Child Abuse & Neglect* 18, 705–714; Tom Luster & Stephen A. Small (1997). Sexual abuse history and problems in adolescence: Exploring the effects of moderating variables, *Journal of Marriage and the Family* 59, 131–142.

211. Id.

212. Linda Myers Williams & Ronald A. Farrell (1990). Legal response to child sexual abuse in day care, *Criminal Justice and Behavior* 17, 284–302.

213. Roger J. R. Levesque (1994). Sex differences in the experience of child sexual victimization, *Journal of Family Violence* 9, 357–369.

214. Judith V. Becker (1994). Offenders: Characteristics and treatment, *Future of Children* 4, 176–197.

215. Deborah A. Daro (1994). Prevention of child sexual abuse, *Future of Children* 4, 198–223.

216. Gregory J. Skibinski & Joan E. Esser-Stuart (1993). Public sentiment toward innovative child sexual abuse intervention strategies: Consensus and conflict, *Juvenile & Family Court Journal* 44, 17–26.

217. Daro (1994) *supra* (216).

218. Bill Watkins & Arnon Bentovim (1992) *supra*.

219. Cf. David A. Wolfe (1993). Child abuse intervention research: Implications for policy. In D. Cicchetti, S. L. Toth & I. E. Sigel (Eds.) *Child Abuse, Child Development, and Social Policy, Advances in Applied Developmental Psychology* (369–397). Norwood, NJ: Ablex Publishing.

220. George J. Skibinski (1994). Intrafamilial child sexual abuse: Intervention programs for first time offenders and their families, *Child Abuse & Neglect* 18, 367–75.

221. James M. Allan & Keven D. Browne (1998). Evaluating community-based treatment programmes for men who sexually abuse children, *Child Abuse Review* 7, 13–29.

222. Lucy Berliner, Donna Schram, Lisa L. Miller & Cheryl Darling Milloy (1995). A sentencing alternative for sex offenders: A study of decision making and recidivism, *Journal of Interpersonal Violence* 10, 487–502.

223. Richard Famularo, Robert Kinscherff, Doris Bunshaft, Gayle Spivak & Terrence Fenton (1989). Parental compliance to court-ordered treatment interventions in cases of child maltreatment, *Child Abuse & Neglect* 13, 507–514; Mark Chaffin (1992). Factors associated with treatment completion and progress among intrafamilial sexual abusers, *Child Abuse & Neglect* 16, 251–64.

224. Jon Kear-Colwell & Philip Pollock (1997). Motivation or confrontation: Which approach to the child sex offender? *Criminal Justice and Behavior* 24, 20–33.

225. F. Berlin, H. Malin & S. Dean (1991). Effects of statutes requiring psychiatrists to report suspected sexual abuse of children, *American Journal of Psychiatry* 148, 449–453.

226. Murray Levine & Eric Doherty (1991). Professional issues: The Fifth Amendment and therapeutic requirements to admit abuse. *Criminal Justice and Behavior* 18, 98–112.

227. Melton (1994) *supra*.

228. Judith Masson (1997). Introducing non-punitive approaches into child-protection: Legal issues. In Nigel Parton (Ed.) *Child Protection and Family Support: Tensions, Contradictions and Possibilities* (92–108). NY: Routledge.

229. For example, the most recent study reveals that rates of incarceration for first-degree child molestation are under 60 percent and that rates are under 30 percent for second-degree molestation. Ross E. Cheit & Erica B. Goldschmidt (1997). Child molesters in the criminal justice system: A comprehensive case-flow analysis of the Rhode Island docket (1985–1993), *Journal of Criminal and Civil Confinement*, 23, 267–301.

230. Id.

231. Karen McCurdy & Deborah Daro (1994). Child maltreatment: A national survey of reports and fatalities, *Journal of Interpersonal Violence* 9, 75–94.

232. Beutler, Williams & Zetzer (1994) *supra*.

233. Elwell & Ephross (1987) *supra*.

234. Craig McNulty & Jane Wardle (1994). Adult disclosure of sexual abuse: A primary cause of psychological distress? *Child Abuse & Neglect* 18, 549–555.

235. Douglas J. Besharov (1994). Responding to child sexual abuse: The need for a balanced approach, *Future of Children* 4, 135–155; David L. Kerns, Douglas L. Terman & Carol S. Larson (1994). The role of physicians in reporting and evaluating child sexual abuse cases, *Future of Children* 4, 119–134.

236. Corrine Wattam (1997) Can filtering processes be rationalized? In Parton (Ed.) *Child Protection and Family Support* (109–125) *supra*.

237. For a similar argument, see Jean Sybil La Fontaine (1990). *Child Sexual Abuse*. Cambridge: Polity Press.

238. U.S. Advisory Board on Child Abuse and Neglect (ABCAN) (1993). *Neighbors Helping Neighbors* (*supra* note).

239. Theodore P. Cross, Edward DeVos & Debra Whitcomb (1994). Prosecution of child sexual abuse: Which cases are accepted, *Child Abuse & Neglect* 18, 663–667.

240. Corrine Wattam (1992). *Making a Case in Child Protection*. Harlow: Longman. Current intervention efforts attempt to fit patients to their cures, rather than the reverse. As we have seen, proper tailoring of assistance is particularly important when providing therapeutic services to child sexual abusers; see David A. Wolfe (1994). The role of intervention and treatment services in the prevention of child abuse and neglect. In Gary B. Melton & Frank D. Barry (Eds.) *Protecting children from abuse and neglect: Foundations for a new national strategy* (224–303). NY: Guilford.

241. Levesque (1995). Prosecuting sex crimes, *supra*.

242. Id.

243. *Prince v. Mass.*, 321 U.S. 158 (1944) (p. 170).

244. Levesque (1994). The sexual use, abuse and exploitation, *supra*.

245. Id.

246. Ross A. Thompson (1993). Developmental research and legal policy: Toward a two-way street. In D. Cicchetti, S. L. Toth, & I. E. Sigel (Eds.) *Child Abuse, Child Development, and Social Policy, Advances in Applied Developmental Psychology* (75–115). Norwood, NJ: Ablex Publishing.

247. Levesque (1996) *supra*.

248. See, e.g., Levesque (1995). Prosecuting sex crimes, *supra*.

249. U.S. Advisory Board on Child Abuse and Neglect (ABCAN) (1993). *Neighbors helping neighbors, supra*.

250. Mark A. Small (1992). Policy review of child abuse and neglect statutes, *Law & Policy* 14, 129–152; Melton (1994) *supra*.

251. Penelope Trickett & Frank W. Putnam (1993). Impact of child sexual abuse on females: Toward a developmental, psychobiological integration, *Psychological Science* 4, 81–87; Pat Gilmartin (1994). *Rape, Incest, and Child Sexual Abuse: Consequences and Recovery*. NY: Garland.

252. Gary B. Melton & Mary Fran Flood (1994). Research policy and child maltreatment: Developing the scientific foundation for effective protection of children, *Child Abuse & Neglect* 18 Suppl., 1–28.

253. Robert Dingwall, John Eekelaar & Topsy Murray (1995). *The Protection of Children: State Intervention in Family Life* (2nd ed.). London: Avebury.

254. In England, for example, the "Cleveland Affair" resulted in the removal of over a hundred children from their homes based on an inappropriate diagnosis of child sexual abuse. See Parton (1997) *supra*. Similar instances have occurred in the U.S.; see John E. B. Myers (1994). Definitions and origins of the backlash against child protection. In John E. B. Myers (Ed.) *The Backlash: Child Protection under Fire* (17–30). Thousand Oaks, CA: Sage.

255. Masson (1997) *supra*.

256. Jane Rosien, Lelia Helms & Carolyn Wanat (1993). Intent v. Practice: Incentives and disincentives for child abuse reporting by school personnel, *Brigham Young Education and Law Journal* 1993, 102–125.

257. Vitit Muntarbhorn (1993). *Sale of Children: Visit by the Special Rapporteur to Australia.* E/CN.4/1993/67/Add.1; Neil Gilbert (Ed.) (1997). *Combatting Child Abuse: International Perspectives and Trends.* NY: Oxford University Press.

258. Erna Olafson, David L. Corwin & Roland C. Summit (1993). Modern history of child sexual abuse awareness: Cycles of discovery and suppression, *Child Abuse & Neglect* 17, 7–24. Lucy S. McGough (1994). *Child Witness: Fragile Voices in the American Legal System.* New Haven: Yale University Press.

259. Richard M. Lerner (1995). *America's Youth in Crisis: Challenges and Options for Programs and Policies.* Thousand Oaks, CA: Sage; Children's Defense Fund (CDF) (1994). *The State of America's Children.* Washington, DC: Children's Defense Fund; Roger J. R. Levesque (1994). Targeting "deadbeat" dads: The problem with the direction of welfare reform, *Hamline Journal of Public Law and Policy* 15, 1–53.

260. Robert Haveman, & Barbara Wolfe (1994). *Succeeding Generations: On the Effects of Investments in Children.* NY: Russell Sage Foundation.

261. Jane Tunstill (1997). Implementing the family support clauses of the 1989 Children Act: Legislative, professional and organizational obstacles. In Parton (39–58) *supra.* There is increasing support for this claim: as reports of abuse increase, the number of out-of-home placement rates diminishes, with the U.S. being the notable exception. Neil Gilbert (Ed.) (1997). *Combatting Child Abuse: International Perspectives and Trends.* NY: Oxford University Press.

262. For a detailed examination of the development and current notions of family privacy, see Roger J. R. Levesque (1994). The Supreme Court, U.S. Constitution, and Family Life. Paper presented a the Second International Study Group on Ideologies of Children's Rights, Spring, 1994, Charleston, SC.

263. Daro (1994) *supra.*

264. Although this undoubtedly may be true, commentators and researchers at the forefront of efforts to respect the different rights involved in child protection efforts have noted how intervention may lead to counterproductive intrusions into family life. Douglas J. Besharov (1994). Responding to child sexual abuse: The need for a balanced approach, *Future of Children* 4, 135–155. Although in the short run it may be possible to ignore the problem of overzealous intervention, in the long run, "continued support for child protective efforts will surely erode" (137). The increasing backlash against child protection efforts underscores the need to balance the rights of children, which urge intervention, with those of other family members. John E. B. Myers (1994). Definitions and origins of the backlash against child protection. In John E. B. Myers (Ed.) *The backlash: Child protection under fire* (17–30). Thousand Oaks, CA: Sage.

265. Mark Hardin (1988). Legal barriers in child abuse investigations: State powers and individual rights, *Washington Law Review* 63, 493–605.

266. Jessica Yelas (1994). Mandatory reporting of child abuse and the public/private distinction, *Auckland University Law Review* 7, 781–802.

267. Haugaard & Reppucci (1988) *supra.*

268. Michael E. Lamb, Kathleen Sternberg & P. W. Esplin (1994). Factors influencing the reliability and validity of statements made by young victims of sexual maltreatment, *Journal of Applied Developmental Psychology* 15, 255–280.

269. Louise Armstrong (1993). *And They Call it Help: The Psychiatric Policing of America's Children.* Reading, MA: Addison-Wesley; Candice Fiering, Lynn Taska & Michael Lewis (1996). A process model for understanding adaptation to

sexual abuse: The role of shame in defining stigmatization, *Child Abuse & Neglect* 20, 767–782.

270. Louise Armstrong (1994). *Rocking the Cradle of Sexual Politics*. Reading, MA: Addison-Wesley (266).

271. Id.

272. Recent efforts targeted at dead beat dads, for example, clearly move financial responsibility from the state to individuals. There are recurrent calls for parents to be legally responsible for children's disruptive behavior. Moreover, the current climate is one of increasing privatization and reduction of welfare services and benefits. Levesque (1995) *supra*.

273. Masson (1997) *supra*.

274. Some of them have led to litigation; see Thomas G. Eschweiler (1995). Educational malpractice in sex education, *Southern Methodist University Law Review* 49, 101–132.

275. Ronald Goldman & Juliette Goldman (1982). *Children's Sexual Thinking: A Comparative Study of Children Aged 5 to 15 Years in Australia, North America, Britain and Sweden*. London: Routledge & Kegan Paul.

276. The lack of understanding becomes problematic, particularly with efforts to deal with victimization that deny child sexuality. In a society in which children are given values about sex that are predominately negative—sex must be contained, sex is dangerous, sex is wrong, sexual relationships are exploitative—we should not be surprised to find sexual responsiveness diversified. Sexual interest in children is one possible consequence of such a developmental process. John Bancroft (1992). The sexuality of sexual offending: The social dimension, *Criminal Behavior and Mental Health* 1, 181–191. Yet, the prevailing image tends to hide that anything could occur between an adult and a child, and between children. The effects of the denial reverberate. The need to see these actions as something alien to our society is part of the highly vested interest in keeping sexuality out of the family. Sexuality within the family is deeply threatening, a result of which is the highly negative views about sexuality. Id. Thus the public remains unwilling to believe that offenders are found in a variety of communities; see Daro (1994) *supra*.

277. Sandy K. Wurtele (1993). Enhancing children's sexual development through child sexual abuse prevention programs, *Journal of Sex Education and Therapy* 19, 37–46.

278. Gregory J. Skibinski & Joan E. Esser-Stuart (1993). Public sentiment toward innovative child sexual abuse intervention strategies: Consensus and conflict, *Juvenile & Family Court Journal* 44, 17–26.

279. Barry Trutte, Elizabeth Adkins & George MacDonald (1996). Professional attitudes regarding treatment and punishment of incest: Comparing police, child welfare, and community mental health, *Journal of Family Violence* 11, 237–249.

280. The demand for greater innovation is unlikely to change any time soon, especially since the Supreme Court has approved of these innovative reforms on the rationale that states are given considerable discretion in devising methods to protect their children. *Maryland v. Craig*, 497 U.S. 836 (1990).

7. Abuse by Young Offenders

1. Michael L. Bourke & Brad Donohue (1996). Assessment and treatment of juvenile sex offenders: An empirical review, *Journal of Child Sexual Abuse* 5, 47–70;

Gail Ryan, Thomas J. Miyoshi, Jeffrey L. Metzner, Richard D. Krugman & George Fryer (1996). Trends in a national sample of sexually abusive youths, *Journal of the American Academy of Child and Adolescent Psychiatry* 35, 17–25.

2. William Breer (1987). *The Adolescent Molester.* Springfield, IL: C. C. Thomas.

3. Studies of juvenile sexual offenders date to the early 1940s. Lewis Jacob Doshay (1943). *The Boy Sex Offender and His Later Career.* NY: Grove & Stratton; Raymond W. Waggoner & David A. Boyd, Jr. (1941). Juvenile aberrant sexual behavior, *American Journal of Orthopsychiatry* 11, 275–291.

4. Children's Convention (1990), Article 4.

5. Texts on child welfare and child maltreatment do not even include peer abuse. Cynthia Crosson Tower (1996). *Understanding Child Abuse and Neglect.* Boston: Allyn and Bacon; Harvey Wallace (1996). Family violence: Legal, medical and social perspectives. Boston: Allyn and Bacon; Susan Whitelaw Downs, Lela B. Costin, Emily Jean McFadden (1996). *Child Welfare and Family Services: Policies and Practice* (5th Ed.). White Plains, NY: Longman.

6. Research indicates that unwanted sexual experiences begin in early childhood and continue through adolescence and adulthood. Perpetrators change from being family members and acquaintances to boyfriends and relationship partners. Wendy Patton & Mary Mannison (1995). Sexual coercion in dating situations among university students: Preliminary Australian data, *Australian Journal of Psychology* 47, 66–72; William R. Downs (1993). Developmental considerations for the effects of childhood sexual abuse, *Journal of Interpersonal Violence* 8, 331–345.

7. See Roger J. R. Levesque (1997). Dating violence, adolescents, and the law, *Virginia Journal of Social Policy and Law* 4, 339–379.

8. Bruce Roscoe & John E. Callahan (1985). Adolescents' self-report of violence in families and dating relations, *Adolescence* 20, 545–553; Denise Gamache (1991). Domination and control: The social context of dating violence. In Barrie Levy (Ed.) *Dating Violence: Young Women in Danger* (73–83). Seattle, WA: Seal Press. Despite statistics revealing high incidence and prevalence rates, only a small fraction, as low as 7 percent, of violent episodes is ever reported to officials, authorities, and others who could render assistance. Chad LeJeune & Victoria Follette (1994). Taking responsibility: Sex differences in reporting dating violence, *Journal of Interpersonal Violence* 9, 122–140.

9. Ileanna Arias, Mary Samios & K. Daniel O'Leary (1987). Prevalence and correlates of physical aggression during courtship, *Journal of Interpersonal Violence* 2, 82–90. For a review, see David B. Sugarman & Gerald T. Hotaling (1989). Dating violence: Prevalence, context, and risk markers. In Maureen A. Pirog-Good & Jan E. Stets (Eds.) *Violence in Dating Relationships: Emerging Social Issues* (3–32). NY: Praeger.

10. Jacquelyn W. White & Marry P. Koss (1992). Courtship violence: Incidence in a national sample of higher education students, *Violence and Victims* 6, 247–256.

11. Teresa M. Bethke & David M. DeJoy (1993). An experimental study of factors influencing the acceptability of dating violence, *Journal of Interpersonal Violence* 8, 36–51.

12. Carol K. Sigelman, Carol J. Berry, & Katherine A. Wiles, (1984). Violence in college students' dating relationships, *Journal of Applied Psychology* 14, 530–548. Jacqueline D. Goodchilds & Gail L. Zellman (1984). Sexual signalling and sexual

aggression in adolescent relationships. In N. Malamuth & E. Donnerstein (Eds.) *Pornography and Sexual Aggression* (233–243). Orlando: Academic Press.

13. LeJeune & Follette (1994) *supra*.

14. As many as 50 percent of dating relationships do not terminate after violent episodes. Nona K. O'Keeffe, Karen Broackopp, & Esther Chew (1986). Teen dating violence, *Social Work* 31, 465–468. Likewise, over 75 percent of victims involved in violent dating relationships expect to marry their abusers. Waiping Alice Lo & Michael J. Sporakowski (1989). The continuation of violent dating relationships among college students, *Journal of College Student Development* 30, 432–439. In addition, half that number actually do marry partners who have abused them before marriage. Bruce Roscoe & Nancy Benaske (1985). Courtship violence experienced by abused wives: Similarities in patterns of abuse, *Family Relations* 34, 680–700.

15. Vangie A. Foshee (1996). Gender differences in adolescent dating abuse prevalence, types and injuries, *Health Education Research: Theory & Practice* 11, 275–286.

16. Donald G. Dutton & Susan Painter (1993). Emotional attachments in abusive relationships: A test of traumatic bonding theory, *Violence and Victims* 8, 105–120.

17. Dee L. R. Graham & Edna I. Rawlings (1991). Bonding with abusive dating partners: Dynamics of Stockholm Syndrome. In Barrie Levy (Ed.) *Dating Violence: Young Women in Danger* (119–135). Seattle, WA: Seal Press.

18. For example, research indicates that relationships are ripe for maltreatment when men and women, respectively, assume dominant and submissive roles. Peter J. Burke, Jan E. Stets & Maureen A. Pirog-Good (1989). Gender identity, self-esteem, and physical and sexual abuse. In Maureen A. Pirog-Good & Jan E. Stets (Eds.) *Violence in Dating Relationships: Emerging Social Issues* (72–93). NY: Praeger. Extensive research indicates that these roles are intensified during adolescence, as youth tend to conform to extreme stereotypic gender roles. Nancy L. Galambos, David M. Almeida & Anne C. Peterson (1990). Masculinity, femininity, and sex role attitudes in early adolescence: Exploring Gender Intensification, *Child Development* 61, 1905–1914; Ann C. Crouter, Beth A. Manke & Susan M. McHale (1995). The family context of gender intensification in early adolescence, *Child Development* 66, 317–326. Intensified gender roles result in the expectation that in romantic relationships, girls are to be supportive and responsible for the success (and failure) of the relationships. Roger J. R. Levesque (1993). The romantic experiences of adolescents in satisfying love relationships, *Journal of Youth and Adolescence* 22, 219–251. Thus, adolescent relationships may be more prone to maltreatment because of intensified sexism seemingly inherent in gender norms and because of limits placed on adolescents that make victims responsible for relationship maintenance. Research reveals that adolescent relationships tend to generate the expectation that young women are "gatekeepers" and young men are the "initiators" of sexual intimacy. This adversarial approach to intimacy has been linked to other forms of relationship violence, such as youths' tendency to believe that males may be justified in their use of force to obtain sex in dating situations. Beverly Miller (1988). Date rape: Time for a new look at prevention, *Journal of College Student Development* 29, 535–555. In addition to intensified gender roles and the tendency to exhibit acceptance for traditional gender roles, adolescent partners' dependency on each other for social acceptance and self-esteem places them at risk for violence. Adolescence is marked by attempts to conform to peer norms

and pressure to be involved in relationships. Susan Moore & Doreen Rosenthal (1993). *Sexuality in Adolescence.* NY: Routledge; Thomas J. Berndt & Richard C. Savin-Williams (1993). Peer relations and friendships. In Patrick H. Tolan & Bertram J. Cohler (Eds.) *Handbook of Clinical Research and Practice with Adolescents* (203–219). NY: Wiley. These social demands placed on adolescents, especially the need for conformity, render teens susceptible to battering.

19. Lenore E. Walker (1989). Psychology and violence against women, *American Psychologist* 44, 695–702.

20. Vangie A. Foshee (1996). Gender differences in adolescent dating abuse prevalence, types and injuries, *Health Education Research: Theory & Practice* 11, 275–286.

21. Jeffrey Arnett (1995). The young and the reckless: Adolescent reckless behavior, *Current Directions in Psychological Science* 4, 67–71. A common manifestation of these normal developments is experimentation with prohibited substances. Adolescent experimentation with these substances and attempts to "do adult things" invariably increase the risk of relationship violence. Research indicates that alcohol and drug use are associated highly with abusive episodes. James M. Makepeace (1987). Social factor and victim-offender differences in courtship violence, *Family Relations* 36, 87–91. Although the use of alcohol and drugs may not cause the violence, they clearly help intensify abuse. Sugarman & Hotaling (1989) *supra.* Evidence that alcohol has been a consistent risk marker for dating violence and that adolescents are beginning to experiment and control their exposure to alcohol, then, suggests adolescents are at increased risk for relationship violence.

22. Patricia Noller & Victor Callan (1991). *The Adolescent in the Family.* NY: Routledge. However, youth rely on families for important sources of support. Robert M. Galatzer-Levy & Bertram J. Cohler (1993). *The Essential Other: A Developmental Psychology of Self.* NY: Basic Books.

23. Turning to families may be more difficult for youth from cultures in which dating and sexuality, as well as alternative forms of relationships, are restricted and may be possible sources of shame. Caroline K. Waterman, Lori J. Dawson & Michael J. Bologna (1989). Sexual coercion in gay male and lesbian relationships: Predictors and implications for support services, *Journal of Sex Research* 26, 118–124. Feelings of shame and helplessness play a decisive role in keeping adolescents from seeking assistance from familial sources, as reflected in the high number of youth who do not even disclose the sexual nature of dating relationships to parents who comfortably discuss sexuality. Roger J. R. Levesque (1996). The peculiar place of adolescents in the HIV-AIDS epidemic: Unusual progress & usual inadequacies in "Adolescent Jurisprudence," *Loyola University Chicago Law Journal* 27, 701–739. To complicate matters even further, if parents do intervene when they suspect abusive behavior, there is the danger that intervention will reinforce the romantic bond. Richard Driscoll, Keith E. Davis & Milton Lipetz (1972). Parental interference and romantic love: The Romeo and Juliet Effect, *Journal of Personality and Social Psychology* 24, 1–10.

24. Levesque (1996) *supra.*

25. Levesque (1993) *supra.*

26. Sugarman & Hotaling (1989) *supra.*

27. Faced with life-threatening situations, adolescents are prone to deny, rather than confront and systematically deal with the situation. Levesque (1996) *supra.*

28. David R. Jezl, Christian E. Molidor & Tracy L. Wright (1996). Physical, sex-

ual and psychological abuse in high school dating relationships: Prevalence rates and self-esteem issues, *Child and Adolescent Social Work Journal* 13, 69–87.

29. James M. Makepeace (1989). Dating, living together, and courtship violence. In Maureen A. Pirog-Good & Jan E. Stets (Eds.) *Violence in Dating Relationships: Emerging Social Issues* (94–107). NY: Praeger. At 106. Episodes become more injurious in the later stages of courtship, when relationship investment increases and leaving the relationship becomes difficult. Mary Reige Laner (1989). Competition and combativeness in courtship: Reports from men, *Journal of Family Violence* 4, 47–62. Given that even the normal process of breaking up involves very sophisticated maneuvering, it should be no surprise that the process of breaking from violent and dependent relationships is even more intensified and more likely to lead to harm. Evidence from adult victims of abuse are illustrative. Separated battered women report being battered fourteen times as often as women still living with their partners; Caroline Wolfe Harlow (1991). *Female Victims of Violent Crime.* Washington, DC: Bureau of Justice Statistics. In addition, a battered woman's chance of being killed by her partner rises more than thirtyfold after she leaves him. George W. Barnard, Hernan Vera, Maria I. Vera, & Gustave Newman (1982). Till death do us part: A study of spouse murder, *Bulletin of the American Academy of Psychiatry and the Law* 10, 271–280.

30. Phyllis Goldfarb (1996). Describing without circumscribing: Questioning the construction of gender in the discourse of intimate violence, *George Washington Law Review* 64, 582–631. Suzanne Pharr (1988). *Homophobia: A Weapon of Sexism.* Little Rock, AR: Chardon Press; Claire M. Renzetti (1992). *Violent Betrayal: Partner Abuse in Lesbian Relationships.* Newbury Park, CA: Sage.

31. Richard Gelles (1988). Violence and pregnancy: Are pregnant women at greater risk of abuse? *Journal of Marriage and the Family* 50, 841–847; Judith McFarlane (1989). Battering in pregnancy: The tip of the iceberg, *Women and Health* 15, 69–84.

32. Barrie Levy (1993). *In Love and in Danger: A Teen's Guide to Breaking Free of Abusive Relationships.* Seattle, WA: Seal Press. Existing research lends some support to the proposition that battering teenagers tend to report their behavior to peer groups and actually receive support for it. Martin S. Keseredy (1988). Women abuse in dating relationships: The relevance of social support theory, *Journal of Family Violence* 3, 1–14. The link between media and adolescent violence remains less clear. Victor C. Strasburger (1995). *Adolescents and the Media: Medical and Psychological Impact.* Thousand Oaks, CA: Sage. However, media portrayals of adolescent relationships do tend to be adversarial. Monique L. Ward (1995). Talking about sex: Common themes about sexuality in the prime-time television programs children and adolescents view most, *Journal of Youth and Adolescence* 24, 595–615. Media portrayals do have an impact on youths' views of dating violence. James D. Johnson, Mike S. Adams, Leslie Ashburn & William Reed (1995). Differential gender effects of exposure to rap music on African American adolescents' acceptance of teen dating violence, *Sex Roles* 33, 597–605.

33. This research receives support from extensive investigations of the development of antisocial behavior. Considerable research indicates that child-rearing environments marked by negative affect and use of arbitrary, restrictive, and punitive parenting strategies fail to promote cooperative or healthy relationships; nor do they foster empathic or altruistic responses to and from others. Kenneth A. Dodge, Gregory S. Petit, & John E. Bates (1994). Effects of physical maltreatment on development of

peer relations, *Development and Psychopathology* 6, 43–55; Scott Feldman & Geraldine Downey (1994). Rejection sensitivity as a mediator of the impact of childhood exposure to family violence on adult attachment behavior, *Development and Psychopathology* 6, 231–247; Fred A. Rogosch, Dante Cicchetti & J. Lawrence Aber (1995). The role of child maltreatment in early deviations in cognitive and affective processing abilities and later peer relationship problems, *Development and Psychopathology* 7, 591–609. These relational styles continue to be linked to antisocial behavior, including domestic violence. Theodore Dix (1991). The affective organization of parenting: Adaptive and maladaptive processes, *Psychological Bulletin* 110, 3–25; S. Vuchinich, L. Bank & G. R. Patterson (1992). Parenting, peers, and the stability of antisocial behavior in preadolescent boys, *Developmental Psychology* 28, 510–521; Matthew T. Greenberg, Mark L. Speltx & Michelle DeKlyen (1993). The role of attachment in early development of disruptive behavior problems, *Development and Psychopathology* 5, 191–213.

34. See Roger J. R. Levesque (1997). Dating violence, adolescents, and the law, *Virginia Journal of Social Policy and Law* 4, 339–379.

35. For reviews, see N. Zoe Hilton (Ed.) (1993). *Legal Responses to Wife Assault.* Newbury Park, CA: Sage; Albert R. Roberts (Ed.) *Helping Battered Women: New Perspectives and Remedies.* NY: Oxford University Press.

36. The exclusion effectively prohibits youth from obtaining relief from truly remarkable legal developments that aim to curb the incidence of violence and assist victims through harnessing the powers and resources of the legal system. For example, in the context of dating violence, youth cannot benefit from several statutory reforms, such as mandatory arrest policies in domestic violence situations, restraining order violations, and more stringent penalties for batterers. Likewise, the exclusion also means that maltreated adolescents may not avail themselves of critical services organized and funded by the state to care for domestic violence victims, including domestic violence shelters and nonresidential programs that provide referrals, medical assistance, and counseling. In addition, and perhaps even more importantly, most states offer guardians ad litem, mandate the use of simplified forms or offer other assistance in filing petitions when *adults* are victimized by relationship violence.

37. See Roger J. R. Levesque (1997). Dating violence, adolescents, and the law, *Virginia Journal of Social Policy and Law* 4, 339–379.

38. Id.

39. Id.

40. These state statutes do not address how orders are to be enforced against minor defendants. The failure to clarify the nature of enforcement has important consequences. For example, the statutes fail to indicate whether minors can be held in criminal contempt, and if so, whether such cases must be adjudicated in juvenile court. If minors are adjudicated in juvenile courts, the proceedings and dispositions tend to be more informal and flexible than those of criminal courts. The result is that the current focus on holding batterers accountable by relying on aggressive law enforcement is not practicable for adolescents.

41. Arguably, minors will be adjudicated in criminal courts only when charges are brought in states with criminal domestic violence statutes. This is important, given that some states define victims of domestic violence differently in civil and criminal statutes. For example, different age or relationship requirements may be imposed in civil or criminal statutes. Several states limit the use of criminal codes by imposing age or relationship requirements that they do not require for civil codes. On

the other hand, some states have more inclusive criminal codes. Despite these differences, it remains unclear how juveniles will be adjudicated.

42. For example, domestic violence statutes clearly reflect a trend toward a "preferred arrest policy." J. David Hirschel & Ira Hutchinson (1991). Police-preferred arrest policies. In Michael Steinman (Ed.) *Woman Battering: Policy Responses* (49–72). Cincinnati, OH: Anderson.

43. Thus, behaviors may include sexual comments, looks or gestures, sexual touching, offensive sexual advances, solicitation of sexual activity, coercion of sexual activity, sexual assault, and physical violence based on the person's sexuality. Judith Berman Brandenburg (1997). *Confronting Sexual Harassment: What Schools and Colleges Can Do.* NY: Teachers College Press.

44. This tends to be the approach adopted by courts. For a review of definitions, see Stacey R. Rinestine (1994). Terrorism on the Playground: What can be done? *Duquesne Law Review* 32, 799–832.

45. See Connie C. Flores (1997). The Fourteenth Amendment and Title IX: A solution to peer sexual harassment, *St. Mary's Law Journal* 29, 153–206.

46. See Jehan A. Abel-Gawad (1997). Kiddie sex harassment: How Title IX could level the playing field without leveling the playground, *Arizona Law Review* 39, 727–768.

47. Sexual harassment guidance, harassment of students by school employees, other students, or third parties, *Federal Register* 62, 12034–12040 (12038).

48. The Canadian study revealed that 60 to 65 percent of victims have been "touched, grabbed or pinched in a sexual way." Chantal Richard (1996). Surviving student to student sexual harassment: Legal remedies and prevention programs, *Dalhousie Law Journal* 19, 169–197. 174.

49. There still remains the difficulty of recognizing visual harassment, such as leering or staring, or displaying demeaning graffiti and pornographic materials. Yet, these can clearly be involved in sexually harassing behavior.

50. Richard (1996) *supra.* Eighty percent of female students had experienced sexual harassment. While the problem appears to be widespread at the high school level, most students begin to experience sexually harassing behavior in elementary and junior high schools. The study also reports that 90 percent of incidents occur in school hallways, but classrooms, school transportation, and cafeterias commonly provide contexts for victimization.

51. Carrie M. H. Herbert (1989). *Talking of Silence: The Sexual Harassment of Schoolgirls.* NY: Falmer Press.

52. The foundational study was conducted and reported by the American Association of University Women (1993). *Hostile Hallways: The AAUW Survey on Sexual Harassment in America's Schools.* For are review of studies, see Brandenburg (1997) *supra.*

53. Id. at 7.

54. Id. Of that group, 44 percent were boys.

55. Id. Sixty-six percent of the boys and 52 percent of the girls surveyed admitted to perpetration. AAUW (1993) *supra.*

56. Valerie E. Lee, Robert G. Croninger, Eleanor Linn & Xianglei Chen (1996). The culture of sexual harassment in secondary schools, *American Educational Research Journal* 33, 383–417.

57. Researchers and commentators assume girls to be the only victims of har-

assing behavior. Herbert (1989); June Larkin (1994). Walking through walls: The sexual harassment of high school girls, *Gender and Education* 6, 263–280; Lee & Coninger (1996) *supra*.

58. AAUW (1993) *supra* (16–17).

59. Id. at 18.

60. One-third of the girls and 13 percent of the boys reported these reactions. Id. at 18.

61. Study cited in Richard (1996) *supra*.

62. Vita C. Rabinowitz (1990). Coping with sexual harassment. In Michelle A. Paludi (Ed.) *Ivory Power: Sexual Harassment on Campus* (103–118). Albany, NY: State University of New York Press. The syndrome includes the following symptoms: general depression, as manifested by changes in eating and sleeping patterns, and vague complaints of aches and pains that prevent the student from attending class or completing work; undefined dissatisfaction with class; sense of powerlessness, help-lessness, and vulnerability; loss of academic self-confidence and decline in academic performance; feelings of isolation from other students; irritability with family and friends; fear and anxiety; inability to concentrate, etc. Id. 112–113.

63. Herbert (1989) *supra*.

64. AAUW (1993) *supra*.

65. Herbert (1989) *supra*.

66. June Larkin (1994). Walking through walls: The sexual harassment of high school girls, *Gender and Education* 6, 263–280.

67. Girls are taught to look for approval for their appearance in a culture that consistently sanctions the treatment of women as sexual objects. Peggy Orenstein (1994). *School Girls: Young Women, Self-esteem and the Confidence Gap*. NY: Doubleday.

68. Harassment based on sexual orientation uniquely effects several youth. Gay and lesbian students can be hurt by the behavior even when they are not singled out as the object of homophobic harassment. For example, homophobic slurs against students based on sexual stereotypes are common and indirectly affect the homosexual students who witness the behaviors. Kelli Kristine Armstrong (1994). The silent minority within a minority: Focusing on the needs of gay youth in our public schools, *Golden Gate University Law Review* 41, 67–97. James W. Button, Barbara A. Rienzo & Kenneth D. Wald (1997). *Private Lives, Public Conflicts: Battles over Gay Rights in American Communities*. Washington, DC: Congressional Quarterly Press.

69. For example, school personnel dismiss harassing behavior as normal courtship, even when the youth are not dating. Nan Stein (1995). Sexual harassment in school: The public performance of gendered violence, *Harvard Educational Review* 65, 145–162.

70. Lee, Croninger, Linn & Chen (1996) *supra*.

71. Lin Farley (1978). *Sexual Shakedown: The Sexual Harassment of Women on the Job*. NY: Warner Books.

72. However, the typical image of student sexual harassment continues to be lecherous professors who demand sexual favors in return for grades. Billie Wright Dziech & Linda Weiner (1990). *The Lecherous Professor: Sexual Harassment on Campus* (2nd ed.). Chicago: University of Illinois Press. Student-to-student harass-ment remains more frequent, up to four times more likely. An American study suggests that students are four times more likely to be harassed by other students than by school employees. AAUW (1993) *supra*.

73. Numerous articles now champion a need to recognize and more appropriately respond to peer sexual harassment. See Verna L. Williams & Deborah L. Brake (1997). When a kiss isn't just a kiss: Title IX and student-to-student harassment, *Creighton Law Review* 30, 423–456; Alexandra A. Bodnar (1996). Arming students for battle: Amending Title IX to combat the sexual harassment of students by students in primary and secondary school, *Southern California Review of Law and Women's Studies* 5, 549–589; Karen Mellencamp Davis (1994). Reading, writing, and sexual Harassment: Finding a constitutional remedy when schools fail to address peer abuse, *Indiana Law Journal* 69, 1123–1163; Kirsten M. Eriksson (1995). What our children are really learning in school: Using Title IX to combat peer sexual harassment, *Georgetown Law Journal* 83, 1799–1820; Carrie N. Baker (1994). Proposed Title IX guidelines on sex-based harassment of students, *Emory Law Journal* 43, 271–323; Monica L. Sherer (1993). No longer child's play: School liability under Title IX for peer sexual harassment, *University of Pennsylvania Law Review* 141, 2119–2168.

74. Id.

75. Herbert (1989) *supra.*

76. Although few schools and school districts have such policies, some have begun to address the issue. Some districts have started sexual harassment prevention programs. Likewise, schools recently have enacted policies to deal with abuse once it has occurred. See Amy M. Rubin (1997). Peer sexual harassment: Existing harassment doctrine and its application to school children, *Hastings Women's Law Journal* 8, 141–158.

77. For example, literature on the experiences of gay youths' relationships with their parents reveals a high degree of rejection and harassment. Sonia Renee Martin (1996). A child's right to be gay: Addressing the emotional maltreatment of queer youth, *Hastings Law Journal* 48, 167–196.

78. *Doe. v. Petaluma City School District*, 830 F. Supp. 1560 (N.D. Cal. 1993).

79. Karen Mellencamp Davis (1994). Reading, writing, and sexual harassment: Finding a constitutional remedy when schools fail to address peer abuse, *Indiana Law Journal* 69, 1123–1163; Kirsten M. Eriksson (1995). What our children are really learning in school: Using Title IX to combat peer sexual harassment, *Georgetown Law Journal* 83, 1799–1820; Carrie N. Baker (1994). Proposed Title IX guidelines on sex-based harassment of students, *Emory Law Journal* 43, 271–323; Monica L. Sherer (1993). No longer child's play: School liability under Title IX for peer sexual harassment, *University of Pennsylvania Law Review* 141, 2119–2168.

80. Helena K. Dolan (1994). The fourth R—Respect: Combatting peer harassment in the public schools, *Fordham Law Review* 63, 223–245; Ashley Smith (1997). Students hurting students: Who will pay? *Houston Law Review* 34, 579–607; Robert L. Phillips (1995). Peer abuse in public schools: Should schools be liable for student to student injuries under section 1983? *Brigham Young University Law Review* 1995, 237–267; Stephanie Easland (1994). Attacking the "boys will be boys" attitude: School liability under section 1983 for per sexual harassment, *Journal of Juvenile Law* 15, 119–149.

81. The major case is *Franklin v. Gwinnett County Public Schools*, 911 F. 2d 617 (11th Cir. 1990), which dealt with student and teacher harassment. See Williams and Brake (1997) *supra.* See Joseph Beckham (1996). Liability for sexual harassment involving students under federal civil rights law, *Education Law Reporter* 4, 521–533.

82. For a similar analysis and recommendation for an amendment to Title IX

that would require sexual harassment policies in primary and secondary schools, see Bodnar (1996) *supra*.

83. For a review of these cases, see Smith (1997) *supra*; Bodnar (1996) *supra*; Bechkam (1996) *supra*.

84. Jeff Horner (1996). A student's right to protection form violence or sexual abuse by other students, *Educational Law Reporter* 4, 110–114. 114.

85. See JoAnn Strauss (1992). Peer sexual harassment of high school students: A reasonable student standard and an affirmative duty imposed on educational institutions, *Law and Inequality* 10, 163–186. Some propose that the unwelcomeness standard simply should not apply to children's relationships. See Rubin (1997) *supra*; Bodnar (1996) *supra*.

86. For reviews of important cases, see *supra*.

87. Lee, Croninger, Linn & Chen (1996) *supra*.

88. Id.

89. These states are California, Cal Educ. Code § 48900.2 (West 1995); Minnesota, Minn. Stat. § 127.46 (West 1994); Florida, Fla. Stat. Ann. § 230.23 (West 1996); Washington, Wash. Rev. Stat. Ann. §Sec. 28A.640.020 (West 1996); and Michigan, Mich. Comp. Laws Ann. § 380.1300A (West 1996).

90. Minnesota Statute § 127.46 (West 1997).

91. Washington Revised Code § 28A.640.020(2)(a)–(f) (West 1997).

92. Abdel-Gawad (1997) *supra*.

93. Id.

94. Martin D. Schwartz & Walter S. DeKeseredy (1997). *Sexual Assault on the College Campus: The Role of Male Peer Support*. Thousand Oaks, CA: Sage.

95. Mary P. Koss (1989). Hidden rape: Sexual aggression and victimization in a national sample of students in higher education. In Maureen A. Pirog-Good & Jan E. Stets (Eds). *Violence in Dating Relationships: Emerging Social Issues* (145–168). NY: Praeger.

96. In Canada, for example, only four out of ten sexual assaults involve adults; see infra section on Canada. See also Barrie Levy (Ed.) (1991). *Dating Violence: Young Women in Danger*, Seattle, WA: Seal Press; Johnson & Sigler (1997) *supra*.

97. Suzanne S. Ageton (1988). Vulnerability to sexual assault. In Ann Wolbert Burgess (Ed.) *Rape and Sexual Assault II* (221–244). NY: Garland,

98. Reports from the 1950s indicate that 62 percent of women reported sexually assaultive victimization during their last year of high school dating and 21 percent of those acts involved attempted or completed forced intercourse. Eugene Kanin (1957). Male aggression in dating-courtship relations, *Journal of Sociology* 63, 197–204. These findings have been highly cited and replicated through other studies and national samples. See Ida M. Johnson & Robert T. Sigler (1997). *Forced Sexual Intercourse in Intimate Relationships*. Brookfield, VT: Ashgate. Stephen A. Small & Donell Kerns (1993). Unwanted sexual activity among peers during early and middle adolescence: Incidence and risk factors, *Journal of Marriage and the Family* 55, 941–952; Melissa J. Himelein, Ron E. Vogel & Dale G. Wachowiak (1994). Nonconsensual sexual experiences in precollege women: Prevalence and risk factors, *Journal of Counseling and Development* 72, 411–415.

99. A major criticism charges that studies use very broad definitions of assault. For example, the most comprehensive and influential study that focused on women indexed all unwanted or nonconsensual sexual acts and assaults as part of rape, even

though the women involved did not classify them as such. See Neil Gilbert (1992). Realities and mythologies of rape, *Society* 29, 4–10.

100. In a study of high school students, nearly half of the sample of students reported forced sexual experiences ranging from forced kissing to sexual intercourse. Jill Rhynard, Marlene Krevs & Julie Glover (1997). Sexual assault in dating relationships, *Journal of School Health* 67(3), 89–93. See also David R. Jexl, Christian E. Milidor & Tracy L. Wright (1996). Physical, sexual and psychological abuse in high school dating relationships: Prevalence rates and self-esteem issues, *Child and Adolescent Social Work Journal* 13, 69–87.

101. Terry C. Davis, Gary Q. Peck & John M. Storment (1993). Acquaintance rape and the high school student, *Journal of Adolescent Health* 12, 220–224.

102. Davis, Peck & Storment (1993) *supra*. For example, if she led him on, 36 percent m and 18 percent f agree that the boy can coerce sex; if she got him sexually excited, 37 percent m and 23 percent f; if they had sex before, 39 percent m and 12 percent f; if she wore revealing clothing, 27 percent m and 9 percent f. See also Susan K. Telljohann, James H. Price, Jodi Summers, Sherry A. Everett & Suzanne Casler (1995). High school students' perceptions of nonconsensual sexual activity, *Journal of School Health* 65(3), 107–112.

103. Id. For an analysis of these studies in legal contexts, see Steven I. Friedland (1991). Date rape and the culture of acceptance, *Florida Law Review* 43, 487–527.

104. Jeanne Boxley, Lynette Lawrance & Harvey Gruchow (1995). A preliminary study of eighth grade students' attitudes toward rape myths and women's roles, *Journal of School Health* 65, 96–100; Linda Cassidy & Rose Marie Hurell (1995). The influence of victim's attire on adolescents' judgments of date rape, *Adolescence* 30, 319–323. For a review, see Paul Pollard (1992). Judgements about victims and attackers in depicted rapes: A review, *British Journal of Social Psychology* 31, 307–326.

105. Martin D. Schwartz & Victoria L. Pitts (1995). Exploring a feminist routine activities approach to explaining sexual assault, *Justice Quarterly* 12, 9–31.

106. See Martin D. Schwartz & Walter S. DeKeseredy (1997). *Sexual Assault on the College Campus: The role of Male Peer Support*. Thousand Oaks, CA: Sage.

107. A characteristic found across several large-sample studies is acceptance of interpersonal aggression. For a review, see Mary E. Craig (1990). Coercive sexuality in dating relationships: A situational model, *Clinical Psychology Review* 10, 395–423. In this context, an important and growing area of research links early socialization experiences, particularly in the contexts of peer groups, and the development of rape supportive attitudes and cultures. For a thorough analysis of rape supportive cultures in the lives of college students, see Schwartz & DeKeseredy (1997) *supra*.

108. Friedland (1991) *supra*.

109. Victoria L. Pitts & Martin D. Schwartz (1993). Promoting self-blame among hidden rape survivors, *Humanity & Society* 17, 383–398.

110. Carol K. Sigelman, Carol J. Berry & Katharine A. Wiles (1984). Violence in college students' dating relationships, *Journal of Applied Social Psychology* 14, 530–548.

111. For a review, see Linda Brookover Bourque (1989). *Defining Rape*. Durham, NC: Duke University Press.

112. For example, victims engaged in unwanted relations may ignore the request, plead indisposition, remain passive, and adopt a variety of survival strategies; their partners may take these signs as consent, or at least acquiescence.

113. Jurors rely on their own social conditioning and gender biases to interpret relevant (and irrelevant) nonverbal cues. For example, to determine whether a situation is coercive, the presence of physical force is often used as a linchpin. See, for example, a study of 360 jurors who had decided rape cases that confirms the considerable role of latent gender bias in decision-making. Gary D. LaFree (1989). *Rape and Criminal Justice: The Social Construction of Social Sexual Assault.* Belmont, CA: Wadsworth. Robin Warsaw (1988). *I Never Called It Rape: The Ms. Report on Recognizing, Fighting, and Surviving Date and Acquaintance Rape.* NY: Harper & Row.

114. Linda A. Fairstein (1993). *Sexual Violence: Our War against Rape.* NY: William Morrow.

115. New Jersey stands as a prime example. See *In Re M. T. S.,* 609 A.2d 1266 (1992).

116. Cheryl A. Whitney (1996). Non-stranger, non-consensual assaults: Changing legislation to ensure that acts are criminally punished, *Rutgers Law Journal* 27, 417–445.

117. Garthe E. Hire (1996). Holding husbands and lovers accountable for rape: Eliminating the "defendant" exception of rape shield laws, *Review of Law and Women's Studies* 5, 591–610.

118. Susan Estrich (1987). *Real Rape.* Cambridge: Harvard University Press; Beverly Balos & Mary Louise Fellows (1991). Guilty of the crime of trust: Non-stranger rape, *Minnesota Law Review* 75, 599–619; Friedland (1991) *supra*; John Dwight Ingram (1993). Date rape: It's time for "No" to really mean "No," *American Journal of Criminal Law* 21, 3–36; Karen M. Kramer (1994). Rule by myth: The social and legal dynamics governing alcohol-related acquaintance rapes, *Stanford Law Review* 47, 115–160.

119. Johnson & Sigler (1997) *supra*.

120. Jeanne C. Marsh, Allison Geist & Nathan Caplan (1992). *Rape and the Limits of Law Reform.* Boston: Auburn House; Cassia Spohn & Julie Horney (1992). *Rape Law Reform: A Grassroots Revolution and Its Impact.* NY: Plenum; Gregory M. Matoesian (1993). *Reproducing Rape: Domination through Talk in the Courtroom.* Cambridge: Polity Press. See also Ronet Bachman & Raymond Paternoster (1993). A contemporary look at the effects of rape law reform: How far have we really come? *Journal of Criminal Law and Criminology* 81, 554–74.

121. Id. Not all forms of rape are viewed similarly. The image of "real rape" is one in which a stranger puts a gun to the head of his victim, threatens to kill or beat her, and then forces her to engage in intercourse. The victim looks like a "real rape" victim: bruises, cuts, and torn clothing indicate struggle, resistance, and lack of consent. Susan Estrich (1987) *supra*. Despite rape law reform, police still fail to view non-physically coercive sexual experiences as rapes; they tend to regard these assaults as false or simply believe that the victim precipitated the rape. Lani A. Remik (1992). Read her lips: An argument for a verbal consent standard in rape, *University of Pennsylvania Law Review* 141, 1103–1151. The "one-on-one" nature of the crime, victim credibility, and reluctance of victims to pursue prosecution to completion create practical problems, even to the extent that some police and prosecutors discourage victims from pressing charges. That they do so has been well documented; see Marsh et al. (1982) *supra*. Importantly, without proper recognition, juries will not address violence properly either. Victims who have been sexually active, despite the direction the laws have taken, are viewed as being of "questionable moral character" and are not believed. Fairstein (1993) *supra*. Victims' behaviors, even including dating and talk-

ing with men at parties, make juries hesitant to convict. See Estrich (1987) *supra*. The result is an undeniable "acquaintance discount:" those who rape nonstrangers actually face a 35 percent decrease in the rates of arrest, prosecution and conviction. Jennifer K. Trucano (1993). Force, consent and victims' rights: How state of New Jersey in Re M. T. S. reinterprets rape statutes, *South Dakota Law Review* 38, 203–225. 204. See also Bachman & Paternoster (1993) *supra*.

122. Kathleen F. Cairney (1995). Addressing acquaintance rape: The new direction of the rape law reform movement, *St. John's Law Review* 69, 291–326.

123. See Longsway and Fitzgerald (1994) *supra*. For a similar analysis in the context of harassment, see Herbert (1989). Talking of silence, *supra*.

124. Estrich (1987) *supra*.

125. For a list of statues, see Whitney (1996) *supra*, n. 108.

126. Lynne Henderson (1992). Rape and responsibility, *Law and Philosophy* 11, 127–178.

127. Monica L. Oberman (1994). Turning girls into women: Re-evaluating modern statutory rape law, *Journal of Criminal Law & Criminology* 85, 15–79.

128. If aggression and submission are part of what is "normal" seduction, then pressured sex is viewed as consensual. Some contend that it is not reasonable for a women to agree to coerced or pressured sex. For example, if the sexual encounter is not communicative, then the woman cannot consent and it is unreasonable for the offender to assume consent. See Lois Pineau (1989). Date rape: A feminist analysis, *Law and Philosophy* 8, 217–43; David M. Adams (1996). Date rape and erotic discourse. In Leslie Francis (Ed.) *Date Rape: Feminism, Philosophy, and the Law* (27–39). University Park: Pennsylvania State University Press. Others propose that it is paternalistic to assume that communication is the only way for a woman to consent to sexual activity. Id. Likewise, there is still the real possibility that even with communication, the communication and consent undoubtedly could take place, as several have argued, against a background of the use of sexuality as a means of oppression and disempowerment of women. Catharine MacKinnon (1991). Reflections on sex and equality under law, *Yale Law Journal* 100, 1281–328. The model also has been challenged as inappropriately essentialist: it assumes one model of "good sex." Catherine Pierce Wells (1996). Date rape and the law: Another feminist view. In Leslie Francis (Ed.) *Date Rape: Feminism, Philosophy, and the Law* (41–50) *supra*. Clearly, the communicative approach assumes a paradigm of liberal autonomy: people understand, communicate, think, and rethink their goals. This Kantian approach has been challenged, particularly from a communitarian perspective. See Michael Sandel (1982). *Liberalism and the Limits of Justice*. NY: Cambridge University Press. The models of self as freely choosing and rechoosing ends does not necessarily apply well to adolescents and children, for whom the contexts in which sexual relationships occur are multiple and necessarily determined by power dynamics.

129. Oberman (1994) *supra*. Heidi Kitrosser (1997). Meaningful consent: Toward a new generation of statutory rape laws, *Virginia Journal of Social Policy & the Law* 4, 287–338.

130. Oberman (1994) *supra*.

131. Kimberly A. Longsway & Louise F. Fitzgerald (1994). Rape myths: A review, *Psychology of Women Quarterly* 18, 133–164.

132. Maryanne Lyons (1992). Adolescents in jeopardy: An analysis of Texas' promiscuity defense for sexual assault, *Houston Law Review* 29, 583–632. Note, however, that these reforms have not affected defense attorneys' trial tactics; see

Andrew E. Taslitz (1996). Patriarchal stories I: Cultural rape narratives in the court-room, *Southern California Review of Law and Women's Studies* 5, 389–500.
133. Alice Susan Andre-Clark (1992). Whither statutory rape laws: of *Michael M.*, the Fourteenth Amendment, and protecting women from sexual aggression, *Southern California Law Review* 65, 1933–1992.
134. Nicole A. Rapp (1994). Teenage sex in California: Thirteen years after *Michael M.*, *Journal of Juvenile Law* 15, 197–221.
135. Davis & Leitenberg (1987) *supra*. Mary Ellen Fromuth, Barry R. Burkhart & Catherine Webb Jones (1991). Hidden child molestation: An investigation of adolescent perpetrators in a nonclinical sample, *Journal of Interpersonal Violence* 6, 376–384; Wayne R. Smith & Caren Monastersky (1986). Assessing juvenile offenders' risk for re-offending, *Criminal Justice and Behavior* 13, 115–140; Eileen Vizard, Elizabeth Monck & Peter Misch (1995). Child and adolescent sexual abuse perpetrators: A review of the research literature, *Journal of Child Psychology and Psychiatry* 36, 731–756.
136. Gail Ryan, Thomas J. Miyoshi, Jeffrey L. Metzner, Richard D. Krugman & George Fryer (1996). Trends in a national sample of sexually abusive youths, *Journal of the American Academy of Child and Adolescent Psychiatry* 35, 17–25. See also Glen E. Davis & Harrold Leitenberg (1987). Adolescent sex offenders, *Psychological Bulletin* 101, 417–427; T. Kempton & R. Forehand (1992). Juvenile sex offenders: Similar to, different from other incarcerated delinquent offenders? *Behavior Research and Therapy* 30, 533–536; Robert Dube & Martin Hebert (1988). Sexual abuse of children under 12 years of age: A review of 511 cases, *Child Abuse & Neglect* 12, 321–330.
137. For example, a recent catchment study that included all reported sex crimes for one year in Liverpool, England, found that adolescents and preadolescents perpetrate far more sexual abuse than any comparable age groupings. David Glasgow, Louise Horne, Rachel Calam & Antony Cox (1994). Evidence, incidence, gender and age in sexual abuse of children perpetrated by children, *Child Abuse Review* 3, 196–219.
138. Michael L. Bourke & Brad Donohue (1996). Assessment and treatment of juvenile sex offenders: An empirical review, *Journal of Child Sexual Abuse* 5, 47–70; Mary Ellen Fromuth, Barry R. Bukhart & Charlene Webb Jones (1991). Hidden child molestation: An investigation of adolescent perpetrators in a non-clinical sample, *Journal of Interpersonal Violence* 6, 376–384.
139. For groundbreaking research in this area, see A. Nicholas Groth, Robert E. Longo & J. Bradley McFaddin (1982). Undetected recidivism among rapists and child molesters, *Crime and Delinquency* 28, 450–458.
140. Peter A. Fehrenbach, Wayne Smith, Caren Monastersky & Robert W. Deisher (1986). Adolescent sexual offenders: Offender and offense characteristics, *American Journal of Orthopsychiatry* 56, 225–233.
141. Id. Davis & Harrold Leitenberg (1987) *supra*. According to other researchers, the percentage of female offenders actually may be higher, as revealed by female offenders who admit offenses for which they have not been identified. Timothy J. Kahn & M. A. Lanfond (1988). Treatment of the adolescent sex offender, *Child and Adolescent Social Work* 5, 135–148. Importantly, when girls do offend, they are likely to do so with male co-offenders. Peter A. Fehrenbach & Caren Monastersky (1988). Characteristics of female adolescent sexual offenders, *American Journal of Orthopsychiatry* 58, 148–151.

142. Fehrenbach, Smith, Monastersky & Deisher (1986) *supra*; Judith Becker, Jerry Cunningham-Rathner & Meg S. Kaplan (1986). Adolescent sexual offenders, *Journal of Interpersonal Violence* 1, 431–435. Richard J. Kavoussi, Meg Kaplan & Judith V. Becker (1988). Psychiatric diagnoses in adolescent sex offenders, *Journal of the American Academy of Child and Adolescent Psychiatry* 27, 241–243.

143. Davis & Leitenberg (1987) *supra*.

144. Samples finding incestuous relationships range from 40 to 60 percent. Toni Cavanagh Johnson (1988). Child perpetrators: Children who molest other children: Preliminary findings, *Child Abuse & Neglect* 12, 219–229; Lois H. Pierce & Robert L. Pierce (1987). Incestuous victimization by juvenile sex offenders, *Journal of Family Violence* 2, 351–364. For example, in a study of 350 young sex offenders, 95 percent of victims were either siblings or children for whom the offender was babysitting. Kahn & Lanfond (1988) *supra*. See also Leslie Margolin & John L. Craft (1990). Child abuse by adolescent caregivers, *Child Abuse & Neglect* 14, 365–373.

145. Id.

146. Judith V. Becker (1988). The effects of child sexual abuse on adolescent sexual offenders. In G. E. Wyatt & G. J. Powell (Eds.) *Lasting Effects of Child Sexual Abuse* (193–207). Beverly Hills: Sage. See also Ryan (1997) *supra*; Judith V. Becker, Meg S. Kaplan, Jerry Cunningham-Rathner & Richard Kavoussi (1986). Characteristics of adolescent incest sexual perpetrators, *Journal of Family Violence* 1, 85–97.

147. Johnson (1988) *supra*.

148. See previous chapter.

149. Less than 5 percent have been identified as suffering mental illness. Gail Ryan (1997). Sexually abusive youth: Defining the problem. In Gail Ryan & Sandy Lane (Eds.) *Juvenile Sexual Offending: Causes, Consequences, and Corrections* (Rev. edition) (3–9). San Francisco: Jossey-Bass. Researchers find several diagnoses with co-morbid conditions, including conduct disorder, antisocial personality disorder, narcissistic personality disorder, as well as learning disabilities. Richard J. Kavoussi, Meg Kaplan & Judith V. Becker (1988). Psychiatric diagnoses in adolescent sex offenders, *Journal of the American Academy of Adolescent Psychiatry* 2, 241–243; Roy J. O'Shaughnessy (1992). Clinical aspects of forensic assessment of juvenile sex offenders, *Psychiatric Clinics of North America* 15, 721–735; George A. Awad & Elisabeth B. Saunders (1991). Male adolescent sexual assaulters: Clinical observations, *Journal of Interpersonal Violence* 6, 446–460; John A. Hunter & Dennis W. Goodwin (1992). The clinical utility of satiation therapy in the treatment of juvenile sex offenders: Variations and efficacy, *Annals of Sex Research* 5, 71–80; E. Osuna & A. Luna (1993). Psychological traits and criminal profiles, *Medicine and Law* 12, 171–180.

150. O'Shaughnessy (1992) *supra*; Dennis R. Carpenter, Steven F. Peed & Brenda Eastman (1995). Personality characteristics of adolescent sexual offenders: A pilot study, *Sexual Abuse: A Journal of Research and Treatment* 7, 195–203; Charlayne L. Cooper, William D. Murphy & Mary R Haynes (1996). Characteristics of abused and nonabused adolescent sexual offenders, *Sexual Abuse: A Journal of Research and Treatment* 8, 105–119.

151. Steven Spaccarelli, Blake Bowden, J. Douglas Coatsworth & Soni Kim (1997). Psychosocial correlates of male sexual aggression in a chronic delinquent sample, *Criminal Justice and Behavior* 24, 71–95; Jeffrey Fagan & Sandra Wexler (1988). Explanations of sexual assault among violent delinquents, *Journal of Adolescent Research* 3, 363–385; G. Awad, J. Saunders & J. Levine (1984). A clinical study of male adolescent sex offenders, *International Journal of Offender Therapy and Comparative*

Criminology 28, 105–116; W. R. Smith (1988). Delinquency and abuse among juvenile sexual offenders, *Journal of Interpersonal Violence* 3, 400–413. Cathy S. Widom (1996). Childhood sexual abuse and its criminal consequences, *Society* 33(4), 47–53. The abusiveness derives from an interaction of what individuals bring to their life experience and what surrounds them. William L. Marshall, Stephen M. Hudson & Sharon Hodkinson (1993). The importance of attachment bonds in the development of juvenile sex offending. In Howard E. Barbaree, William I. Marshall & Stephen M. Hudson (Eds). *Juvenile Sex Offending* (164–181). NY: Guilford; T. Ward, S. Hudson, W. Marashall & R. Siegert (1995). Attachment factors in the development of psychopathology in victims of child sexual abuse, *Sexual Abuse: A Journal of Research and Treatment* 8(4). Much of the research reveals that over half of all juvenile offenders were themselves victims of sexual abuse. Lois H. Pierce & Robert L. Pierce (1987). Incestuous victimization by juvenile sex offenders, *Journal of Family Violence* 2, 351–364; Timothy J. Kahn & Mary A. Lafond (1988). Treatment of the adolescent sexual offender, *Child and Adolescent Social Work* 5, 135–148. Researchers report a very high incidence of trauma that sets the path for maladaptive child development. Colin Hawkes, Jilles Ann Jenkins & Eileen Vizard (1997). Roots of sexual violence in children and adolescents. In Ved Varma (Ed.) *Violence in Children and Adolescents* (84–102). London: Jessica Kingsley.

152. In Fehrenback et al. (1986) *supra*, 32 percent reported no friends and nearly two-thirds showed evidence of social isolation. These results have been supported by several other researchers. See Kahn and Lafond (1988). *supra*; Roger Graves, D. Kim Openshaw & Gerald R. Adams (1992). Adolescent sex offenders and social skills training, *International Journal of Offender Therapy and Comparative Criminology* 36, 139–153.

153. Roger C. Katz (1990). Psychological adjustment in adolescent child molesters, *Child Abuse and Neglect* 14, 567–575; Jeffrey Fagan & Sandra Wexler (1988). Explanations of sexual assault among violent delinquents, *Journal of Adolescent Research* 3, 363–385.

154. It is these two themes that are important to understanding the abusive cycles and the way children become abusive. For a review, see Sandy Lane (1997). The sexual abuse cycle. In Gail Ryan & Sandy Lane (Eds.) *Juvenile Sexual Offending: Causes, Consequences, and Corrections* (Rev. ed.) (77–121). San Francisco: Jossey-Bass.

155. Judith V. Becker & Robert M. Stein (1991). Is sexual erotica associated with sexual deviance in adolescent males? *International Journal of Law and Psychiatry* 14, 85–95; Charlayne L. Cooper, William D. Murphy & Mary R Haynes (1996). Characteristics of abused and nonabused adolescent sexual offenders, *Sexual Abuse: A Journal of Research and Treatment* 8, 105–119.

156. For a review, see Eilana Gil (1993). Etiological theories. In Eliana Gil & Toni Cavanagh Johnson (Eds.) *Sexualized Children: Assessment and Treatment of Sexualized Children and Children Who Molest* (53–66). Pockville, MD: Launch Press; Gail Ryan (1997). Theories of etiology. In Ryan & Lane (1997) *supra* (19–35); Brandt F. Steele & Gail Ryan (1997). Deviancy: Development gone wrong. In Ryan & Lane (1997) *supra* (59–76); Sharon K. Araji (1997). *Sexually Aggressive Children: Coming to Understand Them*. Thousand Oaks, CA: Sage.

157. Gail Ryan, Sandy Lane, John Davis & Connie Issac (1987). Juvenile sex offenders: Development and correction, *Child Abuse & Neglect* 11, 385–395.

158. National Adolescent Perpetrator Network (1993). The Revised Report

from the National Task Force on Juvenile Sexual Offending, *Juvenile and Family Court Journal* 44(4), 5–120.

159. Prentky, Knight, Straus, Rokous, Cerce, & Sims-Knight (1989) *supra*.

160. National Adolescent Perpetrator Network (1993) *supra*. See Gail Ryan (1986). Annotated bibliography: Adolescent perpetrators of sexual molestation of children, *Child Abuse and Neglect* 10, 124–132. Much of the research has been conducted in the United States. Vizard et al. (1995) *surpa*. For an analysis of responses in England, see Helen Mason (1995). Children and adolescents who sexually abuse other children: Responses to an emerging problem, *Journal of Social Welfare and Family Law* 17, 325–336.

161. Howard E. Barbaree, Stephen M. Hudson & Micheal C. Seto (1993). Sexual assault in society: The role of the juvenile offender. In Howard E. Barbaree, William I. Marshall & Stephen M. Hudson (Eds). *Juvenile sex offending* (1–24). NY: Guilford.

162. For a review, see Mark J. Swearingen (1997). Megan's law as applied to juveniles: Protecting children at the expense of children? *Seton Hall Constitutional Law Journal* 7, 525–575; Sander N. Rothchild (1996). Beyond incarceration: Juvenile sex offender treatment programs offer youths a second chance, *Journal of Law and Policy* 4, 719–758.

163. Roger J. R. Levesque & Alan J. Tomkins (1995). Revisioning juvenile justice: Implications of the new child protection movement, *Journal of Urban and Contemporary Law* 48, 87–116. Roger J. R. Levesque (1996). Is there still a place for violent youth in juvenile justice? *Aggressive and Violent Behavior* 1, 69–79.

164. *In re B.g.* 289 N.J. Super. 361, 674 S.2d 178 (App. Div. 1996).

165. Id. at 674 A.2d at 180–181.

166. N.J. Stat Ann. § 2C:7-2(f) (1995).

167. For example, public notification laws are meant to ostracize offenders from their communities. In the case of juveniles, the ostracism undermines efforts to rehabilitate and increase the risk of recidivism. For a review of these laws, see Robert E. Freeman-Longo (1997). Reducing sexual abuse in America: Legislating tougher laws or public education and prevention, *New England Journal on Criminal and Civil Confinement* 23, 303–331.

168. 42 U.S. C. §§ 14701, 14701(f)91) (1995).

169. See Swearingen (1997) *supra*. As of mid 1997, only Nebraska had no law covering the registration and notification of sex offenders. The states that exclude juvenile includes Alabama, Kansas, Kentucky, Louisiana, and Wyoming.

170. For a review, see Levesque (1996). Is there still a place, *supra*.

171. Honey Knopp, Rob Freeman-Long, Sandy Lane (1997). Program development. In Ryan & Lane (1997) *supra* (183–200).

172. For a review, see Rothchild (1996) *supra*.

173. For a review of these statues, see Levesque & Tomkins (1995) *supra*.

174. Levesque & Tomkins (1995) *supra*.

175. Patricia Stenson & Carolyn Anderson (1987). Treating juvenile sex offenders and preventing the cycle of abuse, *Journal of Child Care* 3, 91–102. Barry Morenz & Judith Becker (1995). The treatment of youthful sexual offenders, *Applied & Preventive Psychology* 4, 247–256; Kevin Epps (1991). The residential treatment of adolescent sex offenders, *Issues in Criminological and Legal Psychology* 17, 58–67; Carolyn S. Swift & Kimberly Ryuan-Finn (1995). Perpetrator Prevention: Stopping the development of sexually abusive behavior, *Prevention in Human Services* 12, 13–44;

J. Bremmer (1992). Serious juvenile sex offenders: Treatment and long term follow-up, *Psychiatric Annals* 22, 326–332; Garry P. Perry & Janet Orchard (1992). *Assessment and Treatment of Adolescent Sex Offenders*. Sarasota, FL: Professional Resource Press.

176. For a review of treatment approaches, see Michael L. Bourke & Brad Donohue (1996). Assessment and treatment of juvenile sex offenders: An empirical review, *Journal of Child Sexual Abuse* 5, 47–70; Eileen Vizard, Elizabeth Monck & Peter Misch (1995). Child and adolescent sexual abuse perpetrators: A review of the research literature, *Journal of Child Psychology and Psychiatry* 36, 731–756. See also Rothchild (1996) *supra*.

177. For an empirical analysis of existing adolescent sex offender treatment programs, see Vizard et al. (1995) *supra*.

178. Charles M. Borduin, Scott W. Henggeler, David M. Blaske & Risa J. Stein (1990). Multisystemic treatment of adolescent sexual offenders, *International Journal of Offender Therapy and Comparative Criminology* 34, 105–113.

179. Janis F. Bremer (1992). Serious juvenile sex offenders: Treatment and long-term follow-up, *Psychiatric Annals* 22, 326–332; Timothy J. Kahn & Heather J. Chambers (1991). Assessing reoffense risk with juvenile sexual offenders, *Child Welfare* 70, 333–345.

180. Kahn & Chambers (1991) *supra*; Davis & Leitenberg (1987) *supra*.

181. Recent texts on sexually aggressive children ignore the issue; see Araji (1997) *supra*.

182. For a review of programs, see Sandra K. Wurtele & Cynthia L. Miller-Perrin (1992). *Preventing Child Sexual Abuse: Sharing the Responsibility*. Lincoln: University of Nebraska Press.

183. For a discussion, see Gail Ryan (1997). Perpetration prevention: Primary and secondary. In Ryan & Lane (1997) *supra* (433–454).

184. Id. Betty N. Gordon & Carolyn S. Schroeder (1995). *Sexuality: A Developmental Approach to Problems*. NY: Plenum.

185. Roger J. R. Levesque (1996). Future visions of juvenile justice: Lessons from international and comparative law, *Creighton Law Review* 29, 1563–1585. Most of the commentaries have limited themselves to individual countries; for important citations, see id. Recent comparative attempts have emerged; see Donald J. Shoemaker (1996). *International Handbook on Juvenile Justice*. Westport, CT: Greenwood Press.

186. The first major source of juvenile rights appears in the International Covenant on Civil and Political Rights. International Covenant on Civil and Political Rights, Dec. 19, 1966, 999 U.N.T.S. 171 (entered into force Mar. 23, 1976). The International Covenant concerns itself mostly with the rights of youth actually involved in judicial systems and aims to ensure procedural rights and proper punishments. Article 10 (2)(b) urges Nation States to separate juveniles from adults and speedily adjudicate claims. Article 14(4) requires that states adopt different trial procedures for juveniles, consider the juvenile's age, and promote rehabilitation. These significant steps moved international law into intra-state behavior and recognized children's due process rights even before the United States' groundbreaking Supreme Court decisions addressing the rights of minors adjudicated in juvenile courts. Note, for example, that these procedural protections were offered even before the United States accorded delinquents such protections; see *In re Gault*, 387 U.S. 1 (1967) (landmark children's rights case in which the Court extended extensive due process protections to children involved in juvenile justice systems). The Covenant was followed by the 1985 Beijing

Rules, which serve as a model for fair and humane responses to problem youth by offering explicit principles to guide the development of juvenile justice systems. United Nations Standard Minimum Rules for the Administration of Juvenile Justice ("The Beijing Rules"), Nov. 29, 1985, resol. 40/33 [hereafter, Beijing Rules]. In *Human Rights: A Compilation of International Instruments*, 356–381. The principles guide all aspects of criminal justice processes: from investigation and prosecution, adjudication and disposition, noninstitutional treatment, institutional treatment, and research planning, to policy evaluation and formulation. The enumerated "rights," however, remain limited—they are better seen as broad principles and are not directly enforceable because they are not in treaty form. Also located in the Children's Convention are the following due process provisions: the presumption of innocence, the right to be informed of charges and to have assistance in preparing a defense, the right to have the matter "determined without delay" by a competent authority, the right to have the determination reviewed by a higher authority, the right to protections against self-incrimination and to examine witnesses, the right to respect for the child's privacy throughout all proceedings. Children's Convention (1990), Article 40(2).

187. Children's Convention (1990) Article 37(b). When deprivation of liberties is deemed necessary, children are to be separated from adults, unless this is not considered in the child's best interest. Art. 37(c).

188. United Nations Guidelines for the Prevention of Juvenile Delinquency ("The Riyadh Guidelines"), Dec. 14, 1990 resol. 45/112. In *Human Rights: A Compilation of International Instruments* (346–355). NY: United Nations.

189. The *Guidelines* does so to the extent that it would not cause "serious damage" to the child or "harm to others." Riyadh Guidelines, § 5.

190. United Nations Guidelines for the Prevention of Juvenile Delinquency (1990). The Riyadh Guidelines, *supra*.

191. Society has an obligation to assist parents and families to ensure that children remain in their families and communities.

192. For example, children are no longer "mere objects of socialization or control." Riyadh Guidelines, *supra* (§ 3). Children have a right to self-determination. When designing and implementing policies affecting children and families, nations are now obligated to take into account individual children's evolving capacities. This is perhaps the most radical aspect of international children's rights. Although it is explicitly stated in article 12 of the Children's Convention, the focus on allowing children to participate in decisions that affect them actually impacts upon most rights enumerated in the Convention. *All* children must participate in decisions that affect them. The right recognized in the Children's Convention, Art. 1, are formal *rights* enshrined in international law and bestowed upon "every child."

193. For analysis of these models that actually have been adopted, see Allison Morris & Gabrielle M. Maxwell (1993). Juvenile justice in New Zealand: A new paradigm, *Australia & New Zealand Journal of Criminology* 26, 72–90; Jean-Benoit Zegers & Catherine Price (1994). Youth justice and the Children, Young Persons, and Their Families Act, *Auckland University Law Review* 7, 803–820. The new approach emphasizes the following needs: to involve families in juvenile justice decisions, to keep children in their homes, to strengthen and maintain child-family relationships, and to promote the development of the child in the family.

194. See Morris & Maxwell (1993) *supra*. For a more cautious evaluation, see Christine Coumarelos & Don Weatherburn (1995). Targeting intervention strategies to reduce juvenile recidivism, *Australia & New Zealand Journal of Crimi-*

nology 28, 55–72. Models reveal that the most promising programs are those which aim to increase youths' accountability. This notion of accountability, however, unlike previous approaches, does not view accountability as a necessary evil associated with taking a punitive approach to juvenile justice. Instead, it focuses on reinforcing youths' obligations and responsibility for their actions and provides the opportunity to address more appropriately juvenile justice concerns by actually involving youth in their rehabilitation and reintegration. Just as importantly, it reinforces the commitment that parents, communities, and institutions have toward youth.

195. Borduin et al. (1990) *supra*.

196. Levesque (1996) Future visions, *supra*; Shoemaker (1996) *supra*.

197. Children's Convention (1990) *supra*, Article 37.

198. Access may be direct or through an appropriate representative. Article 12 of the Children's Convention. The importance of this article increases in light of Article 42, which places an obligation on parties to make the principles and provisions known to children. See A. Glenn Mower, Jr. (1997). *The Convention on the Rights of the Child: International Law Support for Children*. Westport, CT: Greenwood Press.

199. Children's Convention (1990) *supra*, Articles 34, 35, 36, 39.

200. The protection is similar to the International Covenant on Civil and Political Rights' Article 2, as well as the Universal Declaration's Article 2.

201. Levesque (1994) *supra*.

202. See Children's Convention (1990) *supra*, Article 5.

203. Id.

204. Id.

205. Id.

206. Denise Gamache (1991). Domination and control: The social context of dating violence. In Barrie Levy (Ed.) *Dating Violence: Young Women in Danger* (73–83). Seattle, WA: Seal Press. Gamache notes that victims typically tell no adult (80), and that isolation from friends and family is a primary characteristic of dating violence (79); it prohibits victims from making sense of their experiences and causes them to accept blame for the violence.

207. Brenda Scott (1994). *Out of Control: Who's Watching Our Child Protection Agencies?* Lafayette, LA: Huntington House Publishers.

208. For a review of the research, see Levesque (1994). Prosecuting sex crimes, *supra*.

209. Fairstein (1993) *supra* (229).

210. Id.

211. Although this may seem an obvious approach, even the recently approved standards of the Family Law Section of the American Bar Association ignore this form of abuse. See Proposed standards of practice for lawyers who represent children in abuse and neglect cases (1995). *Family Law Quarterly* 29, 375–407. The article cites instances of attorneys representing children.

212. For example, the women's rights movement reflects well how simply expanding women's rights has not changed the nature of male-female relations within the family. Greda Lerner (1986). *The Creation of Patriarchy*. NY: Oxford University Press. Although progress undoubtedly has been made, remaining obstacles are more than legal in nature.

213. Children's Convention (1990), Articles 19, 34, 35, and 36.

214. Roger J. R. Levesque (1995). The failures of foster care reform, *supra*.

215. Howard Davidson (1994). *The Impact of Domestic Violence on Children:*

A Report to the President of the American Bar Association. Washington, DC: American Bar Association; Einat Peled (1997). Intervention with children of battered women: A review of current literature, *Children and Youth Services Review* 19, 277–299.

216. Children's Convention (1990) *supra*, Article 19.

217. Id., Article 29.

218. Schools have difficulty implementing programs that deal with sexuality and sexual relationships.

219. Likewise, the often-touted solution of removing abusers from schools remains complicated. See Anthony H. Mansfield (1996). Juvenile justice gone awry: Expulsion statutes unjustly deny educational rights to children, *New York City Law Review* 1, 203-237. Roni R. Reed (1996). Education and the state constitutions: Alternatives for suspended and expelled students, *Cornell Law Review* 81, 582–622.

220. For a review of general principles, see Walter B. Roberts, Jr. & Diane H. Coursol (1996). Strategies for intervention with childhood and adolescent victims of bullying, teasing, and intimidation in school settings, *Elementary School Guidance & Counseling* 30, 204–212; Einat Peled, Peter G. Jaffe & Jeffrey L. Edleson (Eds.) (1995). *Ending the Cycle of Violence: Community Responses to Children of Battered Women*. Thousand Oaks: CA: Sage; Dorothea M. Ross (1996). *Childhood Bullying and Teasing: What School Personnel, Other Professionals, and Parents Can Do*. Alexandria, VA: American Counseling Association.

221. See, e.g, Vangie A. Foshee, Karl E. Bauman, Ximena B. Arriaga, Russell W. Helms, Gary G. Koch & George Fletcher Linder (1998). An evaluation of Safe Dates, an adolescent dating violence prevention program, *American Journal of Public Health* 88, 45–50; Francine Lavoie, Lucie Vezina, Christiane Piche & Michel Boivin (1995). Evaluation of a prevention program for violence in teen dating relationships, *Journal of Interpersonal Violence* 10, 516–524.

222. June Larkin (1994). Walking through walls: The sexual harassment of high school girls, *Gender and Education* 6, 263–280.

223. Gilbert J. Botvin, Steven Schinke & Mario A. Orlandi (1995). School-based health promotion: Substance abuse and sexual behavior, *Applied & Preventive Psychology* 4, 167–184; Jeffrey H. Coben, Harold B. Weiss, Edward P. Mulvey & Stephen R. Dearwater (1994). A primer on school violence prevention, *Journal of School Health* 64, 309–313.

224. Martin Mac an Ghaill (1996). Toward a reconceptualized sex/sexuality education policy: Theory and cultural change, *Journal of Education Policy* 11, 289–302; Donald E. Greydanus, Helen D. Pratt & Linda L. Dannison (1995). Sexuality education programs for youth: Current state of affairs and strategies for the future, *Journal of Sex Education and Therapy* 21, 238–254. Thomas G. Eschweiler (1995). Educational malpractice in sex education, *Southern Methodist University Law Review* 49, 101–132.

225. Children's Convention (1990) *supra*, Article 24.

226. Children's Convention (1990) *supra*, Article 39.

227. Levy (1991) *supra*; Peled, Jaffe & Edleson (1995) *supra*.

228. See, e.g., Levesque (1997) *supra*.

229. This has probably been the most powerful result of sexual harassment law and rape law reform that deals with adults. See, for example, Spohn & Horney (1992) *supra*, who emphasize how effects of legal reform tend to be modest except for its symbolic effect in contributing to changing attitudes.

230. Richard M. Lerner (1982). Children and adolescents as producers of their own development, *Developmental Review* 2, 342–370. Research highlights the developmental significance of children's own peer cultures, and highlights how parents, let alone other adults, are not necessarily the primary influence in children's lives. Judith Rich Harris (1995). Where is the child's environment? A group socialization theory of development, *Psychological Review* 102, 458–489. The peer influence is rather robust; children's peer relationships even profoundly impact children's relationships with their parents. Anne-Marie Ambert (1994). A qualitative study of peer abuse and its effects: Theoretical and empirical implications, *Journal of Marriage and the Family* 56, 119–130.

Index

ROGER J. R. LEVESQUE is an Assistant Professor in the Department of Criminal Justice at Indiana University. He received a J.D. from Columbia University School of Law and a Ph.D. in Cultural Psychology from the University of Chicago. He has published more than forty scholarly articles and book chapters that deal with human rights, children, and maltreatment. In addition, he is the author of *Adolescents, Sex, and the Law: Rethinking Rights for Changing Realities* (forthcoming).